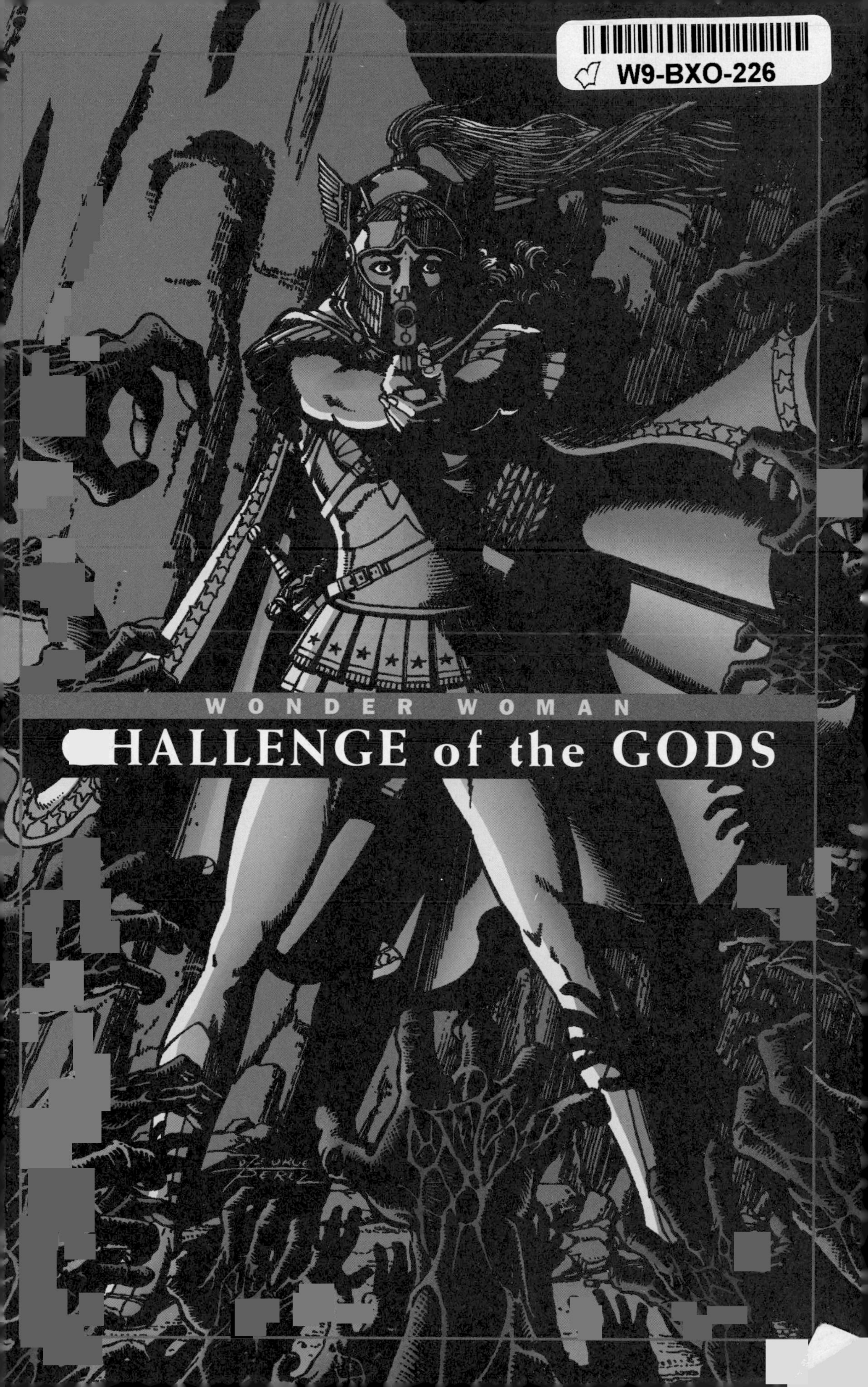
WONDER WOMAN
HALLENGE of the GODS

WONDER WOMAN: CHALLENGE OF THE GODS

Published by DC Comics. Cover and compilation copyright © 2004
DC Comics. All Rights Reserved.

Originally published in single magazine form in WONDER WOMAN #8-14.
Copyright © 1987, 1988 DC Comics. All Rights Reserved. All characters,
names, their distinctive likenesses and related elements are trademarks of
DC Comics. The stories, characters and incidents featured in this publication
are entirely fictional. DC Comics does not read or accept unsolicited
submissions of ideas, stories or artwork.

DC Comics, 1700 Broadway, New York, NY 10019
A Warner Bros. Entertainment Company
Printed in Canada. First Printing.
ISBN: 1-4012-0324-8

Cover art by George Pérez
Cover color by Tom Smith
*Inking reconstruction on pages 29, 31-34, 38-47, 49-52 by Bob Wiacek
Thanks to Phil Jimenez

WONDER WOMAN
CHALLENGE of the GODS

GEORGE PÉREZ   LEN WEIN Writers

GEORGE PÉREZ Penciller

BRUCE PATTERSON Inker

CARL GAFFORD   TATJANA WOOD Colorists

JOHN COSTANZA Letterer

GEORGE PÉREZ Original Series Covers

Bob Wiacek Inking reconstruction on Chapter Two*

Heroic Age Color reconstruction and enhancement

Wonder Woman created by William Moulton Marston

OUR STORY SO FAR...

Over three thousand years ago, the goddess Artemis proposed to the Olympian gods that a new race of mortal human beings be created, which she would call Amazons — a female race that would set an example to the rest of humanity and promote equality between the sexes. Artemis, along with Athena, Aprhodite, Demeter, and Hestia, created the Amazons from the souls of women who were killed before their time due to violence by men. The first to be reborn, Hippolyte, was designated as the queen.

The Amazons founded a city-state called Themyscira, where compassion and justice would reign. But the war god Ares found the Amazons an obstacle to his quest for absolute power, and so had a pawn taunt the demigod Heracles with false reports that Hippolyte was besmirching his reputation. Heracles tricked the Amazons into a celebratory gathering with his warriors — but the Amazons were caught off-guard, and Heracles and his men treacherously attacked, defeated, and enslaved them.

Hippolyte prayed to the goddesses for forgiveness. Athena appeared to her and said she would be free if she rededicated herself to her ideals. Hippolyte escaped her cell, freed the other Amazons, and led them in defeating their captors.

The goddesses decreed that Hippolyte and her Amazons do penance for failing to lead humanity to establish new ways of justice and equality. Therefore, the goddesses sent Hippolyte's Amazons to a distant island, beneath which lay a source of great evil. As long as Amazons served to keep that evil from menacing humanity, the Amazons would be immortal.

Hippolyte's Amazons established a new city-state on Paradise Island, and the Amazons renewed their sense of purpose and self-discipline as the centuries passed. Various Amazons were killed over the years in carrying out the difficult task of keeping the great evil confined underground. During all this time, the Amazons of Paradise Island had no contact with the outside world.

Hippolyte was the only one of the Amazons who was pregnant when she was killed in her previous incarnation. The soul of Hippolyte's unborn daughter was still waiting to be reborn. On Artemis' instructions, Hippolyte formed the image of a baby from the clay of Paradise Island. The five goddesses who were the Amazons' patrons, along with Hermes, endowed the unborn soul with various gifts, including superhuman strength and speed and the power of flight. Then the unborn soul entered the clay image, which came to life as a real baby. The child was named Diana, after a revered warrior who had died to save the Amazon race.

After Hippolyte's daughter had grown to adulthood, the gods revealed to the Amazons that Ares had gone insane and might destroy all of Earth with a terrible source of power. The gods decreed that the Amazons choose through a tournament a champion who could confront Ares in the world outside Paradise Island.

Diana asked to participate in the tournament but was forbidden to do so by Hippolyte. Nonetheless, urged on by Athena, Diana entered the tournament, concealing her identity, and won. Unable to defy the gods' will, Hippolyte agreed to let Diana be the champion to be sent against Ares. Diana was given a costume bearing the standard of her deceased namesake.

Hermes transported Diana to Boston, Massachusetts, where she met a professor of classical Greek history named Julia Kapatelis, who taught her how to speak English and serves as her guide to the modern world. Diana presented herself as an ambassador from Paradise Island to the rest of society, here to teach the ways of her just and peaceful civilization to a violent world.

Diana ultimately accomplished the mission for which she was sent to Man's World, defeating Ares before the god could bring about a third World War. The media dubbed her "Wonder Woman," and she became an overnight sensation — while also gaining a publicist in Myndi Mayer.

Julia and her daughter Vanessa have taken Diana into their home.

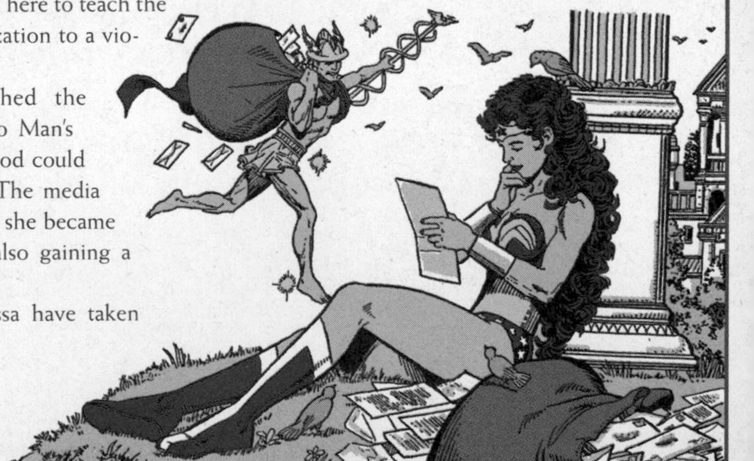

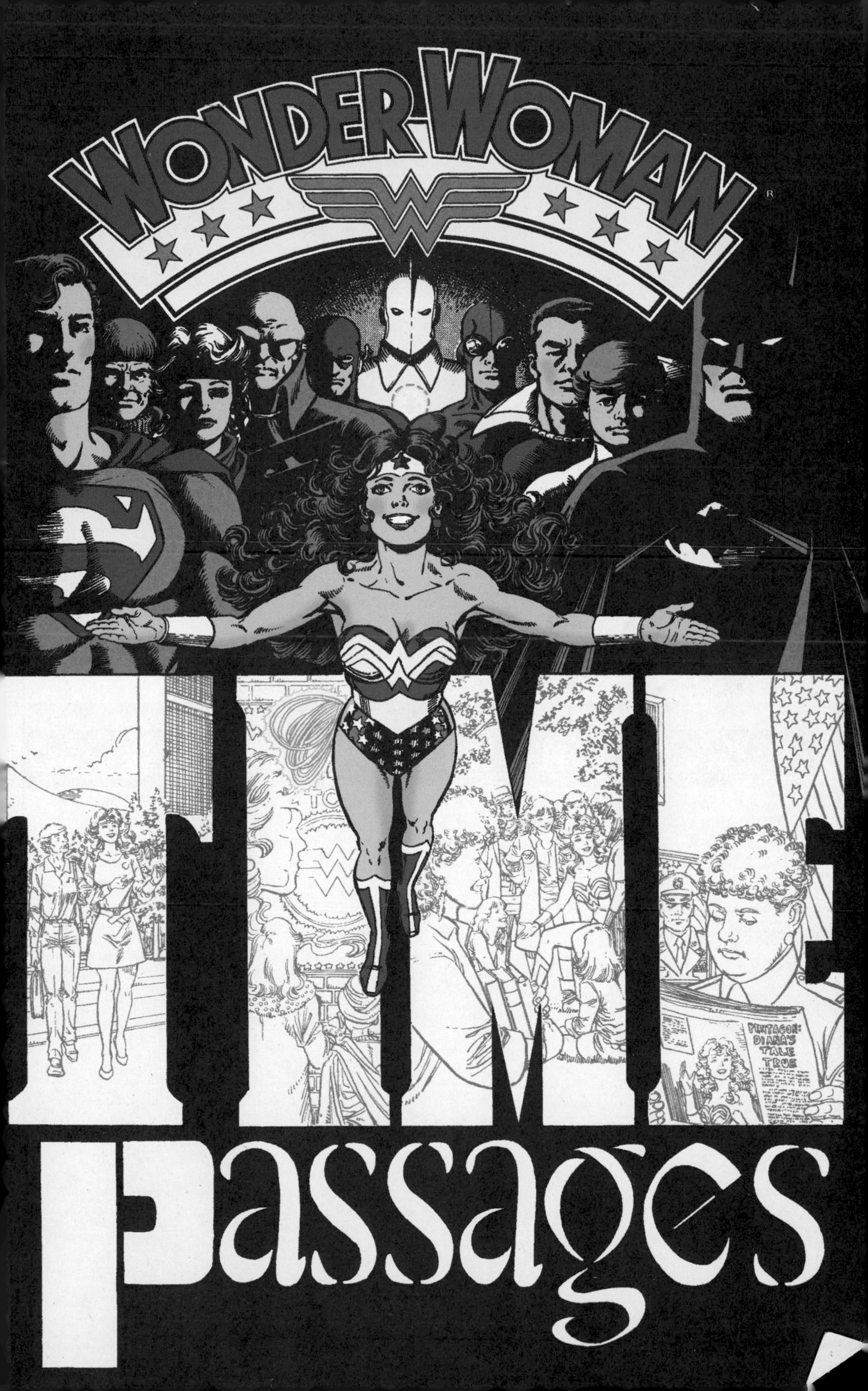
WONDER WOMAN
TIME
Passages
PENTAGON: DIANA'S TALE TRUE

WONDER WOMAN

CHAPTER ONE

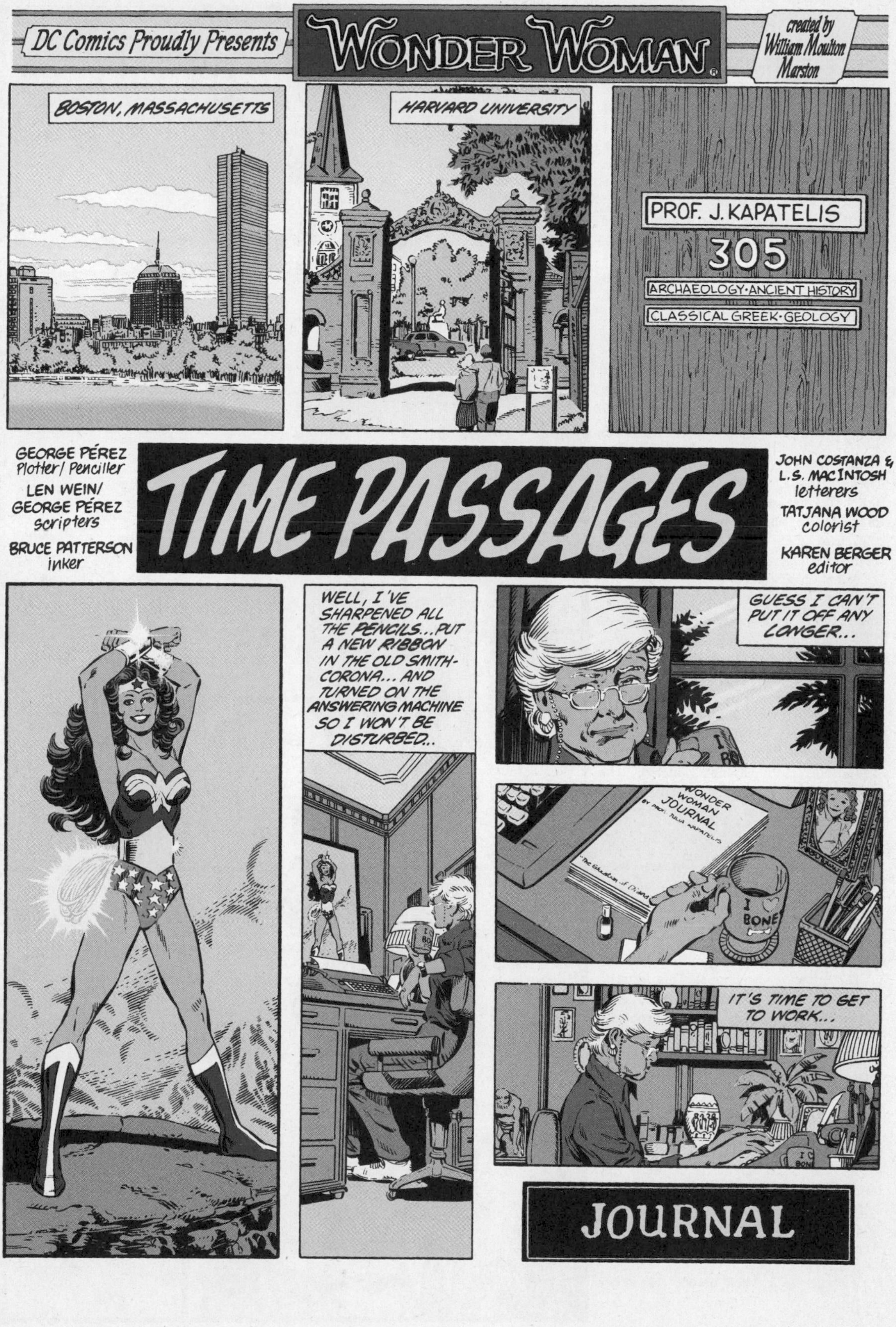

DC Comics Proudly Presents
WONDER WOMAN
created by William Moulton Marston
BOSTON, MASSACHUSETTS
HARVARD UNIVERSITY
PROF. J. KAPATELIS
305
ARCHAEOLOGY · ANCIENT HISTORY
CLASSICAL GREEK · GEOLOGY
GEORGE PÉREZ Plotter/ Penciller
LEN WEIN/ GEORGE PÉREZ scripters
BRUCE PATTERSON inker
TIME PASSAGES
JOHN COSTANZA & L.S. MACINTOSH letterers
TATJANA WOOD colorist
KAREN BERGER editor
WELL, I'VE SHARPENED ALL THE PENCILS... PUT A NEW RIBBON IN THE OLD SMITH-CORONA... AND TURNED ON THE ANSWERING MACHINE SO I WON'T BE DISTURBED...
GUESS I CAN'T PUT IT OFF ANY LONGER...
WONDER WOMAN JOURNAL
I BONE
IT'S TIME TO GET TO WORK...
JOURNAL

APRIL, 1987

I have walked the sands of the Kalahari, inhaled the dust of Tutankhamon's tomb, published four definitive volumes of Greek history, borne a daughter, buried a husband, but nothing I've ever done before has been as difficult as this. There is so much to say about the Princess Diana, so little time to say it.

I sit here studying the stunning poster of Diana that her publicist, Myndi Mayer, commissioned for the Wonder Woman speaking tour. Despite my initial reservations about Ms. Mayer, I have to admit she has done an admirable job of promoting Diana's mission to Man's World (as the Amazons are wont to call it).

It has been a rather intense time for Diana, what with the untold hours we spent in my library to prepare the Princess for her appearance before the United Nations General Assembly. I would have preferred more hours of rehearsal, but the time limit imposed on Diana by her mother, Queen Hippolyte, made that practically impossible. Despite the pressure, I'm still astonished by Diana's ability to assimilate so much information so quickly.

At the UN, Diana insisted I act as her interpreter, since she spoke in her native Themysciran, the Amazon dialect derived from ancient Greek. Diana felt the English language was still too new to her, and she wanted no possible misinterpretation of her message of love and peace.

Unfortunately, Diana soon discovered that, in some backward countries of this supposedly "enlightened" world, the words of a woman, no matter how meaningful or true, simply will not be heard.

To make matters worse, the Russian delegate protested that Diana's star-spangled uniform belied her true political leanings and thus her involvement in the Ares Affair. He casually dismissed the mythological aspects of the Affair as patently absurd and denounced Diana as an American propagandist. This left the Princess more perplexed than ever regarding the strange political problems her costume seemed to generate in Man's World, and she was determined to discover the cause.

Thus, despite my protestations, Diana accepted an invitation from the military to prove that the Ares Assault had been much more than an attempted military coup. The Government requested I not attend this meeting, and I couldn't really blame them, considering how I'd ruined their plans to keep the matter quiet. Still, I accompanied Diana to the airfield to see her off.

It would be a week before I saw her again.

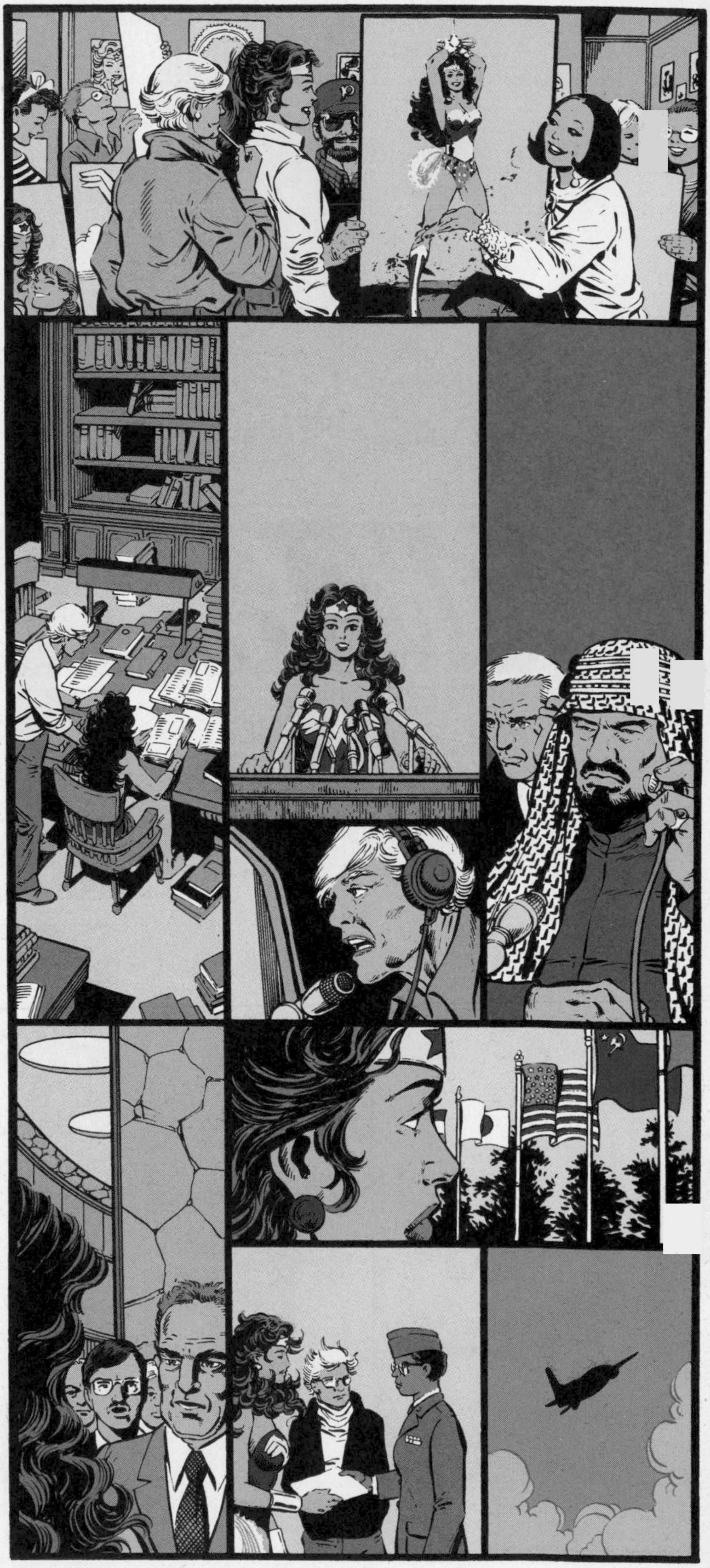

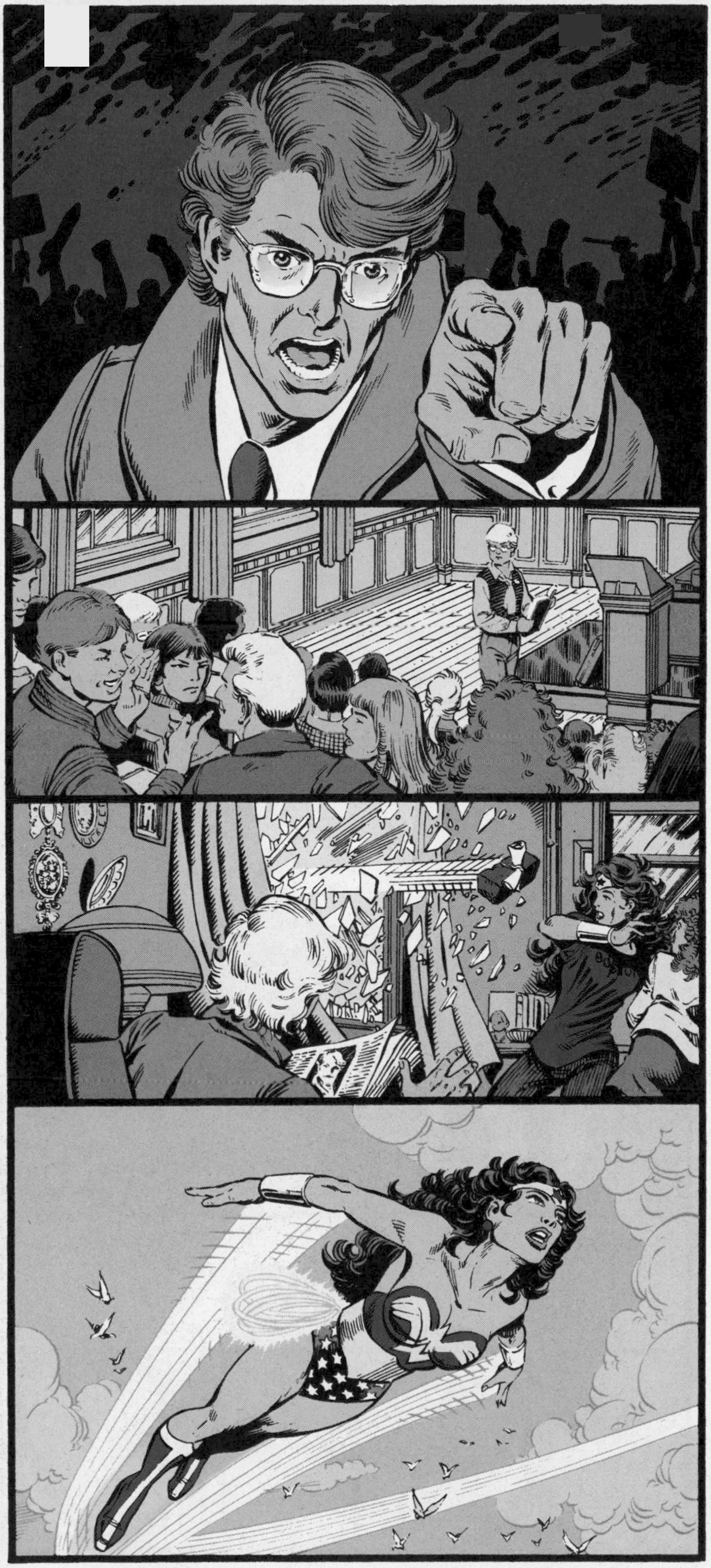

Something happened to Diana while she was away, something that changed her attitude completely. She returned to Boston quite subdued, determined to dedicate herself to quiet, contemplative study. Despite her little time remaining in our world, Diana asked me to call Myndi Mayer and cancel all further public appearances. It seemed the Princess was finally becoming aware of how different this new, troubled world was from her beloved Paradise Island.

In retrospect, I have begun to wonder if Diana has clairvoyant powers as well. For her self-imposed exile came at almost precisely the same moment that the self-styled savior of the Human Race, that fanatical Psychologist who called himself G. Gordon Godfrey, began his nationwide campaign to outlaw all of America's so-called "super-heroes."

Though his one-man campaign seemed almost ludicrous at first, it quickly picked up steam. Suddenly, some of America's foremost political figures were siding with Godfrey, as if all the collective good that these supremely gifted beings had accomplished over the years was being erased from the public consciousness by some form of mass hypnotism.

In my own classroom, I watched helplessly as my students divided themselves into opposing factions. Violent factions. Though the effects of Godfrey's tirades were not universal, it was obvious they were still painfully far-reaching.

Suddenly, because of my relationship with Diana, I found myself under public scrutiny. It reminded me all too much of the infamous Red Scare of the 1950s, an era I had absolutely no desire to relive. I was suddenly considered a subversive by some for harboring a supposed "super-hero" in my home, and they did not hesitate to make their displeasure known.

When the new house that I had rented was brutally attacked, it was more than Diana could tolerate. After weeks of self-imposed silence, the Amazon Princess known to our world as "Wonder Woman" decided the time had finally come for her to fight for her unalienable rights.

Before I could even begin to dissuade her, Diana was once again gone.

Despite her many public appearances, Diana was still very much an enigma to most of the world. Thus, Guy Gardner, the newest -- and, so Diana tells me, the most irritating -- member of the intergalactic Green Lantern Corps, had no idea what to make of the Amazon Princess when she first crossed his path in Washington, D.C., during the height of Gordon Godfrey's anti-heroic madness.

Finally though, G. Gordon Godfrey met his inevitable downfall. When his own arrogance caused him to lose control of the raging mobs he himself had created, Godfrey donned the gleaming golden helmet of the mysterious Doctor Fate -- a helmet purportedly possessed of incredible mystic power -- and, unable to endure such power, Godfrey was reduced to a gibbering mound of flesh.

Suddenly, Diana found herself standing among many of the other costumed heroes who had suffered because of Godfrey's madness, other super-powerful beings such as she. Now, for the first time, it seemed as if Diana might finally find some sense of belonging in Man's World. But, despite their warm welcome, Diana fled this company of heroes even as she was invited to join the newly re-formed Justice League.

Later, I asked Diana why she had refused such an incredible invitation. She told me she did not believe the point of her mission to Man's World was to become a costumed crimefighter. That, she said, implied violence condoned by society in the name of order. Apparently, crime is unknown on Paradise Island, and order there is a state of mutual respect and love. Diana believed her true destiny was to teach the world the Amazon way.

However, from that day forward, Diana was constantly discussing these unique beings. The Black Canary was the first female crimefighter the Princess had ever seen. On Paradise Island, Diana said, the Canary would have been hailed as a great gladiator. Then there was J'onn J'onzz, the Manhunter from Mars, the proud, emerald-skinned alien from that bright red planet named for a god who was Ares in all but name. Diana found the irony most amusing. And, of course, Diana was fascinated by the militarily named Captain Marvel, whose own powers were supposedly derived from the gods of various pantheons. Who were all these others who claimed to be gods, Diana wondered? Now, for the first time, it seemed Diana had begun to better understand the widespread skepticism regarding her own mythic origins.

Most interesting was the strange silence that would come over Diana whenever I mentioned Superman. She would not talk about him -- as if some unspoken secret existed between them.

Maybe some day she'll tell me about it.

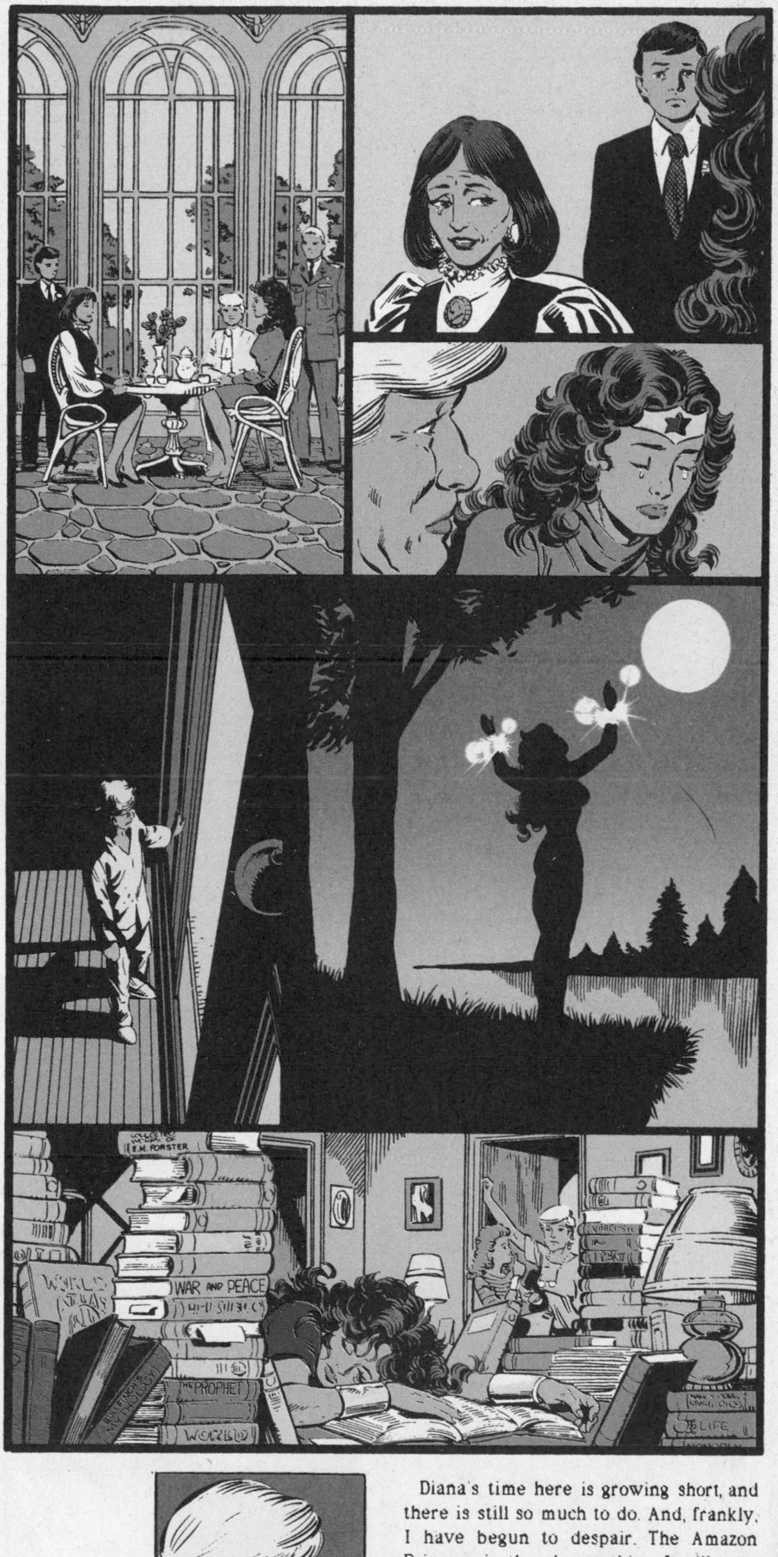
E.M. FORSTER
WAR AND PEACE
THE PROPHET

It was a day or two after the official announcement by the Pentagon Chiefs, acknowledging the veracity of Diana's various claims regarding the Ares Affair, that we received a call from Colonel Matthew Michaelis' widow, Angelina.

Now that the whole insane Affair was finally a matter of public record, she sincerely needed to know the details of how fiercely her husband had fought to save the world, how bravely he had died. And, with both Colonel Steve Trevor and Lieutenant Etta Candy away on special assignment, I was the last person on earth who had seen her husband alive.

That brave woman, still wearing black, smiled proudly through her tears as Diana and I told her of her husband's unwavering loyalty and heroism. He had been gunned down while shielding Lt. Candy and myself from a withering hail of bullets. As Mrs. Michaelis and her young son, Andrew, took some small comfort from our words, I noticed Diana was weeping as well. She would later confide that she had never before experienced the loss of a loved one and that she now understood the terrible fear that must have gripped her mother's heart when Diana was called upon to face almost certain death in battle against Ares. As a widow myself, I knew exactly what she meant.

Some nights thereafter I would awaken to find Diana standing nude on the lawn behind the house, praying to her Amazon gods. I realized then what an amazing contradiction she is. On the one hand, nature's innocent, her very voice like a warm, comforting breeze. On the other hand, desperate energy, forever searching for proper outlets. She is, in short, the living seed of change.

However, despite all her determination and energy, even Diana must eventually face her own humanity. Some nights Vanessa and I have found her sprawled in my library amidst a mountain of books. I suppose even Amazons must sleep.

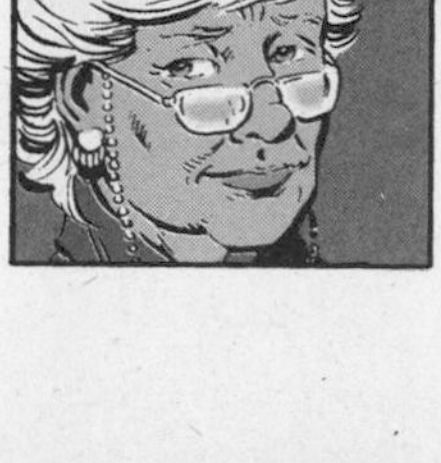

Diana's time here is growing short, and there is still so much to do. And, frankly, I have begun to despair. The Amazon Princess is the closest thing I will ever know to a Goddess; the woman Diana is the closest thing I will ever have to a true friend.

God, how I'm going to miss her.

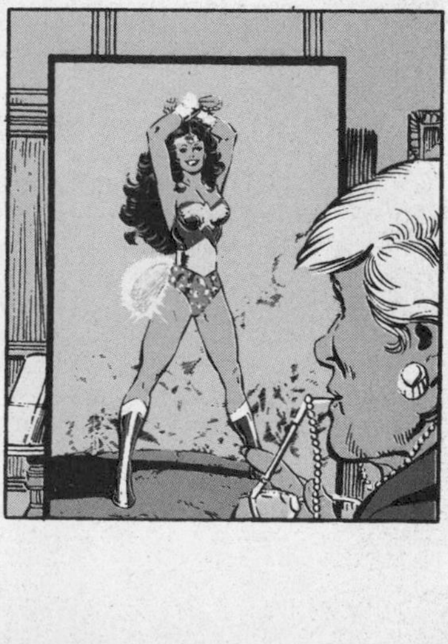

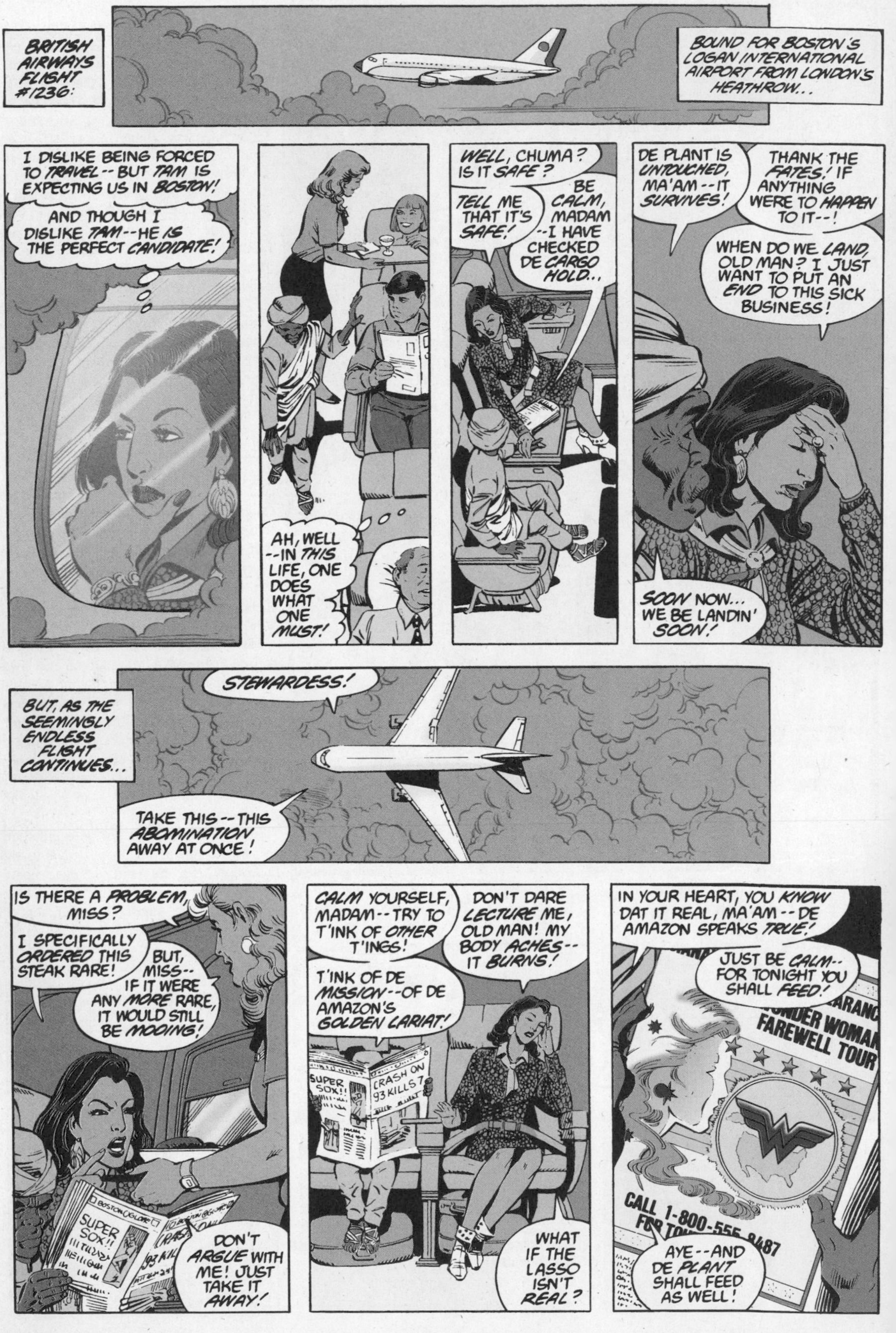
BRITISH AIRWAYS FLIGHT #1236:
BOUND FOR BOSTON'S LOGAN INTERNATIONAL AIRPORT FROM LONDON'S HEATHROW...
I DISLIKE BEING FORCED TO TRAVEL--BUT TAM IS EXPECTING US IN BOSTON!
AND THOUGH I DISLIKE TAM--HE IS THE PERFECT CANDIDATE!
AH, WELL --IN THIS LIFE, ONE DOES WHAT ONE MUST!
WELL, CHUMA? IS IT SAFE?
TELL ME THAT IT'S SAFE!
BE CALM, MADAM --I HAVE CHECKED DE CARGO HOLD...
DE PLANT IS UNTOUCHED, MA'AM--IT SURVIVES!
THANK THE FATES! IF ANYTHING WERE TO HAPPEN TO IT--!
WHEN DO WE LAND, OLD MAN? I JUST WANT TO PUT AN END TO THIS SICK BUSINESS!
SOON NOW... WE BE LANDIN' SOON!
BUT, AS THE SEEMINGLY ENDLESS FLIGHT CONTINUES...
STEWARDESS!
TAKE THIS--THIS ABOMINATION AWAY AT ONCE!
IS THERE A PROBLEM, MISS?
I SPECIFICALLY ORDERED THIS STEAK RARE!
BUT, MISS--IF IT WERE ANY MORE RARE, IT WOULD STILL BE MOOING!
DON'T ARGUE WITH ME! JUST TAKE IT AWAY!
SUPER SOX!!
CALM YOURSELF, MADAM--TRY TO T'INK OF OTHER T'INGS!
DON'T DARE LECTURE ME, OLD MAN! MY BODY ACHES--IT BURNS!
T'INK OF DE MISSION--OF DE AMAZON'S GOLDEN LARIAT!
SUPER SOX!!
CRASH ON 93 KILLS 7
WHAT IF THE LASSO ISN'T REAL?
IN YOUR HEART, YOU KNOW DAT IT REAL, MA'AM--DE AMAZON SPEAKS TRUE!
JUST BE CALM--FOR TONIGHT YOU SHALL FEED!
FAREWELL TOUR
CALL 1-800-555-8487
AYE--AND DE PLANT SHALL FEED AS WELL!

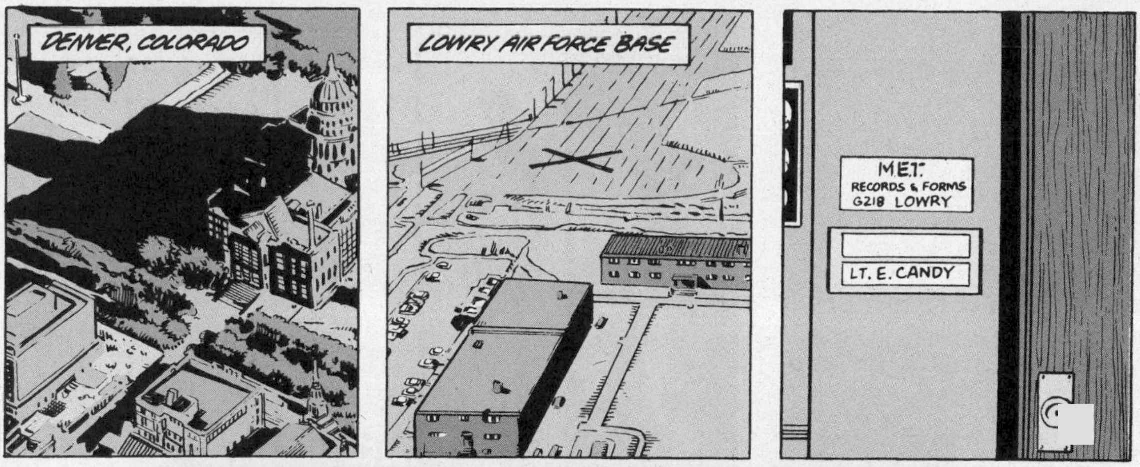
DENVER, COLORADO
LOWRY AIR FORCE BASE
M.E.T. RECORDS & FORMS G218 LOWRY
LT. E. CANDY

TIME PASSAGES

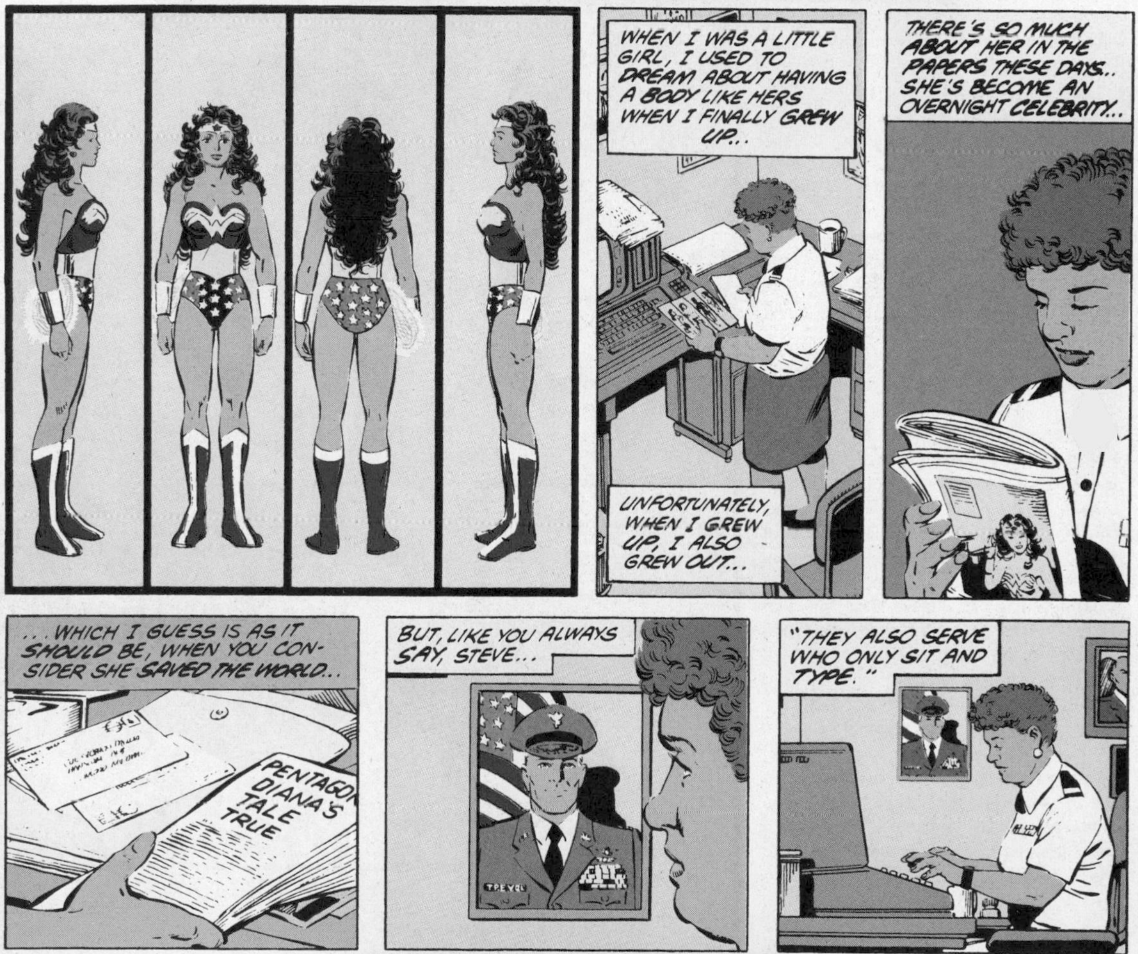
WHEN I WAS A LITTLE GIRL, I USED TO DREAM ABOUT HAVING A BODY LIKE HERS WHEN I FINALLY GREW UP...
UNFORTUNATELY, WHEN I GREW UP, I ALSO GREW OUT...
THERE'S SO MUCH ABOUT HER IN THE PAPERS THESE DAYS... SHE'S BECOME AN OVERNIGHT CELEBRITY...
...WHICH I GUESS IS AS IT SHOULD BE, WHEN YOU CONSIDER SHE SAVED THE WORLD...
PENTAGON: DIANA'S TALE TRUE
BUT, LIKE YOU ALWAYS SAY, STEVE...
"THEY ALSO SERVE WHO ONLY SIT AND TYPE."

Dispatch

Dear Colonel Trevor,

Enclosed with this personal dispatch you'll find the Tribunal's findings and recommendations regarding the so-called "Ares Project / Wonder Woman Affair." Though most of the enclosed information is already public knowledge, I thought you might be interested in my own opinions on the matter.

With your own current duties taking you so far away, I was ordered to serve as an official observer during the now-famous "Wonder Woman Maneuvers." Since the Brass was aware that Princess Diana both knew and trusted me, I guess it was only logical that I attend. Of course, it was under the stipulation that I not voice any personal opinions which might in any way affect Diana's decision to cooperate.

After they had completed taking all of her vital statistics and some photos (see enclosed), General Hillary delivered the Princess into the capable hands of Major Dennis Warren and his research team.

By this point, Diana's English was good enough for her to understand the meaning and necessity of the tests. Nevertheless, an interpreter, a MSgt. Lodicos, was assigned to the Princess in the event of any unforeseen problems. As you may or may not already be aware, the Brass wouldn't approve of Prof. Kapatelis being there because of, quote, the risks to civilian personnel, unquote.

Yeah. Sure.

At any rate, Diana was briefed as to the potential dangers of these tests, but the Amazon was determined to prove her claims in the hope that this would also prove and validate the respective reports you and I filed regarding the various events, natural and otherwise, that culminated at that Missile Base. She was also interested in perhaps learning whether the amazing similarities between our flag and her costume did indeed indicate that an alliance with the U.S. was part of Diana's destiny.

As the transport chopper carried us to the Arizona testing site, I noticed the Princess quietly composed in prayer. I later learned it was a prayer common to the Amazons when they were preparing for contest or battle.

Maybe it was just the intensity of the moment, but I could have sworn the sky suddenly opened then, as if somehow it was actually answering her.

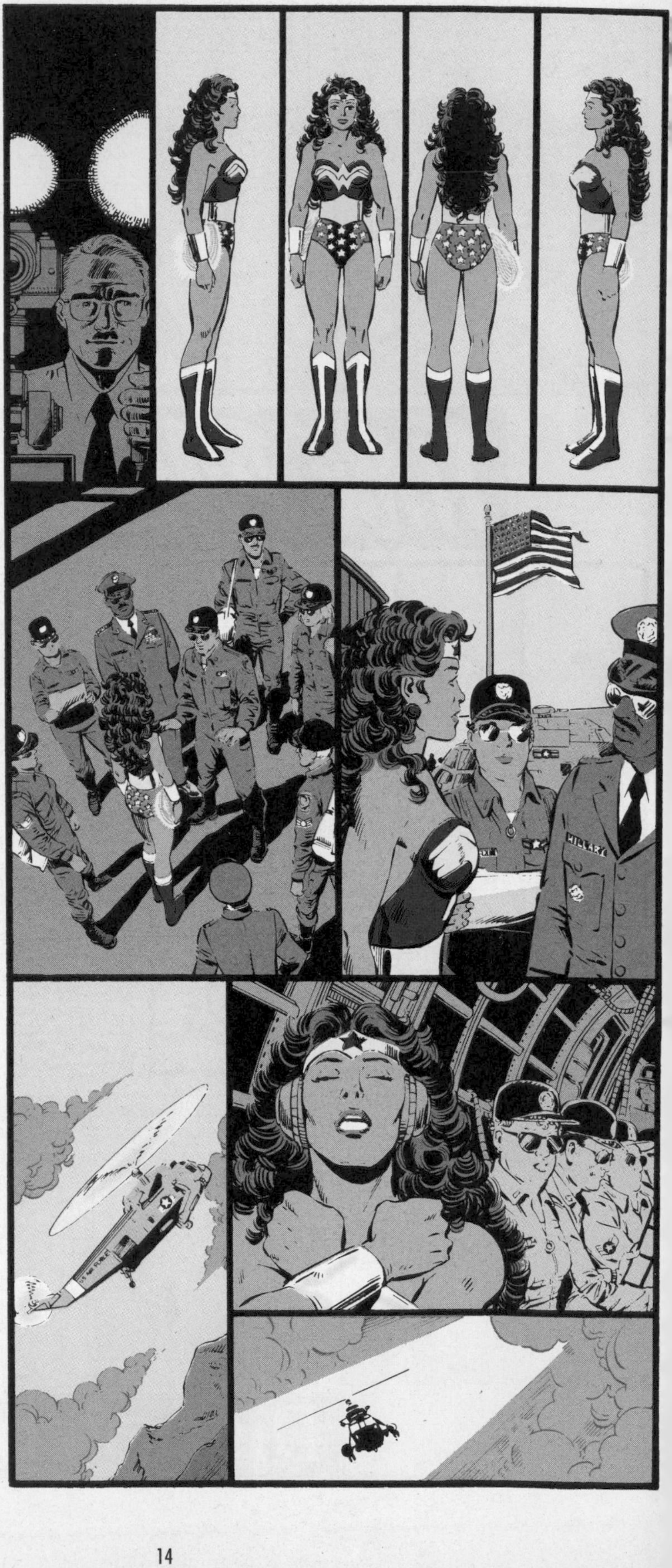
HILLARY

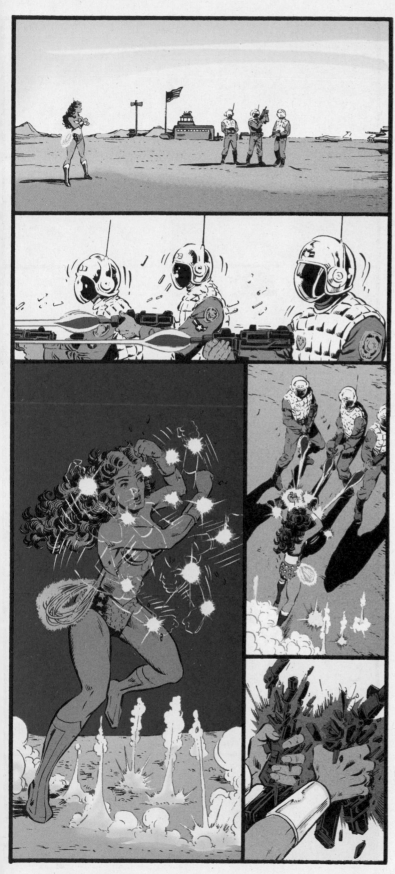

When we got to the test site, preparations had already been made. At the Princess' request, the cameras had been set up in the observation building. Since the first test was going to be "The Flashing Thunder," as Diana called it (military code name: Bullets and Bracelets), she was afraid the equipment might be damaged by ricochets.

The volunteer marksmen were all wearing protective clothing and had been armed with specially modified Uzis. I couldn't believe it. I considered lodging a formal protest against Major Warren for putting the Princess in such danger, but Diana talked me out of it, assuring me she was at no risk.

(A curious aside here: while discussing the impending Bullets and Bracelets tests, Diana mentioned that a simpler version of "The Flashing Thunder" was a test she had faced on Themyscira when competing for the right to challenge Ares. From her description, it sounds like she was shot at with a .45 Magnum, though how such a weapon had come to be on Paradise Island, Diana either couldn't or wouldn't explain. In any case, the Princess said that this particular test had been given specifically to prepare her for possible combat with modern military weaponry. Still, I'd sure love to learn more about that gun.)

Suddenly, at a radioed command, the three marksmen opened fire on Diana -- point blank. I nearly screamed then, but I needn't have worried.

In a frantic flurry of motion even a frame-by-frame playback had difficulty catching, Diana deflected the barrage with her bracelets. I don't know what strange alloy those things are made of, but the bracelets weren't even scratched.

As the bullets flew, the Princess quickly, unexpectedly, charged the riflemen, and not only disarmed them, but also crushed their weapons with her bare hands.

It was at this point, I think, that Major Warren finally started to be impressed.

To be honest though, as impressive as the results of the Bullets and Bracelets test were, even I was stunned at the extent of Diana's abilities that were demonstrated in subsequent tests.

I mean, at one point she actually prevented a Grumman 14A Tomcat -- one they'd commissioned from the Navy specifically for these tests -- from taking off from its runway. She simply lassoed the plane's tail fin with that incredible glowing lariat of hers (the one she says is actually the reforged girdle of the Earth-goddess Gaea), planted her heels firmly against the tarmac, and held her ground. The powerful jet fighter didn't move an inch. In fact, Major Warren finally had to order the pilot to shut down the engine before the bird was damaged from the strain.

When the Princess actually lifted and toppled the Army's new M1 MBT Tank, I knew the Major was certifiably stunned. Interestingly enough, Diana later told me her first instinct was to destroy both the jet and the tank, until she realized they were manned by human crews. Diana's reservations against harming another human being seemed visibly to annoy the Major, who was growing progressively more and more dumbfounded by this enigmatic woman warrior.

For myself, I find I'm growing to respect her more and more.

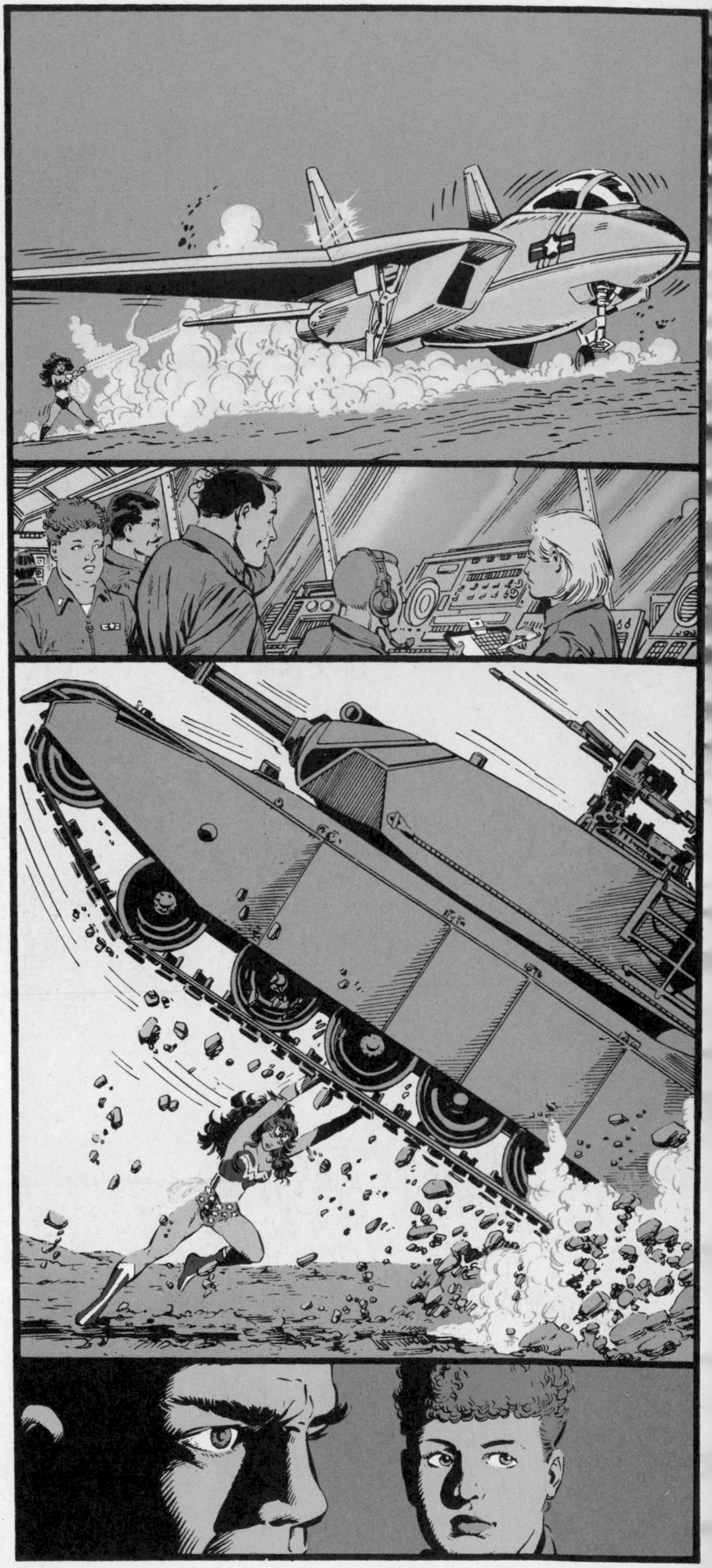

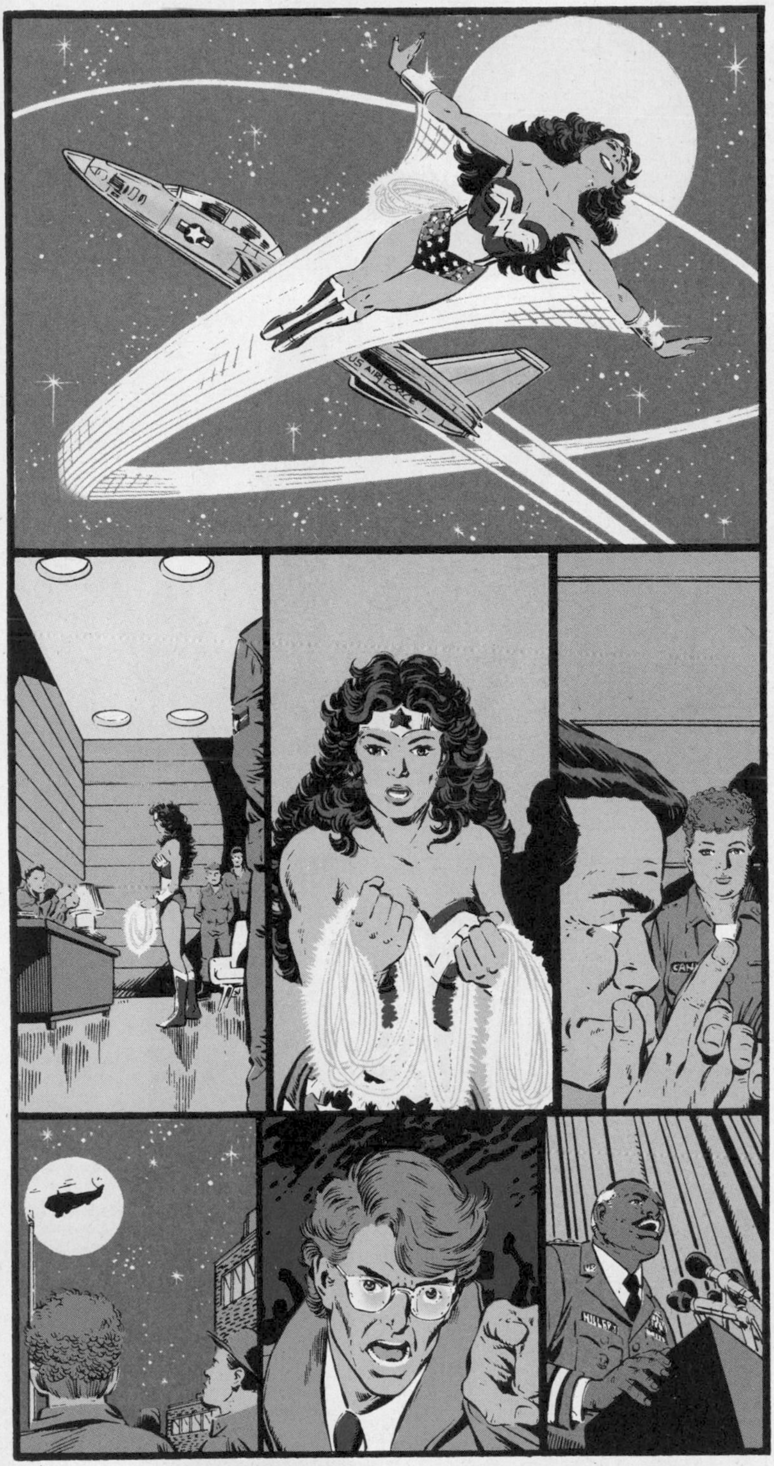
US AIR FORCE

When Diana outperformed that same jet in aerial maneuvers, she actually smiled. She told me this was what she preferred -- a contest of skill which endangered no one -- and besides, she said, she adored the sensation of flying.

With that final test over, Major Warren summoned the Princess to his office. Although he was finally convinced of the truth of Diana's claims, he thought the U.S. should be permitted to examine and, if possible, duplicate the materials used to form her bracelets and lariat.

To say she did not take kindly to that concept is to put it mildly. What were perceived as weapons by the Major were, to Diana, gifts from the Gods and her sister Amazons, and she would permit no one to take them from her.

Frankly, it took all of my composure and military training to keep from telling off the Major myself. Even though Diana had proven herself beyond a doubt, he still seemed strangely ambivalent -- perhaps even antagonistic -- towards her. Nevertheless, he had no choice but to allow Diana to return to Prof. Kapatelis.

Overall, the whole affair seemed to unnerve the Princess, and I felt somewhat ashamed of how she must perceive us. She had come to our world to help us, and here she was, being treated like some sort of subversive. Beyond various televised appearances and such, I haven't seen or spoken to Diana since that day.

In fact, she seemed to disappear for a while, until that strange anti-hero business generated by G. Gordon Godfrey boiled over.

At least Diana's acceptance by the other heroes, including that Martian Manhunter who saved President Reagan's life, opened the way for the announcement by General Hillary, exonerating us and clarifying the events at that Missile Base for the general public.

Steve, this is my last week at Lowry. I'll be back at Hanscom when you return. I opened this letter with a formal greeting, hoping to reaffirm my belief that the Military life is still for you.

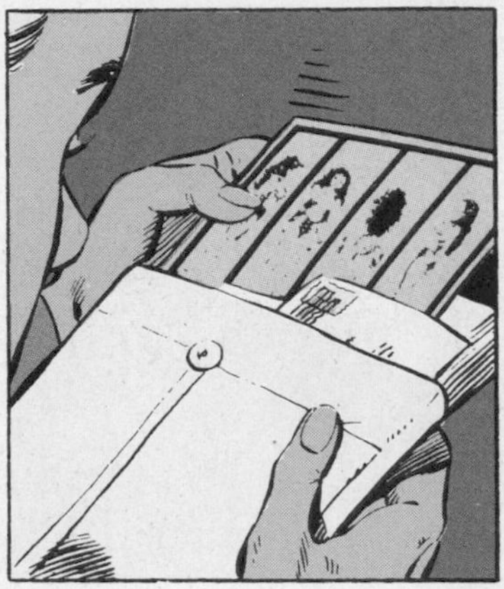

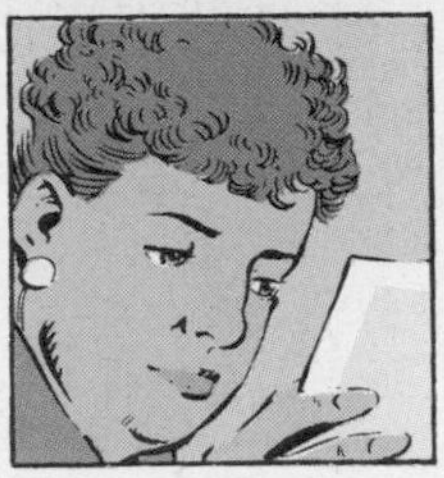

I just hope that past problems won't harden you against the career you once loved so much.

I'm also enclosing some letters from your family, and I hope all is well. I miss you, Steve. More than I can say.

Looking forward to your return.

Respectfully,

Etta

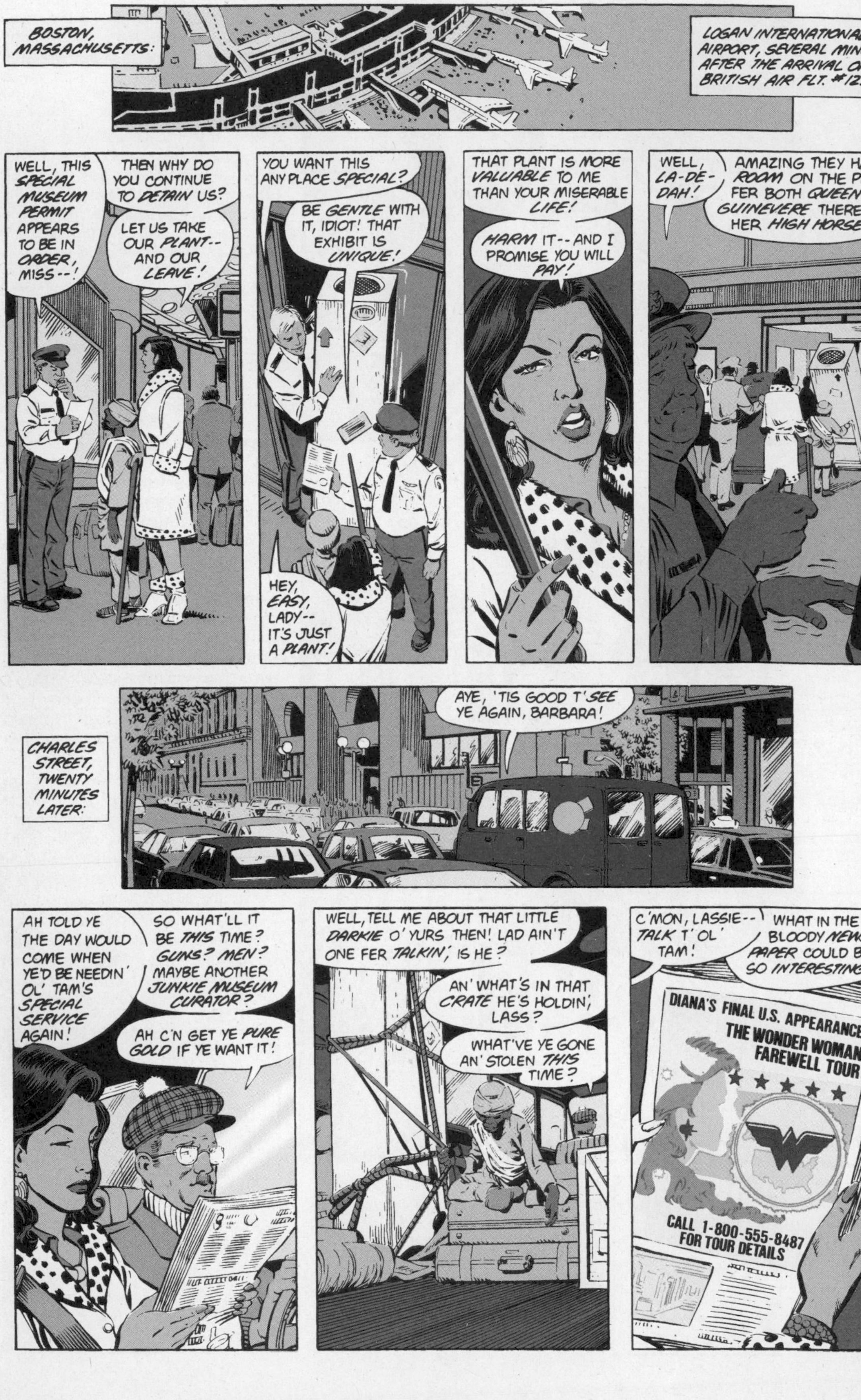
BOSTON, MASSACHUSETTS:
LOGAN INTERNATIONAL AIRPORT, SEVERAL MINUTES AFTER THE ARRIVAL OF BRITISH AIR FLT. #1236...
WELL, THIS SPECIAL MUSEUM PERMIT APPEARS TO BE IN ORDER, MISS--!
THEN WHY DO YOU CONTINUE TO DETAIN US?
LET US TAKE OUR PLANT-- AND OUR LEAVE!
YOU WANT THIS ANY PLACE SPECIAL?
BE GENTLE WITH IT, IDIOT! THAT EXHIBIT IS UNIQUE!
HEY, EASY, LADY-- IT'S JUST A PLANT!
THAT PLANT IS MORE VALUABLE TO ME THAN YOUR MISERABLE LIFE!
HARM IT-- AND I PROMISE YOU WILL PAY!
WELL, LA-DE-DAH!
AMAZING THEY HAD ROOM ON THE PLANE FER BOTH QUEEN GUINEVERE THERE AND HER HIGH HORSE!
CHARLES STREET, TWENTY MINUTES LATER:
AYE, 'TIS GOOD T'SEE YE AGAIN, BARBARA!
AH TOLD YE THE DAY WOULD COME WHEN YE'D BE NEEDIN' OL' TAM'S SPECIAL SERVICE AGAIN!
SO WHAT'LL IT BE THIS TIME? GUNS? MEN? MAYBE ANOTHER JUNKIE MUSEUM CURATOR?
AH C'N GET YE PURE GOLD IF YE WANT IT!
WELL, TELL ME ABOUT THAT LITTLE DARKIE O' YURS THEN! LAD AIN'T ONE FER TALKIN', IS HE?
AN' WHAT'S IN THAT CRATE HE'S HOLDIN', LASS?
WHAT'VE YE GONE AN' STOLEN THIS TIME?
C'MON, LASSIE-- TALK T' OL' TAM!
WHAT IN THE BLOODY NEWSPAPER COULD BE SO INTERESTING?
DIANA'S FINAL U.S. APPEARANCE
THE WONDER WOMAN FAREWELL TOUR
CALL 1-800-555-8487 FOR TOUR DETAILS

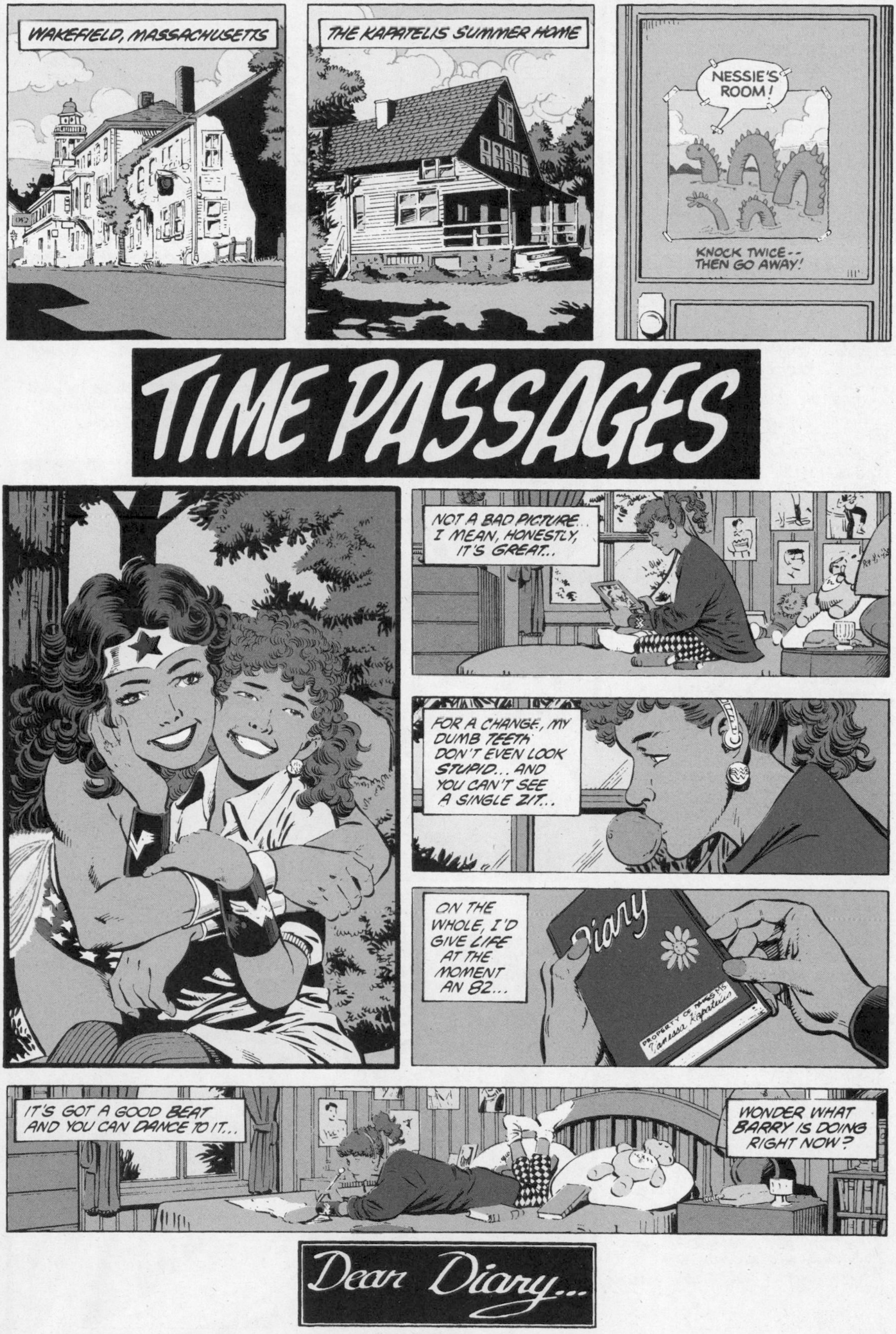
WAKEFIELD, MASSACHUSETTS
THE KAPATELIS SUMMER HOME
NESSIE'S ROOM!
KNOCK TWICE-- THEN GO AWAY!
TIME PASSAGES
NOT A BAD PICTURE... I MEAN, HONESTLY, IT'S GREAT...
FOR A CHANGE, MY DUMB TEETH DON'T EVEN LOOK STUPID... AND YOU CAN'T SEE A SINGLE ZIT...
ON THE WHOLE, I'D GIVE LIFE AT THE MOMENT AN 82...
Diary
IT'S GOT A GOOD BEAT AND YOU CAN DANCE TO IT...
WONDER WHAT BARRY IS DOING RIGHT NOW?
Dear Diary...

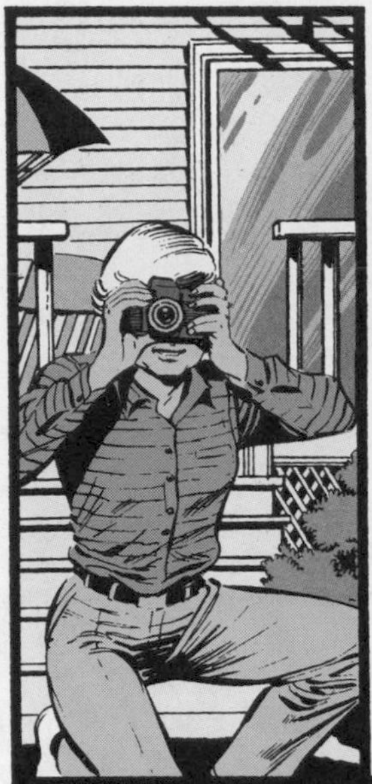

Dear Diary,

Well, just got that picture Mom took of Diana and me the same day I got those special "Wonder Woman" bracelets and earrings from Myndi. The photo looks so excellent! Diana looks great! And so do I!

Y'know, Diary, I never did tell you all about that day. (I was so exhausted, since mom made me do all my homework and stuff before she would take the picture--YUK!)

Anyway, that was the day Diana and me finally had a lo-o-o-ong talk about things, and I found out how really terrific she is. Did I tell you she thinks I'm beautiful? Really! She told me I was the first young girl she'd ever seen, 'cause when she grew up (on Paradise Island), she was the only child and all the other Amazons were all adults. That must have been the pits!

Anyway, she kept telling me what a beautiful place her home is and how the air there is so clean and how you can go swimming there every day and all. (Too bad it was too cold to use the pool!) The not-so-cool part is that they also spend a lot of time doing schoolwork, sort of. Diana says that learning is "part of growing". See, they don't age on Paradise Island--they grow. Isn't that weird? Diana said she'd like to take me there someday, but I don't know. I mean, some of it sounds really neat and all, but there's no movies, no MTV, no clothing stores--NO BOYS!!

Though it DOES sound like an excellent place to get a TAN!

By the way, it seems Diana is also the only Amazon with her special powers. She said they were a gift from the Gods she worshipped (seems the Amazons are really heavy into their religion)! I told her we studied some about Zeus and the other Gods in school, but I never believed they REALLY existed! Now I do.

The saddest part was when Diana asked me about Daddy. She'd seen pictures of him around the house and wondered what it was like to have a father. Listening to her made me feel really lucky that I'd had him for even such a short time before he died.

I mean, we were really getting along, and it made me feel like a real DORK for the way I acted when we first met. Honest, I wouldn't have blamed her if she hadn't saved my life.

Anyway, suddenly, Diana got this most excellent urge, and she picked me up in her arms, and we went flying! Really FLYING!!

Okay, I'll admit I was scared at first--just a LITTLE scared--but after a while it was really awesome.

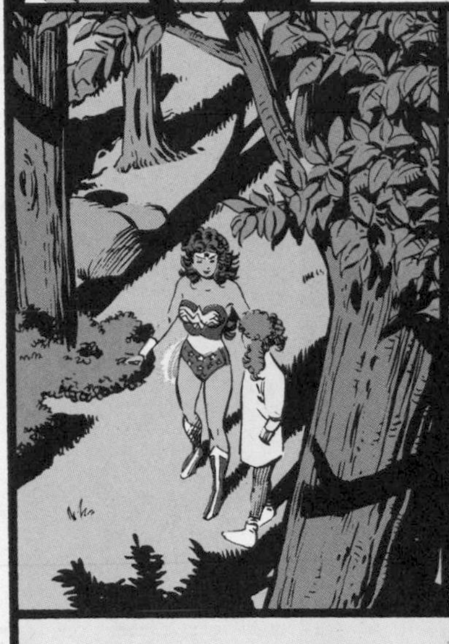

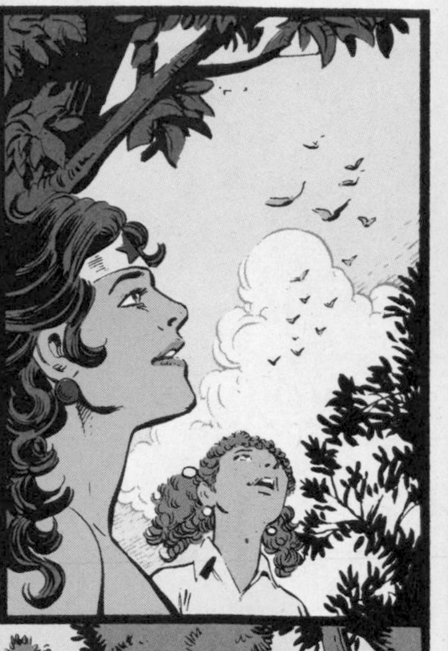

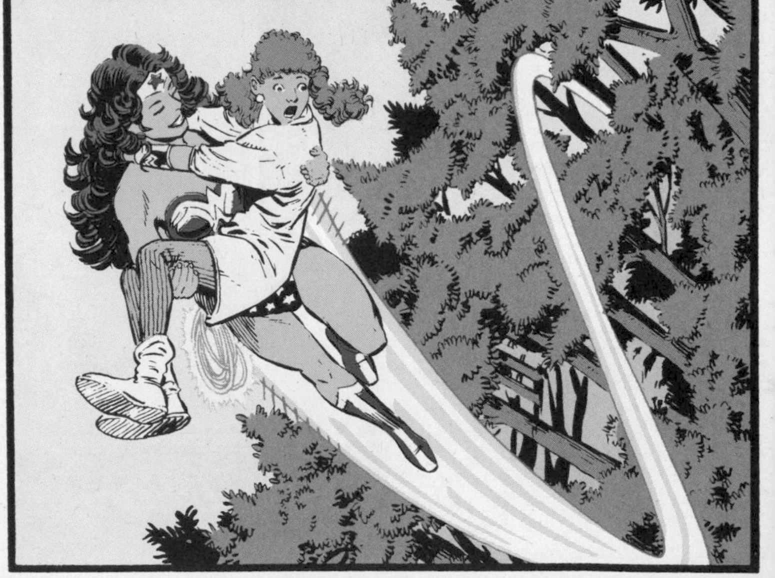

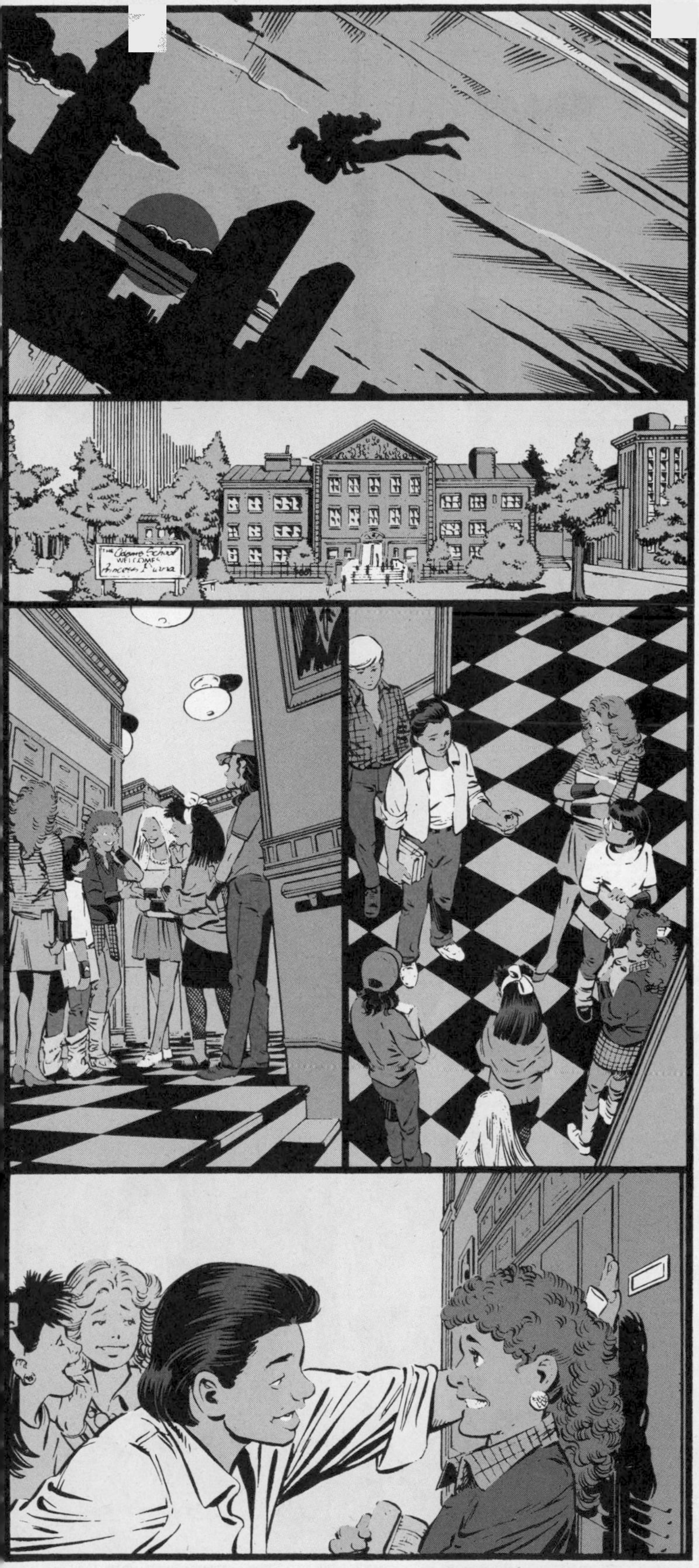

I guess Diana and I flew all over the place for hours, talking about anything that popped into our heads. Diana told me she was nervous about talking at my school (more about that later). She said the English language still confused her some of the time. (Honestly, she speaks it better than me!) I tried talking Greek to her for a while, but my Greek stinks! (Just ask Mom--HA HA!)

Anyway, we came home really late 'cause we got so LOST! Diana said this world was so much bigger than her tiny island, and she thought I knew where we were. Boy, did we laugh. (Even Mom!)

*****

Well, today was the big day! I got to school super-early so I could talk to Joanne, Charlene, and the other girls. I told them all about me and Diana flying over the city and stuff. Boy, were they impressed!

That's when HE walked in! BARRY LOCATELLI! Remember, Diary, how I told you about him? He is absolutely the cutest boy in the whole school! He actually came over to talk to me-- ME!! The other girls were so jealous! I just prayed I wouldn't do anything stupid--like throw up or faint or anything.
I mean, until this morning I thought flying was the biggest thrill of my life! GOD!! I couldn't stand it! Barry leaned towards me, backing my trembling body against the cold lockers. He stared at me with those Rob Lowe eyes of his. Spoke to me with those Michael J. Fox lips. Smiled that Kirk Cameron smile. (I was going to DIE, I just knew it!) He said he had admired me from afar for ages. He said he thought I was cute! (Nope, I wasn't going to die. I was already dead and in Heaven!)
If you don't believe me, just ask the other girls. They all heard him. He said he wanted to sit next to ME at Diana's lecture.

I mean, I tried to be cool. I didn't drool or anything. I think I just nodded my head, because I couldn't say a word. But when he finally walked away, I let out such a SCREAM!

Well, anyway, Diana gave her lecture in the auditorium that afternoon. She was wearing that weird red-white-and-blue costume she wears most of the time. I really wish Mom would let me help buy her some *normal* clothes.

The speech was going just great and Diana had no problem with English like she was afraid she would. Of course, I'd heard it all before when we were flying, but that was okay since the lecture got me out of introductory physics class. All the other girls were really excited and started imitating Diana's Amazon salute (which is when you cross your arms like an X and have the bracelets touch each other). Boy, the local stores must have sold a lot of those bracelets just from *our* school alone.

A lot of boys listened too, except for the usual jerks like Johnny Meekins. He just kept bothering Lisa Choi by pretending to fall asleep while Diana was talking. Honestly, if I was an Amazon, I'd hit him where it 'hurts'!

But then again, if I was an Amazon, I wouldn't have Barry. He was just so beautiful! He actually listened to Diana. I could tell how interested he was. He never took his attention off her for a second. I mean, he's just so *different* from the other boys.

Even though I only just turned 13, he made me feel mature, like I was his equal. (He's 15½, but I've always liked older men). Maybe --oh, PLEASE, God--, maybe he'll even ask me to next month's dance. (I know; I'm going CRAZY, but isn't that what love is all about?)

Anyway, after school, Barry and I went to the yard, where Diana was still talking to some of the kids. Even some of the teachers, like Mr. Kettering from Algebra, were standing around listening.

I told Diana what a hit she'd been. Barry told her too. He's so gorgeous!

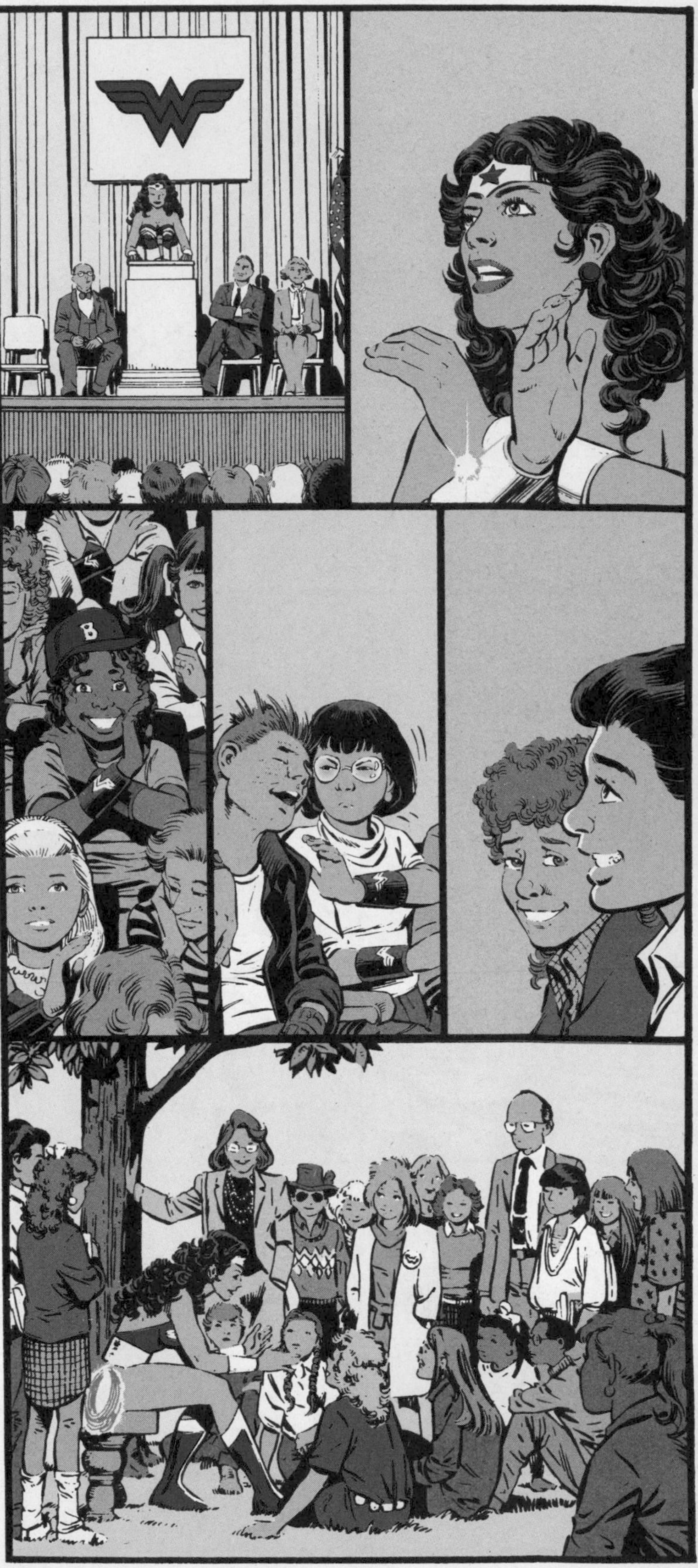

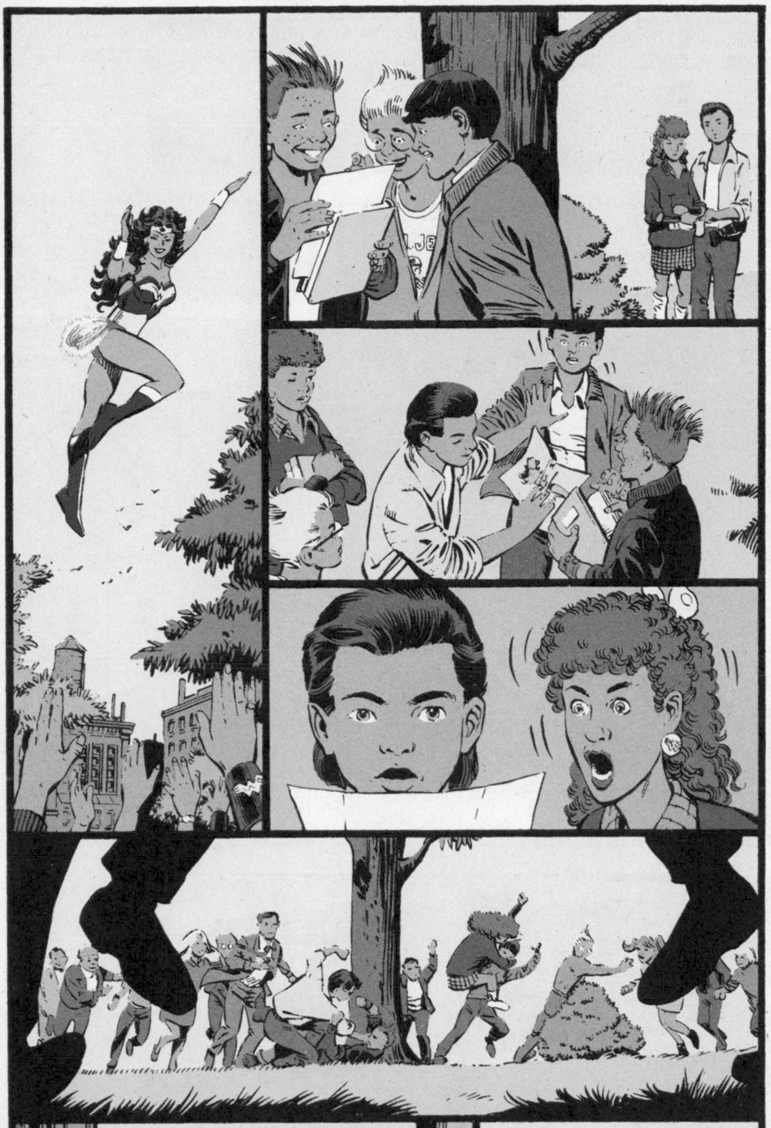

Around 3:30, Diana finally left and I was just kind of walking around with Barry when we saw Johnny Meekins, Louie Lucas, and Vinnie Cafola acting like real goons behind a tree. They were looking at this picture and making all kinds of rude and disgusting noises.

Barry pushed Louie and Vinnie aside and took the picture from Johnny, who looked really scared that Barry was gonna hit him.

When we looked at the picture, I nearly wanted to barf. It was a shot of Diana that those morons had drawn all over to make it look really gross and disgusting. It reminded me of what Diana had said during the lecture, about how the Amazons had been treated by the Greek armies.

Well, I didn't get sick--I just got fighting mad! And so did Barry! We really piled into those creeps like Sigourney Weaver in "Aliens"! While Barry beat on Johnny, I jumped on Vinnie and hit him in the head with my bracelets. I don't know how long we were fighting, but Mr. Nanko stopped us before we clobbered those idiots. Thankfully, Mom used her influence to keep us from getting suspended, but, boy, was she MAD! Mom never yells, y'know--she just LOOKS at you. I swear, you can positively feel her eyes blistering your skin! Mom made me apologize to Johnny and the others. She said that Diana wouldn't have acted that way, and she was right. Diana never uses violence except as a last resort. Mom also grounded me for a whole MONTH!!

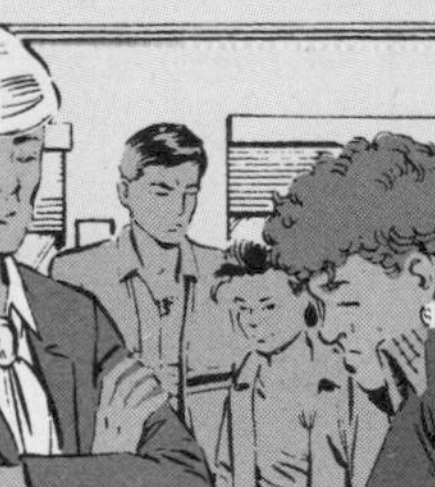

Well, at least I'll still see Barry in school. He thought I was really cool during the fight and he even gave me a picture of him. He said I was his "Wonder Woman"!

Wow, grounded for a whole MONTH!

Y'know something, Dear Diary? It was WORTH it!

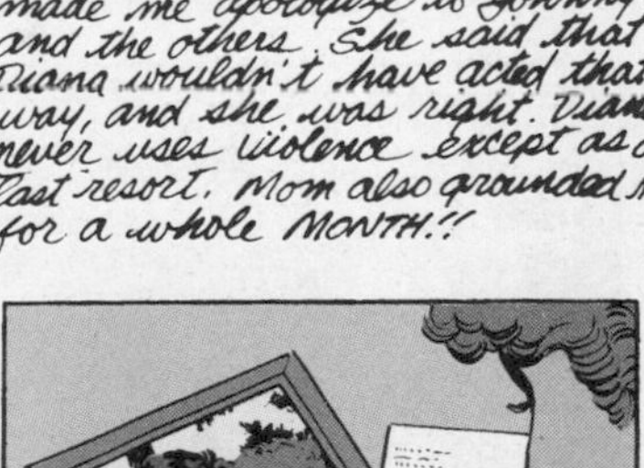
Diary

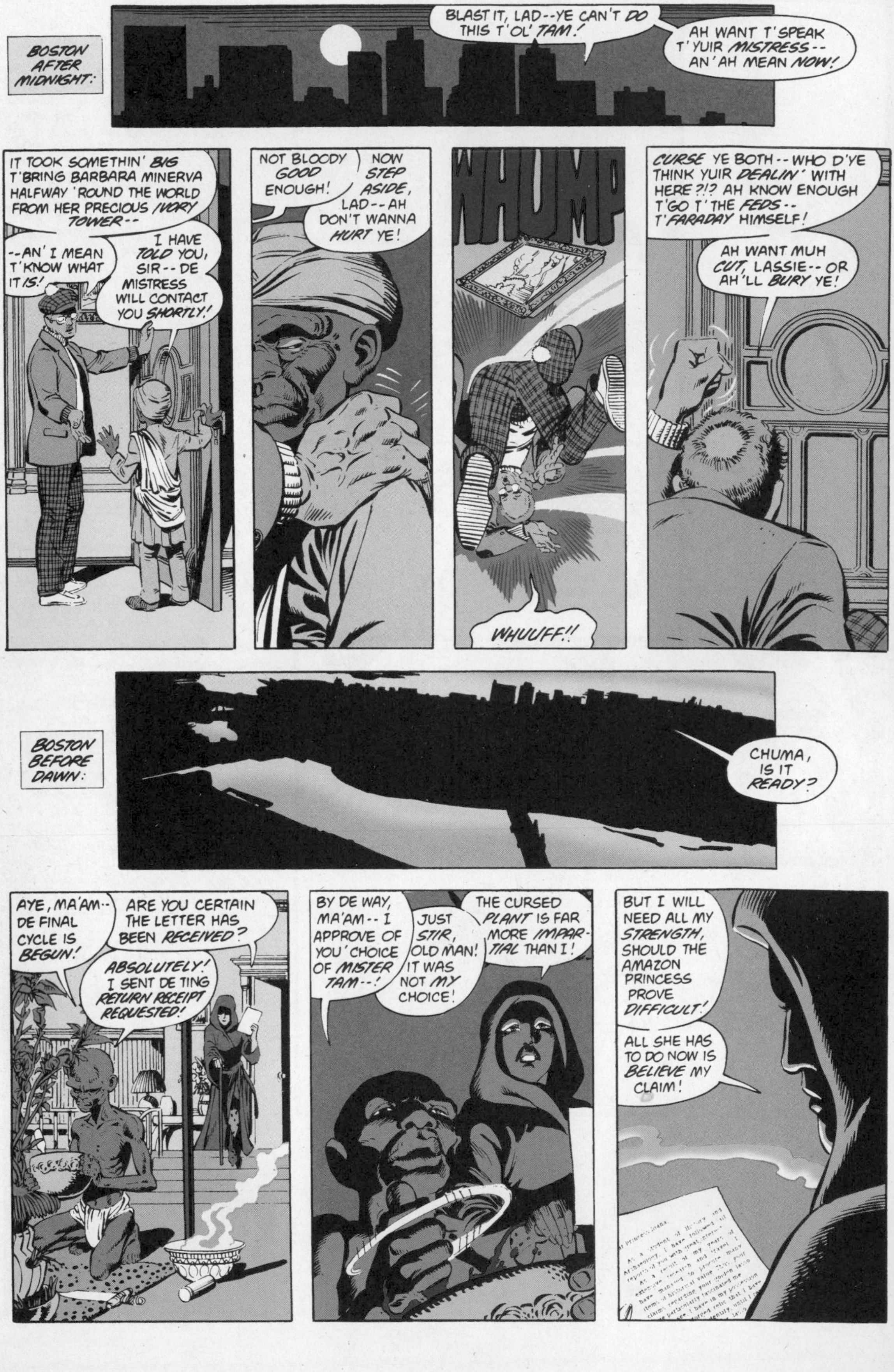
BOSTON AFTER MIDNIGHT:
BLAST IT, LAD--YE CAN'T DO THIS T'OL' TAM!
AH WANT T'SPEAK T'YUIR MISTRESS-- AN'AH MEAN NOW!
IT TOOK SOMETHIN' BIG T'BRING BARBARA MINERVA HALFWAY 'ROUND THE WORLD FROM HER PRECIOUS IVORY TOWER--
--AN' I MEAN T'KNOW WHAT IT IS!
I HAVE TOLD YOU, SIR--DE MISTRESS WILL CONTACT YOU SHORTLY!
NOT BLOODY GOOD ENOUGH!
NOW STEP ASIDE, LAD--AH DON'T WANNA HURT YE!
WHUMP
WHUUFF!!
CURSE YE BOTH--WHO D'YE THINK YUIR DEALIN' WITH HERE?!? AH KNOW ENOUGH T'GO T' THE FEDS-- T'FARADAY HIMSELF!
AH WANT MUH CUT, LASSIE--OR AH'LL BURY YE!
BOSTON BEFORE DAWN:
CHUMA, IS IT READY?
AYE, MA'AM-- DE FINAL CYCLE IS BEGUN!
ARE YOU CERTAIN THE LETTER HAS BEEN RECEIVED?
ABSOLUTELY! I SENT DE TING RETURN RECEIPT REQUESTED!
BY DE WAY, MA'AM--I APPROVE OF YOU' CHOICE OF MISTER TAM--!
JUST STIR, OLD MAN! IT WAS NOT MY CHOICE!
THE CURSED PLANT IS FAR MORE IMPARTIAL THAN I!
BUT I WILL NEED ALL MY STRENGTH, SHOULD THE AMAZON PRINCESS PROVE DIFFICULT!
ALL SHE HAS TO DO NOW IS BELIEVE MY CLAIM!

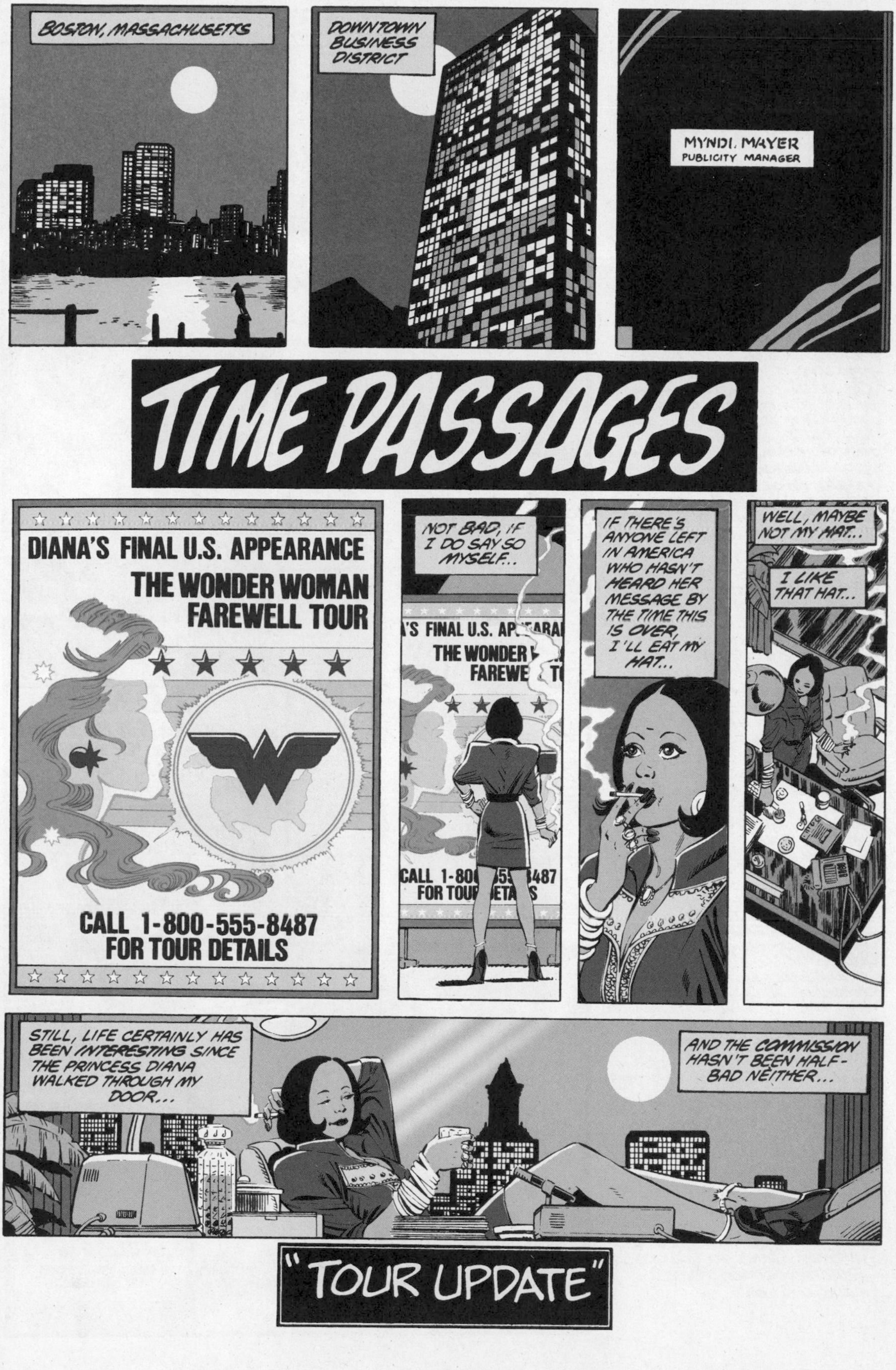
BOSTON, MASSACHUSETTS
DOWNTOWN BUSINESS DISTRICT
MYNDI MAYER
PUBLICITY MANAGER
TIME PASSAGES
DIANA'S FINAL U.S. APPEARANCE
THE WONDER WOMAN FAREWELL TOUR
CALL 1-800-555-8487
FOR TOUR DETAILS
NOT BAD, IF I DO SAY SO MYSELF...
IF THERE'S ANYONE LEFT IN AMERICA WHO HASN'T HEARD HER MESSAGE BY THE TIME THIS IS OVER, I'LL EAT MY HAT...
WELL, MAYBE NOT MY HAT...
I LIKE THAT HAT...
STILL, LIFE CERTAINLY HAS BEEN INTERESTING SINCE THE PRINCESS DIANA WALKED THROUGH MY DOOR...
AND THE COMMISSION HASN'T BEEN HALF-BAD NEITHER...
"TOUR UPDATE"

Darling Julia,

Just to bring you up to date...

With that horrid G. Gordon Godfrey problem finally dealt with, and the military's public acknowledgement of Diana's claims regarding the "Ares Affair," our Wonder Woman Tour couldn't have been better-timed. Especially since the princess' brief period of seclusion had whetted everyone's appetite to learn more about her.

Being all too well-aware of the time limits imposed upon us by Diana's mother, I knew the only way to accomplish Diana's goals was with a juggernaut media blitz.

The press coverage I arranged of Boston's Mayor Flynn presenting the princess with the key to the city was an overwhelmingly positive and her subsequent appearance on the Carson show was a ratings blockbuster. The audience reaction to Diana lifting the entire Tonight show set, complete with Johnny, Ed, Doc, and even -- God help us -- Tommy Newsome still sitting on it, was nothing short of spectacular.

Of course, arranging Diana's meeting with the President was the crowning touch. Because of her hectic schedule, Diana was the only super-hero who had not yet been honored by the Big Man for her participation in the Godfrey affair. By arranging a separate audience for Diana, we assured she wouldn't have to share the spotlight with anyone else.

On the merchandising front, it seems that stores nation-wide can't seem to stock enough Wonder Woman material. Add to that the licensing of Diana's own monthly comic book to be published by DC Comics Inc., as well as licensing her likeness to various Wonder Woman clothing and notions lines, huge profits are being projected across the board for the final two fiscal quarters of this year.

Since Diana claims she'll no longer be with us by year's end, her share of the profits will be channeled toward a "Wonder Woman Foundation" whose principal aim will be to publicize, promote, and encourage the contribution of various women over 40 years old toward equality and advancement.

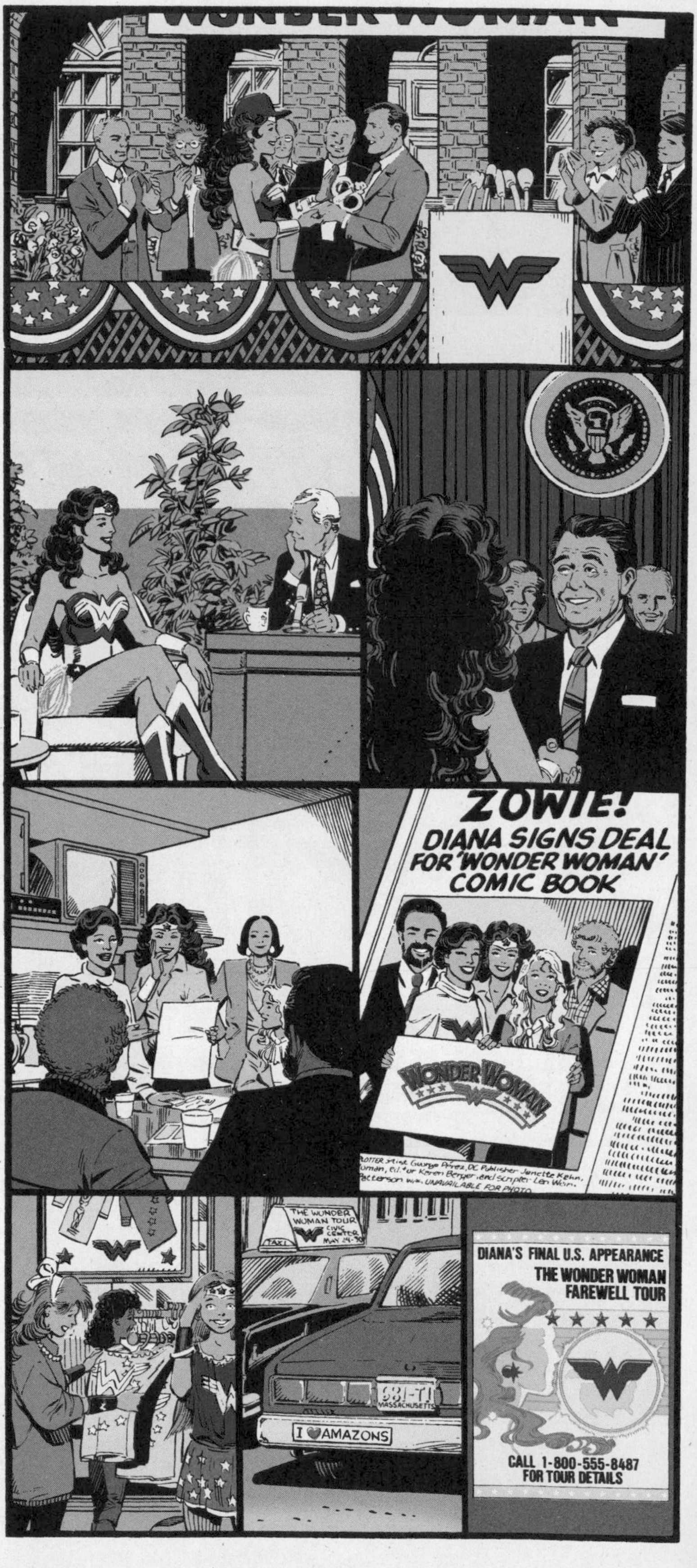
WONDER WOMAN
ZOWIE!
DIANA SIGNS DEAL FOR 'WONDER WOMAN' COMIC BOOK
WONDER WOMAN
...OTTER artist George Pérez, DC Publisher Jenette Kahn, ...oman, editor Karen Berger, and scripter Len Wein. ...Patterson was UNAVAILABLE FOR PHOTO
THE WONDER WOMAN TOUR CIVIC CENTER MAY 24-30
TAXI
MASSACHUSETTS
I ♥ AMAZONS
DIANA'S FINAL U.S. APPEARANCE
THE WONDER WOMAN FAREWELL TOUR
CALL 1-800-555-8487 FOR TOUR DETAILS

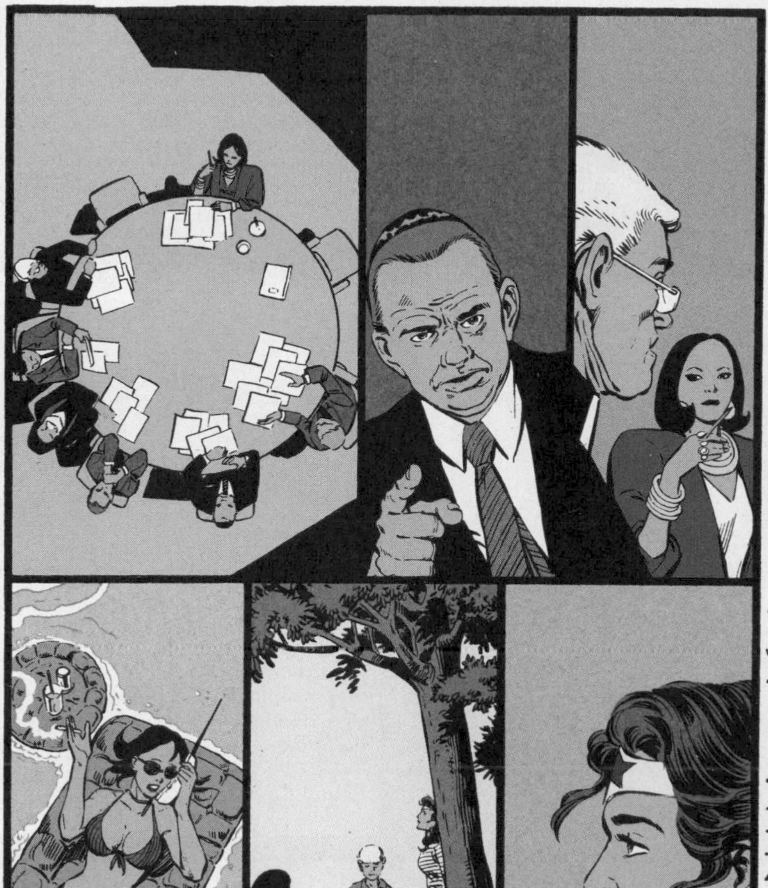
NA'S FINAL U.S. APPEARANCE
THE WONDER WOMAN
FAREWELL TOUR
CALL 1-800-555-
FOR TOUR DETA

Though I'll miss her, it may be just as well that Diana's stay here on "Man's World" is temporary. There has been increasing pressure from various religious spokespeople over the past few weeks, demanding they be allowed to question the Princess regarding her religious beliefs. In a round-table discussion with prominent Christian and Judaic leaders, great concern was expressed regarding the "Pagan" aspects of the Mythic Greek philosophy Diana expounds. While meetings such as these have generally been civil, a growing number of Fundamentalists and even Atheists have called me at all hours of the day to lodge formal complaints.

As you remember that day up at your summer place, I finally had no choice but to tell the Princess about the problem, and it became obvious that the strain of the tour was finally beginning to take its toll. Though I tried to emphasize the potential positive responses we could make, Diana seemed lost in thoughts of male chauvinism, political polarization, anti-heroic prejudice. and now religious persecution, all still so new to her.

Though the tour is finally drawing to a close, the fan mail just keeps pouring in. One letter in particular caught my eye, and I thought I should forward it to you.

It's from a Doctor Barbara Minerva, and it strikes me as just the tonic Diana needs right now.

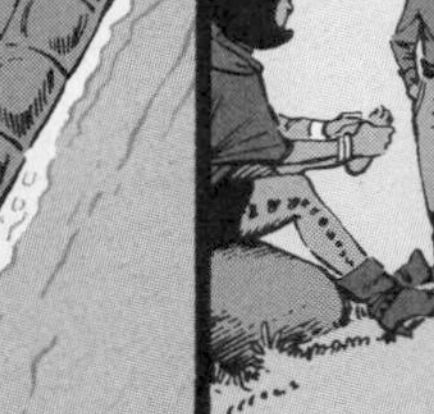

Besides, if Minerva's claims are valid, we've got a nifty new piece of publicity here.

Take care of our Princess, Professor.

Myndi Mayer

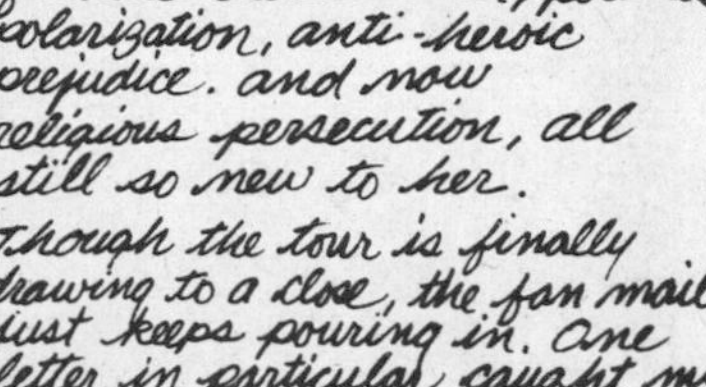
Mayer Publicists, Inc.
Boston, MA 02112
Dear Princess Diana,
As a student of
Archaeology, I have foll
reports of you with great intere
As a result of my years of
extensive research and travel,
have managed to procure
items of historical value.
claims regarding your
have particularly fasc
You see, I hav

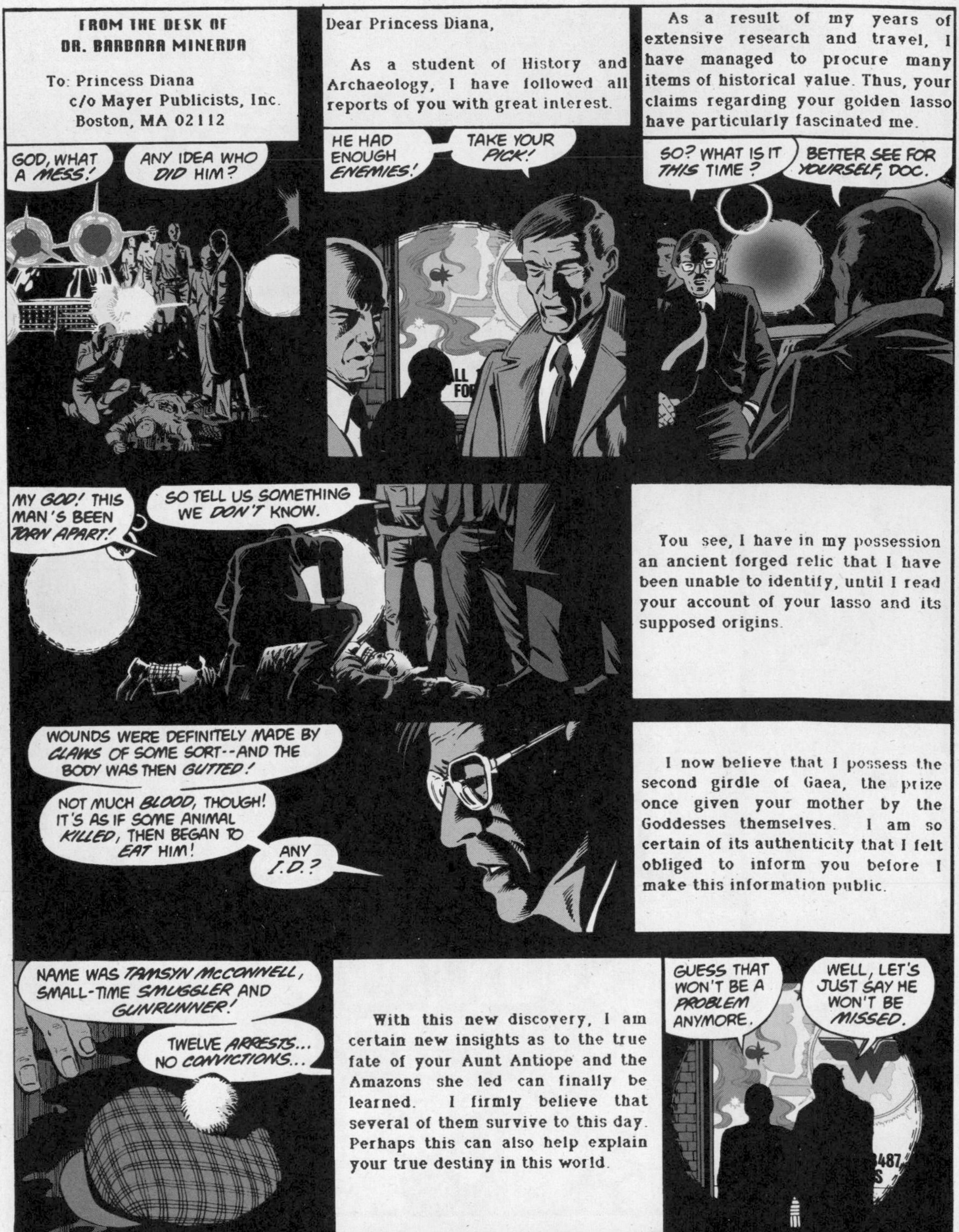
FROM THE DESK OF
DR. BARBARA MINERVA
To: Princess Diana
c/o Mayer Publicists, Inc.
Boston, MA 02112
GOD, WHAT A MESS!
ANY IDEA WHO DID HIM?
Dear Princess Diana,
As a student of History and Archaeology, I have followed all reports of you with great interest.
HE HAD ENOUGH ENEMIES!
TAKE YOUR PICK!
As a result of my years of extensive research and travel, I have managed to procure many items of historical value. Thus, your claims regarding your golden lasso have particularly fascinated me.
SO? WHAT IS IT THIS TIME?
BETTER SEE FOR YOURSELF, DOC.
MY GOD! THIS MAN'S BEEN TORN APART!
SO TELL US SOMETHING WE DON'T KNOW.
You see, I have in my possession an ancient forged relic that I have been unable to identify, until I read your account of your lasso and its supposed origins.
WOUNDS WERE DEFINITELY MADE BY CLAWS OF SOME SORT--AND THE BODY WAS THEN GUTTED!
NOT MUCH BLOOD, THOUGH! IT'S AS IF SOME ANIMAL KILLED, THEN BEGAN TO EAT HIM!
ANY I.D.?
I now believe that I possess the second girdle of Gaea, the prize once given your mother by the Goddesses themselves. I am so certain of its authenticity that I felt obliged to inform you before I make this information public.
NAME WAS TAMSYN McCONNELL, SMALL-TIME SMUGGLER AND GUNRUNNER!
TWELVE ARRESTS... NO CONVICTIONS...
With this new discovery, I am certain new insights as to the true fate of your Aunt Antiope and the Amazons she led can finally be learned. I firmly believe that several of them survive to this day. Perhaps this can also help explain your true destiny in this world.
GUESS THAT WON'T BE A PROBLEM ANYMORE.
WELL, LET'S JUST SAY HE WON'T BE MISSED.
As a woman myself, I am excited by these possibilities and hope you will agree to contact me at the above address.
Very truly yours,
Dr. Barbara Minerva

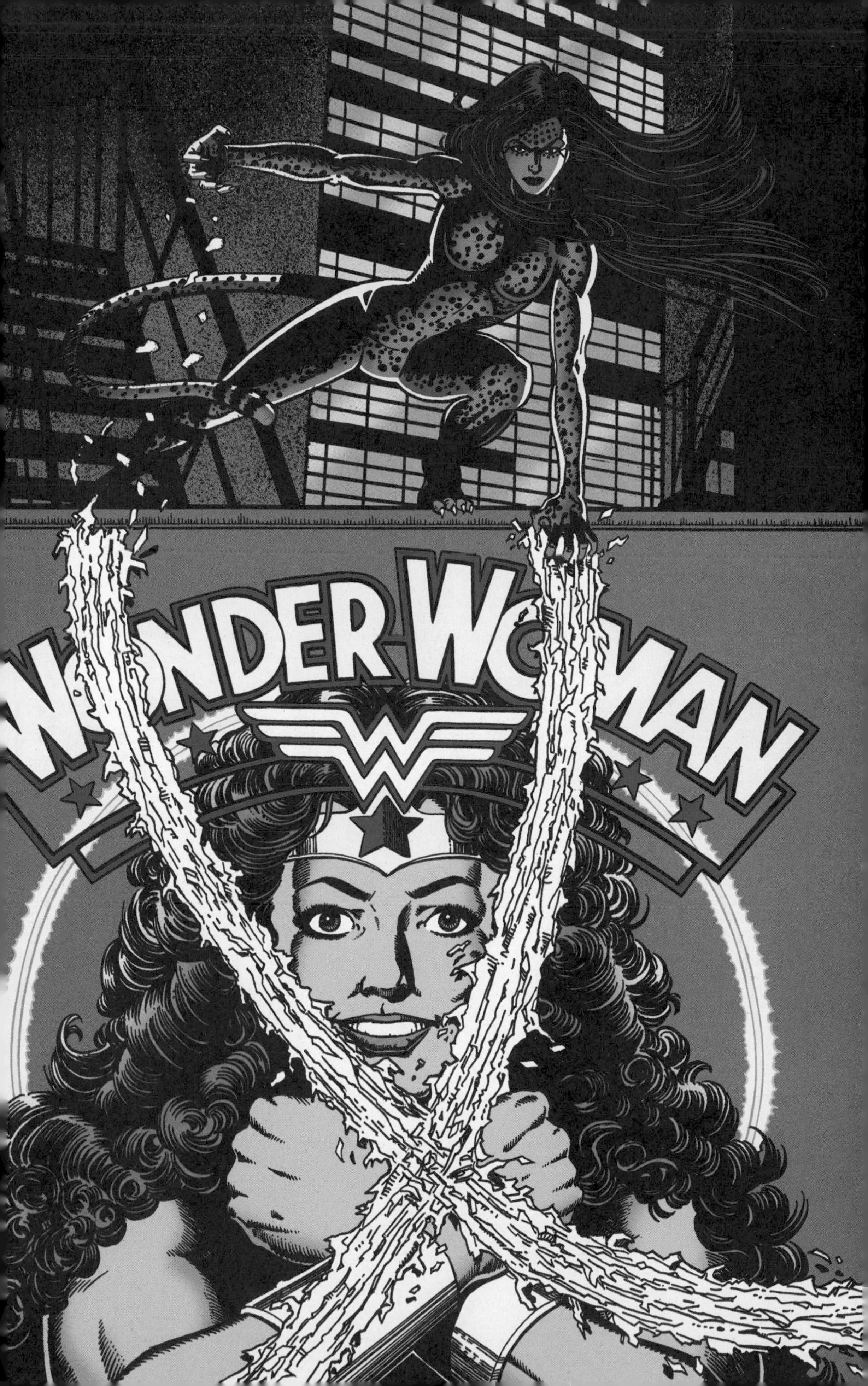
WONDER WOMAN

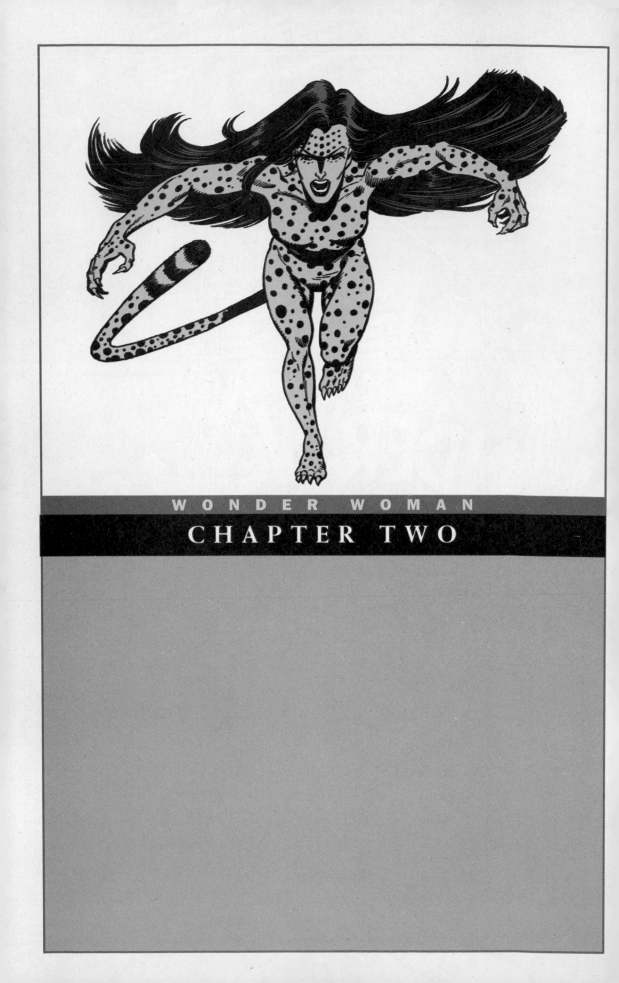

WONDER WOMAN

CHAPTER TWO

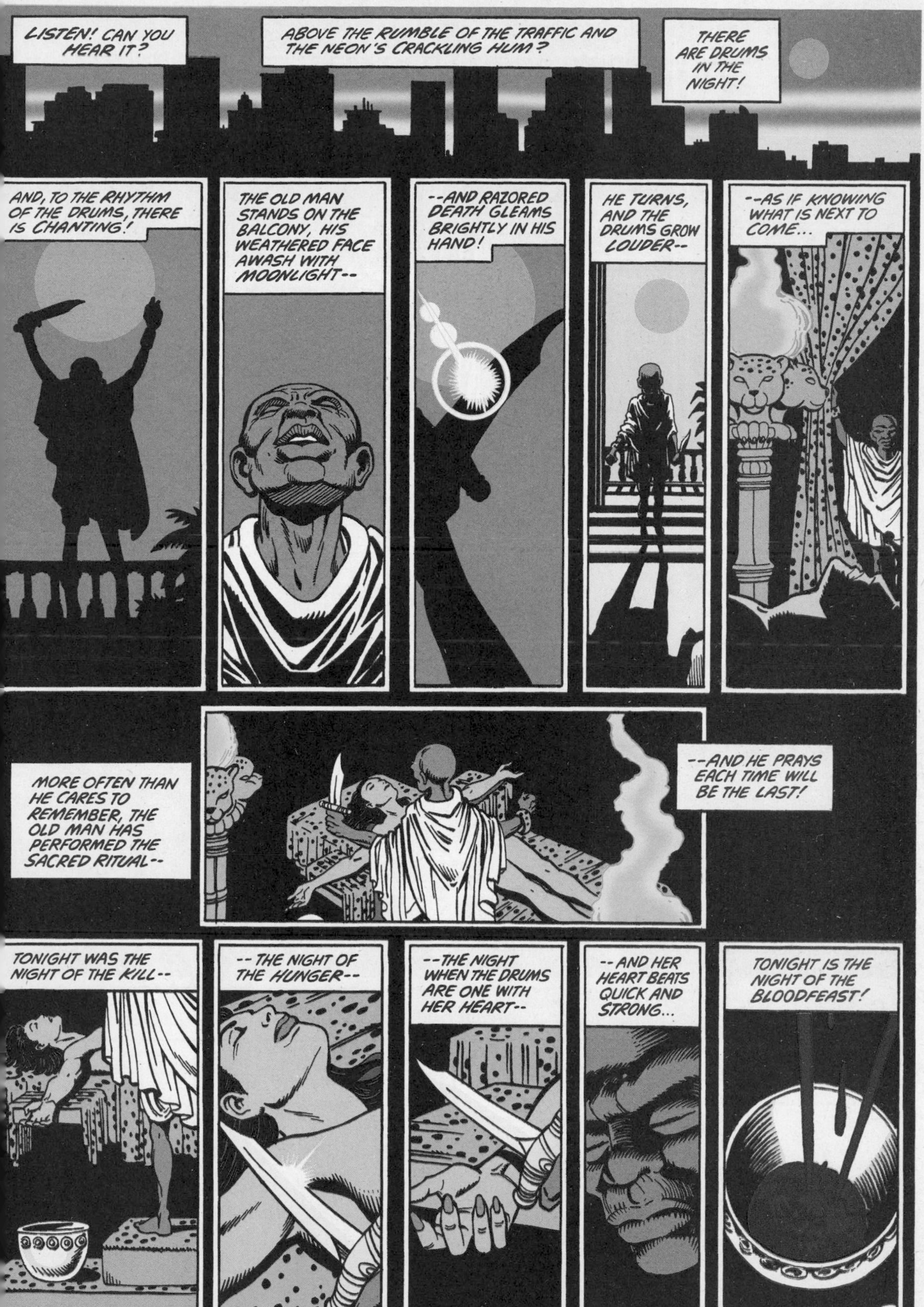
LISTEN! CAN YOU HEAR IT?
ABOVE THE RUMBLE OF THE TRAFFIC AND THE NEON'S CRACKLING HUM?
THERE ARE DRUMS IN THE NIGHT!
AND, TO THE RHYTHM OF THE DRUMS, THERE IS CHANTING!
THE OLD MAN STANDS ON THE BALCONY, HIS WEATHERED FACE AWASH WITH MOONLIGHT--
--AND RAZORED DEATH GLEAMS BRIGHTLY IN HIS HAND!
HE TURNS, AND THE DRUMS GROW LOUDER--
--AS IF KNOWING WHAT IS NEXT TO COME...
MORE OFTEN THAN HE CARES TO REMEMBER, THE OLD MAN HAS PERFORMED THE SACRED RITUAL--
--AND HE PRAYS EACH TIME WILL BE THE LAST!
TONIGHT WAS THE NIGHT OF THE KILL--
--THE NIGHT OF THE HUNGER--
--THE NIGHT WHEN THE DRUMS ARE ONE WITH HER HEART--
--AND HER HEART BEATS QUICK AND STRONG...
TONIGHT IS THE NIGHT OF THE BLOODFEAST!
1

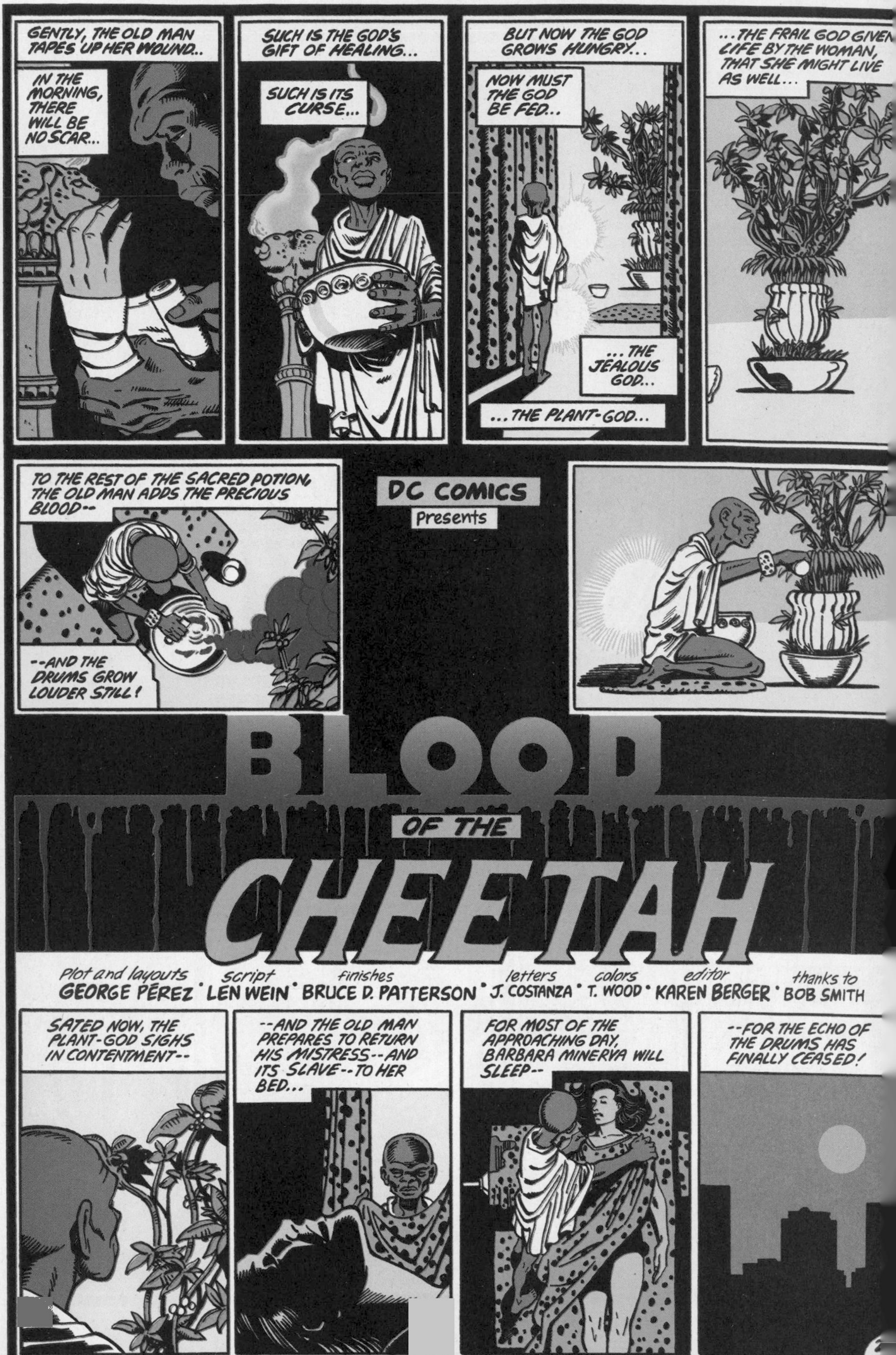
GENTLY, THE OLD MAN TAPES UP HER WOUND..
IN THE MORNING, THERE WILL BE NO SCAR...
SUCH IS THE GOD'S GIFT OF HEALING...
SUCH IS ITS CURSE...
BUT NOW THE GOD GROWS HUNGRY...
NOW MUST THE GOD BE FED...
...THE JEALOUS GOD...
...THE PLANT-GOD...
...THE FRAIL GOD GIVEN LIFE BY THE WOMAN, THAT SHE MIGHT LIVE AS WELL...
TO THE REST OF THE SACRED POTION, THE OLD MAN ADDS THE PRECIOUS BLOOD--
--AND THE DRUMS GROW LOUDER STILL!
DC COMICS
Presents
BLOOD
OF THE
CHEETAH
Plot and layouts GEORGE PÉREZ · script LEN WEIN · finishes BRUCE D. PATTERSON · letters J. COSTANZA · colors T. WOOD · editor KAREN BERGER · thanks to BOB SMITH
SATED NOW, THE PLANT-GOD SIGHS IN CONTENTMENT--
--AND THE OLD MAN PREPARES TO RETURN HIS MISTRESS--AND ITS SLAVE--TO HER BED...
FOR MOST OF THE APPROACHING DAY, BARBARA MINERVA WILL SLEEP--
--FOR THE ECHO OF THE DRUMS HAS FINALLY CEASED!

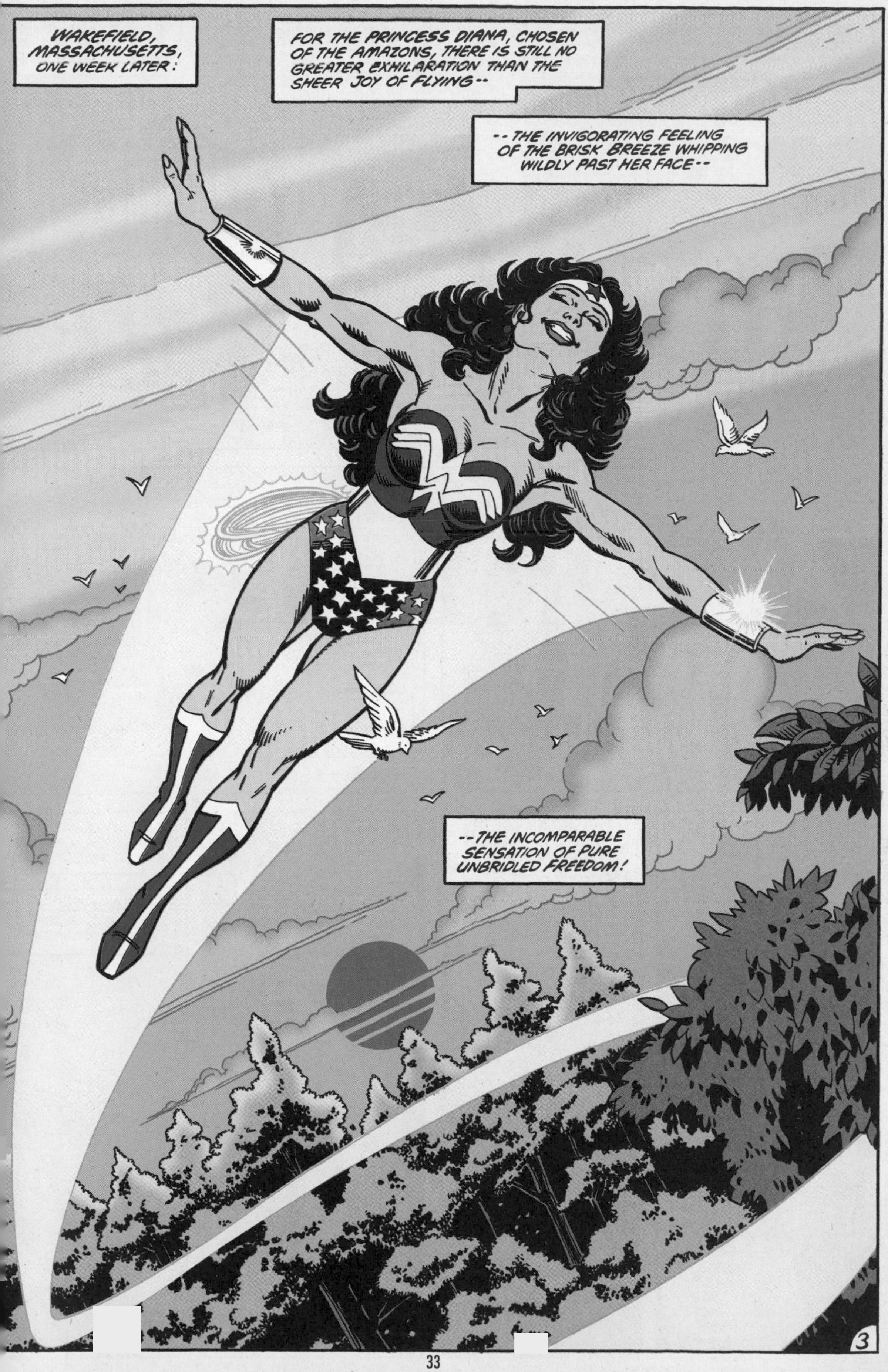
WAKEFIELD, MASSACHUSETTS, ONE WEEK LATER:
FOR THE PRINCESS DIANA, CHOSEN OF THE AMAZONS, THERE IS STILL NO GREATER EXHILARATION THAN THE SHEER JOY OF FLYING--
--THE INVIGORATING FEELING OF THE BRISK BREEZE WHIPPING WILDLY PAST HER FACE--
--THE INCOMPARABLE SENSATION OF PURE UNBRIDLED FREEDOM!
3

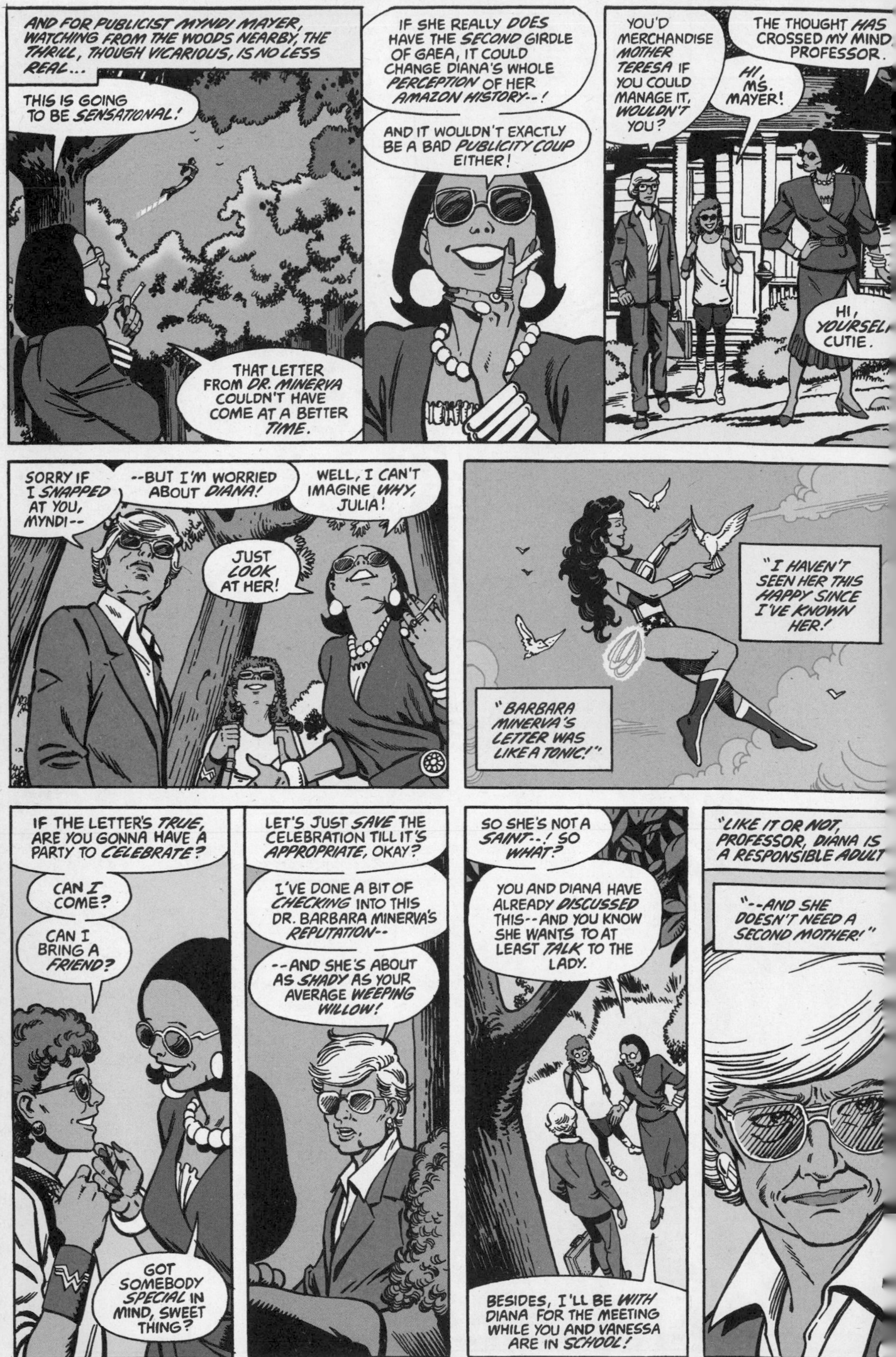
AND FOR PUBLICIST MYNDI MAYER, WATCHING FROM THE WOODS NEARBY, THE THRILL, THOUGH VICARIOUS, IS NO LESS REAL...
THIS IS GOING TO BE SENSATIONAL!
THAT LETTER FROM DR. MINERVA COULDN'T HAVE COME AT A BETTER TIME.
IF SHE REALLY DOES HAVE THE SECOND GIRDLE OF GAEA, IT COULD CHANGE DIANA'S WHOLE PERCEPTION OF HER AMAZON HISTORY--!
AND IT WOULDN'T EXACTLY BE A BAD PUBLICITY COUP EITHER!
YOU'D MERCHANDISE MOTHER TERESA IF YOU COULD MANAGE IT, WOULDN'T YOU?
THE THOUGHT HAS CROSSED MY MIND, PROFESSOR.
HI, MS. MAYER!
HI, YOURSELF, CUTIE.
SORRY IF I SNAPPED AT YOU, MYNDI--
--BUT I'M WORRIED ABOUT DIANA!
WELL, I CAN'T IMAGINE WHY, JULIA!
JUST LOOK AT HER!
"BARBARA MINERVA'S LETTER WAS LIKE A TONIC!"
"I HAVEN'T SEEN HER THIS HAPPY SINCE I'VE KNOWN HER!"
IF THE LETTER'S TRUE, ARE YOU GONNA HAVE A PARTY TO CELEBRATE?
CAN I COME?
CAN I BRING A FRIEND?
GOT SOMEBODY SPECIAL IN MIND, SWEET THING?
LET'S JUST SAVE THE CELEBRATION TILL IT'S APPROPRIATE, OKAY?
I'VE DONE A BIT OF CHECKING INTO THIS DR. BARBARA MINERVA'S REPUTATION--
--AND SHE'S ABOUT AS SHADY AS YOUR AVERAGE WEEPING WILLOW!
SO SHE'S NOT A SAINT--! SO WHAT?
YOU AND DIANA HAVE ALREADY DISCUSSED THIS--AND YOU KNOW SHE WANTS TO AT LEAST TALK TO THE LADY.
BESIDES, I'LL BE WITH DIANA FOR THE MEETING WHILE YOU AND VANESSA ARE IN SCHOOL!
"LIKE IT OR NOT, PROFESSOR, DIANA IS A RESPONSIBLE ADULT
"--AND SHE DOESN'T NEED A SECOND MOTHER!"

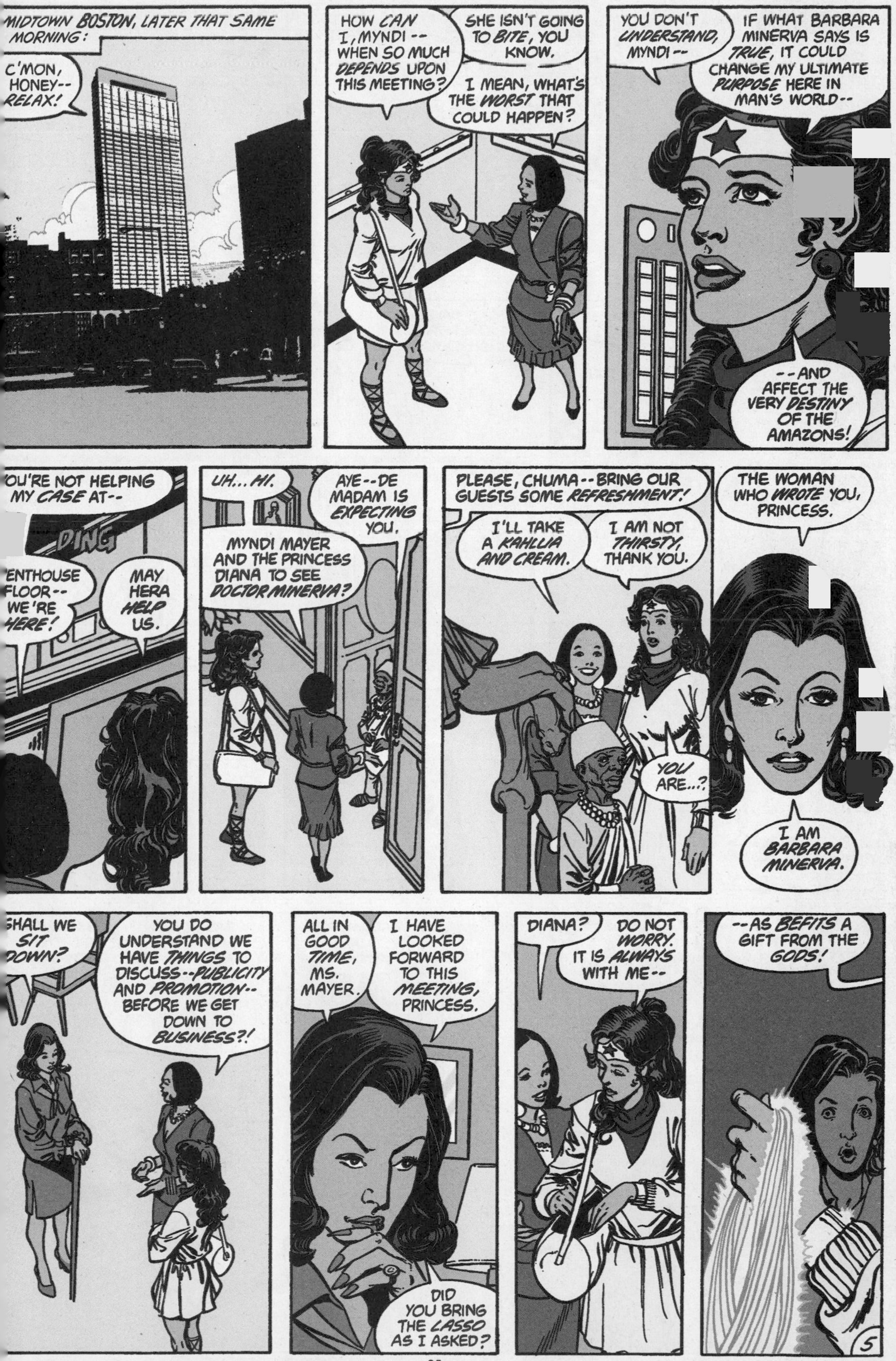
MIDTOWN BOSTON, LATER THAT SAME MORNING:
C'MON, HONEY-- RELAX!
HOW CAN I, MYNDI -- WHEN SO MUCH DEPENDS UPON THIS MEETING?
SHE ISN'T GOING TO BITE, YOU KNOW.
I MEAN, WHAT'S THE WORST THAT COULD HAPPEN?
YOU DON'T UNDERSTAND, MYNDI --
IF WHAT BARBARA MINERVA SAYS IS TRUE, IT COULD CHANGE MY ULTIMATE PURPOSE HERE IN MAN'S WORLD --
-- AND AFFECT THE VERY DESTINY OF THE AMAZONS!
OU'RE NOT HELPING MY CASE AT--
DING
ENTHOUSE FLOOR-- WE'RE HERE!
MAY HERA HELP US.
UH... HI.
MYNDI MAYER AND THE PRINCESS DIANA TO SEE DOCTOR MINERVA?
AYE--DE MADAM IS EXPECTING YOU.
PLEASE, CHUMA--BRING OUR GUESTS SOME REFRESHMENT!
I'LL TAKE A KAHLUA AND CREAM.
I AM NOT THIRSTY, THANK YOU.
YOU ARE...?
THE WOMAN WHO WROTE YOU, PRINCESS.
I AM BARBARA MINERVA.
SHALL WE SIT DOWN?
YOU DO UNDERSTAND WE HAVE THINGS TO DISCUSS--PUBLICITY AND PROMOTION-- BEFORE WE GET DOWN TO BUSINESS?!
ALL IN GOOD TIME, MS. MAYER.
I HAVE LOOKED FORWARD TO THIS MEETING, PRINCESS.
DID YOU BRING THE LASSO AS I ASKED?
DIANA?
DO NOT WORRY. IT IS ALWAYS WITH ME--
--AS BEFITS A GIFT FROM THE GODS!
5

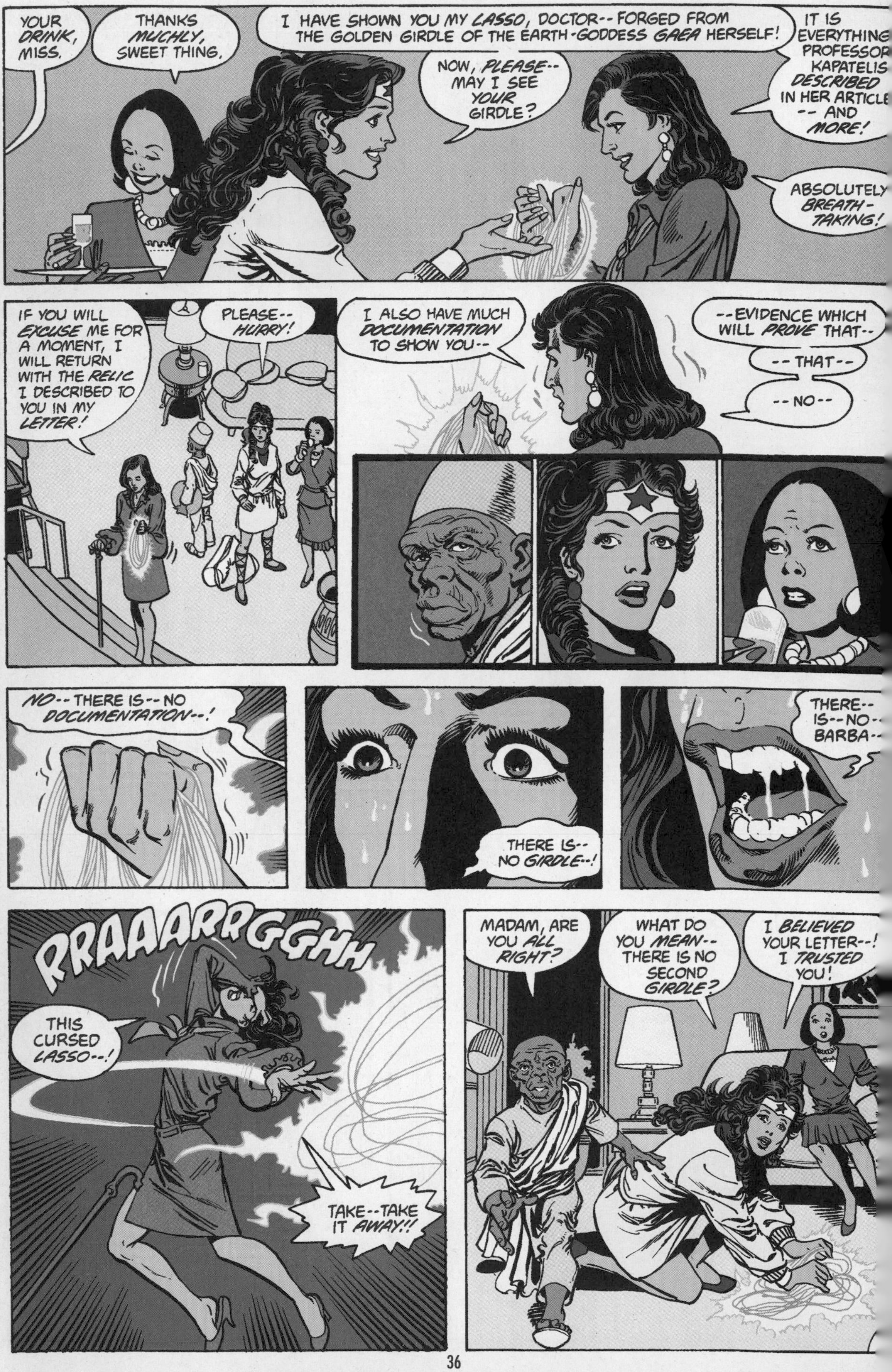
YOUR DRINK, MISS.
THANKS MUCHLY, SWEET THING.
I HAVE SHOWN YOU MY LASSO, DOCTOR-- FORGED FROM THE GOLDEN GIRDLE OF THE EARTH-GODDESS GAEA HERSELF!
NOW, PLEASE-- MAY I SEE YOUR GIRDLE?
IT IS EVERYTHING PROFESSOR KAPATELIS DESCRIBED IN HER ARTICLE -- AND MORE!
ABSOLUTELY BREATH-TAKING!
IF YOU WILL EXCUSE ME FOR A MOMENT, I WILL RETURN WITH THE RELIC I DESCRIBED TO YOU IN MY LETTER!
PLEASE-- HURRY!
I ALSO HAVE MUCH DOCUMENTATION TO SHOW YOU--
--EVIDENCE WHICH WILL PROVE THAT--
-- THAT --
-- NO --
NO-- THERE IS-- NO DOCUMENTATION--!
THERE IS-- NO GIRDLE--!
THERE-- IS--NO-- BARBA--
RRAAARRGGHH
THIS CURSED LASSO--!
TAKE--TAKE IT AWAY!!
MADAM, ARE YOU ALL RIGHT?
WHAT DO YOU MEAN-- THERE IS NO SECOND GIRDLE?
I BELIEVED YOUR LETTER--! I TRUSTED YOU!

WHY WOULD YOU BETRAY ME THIS WAY, DOCTOR? YOU ARE A SISTER?!

I TURNED AWAY FROM JULIA TO MEET YOU!

NO, PLEASE-- WAIT! I ONLY WANTED TO MEET YOU--!

WE HAVE TO TALK--!

SWEET THING-- I'M SORRY!

I THOUGHT SHE WAS LEGIT!

NO, MYNDI-- YOU THOUGHT ONLY OF YOURSELF!

JULIA WAS RIGHT--YOU CARE NOTHING ABOUT ME!

YOU ARE INTERESTED SOLELY IN EXPLOITING ME!

HOW COULD ONE WOMAN DO THAT TO ANOTHER?

< GODDESSES OF OLYMPUS! PRAY GRANT THY WAYWARD DAUGHTER SOME SIGN! >

< HELP ME TO UNDERSTAND THIS MADNESS! >

GREAT.

JUST FREAKING FABULOUS!

BUT QUESTIONS ARE ALL MYNDI MAYER HAS LEFT...

DIANA-- PLEASE!

PLEASE WAIT!

THE ANSWERS ARE ALREADY LONG GONE!

NOW WHAT?

⑦

37

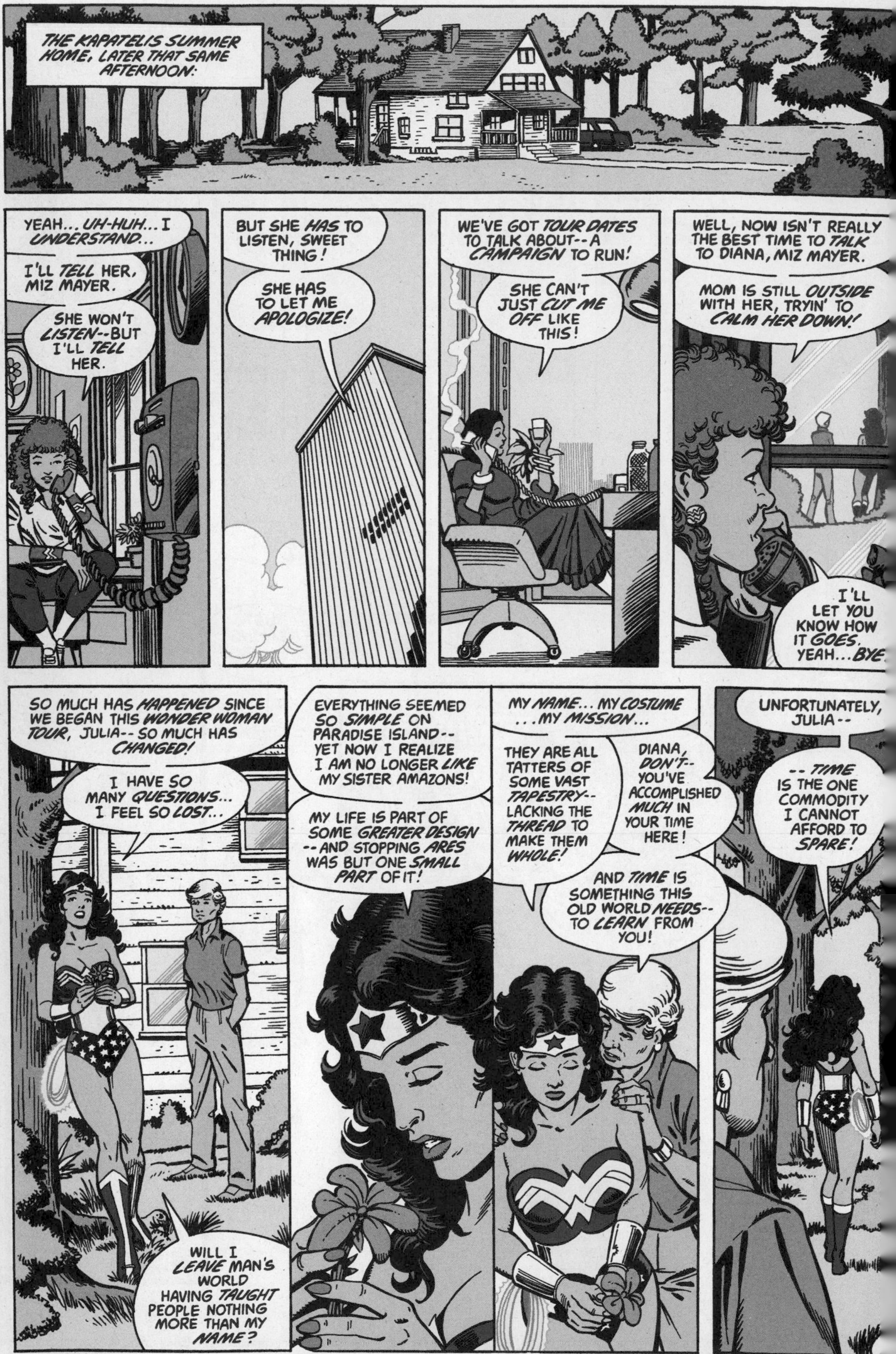
THE KAPATELIS SUMMER HOME, LATER THAT SAME AFTERNOON:
YEAH... UH-HUH... I UNDERSTAND...
I'LL TELL HER, MIZ MAYER.
SHE WON'T LISTEN--BUT I'LL TELL HER.
BUT SHE HAS TO LISTEN, SWEET THING!
SHE HAS TO LET ME APOLOGIZE!
WE'VE GOT TOUR DATES TO TALK ABOUT--A CAMPAIGN TO RUN!
SHE CAN'T JUST CUT ME OFF LIKE THIS!
WELL, NOW ISN'T REALLY THE BEST TIME TO TALK TO DIANA, MIZ MAYER.
MOM IS STILL OUTSIDE WITH HER, TRYIN' TO CALM HER DOWN!
I'LL LET YOU KNOW HOW IT GOES. YEAH... BYE.
SO MUCH HAS HAPPENED SINCE WE BEGAN THIS WONDER WOMAN TOUR, JULIA-- SO MUCH HAS CHANGED!
I HAVE SO MANY QUESTIONS... I FEEL SO LOST...
WILL I LEAVE MAN'S WORLD HAVING TAUGHT PEOPLE NOTHING MORE THAN MY NAME?
EVERYTHING SEEMED SO SIMPLE ON PARADISE ISLAND-- YET NOW I REALIZE I AM NO LONGER LIKE MY SISTER AMAZONS!
MY LIFE IS PART OF SOME GREATER DESIGN --AND STOPPING ARES WAS BUT ONE SMALL PART OF IT!
MY NAME... MY COSTUME ...MY MISSION...
THEY ARE ALL TATTERS OF SOME VAST TAPESTRY--LACKING THE THREAD TO MAKE THEM WHOLE!
DIANA, DON'T-- YOU'VE ACCOMPLISHED MUCH IN YOUR TIME HERE!
AND TIME IS SOMETHING THIS OLD WORLD NEEDS-- TO LEARN FROM YOU!
UNFORTUNATELY, JULIA--
--TIME IS THE ONE COMMODITY I CANNOT AFFORD TO SPARE!

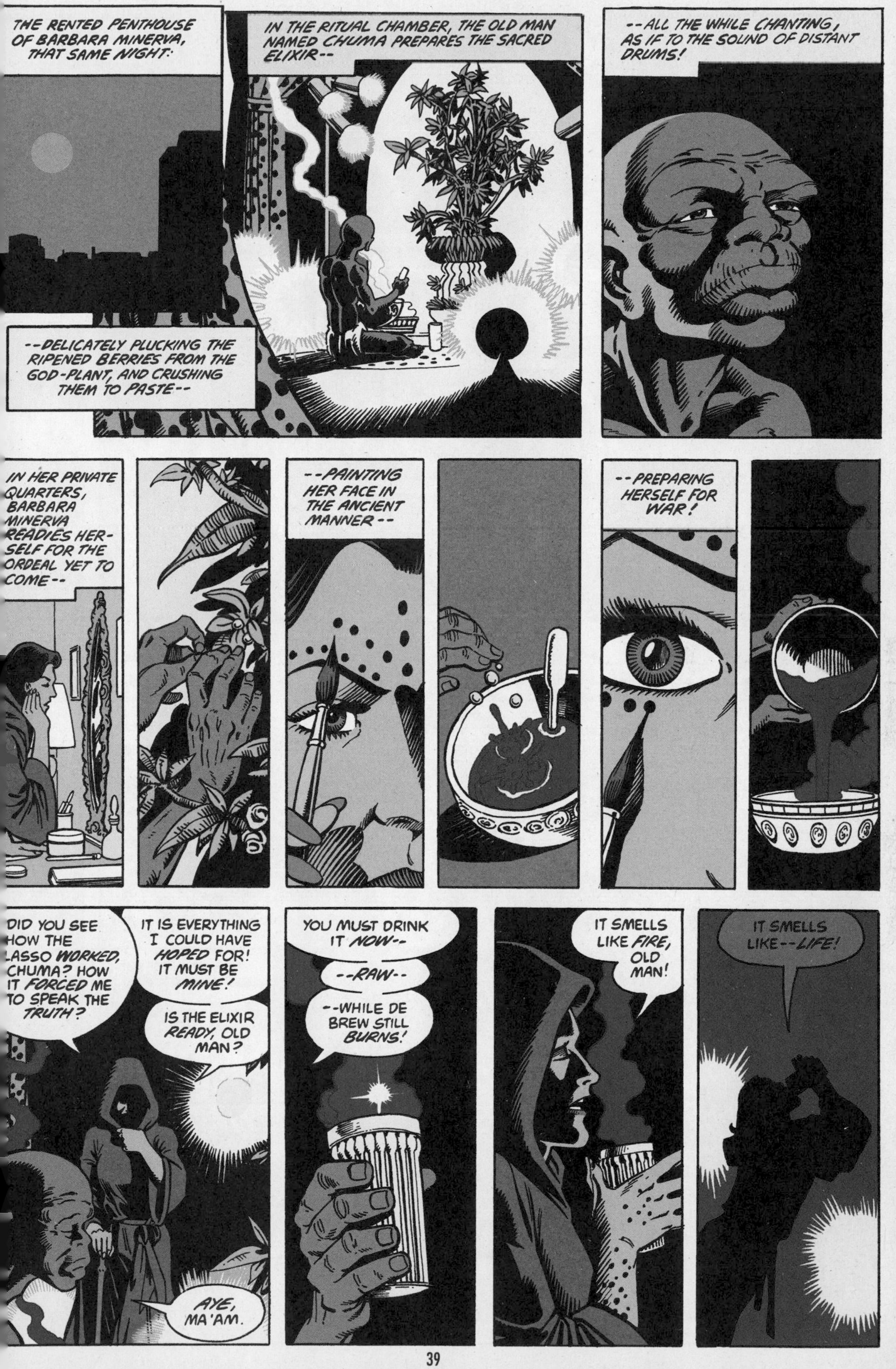

THE RENTED PENTHOUSE OF BARBARA MINERVA, THAT SAME NIGHT:
IN THE RITUAL CHAMBER, THE OLD MAN NAMED CHUMA PREPARES THE SACRED ELIXIR--
--DELICATELY PLUCKING THE RIPENED BERRIES FROM THE GOD-PLANT, AND CRUSHING THEM TO PASTE--
--ALL THE WHILE CHANTING, AS IF TO THE SOUND OF DISTANT DRUMS!
IN HER PRIVATE QUARTERS, BARBARA MINERVA READIES HER-SELF FOR THE ORDEAL YET TO COME--
--PAINTING HER FACE IN THE ANCIENT MANNER--
--PREPARING HERSELF FOR WAR!
DID YOU SEE HOW THE LASSO WORKED, CHUMA? HOW IT FORCED ME TO SPEAK THE TRUTH?
IT IS EVERYTHING I COULD HAVE HOPED FOR! IT MUST BE MINE!
IS THE ELIXIR READY, OLD MAN?
AYE, MA'AM.
YOU MUST DRINK IT NOW--
--RAW--
--WHILE DE BREW STILL BURNS!
IT SMELLS LIKE FIRE, OLD MAN!
IT SMELLS LIKE--LIFE!

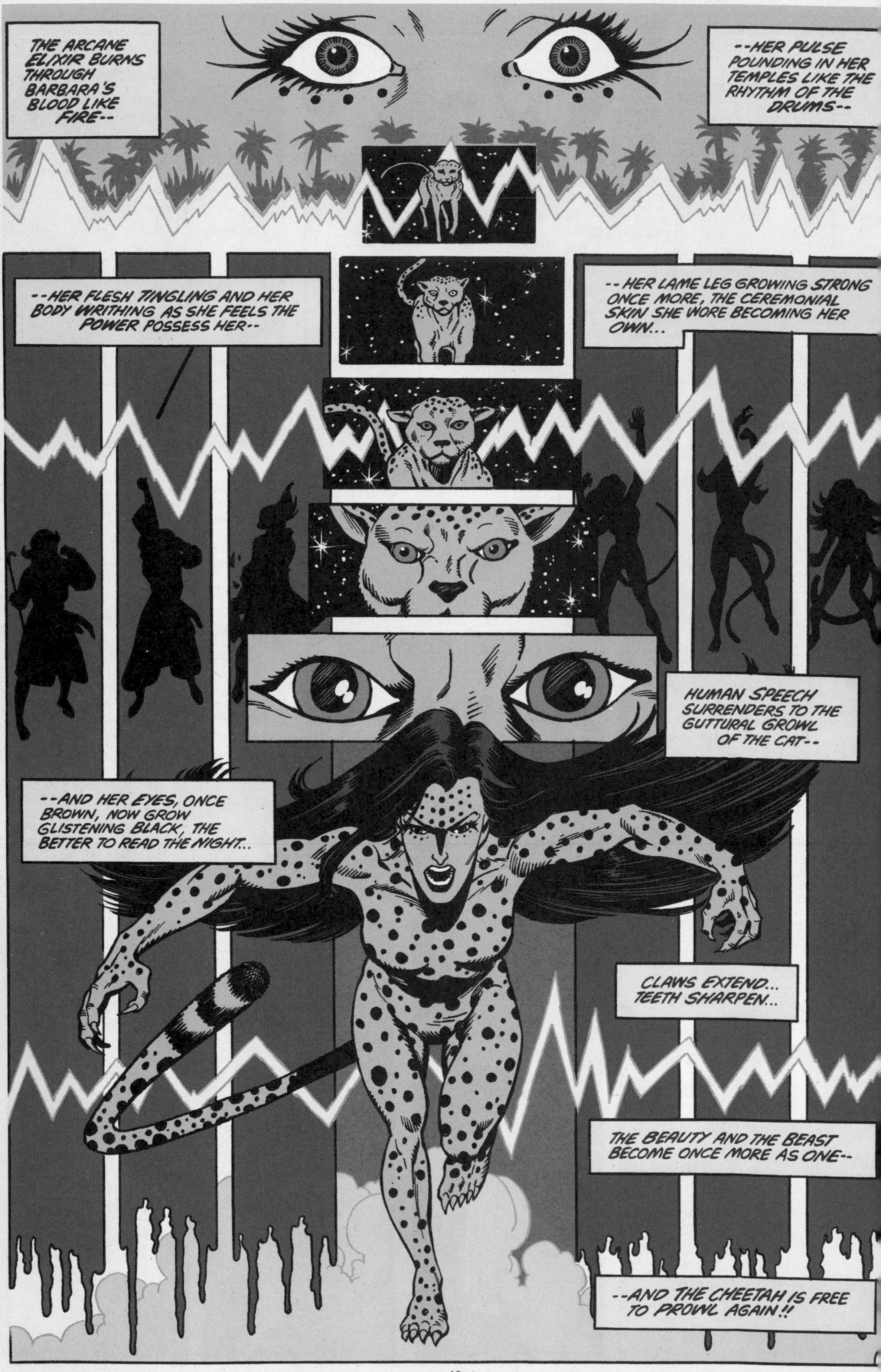
THE ARCANE ELIXIR BURNS THROUGH BARBARA'S BLOOD LIKE FIRE--
--HER PULSE POUNDING IN HER TEMPLES LIKE THE RHYTHM OF THE DRUMS--
--HER FLESH TINGLING AND HER BODY WRITHING AS SHE FEELS THE POWER POSSESS HER--
--HER LAME LEG GROWING STRONG ONCE MORE, THE CEREMONIAL SKIN SHE WORE BECOMING HER OWN...
HUMAN SPEECH SURRENDERS TO THE GUTTURAL GROWL OF THE CAT--
--AND HER EYES, ONCE BROWN, NOW GROW GLISTENING BLACK, THE BETTER TO READ THE NIGHT...
CLAWS EXTEND... TEETH SHARPEN...
THE BEAUTY AND THE BEAST BECOME ONCE MORE AS ONE--
--AND THE CHEETAH IS FREE TO PROWL AGAIN!!

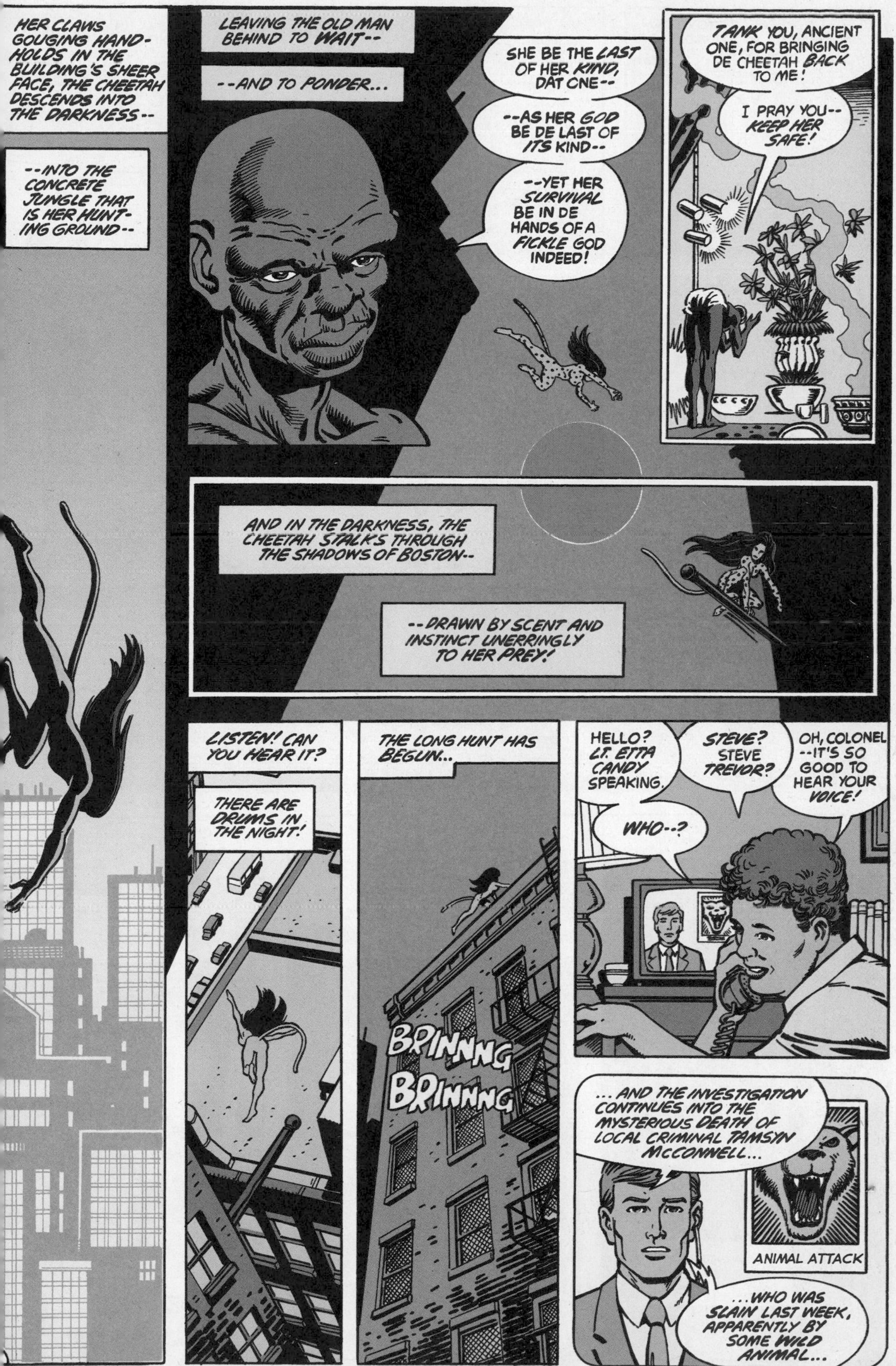
HER CLAWS GOUGING HAND-HOLDS IN THE BUILDING'S SHEER FACE, THE CHEETAH DESCENDS INTO THE DARKNESS--
--INTO THE CONCRETE JUNGLE THAT IS HER HUNTING GROUND--
LEAVING THE OLD MAN BEHIND TO WAIT--
--AND TO PONDER...
SHE BE THE LAST OF HER KIND, DAT ONE--
--AS HER GOD BE DE LAST OF ITS KIND--
--YET HER SURVIVAL BE IN DE HANDS OF A FICKLE GOD INDEED!
TANK YOU, ANCIENT ONE, FOR BRINGING DE CHEETAH BACK TO ME!
I PRAY YOU-- KEEP HER SAFE!
AND IN THE DARKNESS, THE CHEETAH STALKS THROUGH THE SHADOWS OF BOSTON--
--DRAWN BY SCENT AND INSTINCT UNERRINGLY TO HER PREY!
LISTEN! CAN YOU HEAR IT?
THERE ARE DRUMS IN THE NIGHT!
THE LONG HUNT HAS BEGUN...
BRINNNG
BRINNNG
HELLO? LT. ETTA CANDY SPEAKING.
WHO--?
STEVE? STEVE TREVOR?
OH, COLONEL --IT'S SO GOOD TO HEAR YOUR VOICE!
...AND THE INVESTIGATION CONTINUES INTO THE MYSTERIOUS DEATH OF LOCAL CRIMINAL TAMSYN McCONNELL...
ANIMAL ATTACK
...WHO WAS SLAIN LAST WEEK, APPARENTLY BY SOME WILD ANIMAL...

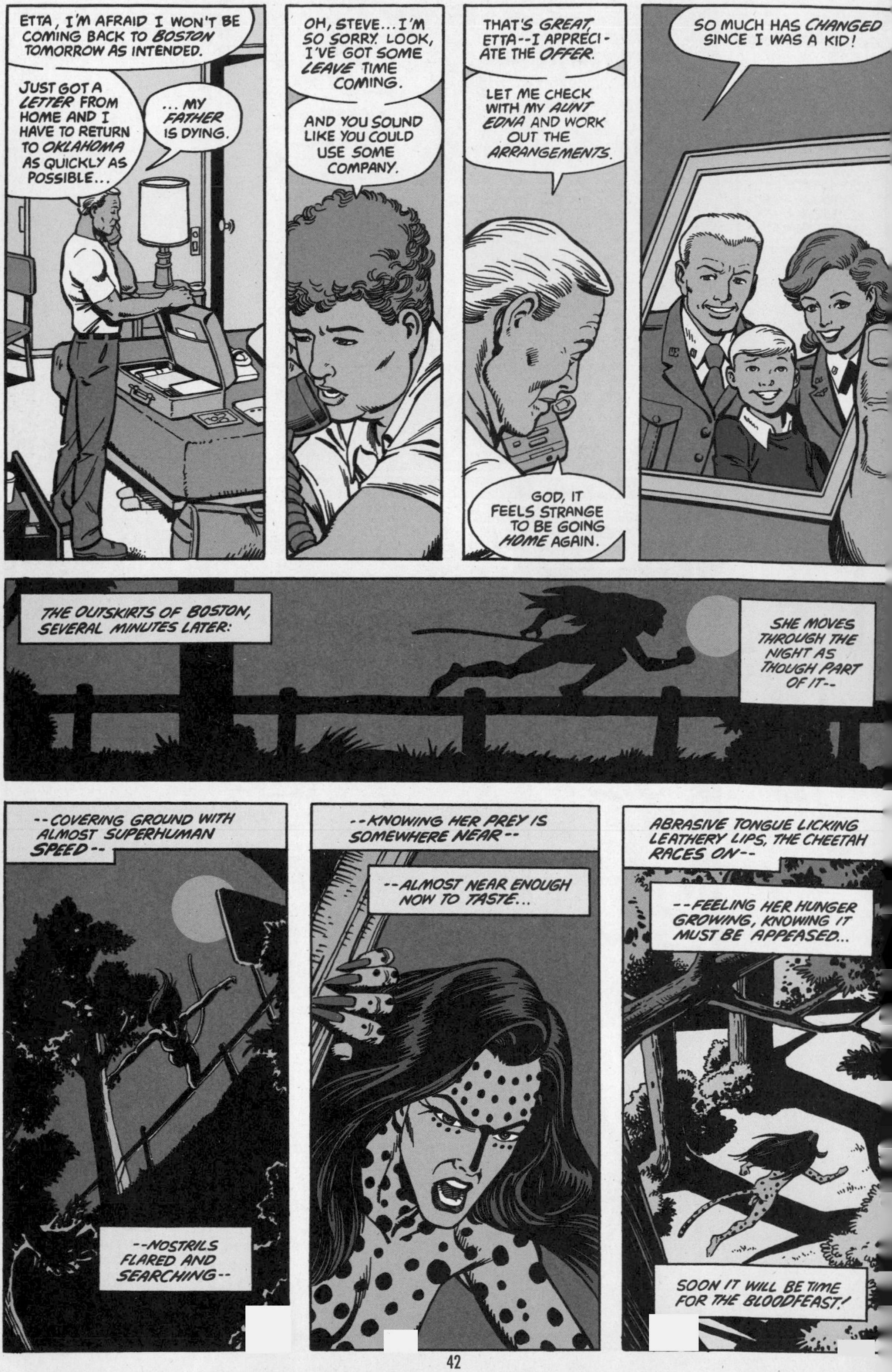
ETTA, I'M AFRAID I WON'T BE COMING BACK TO BOSTON TOMORROW AS INTENDED.
JUST GOT A LETTER FROM HOME AND I HAVE TO RETURN TO OKLAHOMA AS QUICKLY AS POSSIBLE...
...MY FATHER IS DYING.
OH, STEVE... I'M SO SORRY. LOOK, I'VE GOT SOME LEAVE TIME COMING.
AND YOU SOUND LIKE YOU COULD USE SOME COMPANY.
THAT'S GREAT, ETTA--I APPRECIATE THE OFFER.
LET ME CHECK WITH MY AUNT EDNA AND WORK OUT THE ARRANGEMENTS.
GOD, IT FEELS STRANGE TO BE GOING HOME AGAIN.
SO MUCH HAS CHANGED SINCE I WAS A KID!
THE OUTSKIRTS OF BOSTON, SEVERAL MINUTES LATER:
SHE MOVES THROUGH THE NIGHT AS THOUGH PART OF IT--
--COVERING GROUND WITH ALMOST SUPERHUMAN SPEED--
--NOSTRILS FLARED AND SEARCHING--
--KNOWING HER PREY IS SOMEWHERE NEAR--
--ALMOST NEAR ENOUGH NOW TO TASTE...
ABRASIVE TONGUE LICKING LEATHERY LIPS, THE CHEETAH RACES ON--
--FEELING HER HUNGER GROWING, KNOWING IT MUST BE APPEASED...
SOON IT WILL BE TIME FOR THE BLOODFEAST!

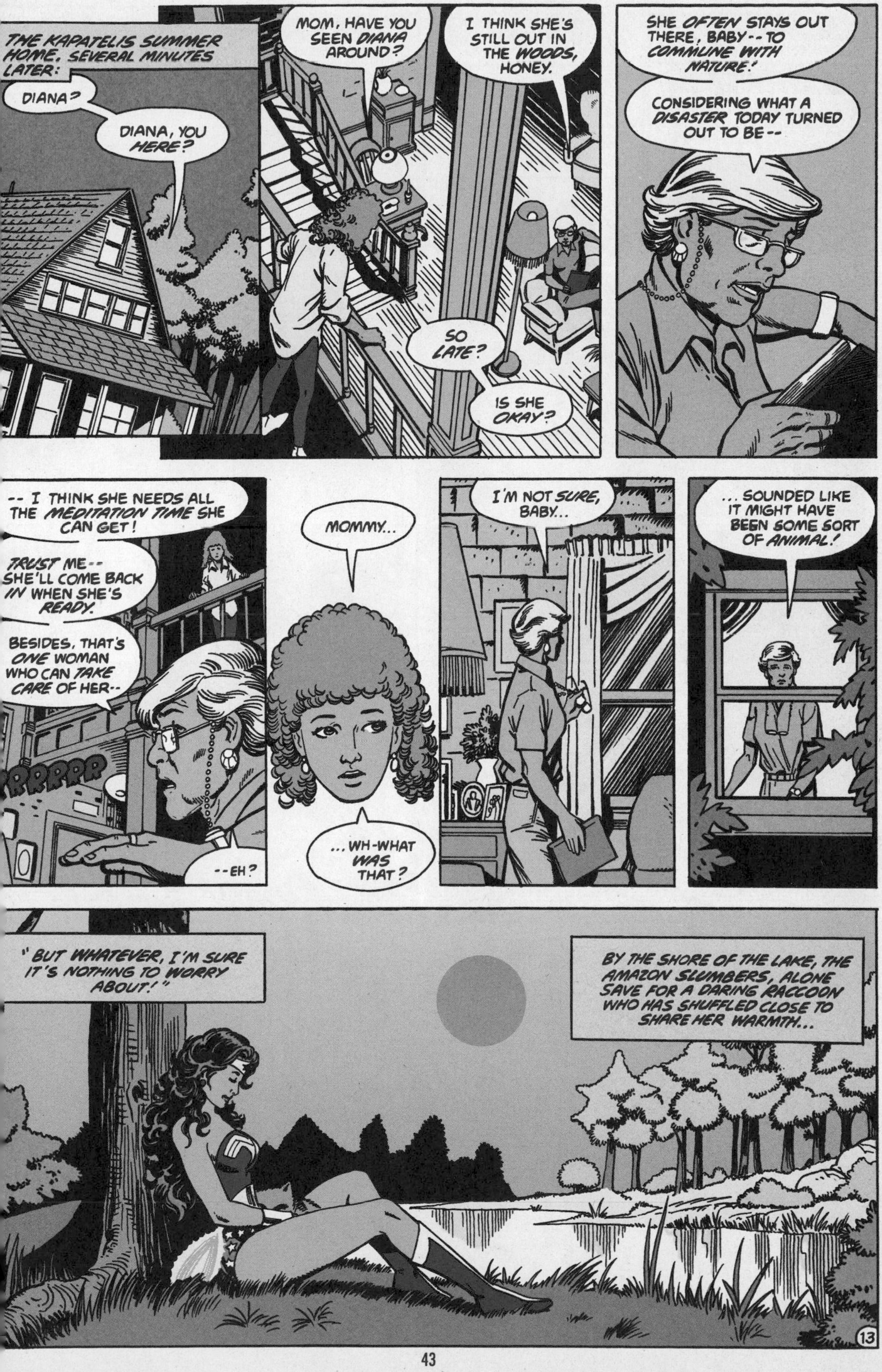
THE KAPATELIS SUMMER HOME, SEVERAL MINUTES LATER:
DIANA?
DIANA, YOU HERE?
MOM, HAVE YOU SEEN DIANA AROUND?
I THINK SHE'S STILL OUT IN THE WOODS, HONEY.
SO LATE?
IS SHE OKAY?
SHE OFTEN STAYS OUT THERE, BABY-- TO COMMUNE WITH NATURE!
CONSIDERING WHAT A DISASTER TODAY TURNED OUT TO BE--
-- I THINK SHE NEEDS ALL THE MEDITATION TIME SHE CAN GET!
TRUST ME-- SHE'LL COME BACK IN WHEN SHE'S READY.
BESIDES, THAT'S ONE WOMAN WHO CAN TAKE CARE OF HER--
RRRRRR
--EH?
MOMMY...
...WH-WHAT WAS THAT?
I'M NOT SURE, BABY...
... SOUNDED LIKE IT MIGHT HAVE BEEN SOME SORT OF ANIMAL!
"BUT WHATEVER, I'M SURE IT'S NOTHING TO WORRY ABOUT!"
BY THE SHORE OF THE LAKE, THE AMAZON SLUMBERS, ALONE SAVE FOR A DARING RACCOON WHO HAS SHUFFLED CLOSE TO SHARE HER WARMTH...
13

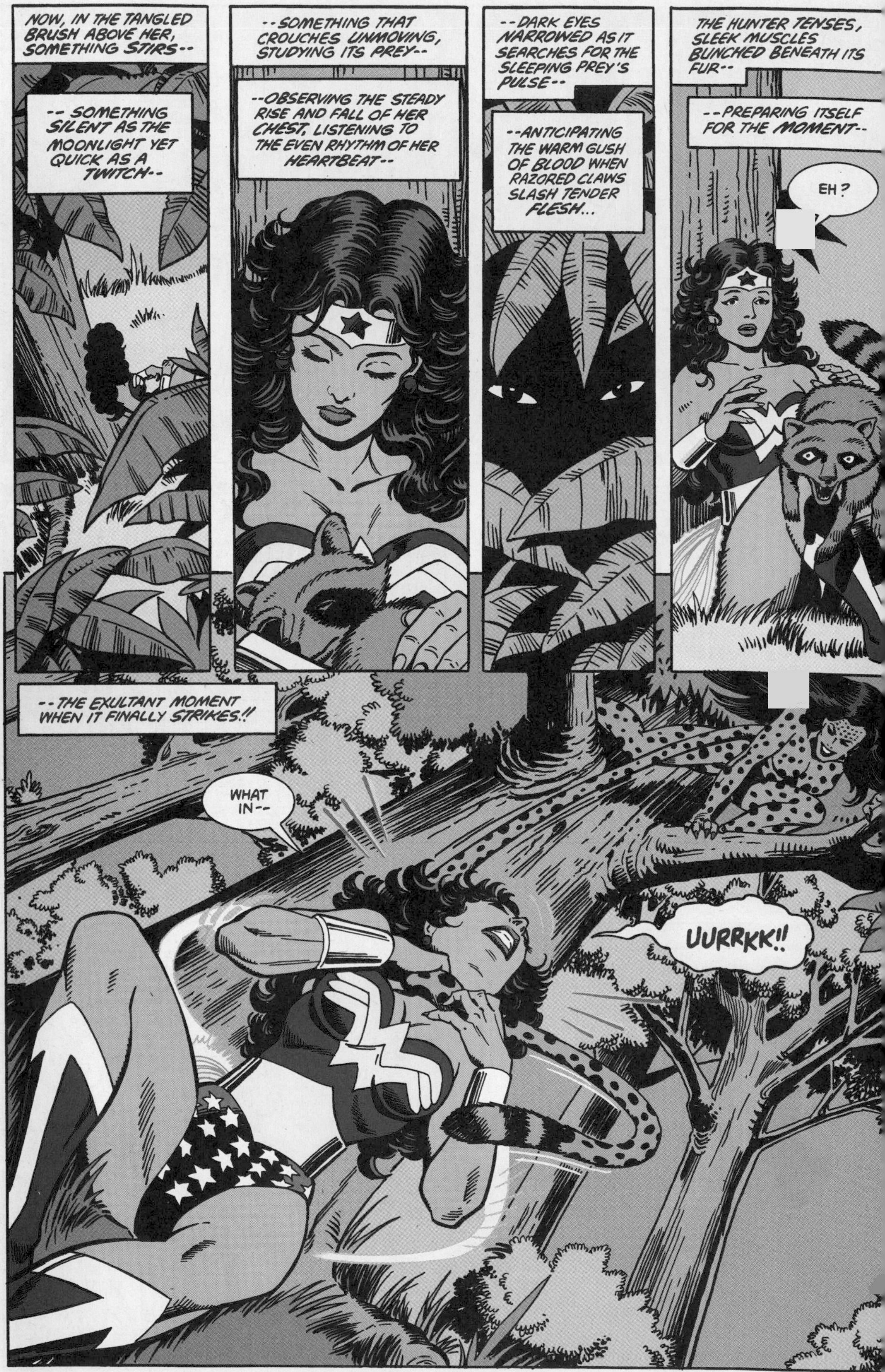
NOW, IN THE TANGLED BRUSH ABOVE HER, SOMETHING STIRS--
-- SOMETHING SILENT AS THE MOONLIGHT YET QUICK AS A TWITCH--
--SOMETHING THAT CROUCHES UNMOVING, STUDYING ITS PREY--
--OBSERVING THE STEADY RISE AND FALL OF HER CHEST, LISTENING TO THE EVEN RHYTHM OF HER HEARTBEAT--
--DARK EYES NARROWED AS IT SEARCHES FOR THE SLEEPING PREY'S PULSE--
--ANTICIPATING THE WARM GUSH OF BLOOD WHEN RAZORED CLAWS SLASH TENDER FLESH...
THE HUNTER TENSES, SLEEK MUSCLES BUNCHED BENEATH ITS FUR--
--PREPARING ITSELF FOR THE MOMENT--
EH?
--THE EXULTANT MOMENT WHEN IT FINALLY STRIKES!!
WHAT IN--
UURRKK!!

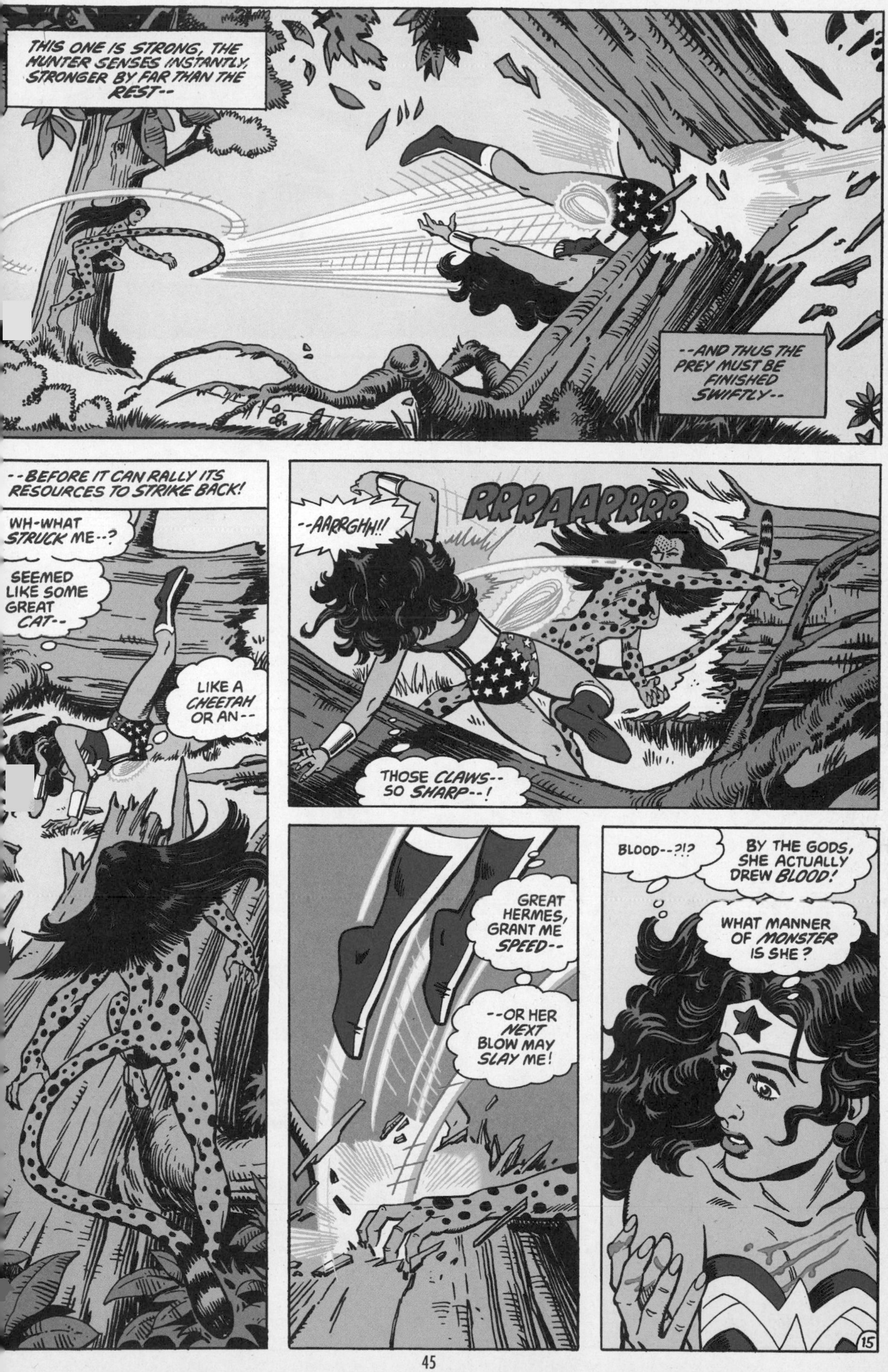
THIS ONE IS STRONG, THE HUNTER SENSES INSTANTLY, STRONGER BY FAR THAN THE REST--
--AND THUS THE PREY MUST BE FINISHED SWIFTLY--
--BEFORE IT CAN RALLY ITS RESOURCES TO STRIKE BACK!
WH-WHAT STRUCK ME--?
SEEMED LIKE SOME GREAT CAT--
LIKE A CHEETAH OR AN--
--AARRGHH!!
RRRAAARRRR
THOSE CLAWS-- SO SHARP--!
GREAT HERMES, GRANT ME SPEED--
--OR HER NEXT BLOW MAY SLAY ME!
BLOOD--?!?
BY THE GODS, SHE ACTUALLY DREW BLOOD!
WHAT MANNER OF MONSTER IS SHE?
15

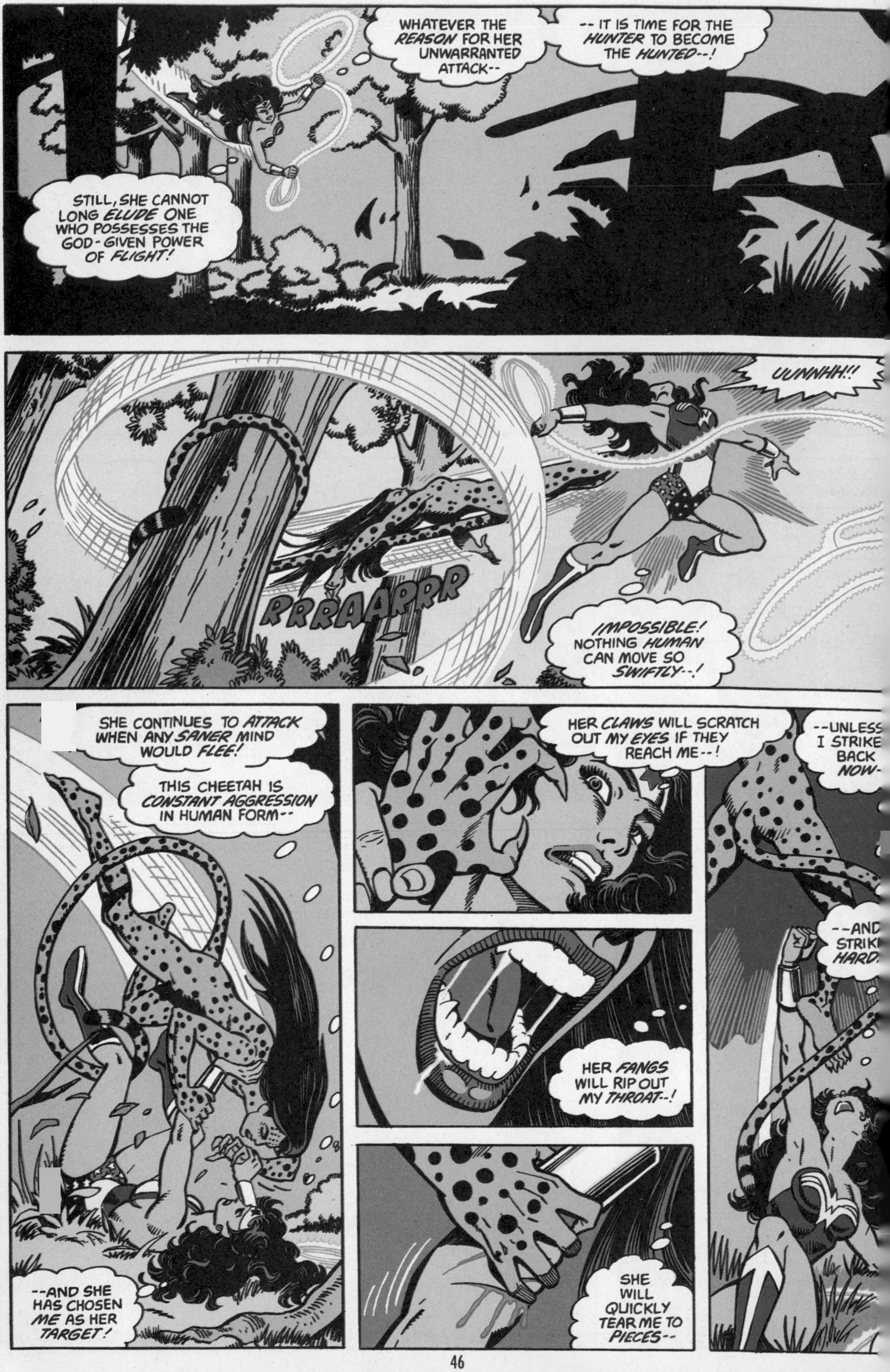
WHATEVER THE REASON FOR HER UNWARRANTED ATTACK--
-- IT IS TIME FOR THE HUNTER TO BECOME THE HUNTED--!
STILL, SHE CANNOT LONG ELUDE ONE WHO POSSESSES THE GOD-GIVEN POWER OF FLIGHT!
UUNNHH!!
RRRAARRR
IMPOSSIBLE! NOTHING HUMAN CAN MOVE SO SWIFTLY--!
SHE CONTINUES TO ATTACK WHEN ANY SANER MIND WOULD FLEE!
THIS CHEETAH IS CONSTANT AGGRESSION IN HUMAN FORM--
--AND SHE HAS CHOSEN ME AS HER TARGET!
HER CLAWS WILL SCRATCH OUT MY EYES IF THEY REACH ME--!
HER FANGS WILL RIP OUT MY THROAT--!
SHE WILL QUICKLY TEAR ME TO PIECES--
--UNLESS I STRIKE BACK NOW-
--AND STRIKE HARD!

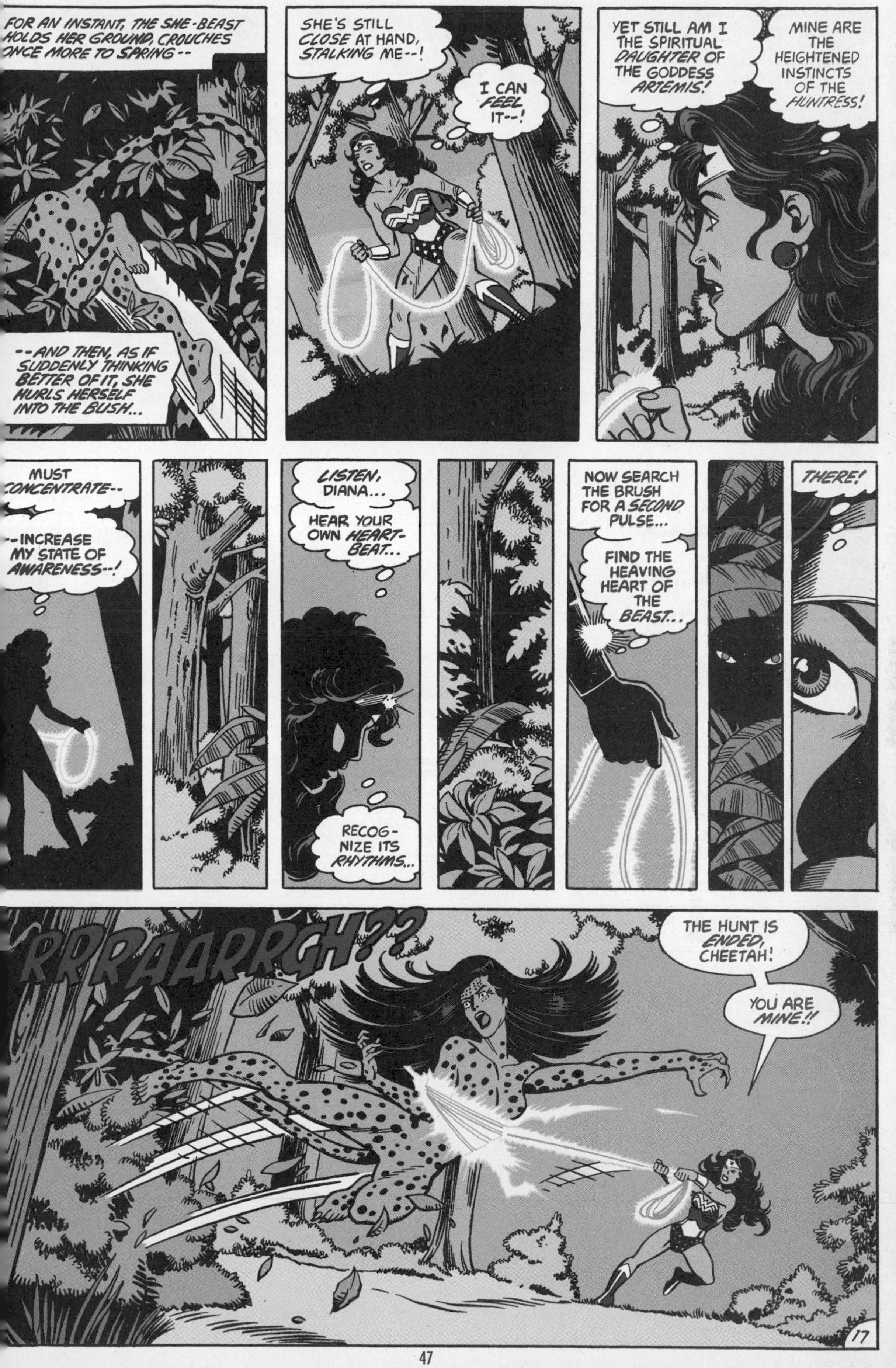
FOR AN INSTANT, THE SHE-BEAST HOLDS HER GROUND, CROUCHES ONCE MORE TO SPRING--
--AND THEN, AS IF SUDDENLY THINKING BETTER OF IT, SHE HURLS HERSELF INTO THE BUSH...
SHE'S STILL CLOSE AT HAND, STALKING ME--!
I CAN FEEL IT--!
YET STILL AM I THE SPIRITUAL DAUGHTER OF THE GODDESS ARTEMIS!
MINE ARE THE HEIGHTENED INSTINCTS OF THE HUNTRESS!
MUST CONCENTRATE--
--INCREASE MY STATE OF AWARENESS--!
LISTEN, DIANA...
HEAR YOUR OWN HEART-BEAT...
RECOG-NIZE ITS RHYTHMS...
NOW SEARCH THE BRUSH FOR A SECOND PULSE...
FIND THE HEAVING HEART OF THE BEAST...
THERE!
RRRAARRGH??
THE HUNT IS ENDED, CHEETAH!
YOU ARE MINE!!
17

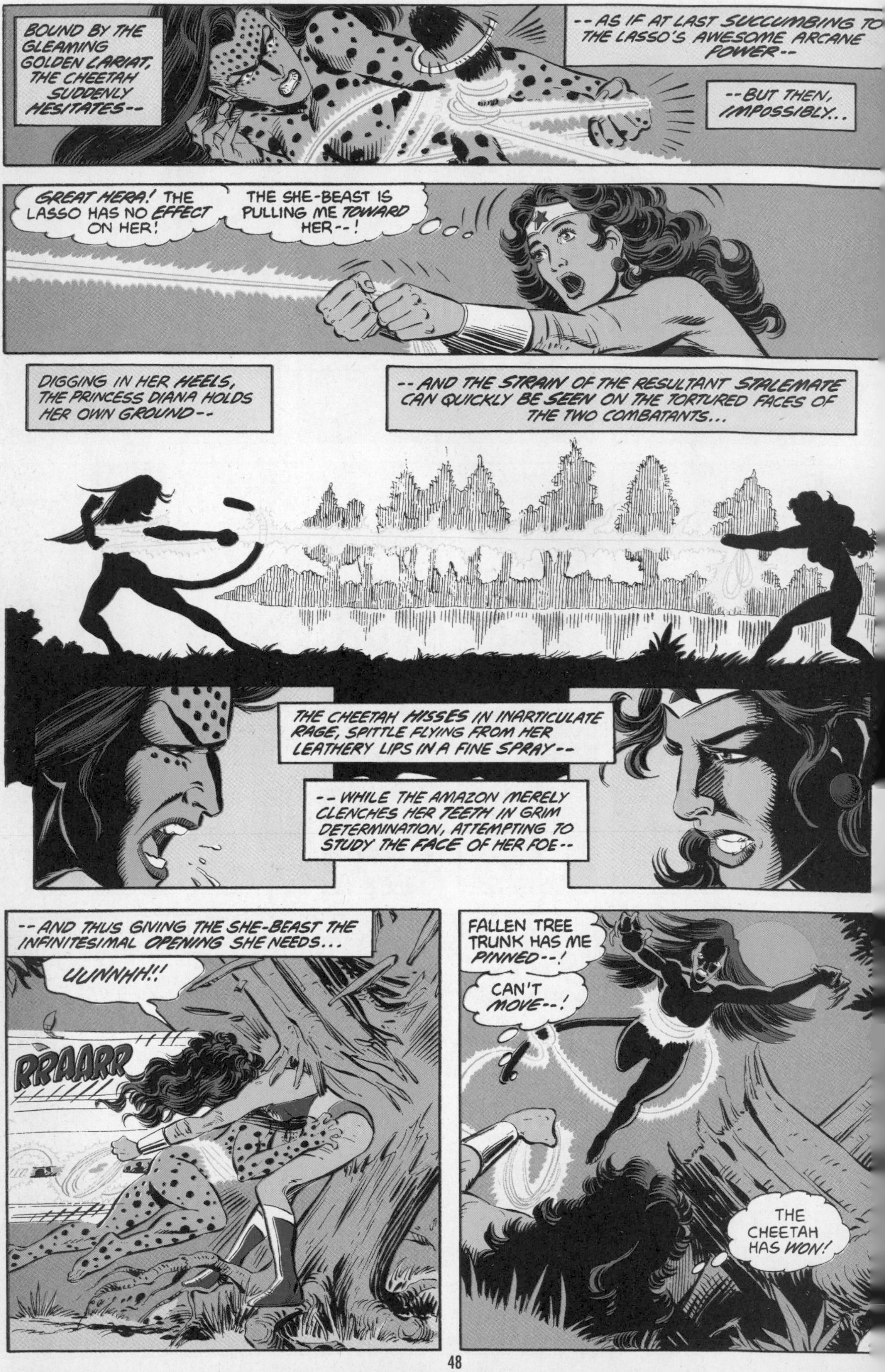
BOUND BY THE GLEAMING GOLDEN LARIAT, THE CHEETAH SUDDENLY HESITATES--
--AS IF AT LAST SUCCUMBING TO THE LASSO'S AWESOME ARCANE POWER--
--BUT THEN, IMPOSSIBLY...
GREAT HERA! THE LASSO HAS NO EFFECT ON HER!
THE SHE-BEAST IS PULLING ME TOWARD HER--!
DIGGING IN HER HEELS, THE PRINCESS DIANA HOLDS HER OWN GROUND--
--AND THE STRAIN OF THE RESULTANT STALEMATE CAN QUICKLY BE SEEN ON THE TORTURED FACES OF THE TWO COMBATANTS...
THE CHEETAH HISSES IN INARTICULATE RAGE, SPITTLE FLYING FROM HER LEATHERY LIPS IN A FINE SPRAY--
--WHILE THE AMAZON MERELY CLENCHES HER TEETH IN GRIM DETERMINATION, ATTEMPTING TO STUDY THE FACE OF HER FOE--
--AND THUS GIVING THE SHE-BEAST THE INFINITESIMAL OPENING SHE NEEDS...
UUNNHH!!
RRAARR
FALLEN TREE TRUNK HAS ME PINNED--!
CAN'T MOVE--!
THE CHEETAH HAS WON!

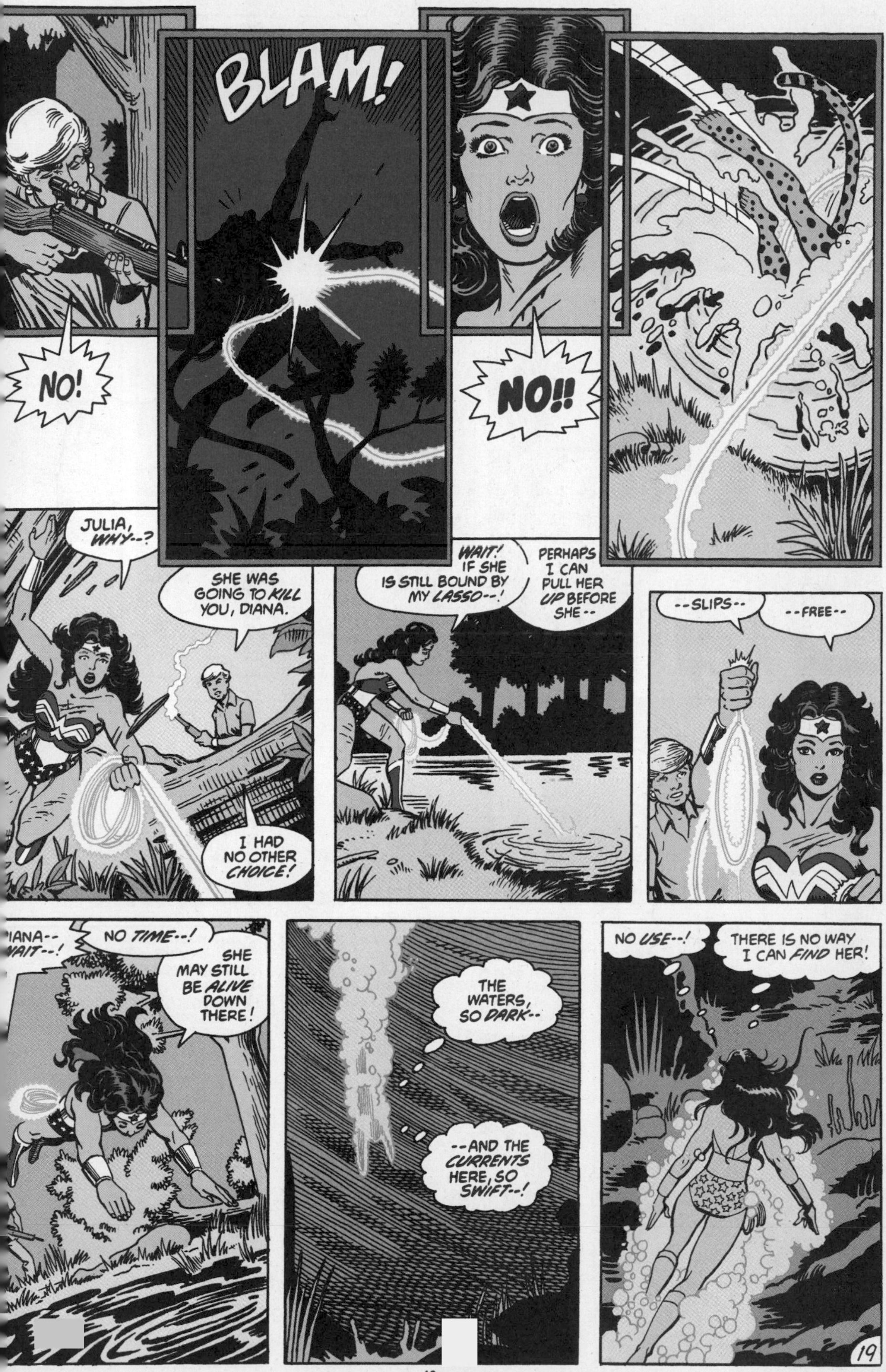
NO!
BLAM!
NO!!
JULIA, WHY--?
SHE WAS GOING TO KILL YOU, DIANA.
I HAD NO OTHER CHOICE!
WAIT! IF SHE IS STILL BOUND BY MY LASSO--!
PERHAPS I CAN PULL HER UP BEFORE SHE --
--SLIPS--
--FREE--
IANA-- WAIT--!
NO TIME--!
SHE MAY STILL BE ALIVE DOWN THERE!
THE WATERS, SO DARK--
--AND THE CURRENTS HERE, SO SWIFT--!
NO USE--!
THERE IS NO WAY I CAN FIND HER!
19

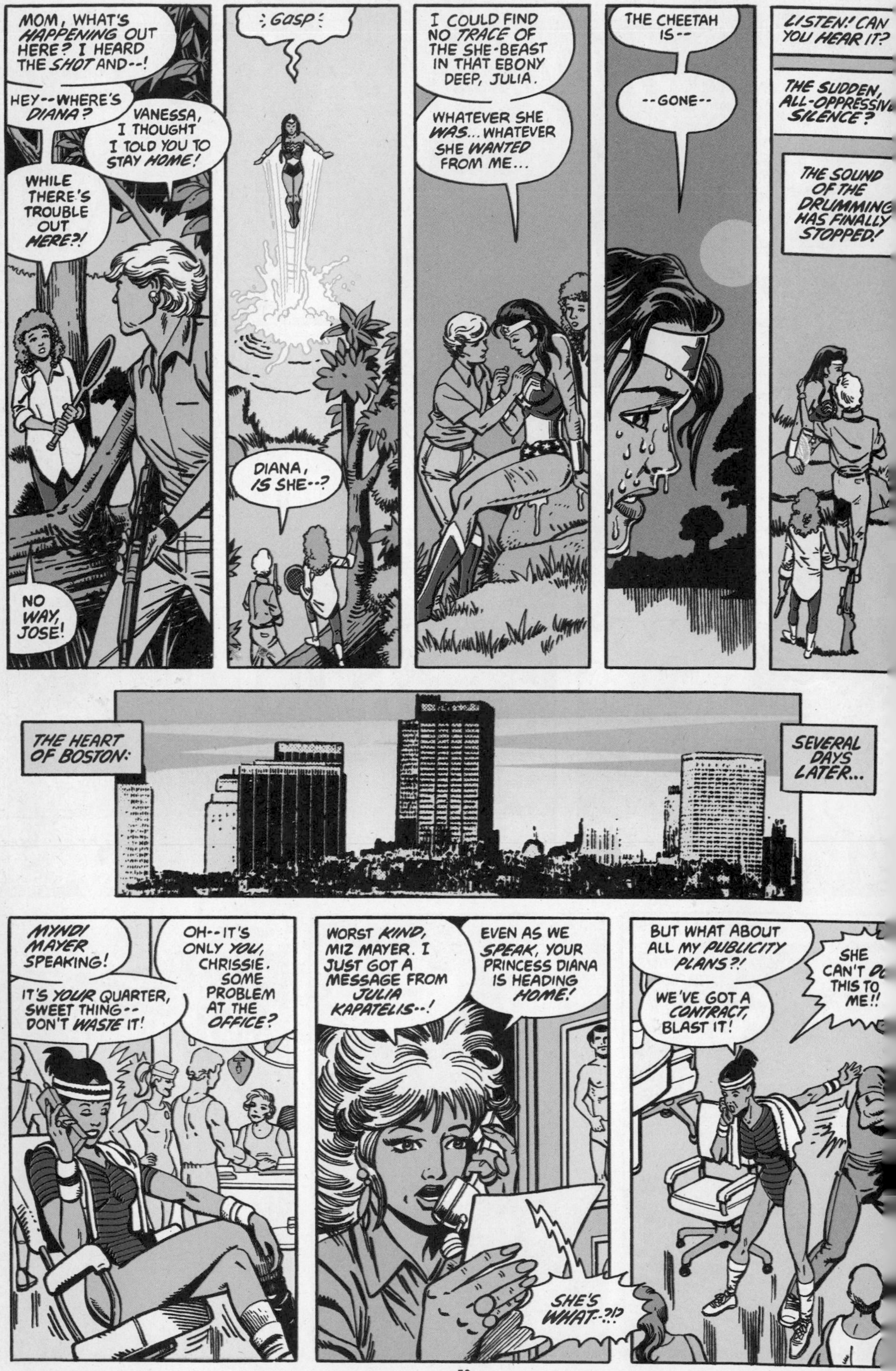

MOM, WHAT'S HAPPENING OUT HERE? I HEARD THE SHOT AND--!
HEY--WHERE'S DIANA?
VANESSA, I THOUGHT I TOLD YOU TO STAY HOME!
WHILE THERE'S TROUBLE OUT HERE?!
NO WAY, JOSE!
Gasp
DIANA, IS SHE--?
I COULD FIND NO TRACE OF THE SHE-BEAST IN THAT EBONY DEEP, JULIA.
WHATEVER SHE WAS... WHATEVER SHE WANTED FROM ME...
THE CHEETAH IS--
--GONE--
LISTEN! CAN YOU HEAR IT?
THE SUDDEN, ALL-OPPRESSIVE SILENCE?
THE SOUND OF THE DRUMMING HAS FINALLY STOPPED!
THE HEART OF BOSTON:
SEVERAL DAYS LATER...
MYNDI MAYER SPEAKING!
IT'S YOUR QUARTER, SWEET THING--DON'T WASTE IT!
OH--IT'S ONLY YOU, CHRISSIE. SOME PROBLEM AT THE OFFICE?
WORST KIND, MIZ MAYER. I JUST GOT A MESSAGE FROM JULIA KAPATELIS--!
EVEN AS WE SPEAK, YOUR PRINCESS DIANA IS HEADING HOME!
SHE'S WHAT--?!?
BUT WHAT ABOUT ALL MY PUBLICITY PLANS?!
WE'VE GOT A CONTRACT, BLAST IT!
SHE CAN'T DO THIS TO ME!!

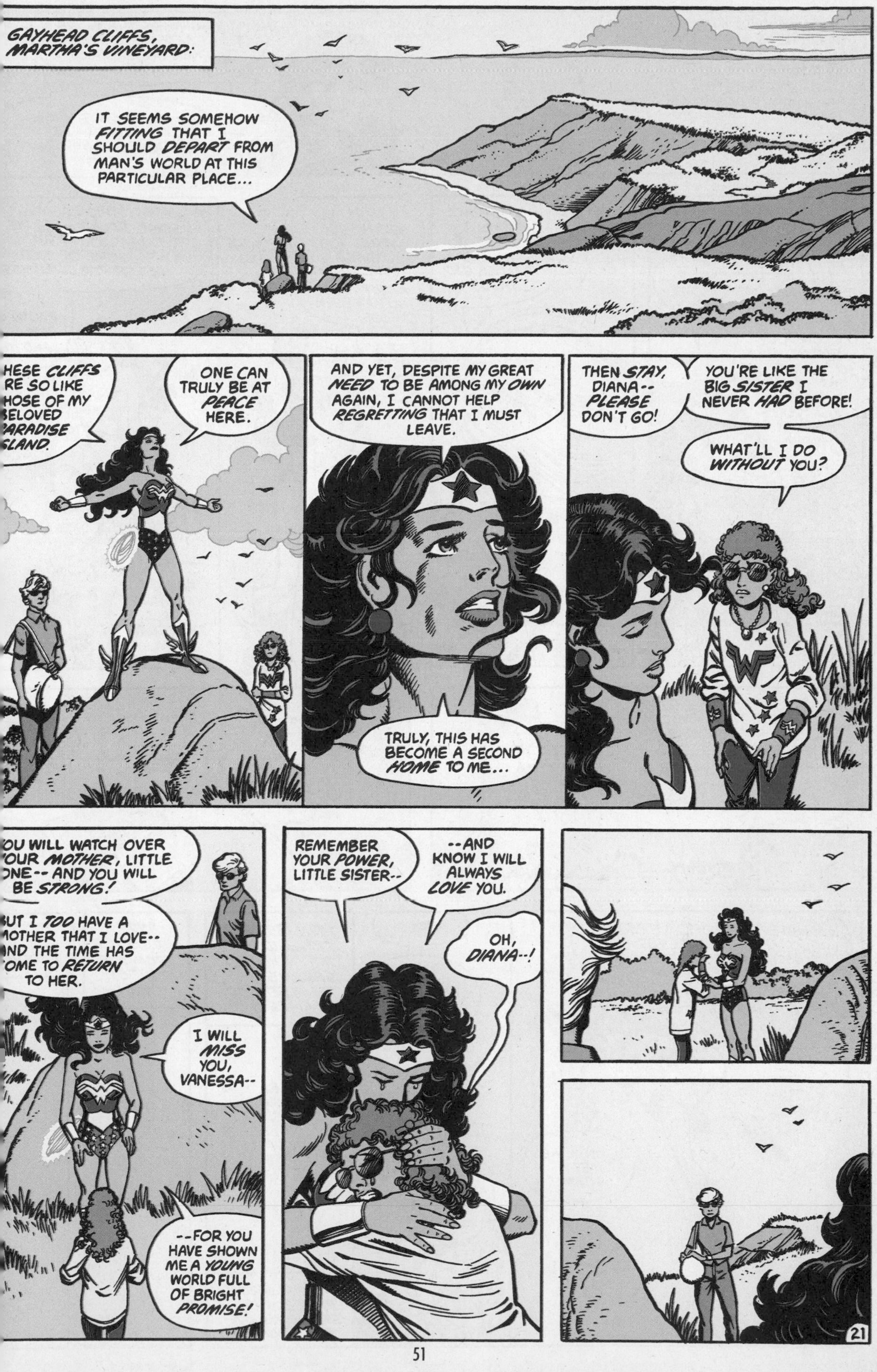
GAYHEAD CLIFFS, MARTHA'S VINEYARD:
IT SEEMS SOMEHOW FITTING THAT I SHOULD DEPART FROM MAN'S WORLD AT THIS PARTICULAR PLACE...
HESE CLIFFS RE SO LIKE HOSE OF MY BELOVED ARADISE SLAND.
ONE CAN TRULY BE AT PEACE HERE.
AND YET, DESPITE MY GREAT NEED TO BE AMONG MY OWN AGAIN, I CANNOT HELP REGRETTING THAT I MUST LEAVE.
TRULY, THIS HAS BECOME A SECOND HOME TO ME...
THEN STAY, DIANA-- PLEASE DON'T GO!
YOU'RE LIKE THE BIG SISTER I NEVER HAD BEFORE!
WHAT'LL I DO WITHOUT YOU?
OU WILL WATCH OVER OUR MOTHER, LITTLE NE-- AND YOU WILL BE STRONG!
UT I TOO HAVE A MOTHER THAT I LOVE-- ND THE TIME HAS OME TO RETURN TO HER.
I WILL MISS YOU, VANESSA--
--FOR YOU HAVE SHOWN ME A YOUNG WORLD FULL OF BRIGHT PROMISE!
REMEMBER YOUR POWER, LITTLE SISTER--
--AND KNOW I WILL ALWAYS LOVE YOU.
OH, DIANA--!
21

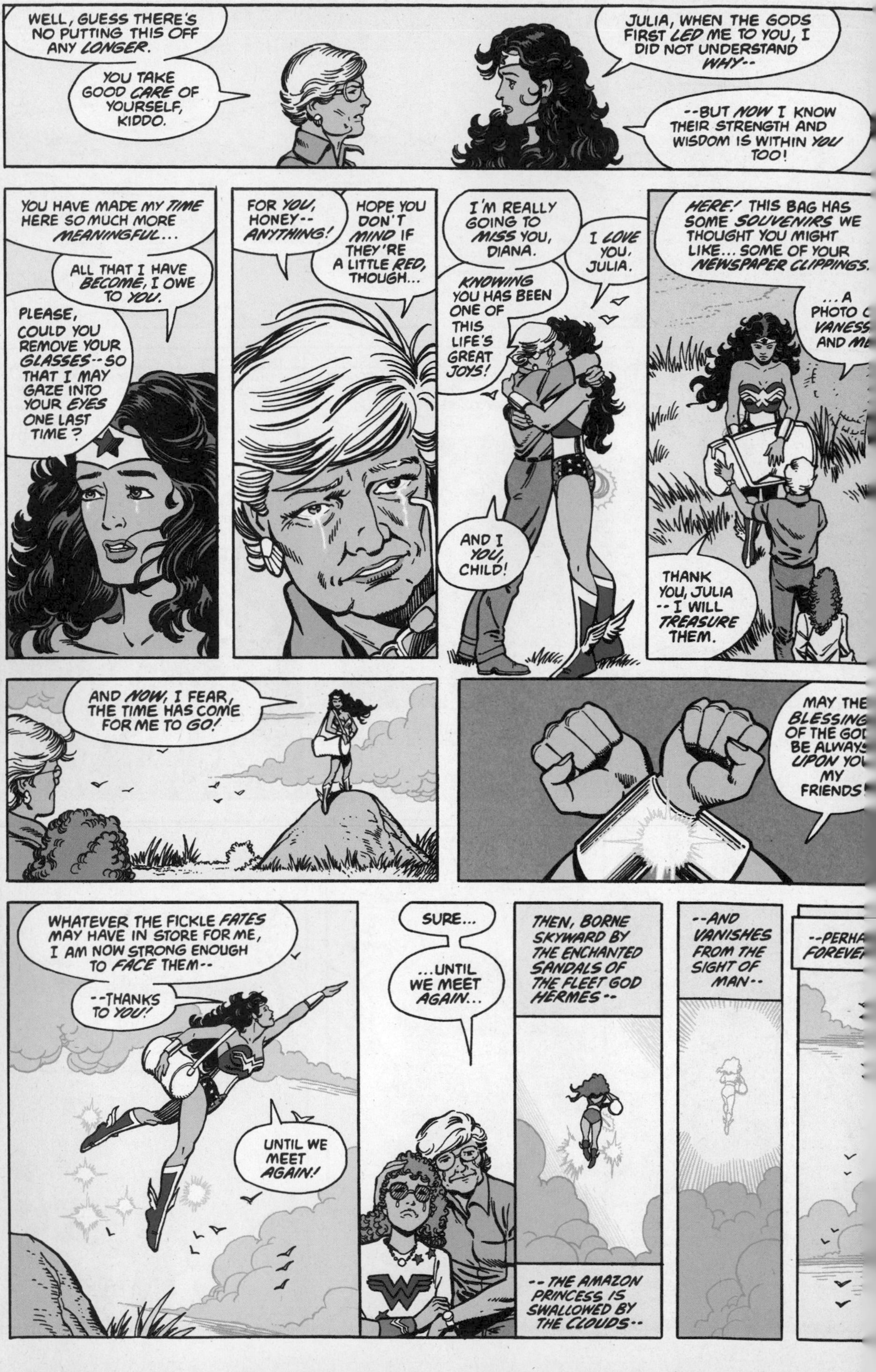

WELL, GUESS THERE'S NO PUTTING THIS OFF ANY LONGER.
YOU TAKE GOOD CARE OF YOURSELF, KIDDO.
JULIA, WHEN THE GODS FIRST LED ME TO YOU, I DID NOT UNDERSTAND WHY--
--BUT NOW I KNOW THEIR STRENGTH AND WISDOM IS WITHIN YOU TOO!
YOU HAVE MADE MY TIME HERE SO MUCH MORE MEANINGFUL...
ALL THAT I HAVE BECOME, I OWE TO YOU.
PLEASE, COULD YOU REMOVE YOUR GLASSES--SO THAT I MAY GAZE INTO YOUR EYES ONE LAST TIME?
FOR YOU, HONEY--ANYTHING!
HOPE YOU DON'T MIND IF THEY'RE A LITTLE RED, THOUGH...
I'M REALLY GOING TO MISS YOU, DIANA.
KNOWING YOU HAS BEEN ONE OF THIS LIFE'S GREAT JOYS!
I LOVE YOU, JULIA.
AND I YOU, CHILD!
HERE! THIS BAG HAS SOME SOUVENIRS WE THOUGHT YOU MIGHT LIKE... SOME OF YOUR NEWSPAPER CLIPPINGS.
...A PHOTO O VANESS AND M
THANK YOU, JULIA --I WILL TREASURE THEM.
AND NOW, I FEAR, THE TIME HAS COME FOR ME TO GO!
MAY THE BLESSING OF THE GOD BE ALWAYS UPON YO MY FRIENDS!
WHATEVER THE FICKLE FATES MAY HAVE IN STORE FOR ME, I AM NOW STRONG ENOUGH TO FACE THEM--
--THANKS TO YOU!
UNTIL WE MEET AGAIN!
SURE...
...UNTIL WE MEET AGAIN...
THEN, BORNE SKYWARD BY THE ENCHANTED SANDALS OF THE FLEET GOD HERMES--
--THE AMAZON PRINCESS IS SWALLOWED BY THE CLOUDS--
--AND VANISHES FROM THE SIGHT OF MAN--
--PERHA FOREVE

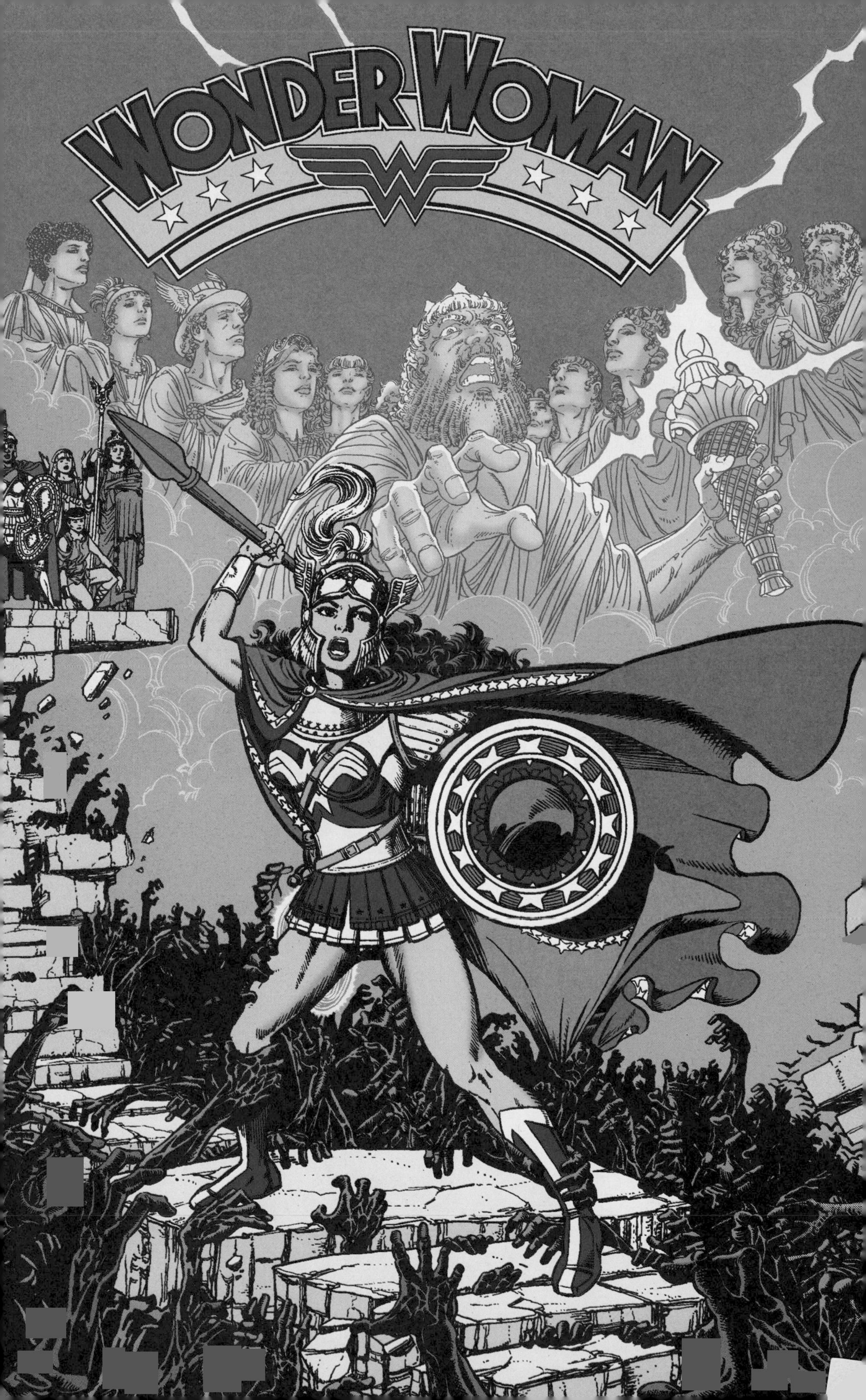
WONDER WOMAN

WONDER WOMAN

CHAPTER THREE

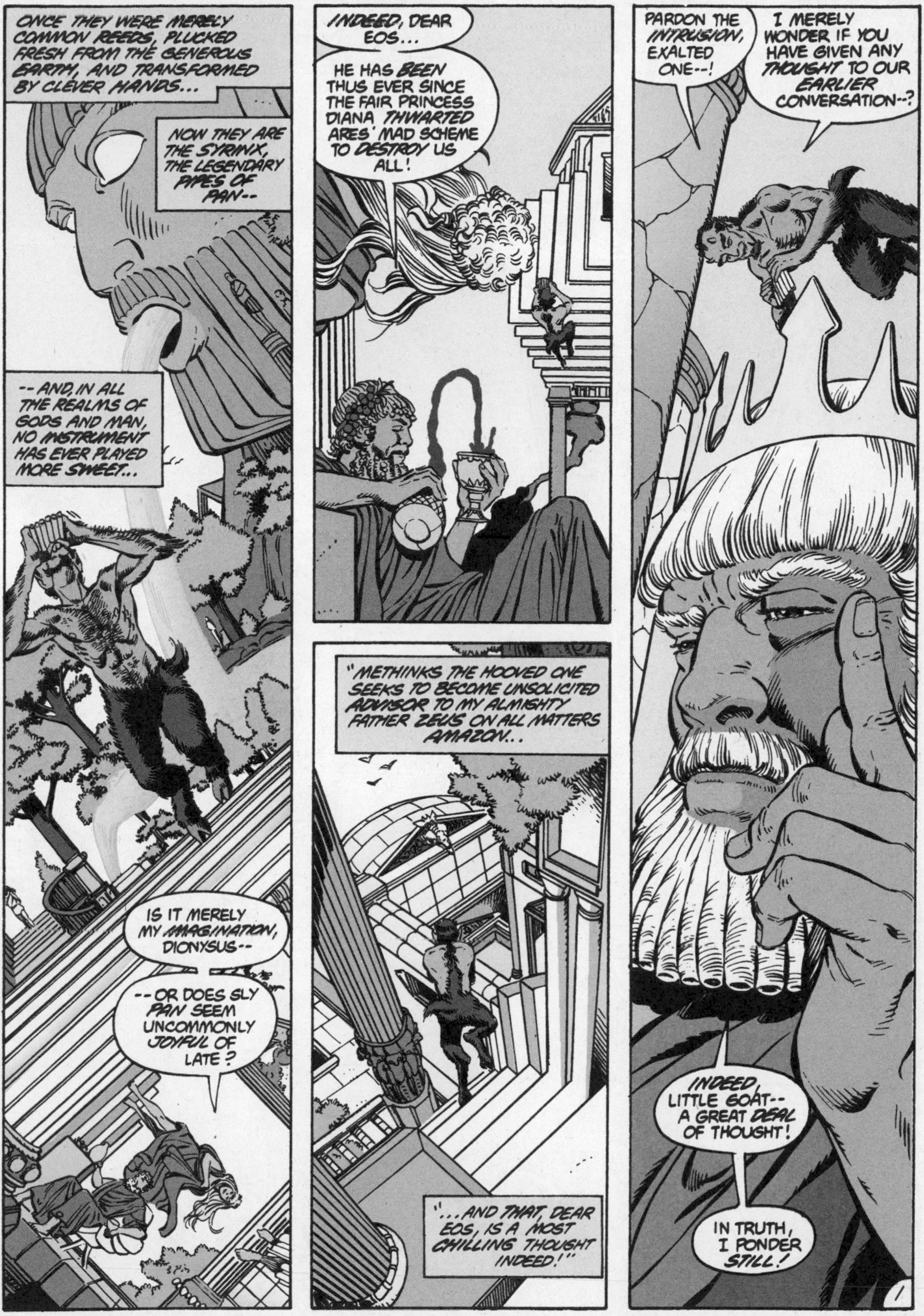
ONCE THEY WERE MERELY COMMON REEDS, PLUCKED FRESH FROM THE GENEROUS EARTH, AND TRANSFORMED BY CLEVER HANDS...
NOW THEY ARE THE SYRINX, THE LEGENDARY PIPES OF PAN--
-- AND, IN ALL THE REALMS OF GODS AND MAN, NO INSTRUMENT HAS EVER PLAYED MORE SWEET...
IS IT MERELY MY IMAGINATION, DIONYSUS--
-- OR DOES SLY PAN SEEM UNCOMMONLY JOYFUL OF LATE?
INDEED, DEAR EOS...
HE HAS BEEN THUS EVER SINCE THE FAIR PRINCESS DIANA THWARTED ARES' MAD SCHEME TO DESTROY US ALL!
"METHINKS THE HOOVED ONE SEEKS TO BECOME UNSOLICITED ADVISOR TO MY ALMIGHTY FATHER ZEUS ON ALL MATTERS AMAZON...
"...AND THAT, DEAR EOS, IS A MOST CHILLING THOUGHT INDEED!"
PARDON THE INTRUSION, EXALTED ONE--!
I MERELY WONDER IF YOU HAVE GIVEN ANY THOUGHT TO OUR EARLIER CONVERSATION--?
INDEED, LITTLE GOAT-- A GREAT DEAL OF THOUGHT!
IN TRUTH, I PONDER STILL!
1

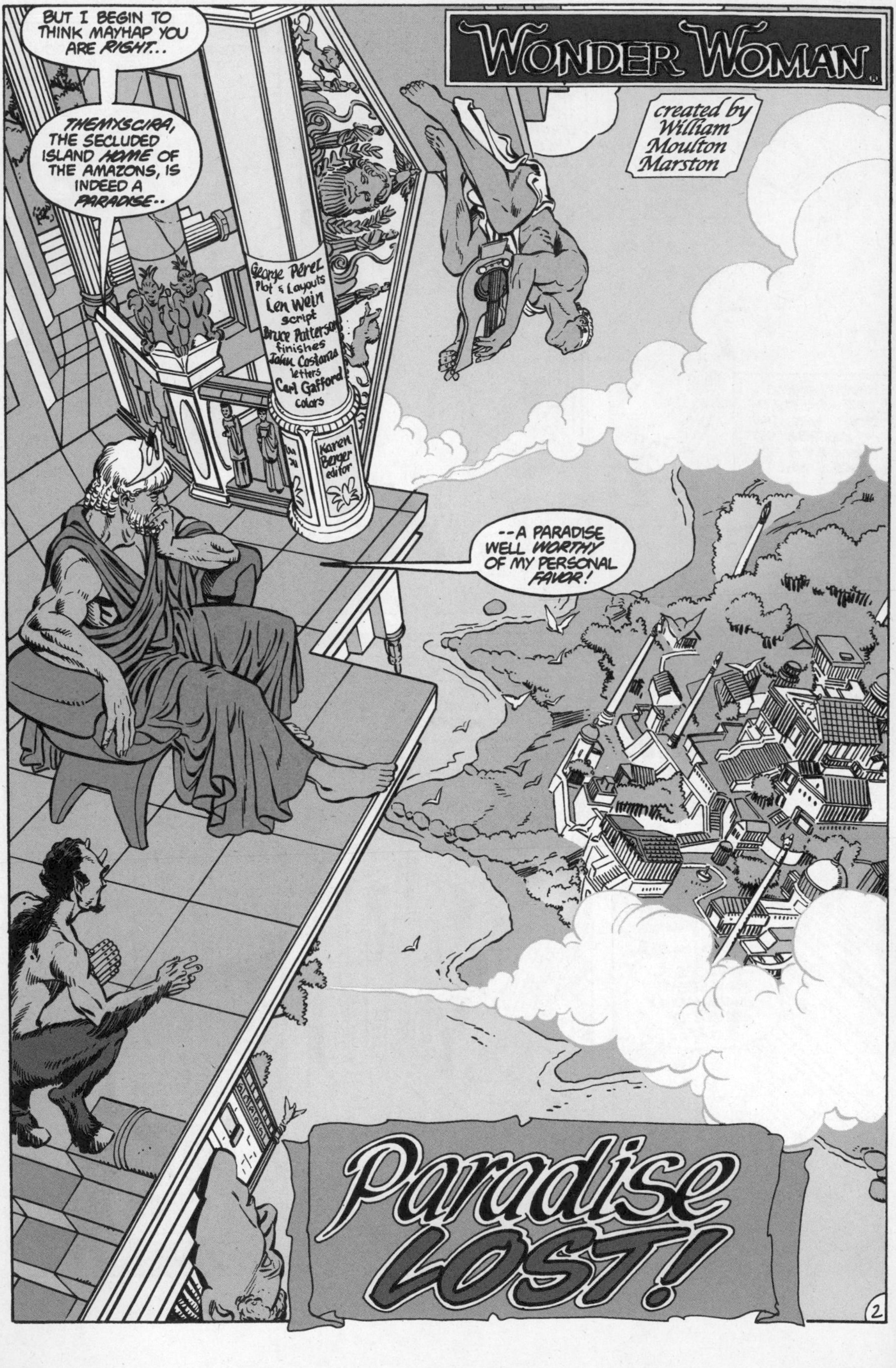
BUT I BEGIN TO THINK MAYHAP YOU ARE RIGHT...
THEMYSCIRA, THE SECLUDED ISLAND HOME OF THE AMAZONS, IS INDEED A PARADISE..
WONDER WOMAN
created by William Moulton Marston
George Pérez Plot & Layouts
Len Wein script
Bruce Patterson finishes
John Costanza letters
Carl Gafford colors
Karen Berger editor
--A PARADISE WELL WORTHY OF MY PERSONAL FAVOR!
Paradise LOST!
2

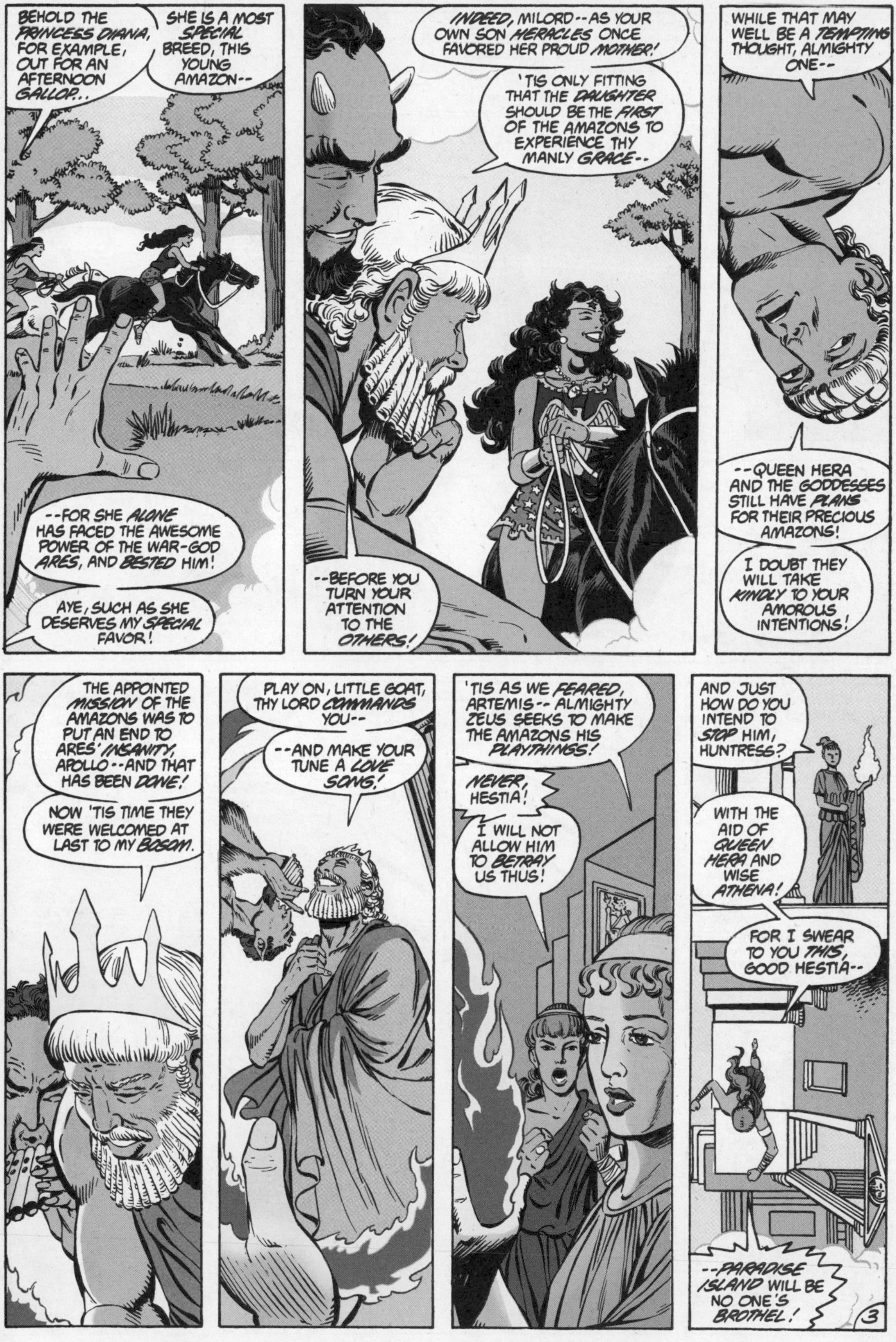
BEHOLD THE PRINCESS DIANA, FOR EXAMPLE, OUT FOR AN AFTERNOON GALLOP..
SHE IS A MOST SPECIAL BREED, THIS YOUNG AMAZON--
--FOR SHE ALONE HAS FACED THE AWESOME POWER OF THE WAR-GOD ARES, AND BESTED HIM!
AYE, SUCH AS SHE DESERVES MY SPECIAL FAVOR!
INDEED, MILORD--AS YOUR OWN SON HERACLES ONCE FAVORED HER PROUD MOTHER!
'TIS ONLY FITTING THAT THE DAUGHTER SHOULD BE THE FIRST OF THE AMAZONS TO EXPERIENCE THY MANLY GRACE--
--BEFORE YOU TURN YOUR ATTENTION TO THE OTHERS!
WHILE THAT MAY WELL BE A TEMPTING THOUGHT, ALMIGHTY ONE--
--QUEEN HERA AND THE GODDESSES STILL HAVE PLANS FOR THEIR PRECIOUS AMAZONS!
I DOUBT THEY WILL TAKE KINDLY TO YOUR AMOROUS INTENTIONS!
THE APPOINTED MISSION OF THE AMAZONS WAS TO PUT AN END TO ARES' INSANITY, APOLLO--AND THAT HAS BEEN DONE!
NOW 'TIS TIME THEY WERE WELCOMED AT LAST TO MY BOSOM.
PLAY ON, LITTLE GOAT, THY LORD COMMANDS YOU--
--AND MAKE YOUR TUNE A LOVE SONG!
'TIS AS WE FEARED, ARTEMIS--ALMIGHTY ZEUS SEEKS TO MAKE THE AMAZONS HIS PLAYTHINGS!
NEVER, HESTIA!
I WILL NOT ALLOW HIM TO BETRAY US THUS!
AND JUST HOW DO YOU INTEND TO STOP HIM, HUNTRESS?
WITH THE AID OF QUEEN HERA AND WISE ATHENA!
FOR I SWEAR TO YOU THIS, GOOD HESTIA--
--PARADISE ISLAND WILL BE NO ONE'S BROTHEL!
3

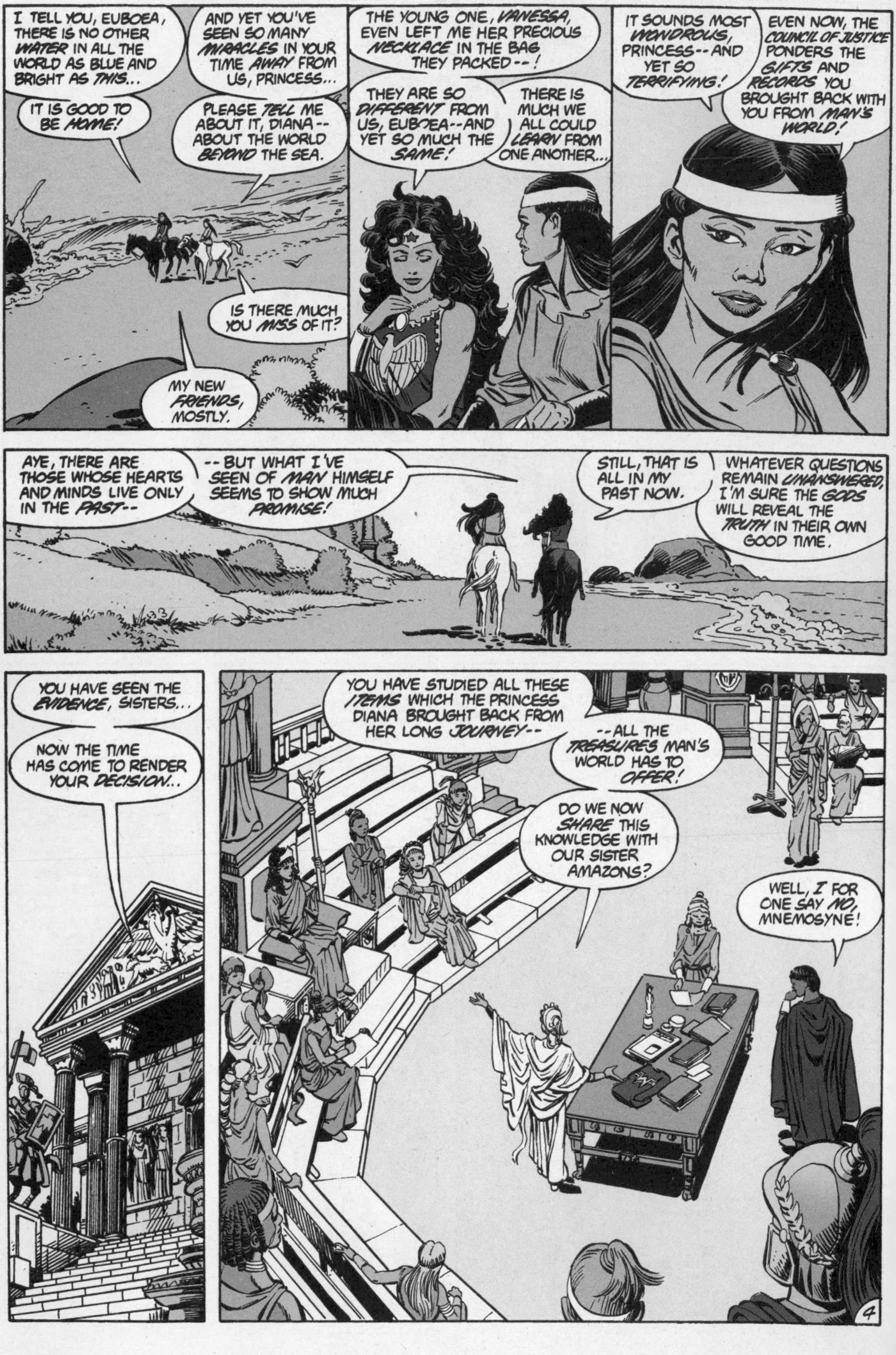

I TELL YOU, EUBOEA, THERE IS NO OTHER WATER IN ALL THE WORLD AS BLUE AND BRIGHT AS THIS...
IT IS GOOD TO BE HOME!
AND YET YOU'VE SEEN SO MANY MIRACLES IN YOUR TIME AWAY FROM US, PRINCESS...
PLEASE TELL ME ABOUT IT, DIANA-- ABOUT THE WORLD BEYOND THE SEA.
IS THERE MUCH YOU MISS OF IT?
MY NEW FRIENDS, MOSTLY.
THE YOUNG ONE, VANESSA, EVEN LEFT ME HER PRECIOUS NECKLACE IN THE BAG THEY PACKED--!
THEY ARE SO DIFFERENT FROM US, EUBOEA--AND YET SO MUCH THE SAME!
THERE IS MUCH WE ALL COULD LEARN FROM ONE ANOTHER...
IT SOUNDS MOST WONDROUS, PRINCESS--AND YET SO TERRIFYING!
EVEN NOW, THE COUNCIL OF JUSTICE PONDERS THE GIFTS AND RECORDS YOU BROUGHT BACK WITH YOU FROM MAN'S WORLD!
AYE, THERE ARE THOSE WHOSE HEARTS AND MINDS LIVE ONLY IN THE PAST--
--BUT WHAT I'VE SEEN OF MAN HIMSELF SEEMS TO SHOW MUCH PROMISE!
STILL, THAT IS ALL IN MY PAST NOW.
WHATEVER QUESTIONS REMAIN UNANSWERED, I'M SURE THE GODS WILL REVEAL THE TRUTH IN THEIR OWN GOOD TIME.
YOU HAVE SEEN THE EVIDENCE, SISTERS...
NOW THE TIME HAS COME TO RENDER YOUR DECISION...
YOU HAVE STUDIED ALL THESE ITEMS WHICH THE PRINCESS DIANA BROUGHT BACK FROM HER LONG JOURNEY--
--ALL THE TREASURES MAN'S WORLD HAS TO OFFER!
DO WE NOW SHARE THIS KNOWLEDGE WITH OUR SISTER AMAZONS?
WELL, I FOR ONE SAY NO, MNEMOSYNE!
4

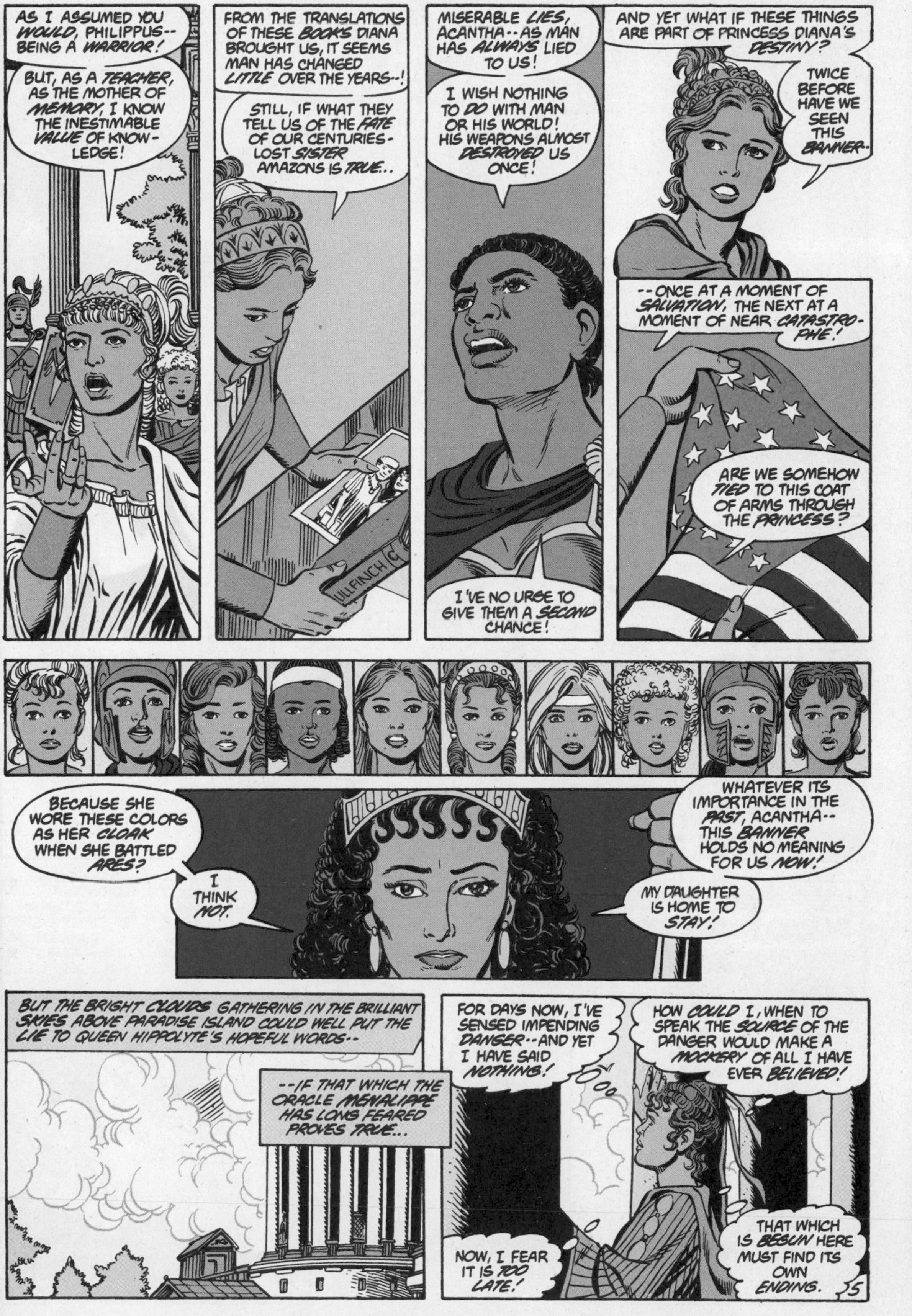

AS I ASSUMED YOU WOULD, PHILIPPUS--BEING A WARRIOR!
BUT, AS A TEACHER, AS THE MOTHER OF MEMORY, I KNOW THE INESTIMABLE VALUE OF KNOW-LEDGE!
FROM THE TRANSLATIONS OF THESE BOOKS DIANA BROUGHT US, IT SEEMS MAN HAS CHANGED LITTLE OVER THE YEARS--!
STILL, IF WHAT THEY TELL US OF THE FATE OF OUR CENTURIES-LOST SISTER AMAZONS IS TRUE...
BULLFINCH
MISERABLE LIES, ACANTHA--AS MAN HAS ALWAYS LIED TO US!
I WISH NOTHING TO DO WITH MAN OR HIS WORLD! HIS WEAPONS ALMOST DESTROYED US ONCE!
I'VE NO URGE TO GIVE THEM A SECOND CHANCE!
AND YET WHAT IF THESE THINGS ARE PART OF PRINCESS DIANA'S DESTINY?
TWICE BEFORE HAVE WE SEEN THIS BANNER--
--ONCE AT A MOMENT OF SALVATION, THE NEXT AT A MOMENT OF NEAR CATASTRO-PHE!
ARE WE SOMEHOW TIED TO THIS COAT OF ARMS THROUGH THE PRINCESS?
BECAUSE SHE WORE THESE COLORS AS HER CLOAK WHEN SHE BATTLED ARES?
I THINK NOT.
WHATEVER ITS IMPORTANCE IN THE PAST, ACANTHA--THIS BANNER HOLDS NO MEANING FOR US NOW!
MY DAUGHTER IS HOME TO STAY!
BUT THE BRIGHT CLOUDS GATHERING IN THE BRILLIANT SKIES ABOVE PARADISE ISLAND COULD WELL PUT THE LIE TO QUEEN HIPPOLYTE'S HOPEFUL WORDS--
--IF THAT WHICH THE ORACLE MENALIPPE HAS LONG FEARED PROVES TRUE...
FOR DAYS NOW, I'VE SENSED IMPENDING DANGER--AND YET I HAVE SAID NOTHING!
HOW COULD I, WHEN TO SPEAK THE SOURCE OF THE DANGER WOULD MAKE A MOCKERY OF ALL I HAVE EVER BELIEVED!
NOW, I FEAR IT IS TOO LATE!
THAT WHICH IS BEGUN HERE MUST FIND ITS OWN ENDING.
5

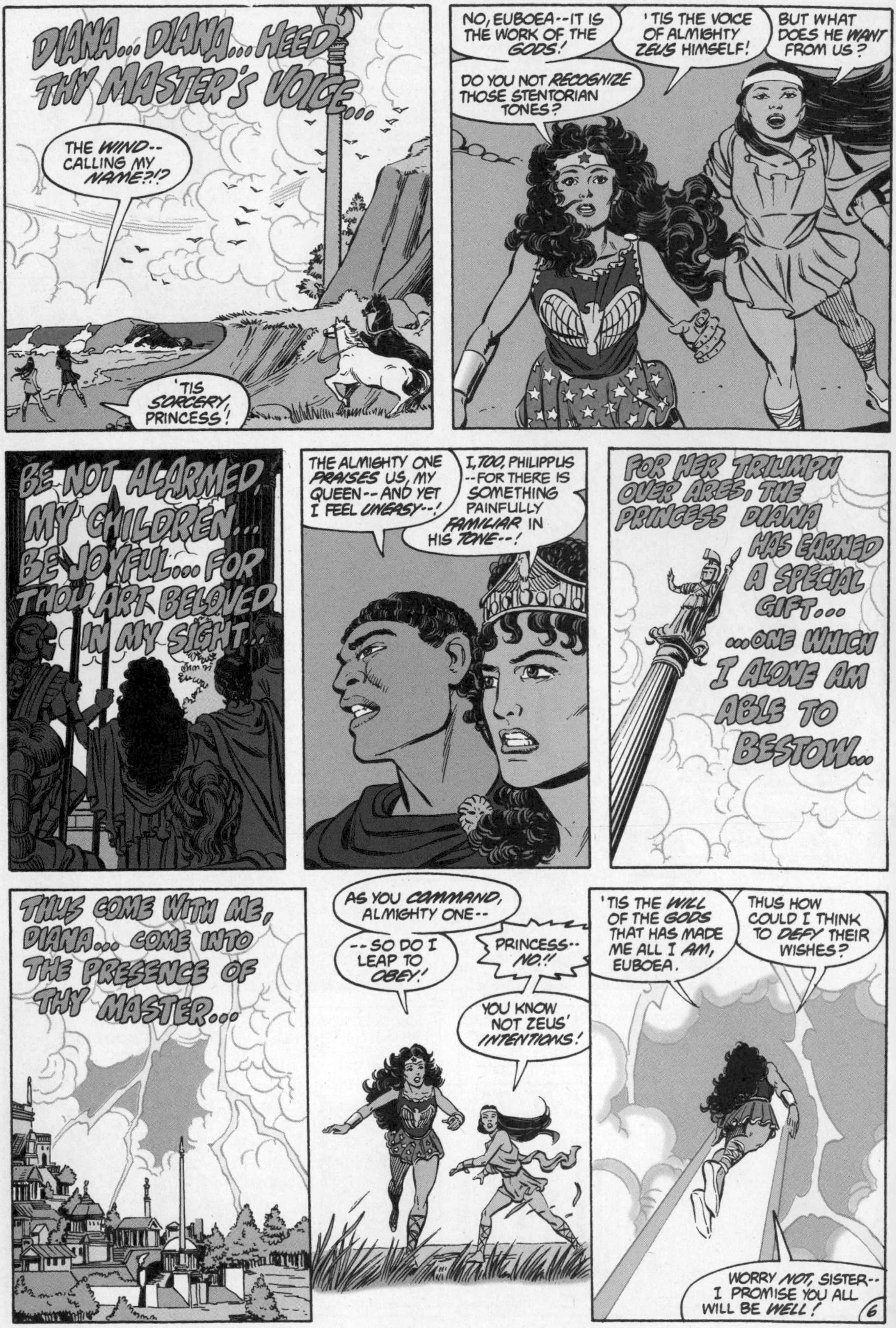

DIANA... DIANA... HEED THY MASTER'S VOICE...
THE WIND-- CALLING MY NAME?!?
'TIS SORCERY, PRINCESS!
NO, EUBOEA--IT IS THE WORK OF THE GODS!
DO YOU NOT RECOGNIZE THOSE STENTORIAN TONES?
'TIS THE VOICE OF ALMIGHTY ZEUS HIMSELF!
BUT WHAT DOES HE WANT FROM US?
BE NOT ALARMED, MY CHILDREN... BE JOYFUL... FOR THOU ART BELOVED IN MY SIGHT...
THE ALMIGHTY ONE PRAISES US, MY QUEEN--AND YET I FEEL UNEASY--!
I, TOO, PHILIPPUS --FOR THERE IS SOMETHING PAINFULLY FAMILIAR IN HIS TONE--!
FOR HER TRIUMPH OVER ARES, THE PRINCESS DIANA HAS EARNED A SPECIAL GIFT...
...ONE WHICH I ALONE AM ABLE TO BESTOW...
THUS COME WITH ME, DIANA... COME INTO THE PRESENCE OF THY MASTER...
AS YOU COMMAND, ALMIGHTY ONE--
--SO DO I LEAP TO OBEY!
PRINCESS-- NO!!
YOU KNOW NOT ZEUS' INTENTIONS!
'TIS THE WILL OF THE GODS THAT HAS MADE ME ALL I AM, EUBOEA.
THUS HOW COULD I THINK TO DEFY THEIR WISHES?
WORRY NOT, SISTER-- I PROMISE YOU ALL WILL BE WELL!
6

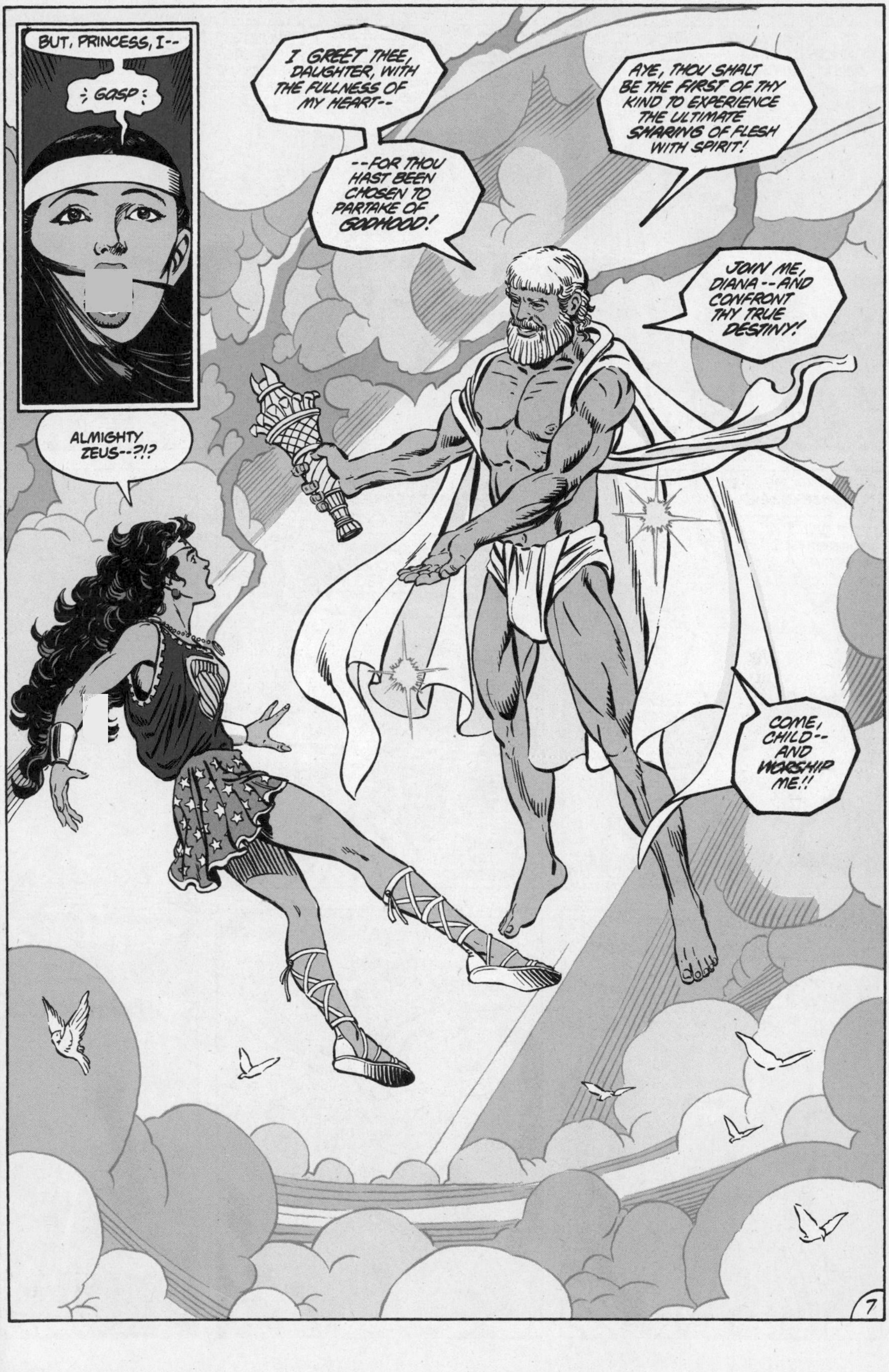
BUT, PRINCESS, I--
GASP
ALMIGHTY ZEUS--?!?
I GREET THEE, DAUGHTER, WITH THE FULLNESS OF MY HEART--
--FOR THOU HAST BEEN CHOSEN TO PARTAKE OF GODHOOD!
AYE, THOU SHALT BE THE FIRST OF THY KIND TO EXPERIENCE THE ULTIMATE SHARING OF FLESH WITH SPIRIT!
JOIN ME, DIANA--AND CONFRONT THY TRUE DESTINY!
COME, CHILD--AND WORSHIP ME!!
7

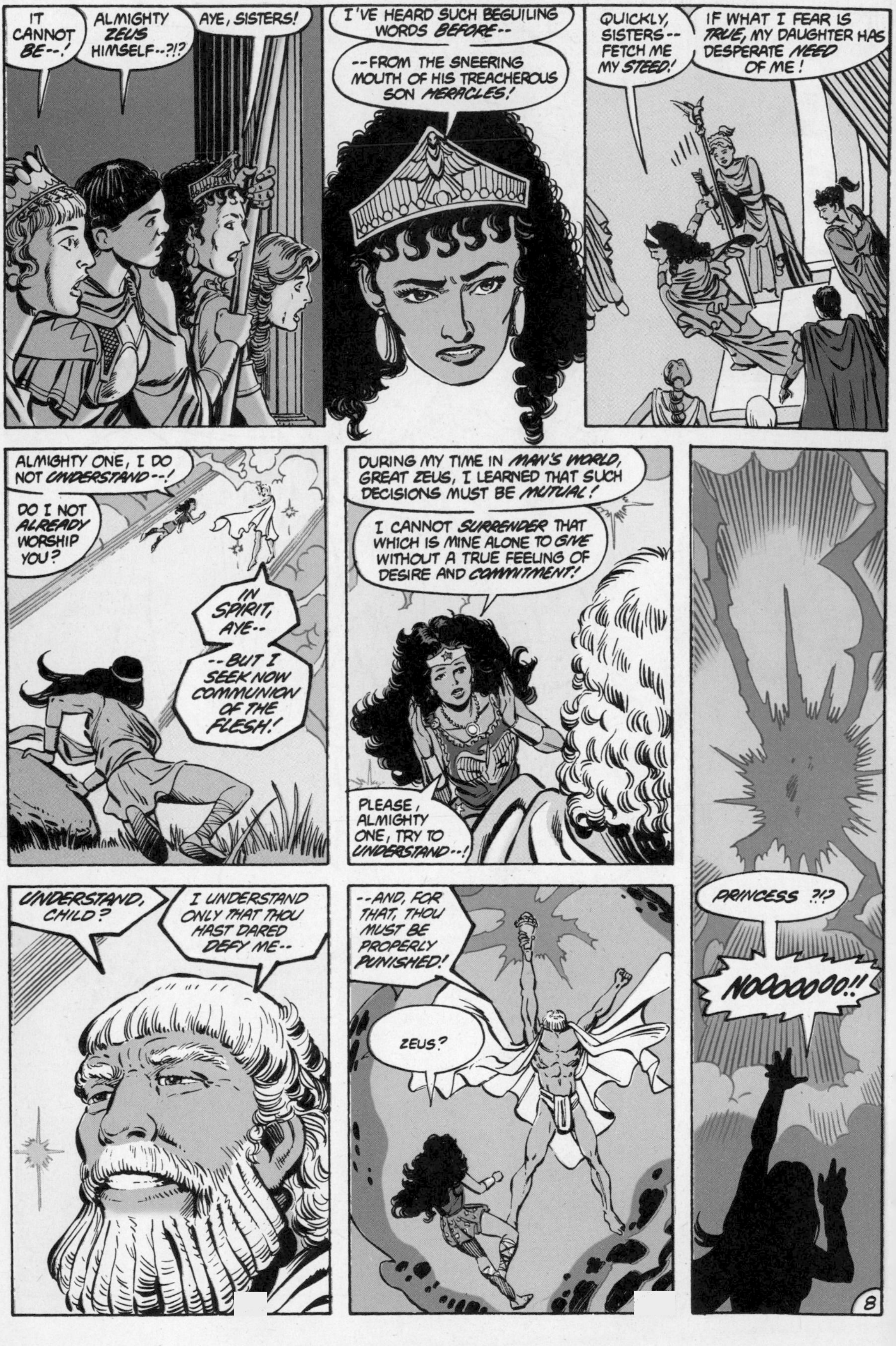

IT CANNOT BE--!
ALMIGHTY ZEUS HIMSELF--?!?
AYE, SISTERS!
I'VE HEARD SUCH BEGUILING WORDS BEFORE--
--FROM THE SNEERING MOUTH OF HIS TREACHEROUS SON HERACLES!
QUICKLY, SISTERS-- FETCH ME MY STEED!
IF WHAT I FEAR IS TRUE, MY DAUGHTER HAS DESPERATE NEED OF ME!
ALMIGHTY ONE, I DO NOT UNDERSTAND--!
DO I NOT ALREADY WORSHIP YOU?
IN SPIRIT, AYE--
--BUT I SEEK NOW COMMUNION OF THE FLESH!
DURING MY TIME IN MAN'S WORLD, GREAT ZEUS, I LEARNED THAT SUCH DECISIONS MUST BE MUTUAL!
I CANNOT SURRENDER THAT WHICH IS MINE ALONE TO GIVE WITHOUT A TRUE FEELING OF DESIRE AND COMMITMENT!
PLEASE, ALMIGHTY ONE, TRY TO UNDERSTAND--!
UNDERSTAND, CHILD?
I UNDERSTAND ONLY THAT THOU HAST DARED DEFY ME--
--AND, FOR THAT, THOU MUST BE PROPERLY PUNISHED!
ZEUS?
PRINCESS ?!?
NOOOOOOO!!
8

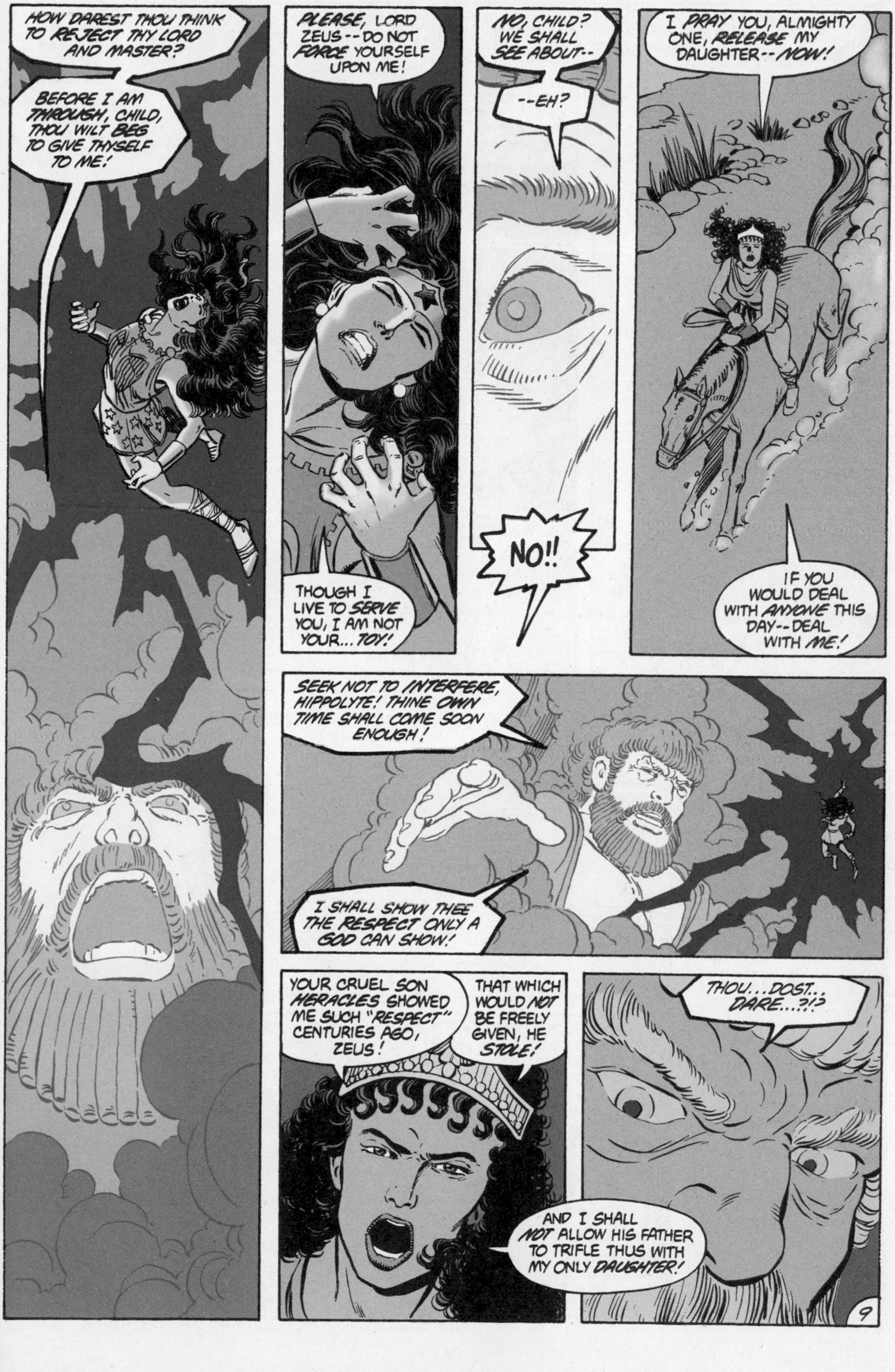
HOW DAREST THOU THINK TO REJECT THY LORD AND MASTER?
BEFORE I AM THROUGH, CHILD, THOU WILT BEG TO GIVE THYSELF TO ME!
PLEASE, LORD ZEUS -- DO NOT FORCE YOURSELF UPON ME!
THOUGH I LIVE TO SERVE YOU, I AM NOT YOUR... TOY!
NO, CHILD? WE SHALL SEE ABOUT--
--EH?
NO!!
I PRAY YOU, ALMIGHTY ONE, RELEASE MY DAUGHTER--NOW!
IF YOU WOULD DEAL WITH ANYONE THIS DAY--DEAL WITH ME!
SEEK NOT TO INTERFERE, HIPPOLYTE! THINE OWN TIME SHALL COME SOON ENOUGH!
I SHALL SHOW THEE THE RESPECT ONLY A GOD CAN SHOW!
YOUR CRUEL SON HERACLES SHOWED ME SUCH "RESPECT" CENTURIES AGO, ZEUS!
THAT WHICH WOULD NOT BE FREELY GIVEN, HE STOLE!
AND I SHALL NOT ALLOW HIS FATHER TO TRIFLE THUS WITH MY ONLY DAUGHTER!
THOU... DOST... DARE...?!?
9

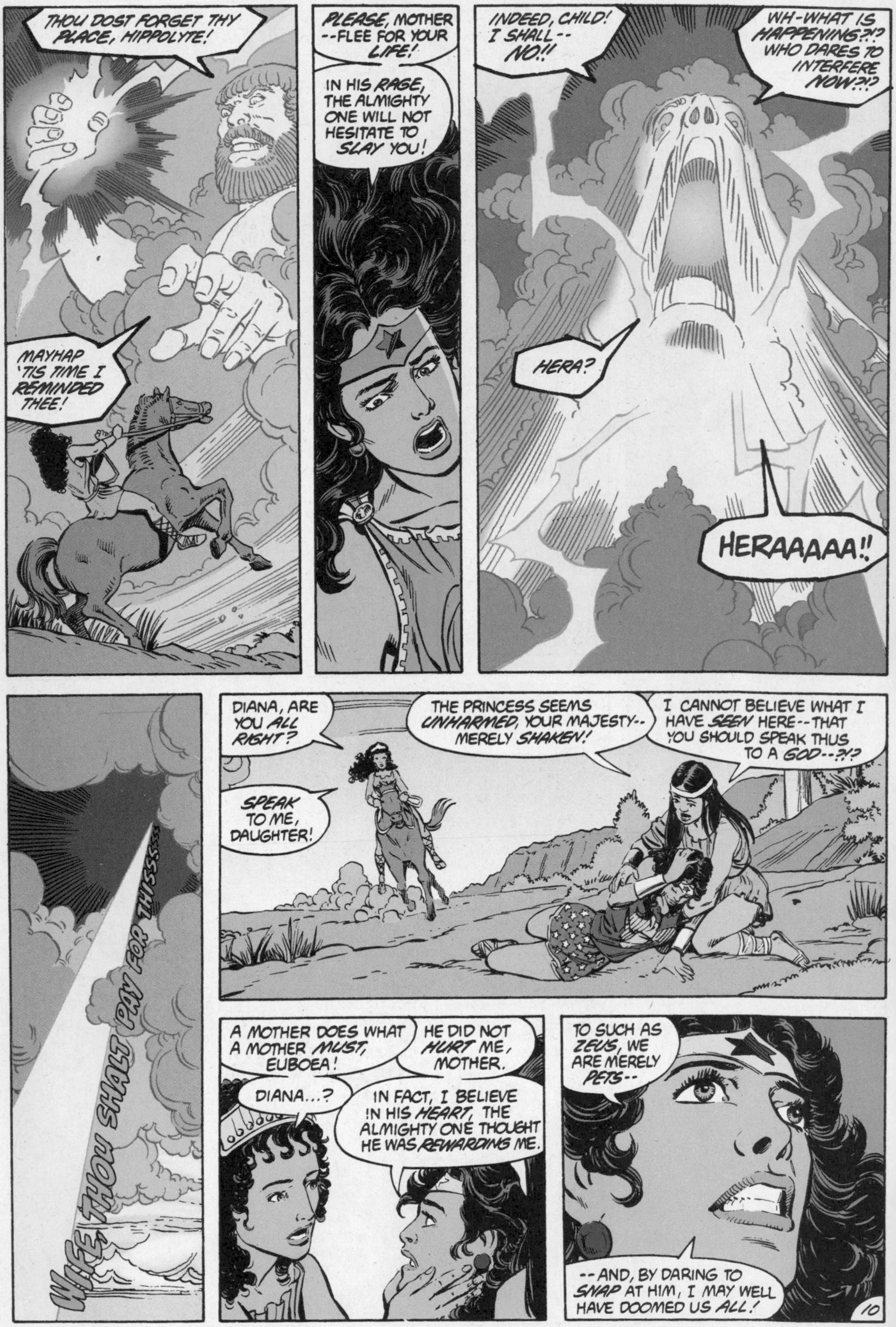
THOU DOST FORGET THY PLACE, HIPPOLYTE!
MAYHAP 'TIS TIME I REMINDED THEE!
PLEASE, MOTHER--FLEE FOR YOUR LIFE!
IN HIS RAGE, THE ALMIGHTY ONE WILL NOT HESITATE TO SLAY YOU!
INDEED, CHILD! I SHALL-- NO!!
WH-WHAT IS HAPPENING?!? WHO DARES TO INTERFERE NOW?!?
HERA?
HERAAAAAA!!
WIFE, THOU SHALT PAY FOR THISSSsss
DIANA, ARE YOU ALL RIGHT?
SPEAK TO ME, DAUGHTER!
THE PRINCESS SEEMS UNHARMED, YOUR MAJESTY-- MERELY SHAKEN!
I CANNOT BELIEVE WHAT I HAVE SEEN HERE--THAT YOU SHOULD SPEAK THUS TO A GOD--?!?
A MOTHER DOES WHAT A MOTHER MUST, EUBOEA!
HE DID NOT HURT ME, MOTHER.
DIANA...?
IN FACT, I BELIEVE IN HIS HEART, THE ALMIGHTY ONE THOUGHT HE WAS REWARDING ME.
TO SUCH AS ZEUS, WE ARE MERELY PETS--
--AND, BY DARING TO SNAP AT HIM, I MAY WELL HAVE DOOMED US ALL!
10

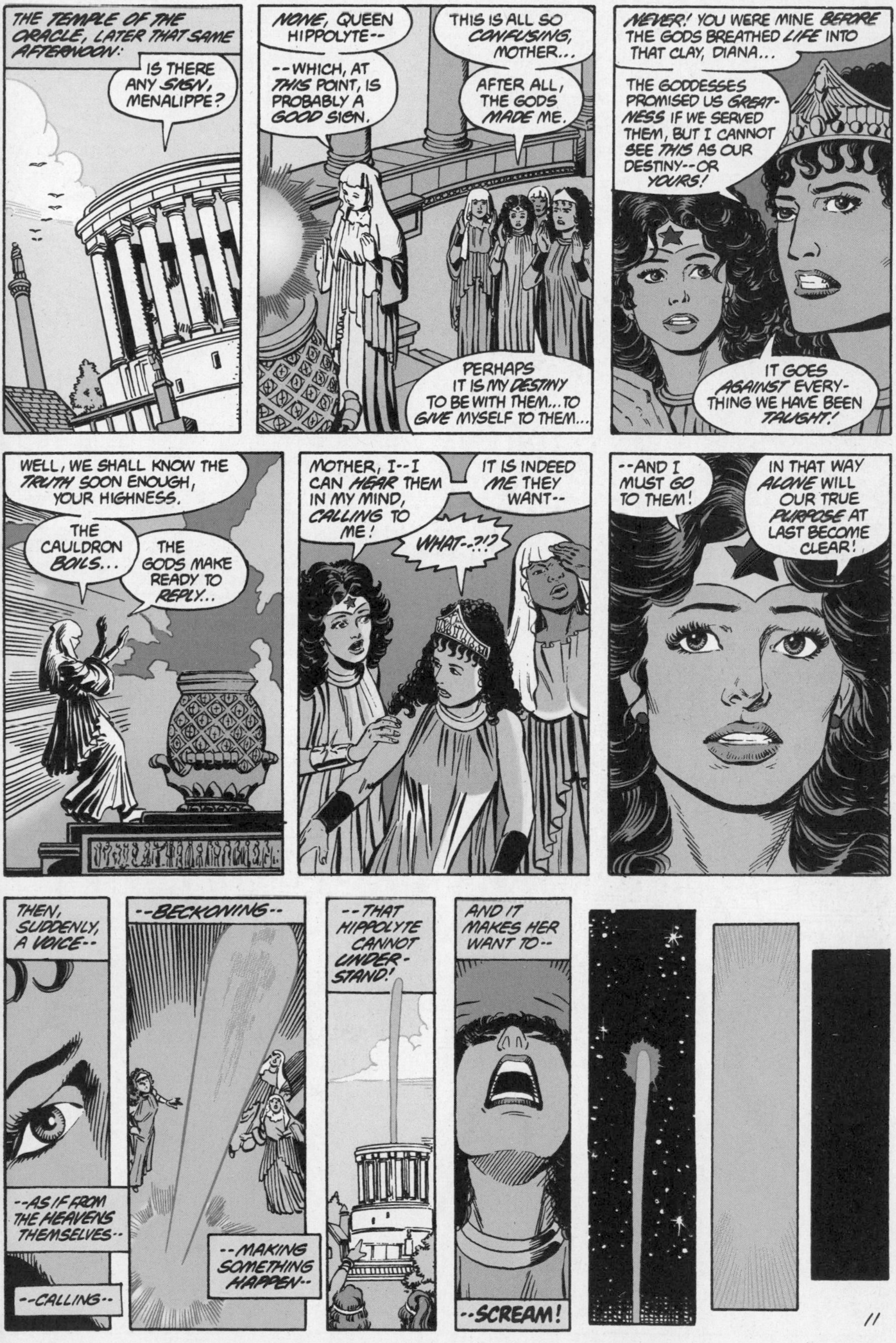
THE TEMPLE OF THE ORACLE, LATER THAT SAME AFTERNOON:
IS THERE ANY SIGN, MENALIPPE?
NONE, QUEEN HIPPOLYTE--
--WHICH, AT THIS POINT, IS PROBABLY A GOOD SIGN.
THIS IS ALL SO CONFUSING, MOTHER...
AFTER ALL, THE GODS MADE ME.
PERHAPS IT IS MY DESTINY TO BE WITH THEM... TO GIVE MYSELF TO THEM...
NEVER! YOU WERE MINE BEFORE THE GODS BREATHED LIFE INTO THAT CLAY, DIANA...
THE GODDESSES PROMISED US GREATNESS IF WE SERVED THEM, BUT I CANNOT SEE THIS AS OUR DESTINY--OR YOURS!
IT GOES AGAINST EVERYTHING WE HAVE BEEN TAUGHT!
WELL, WE SHALL KNOW THE TRUTH SOON ENOUGH, YOUR HIGHNESS.
THE CAULDRON BOILS...
THE GODS MAKE READY TO REPLY...
MOTHER, I--I CAN HEAR THEM IN MY MIND, CALLING TO ME!
IT IS INDEED ME THEY WANT--
WHAT--?!?
--AND I MUST GO TO THEM!
IN THAT WAY ALONE WILL OUR TRUE PURPOSE AT LAST BECOME CLEAR!
THEN, SUDDENLY, A VOICE--
--AS IF FROM THE HEAVENS THEMSELVES--
--CALLING--
--BECKONING--
--MAKING SOMETHING HAPPEN--
--THAT HIPPOLYTE CANNOT UNDERSTAND!
AND IT MAKES HER WANT TO--
--SCREAM!
11

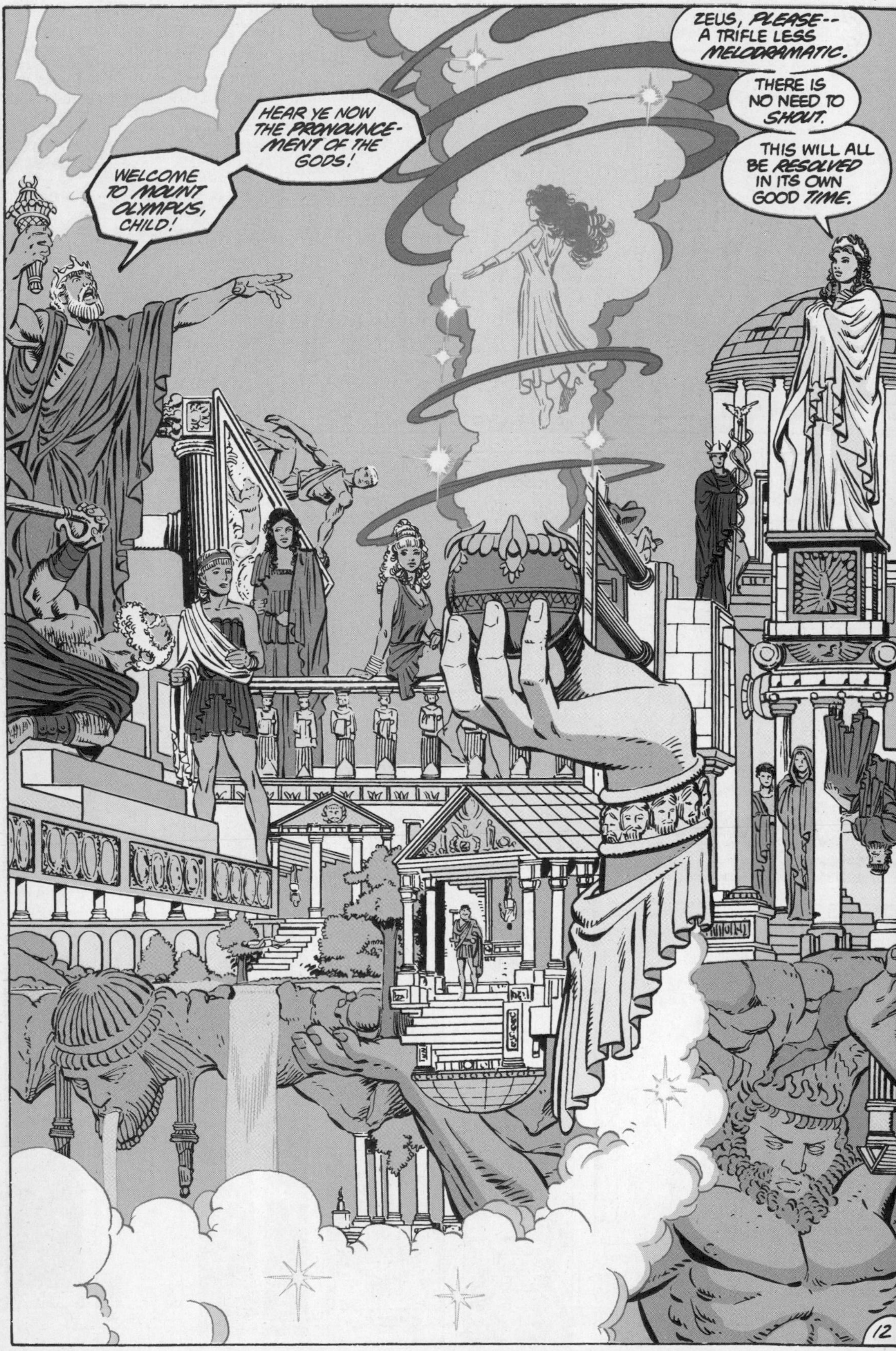
WELCOME TO MOUNT OLYMPUS, CHILD!
HEAR YE NOW THE PRONOUNCEMENT OF THE GODS!
ZEUS, PLEASE-- A TRIFLE LESS MELODRAMATIC.
THERE IS NO NEED TO SHOUT.
THIS WILL ALL BE RESOLVED IN ITS OWN GOOD TIME.
12

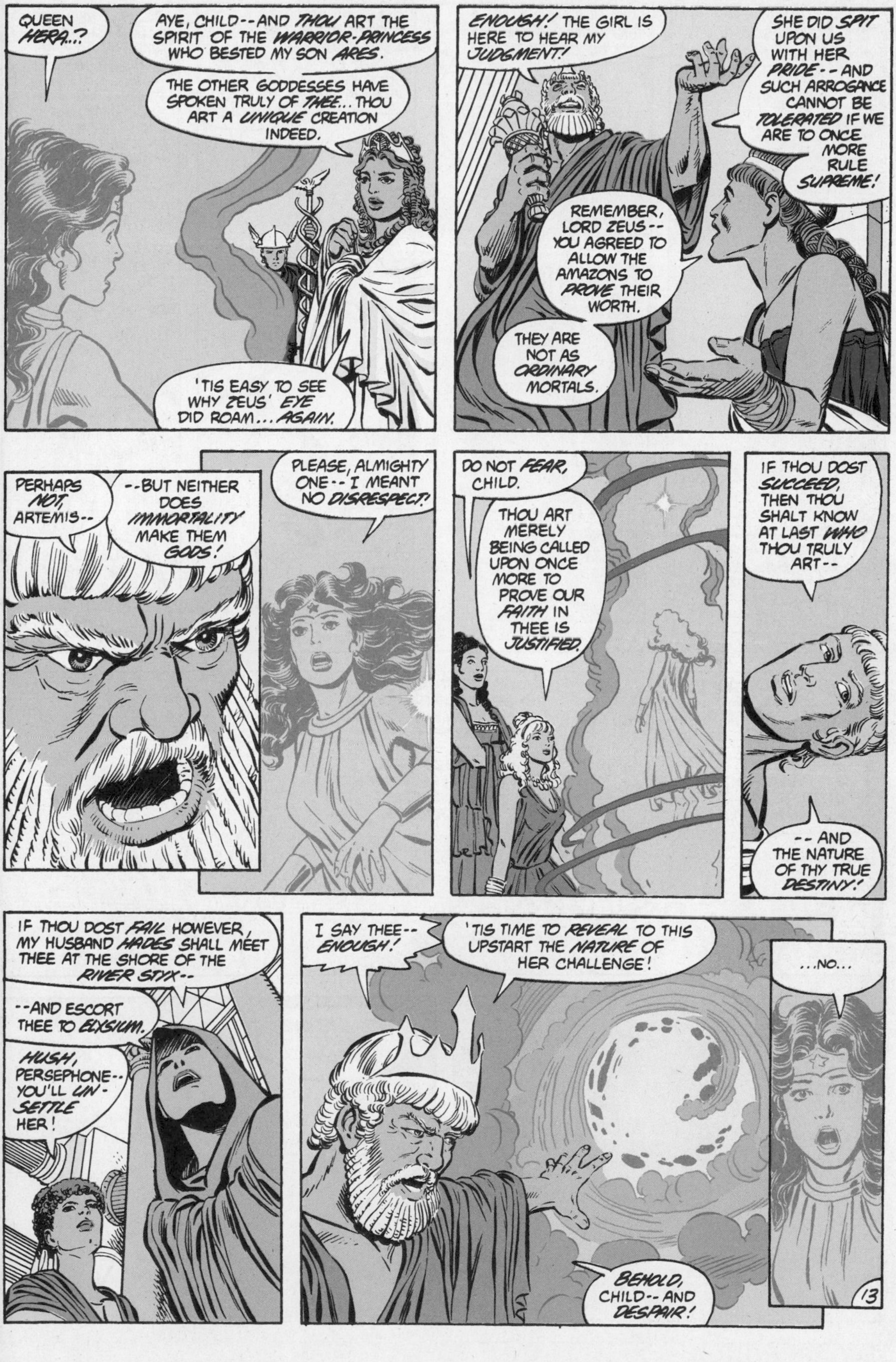
QUEEN HERA..?
AYE, CHILD--AND THOU ART THE SPIRIT OF THE WARRIOR-PRINCESS WHO BESTED MY SON ARES.
THE OTHER GODDESSES HAVE SPOKEN TRULY OF THEE... THOU ART A UNIQUE CREATION INDEED.
'TIS EASY TO SEE WHY ZEUS' EYE DID ROAM... AGAIN.
ENOUGH! THE GIRL IS HERE TO HEAR MY JUDGMENT!
SHE DID SPIT UPON US WITH HER PRIDE--AND SUCH ARROGANCE CANNOT BE TOLERATED IF WE ARE TO ONCE MORE RULE SUPREME!
REMEMBER, LORD ZEUS--YOU AGREED TO ALLOW THE AMAZONS TO PROVE THEIR WORTH.
THEY ARE NOT AS ORDINARY MORTALS.
PERHAPS NOT, ARTEMIS--
--BUT NEITHER DOES IMMORTALITY MAKE THEM GODS!
PLEASE, ALMIGHTY ONE--I MEANT NO DISRESPECT!
DO NOT FEAR, CHILD.
THOU ART MERELY BEING CALLED UPON ONCE MORE TO PROVE OUR FAITH IN THEE IS JUSTIFIED.
IF THOU DOST SUCCEED, THEN THOU SHALT KNOW AT LAST WHO THOU TRULY ART--
--AND THE NATURE OF THY TRUE DESTINY!
IF THOU DOST FAIL HOWEVER, MY HUSBAND HADES SHALL MEET THEE AT THE SHORE OF THE RIVER STYX--
--AND ESCORT THEE TO ELYSIUM.
HUSH, PERSEPHONE--YOU'LL UN-SETTLE HER!
I SAY THEE--ENOUGH!
'TIS TIME TO REVEAL TO THIS UPSTART THE NATURE OF HER CHALLENGE!
...NO...
BEHOLD, CHILD--AND DESPAIR!
13

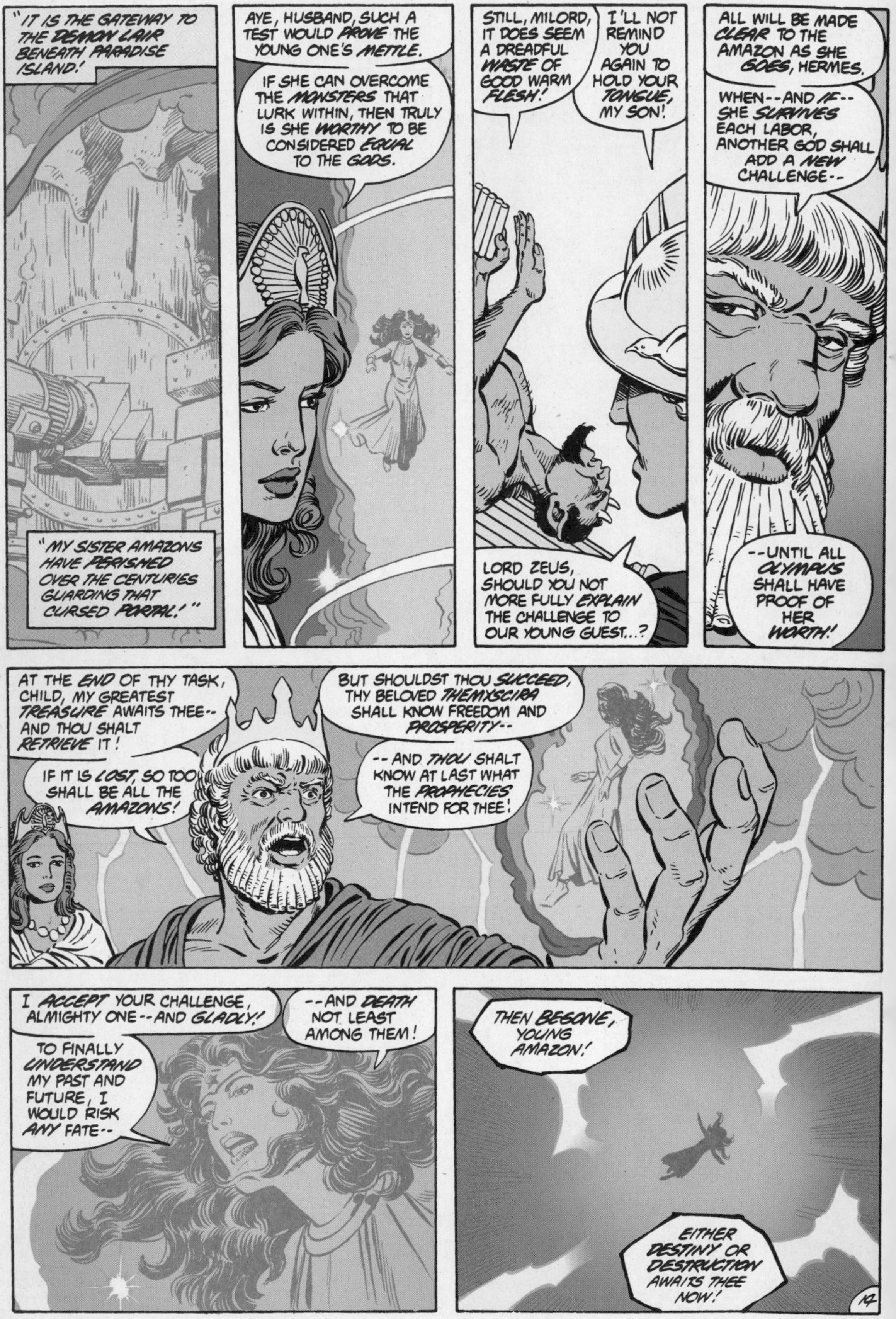
"IT IS THE GATEWAY TO THE DEMON LAIR BENEATH PARADISE ISLAND!
"MY SISTER AMAZONS HAVE PERISHED OVER THE CENTURIES GUARDING THAT CURSED PORTAL!"
AYE, HUSBAND, SUCH A TEST WOULD PROVE THE YOUNG ONE'S METTLE.
IF SHE CAN OVERCOME THE MONSTERS THAT LURK WITHIN, THEN TRULY IS SHE WORTHY TO BE CONSIDERED EQUAL TO THE GODS.
STILL, MILORD, IT DOES SEEM A DREADFUL WASTE OF GOOD WARM FLESH!
I'LL NOT REMIND YOU AGAIN TO HOLD YOUR TONGUE, MY SON!
LORD ZEUS, SHOULD YOU NOT MORE FULLY EXPLAIN THE CHALLENGE TO OUR YOUNG GUEST...?
ALL WILL BE MADE CLEAR TO THE AMAZON AS SHE GOES, HERMES.
WHEN--AND IF--SHE SURVIVES EACH LABOR, ANOTHER GOD SHALL ADD A NEW CHALLENGE--
--UNTIL ALL OLYMPUS SHALL HAVE PROOF OF HER WORTH!
AT THE END OF THY TASK, CHILD, MY GREATEST TREASURE AWAITS THEE--AND THOU SHALT RETRIEVE IT!
IF IT IS LOST, SO TOO SHALL BE ALL THE AMAZONS!
BUT SHOULDST THOU SUCCEED, THY BELOVED THEMYSCIRA SHALL KNOW FREEDOM AND PROSPERITY--
--AND THOU SHALT KNOW AT LAST WHAT THE PROPHECIES INTEND FOR THEE!
I ACCEPT YOUR CHALLENGE, ALMIGHTY ONE--AND GLADLY!
TO FINALLY UNDERSTAND MY PAST AND FUTURE, I WOULD RISK ANY FATE--
--AND DEATH NOT LEAST AMONG THEM!
THEN BEGONE, YOUNG AMAZON!
EITHER DESTINY OR DESTRUCTION AWAITS THEE NOW!
14

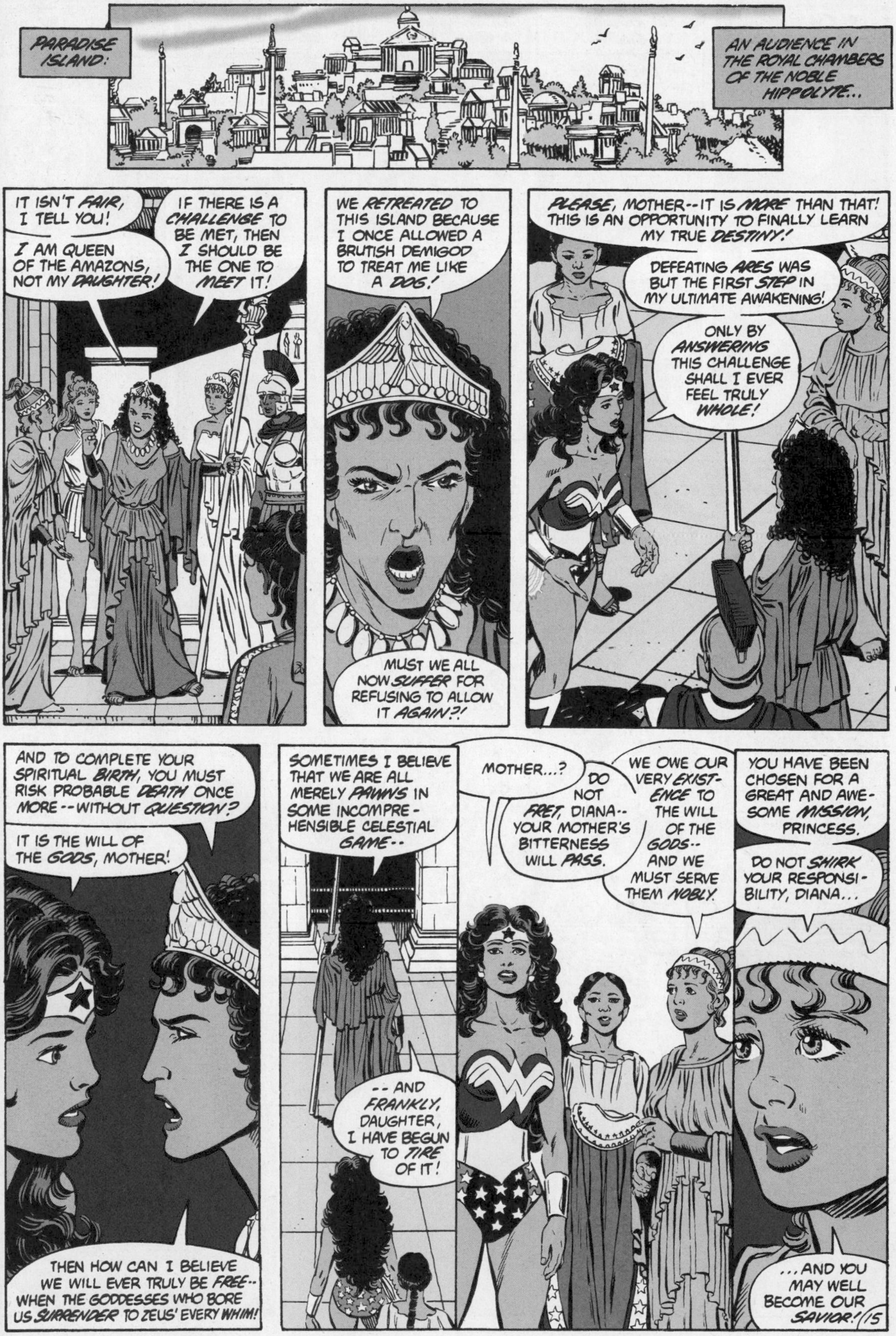
PARADISE ISLAND:
AN AUDIENCE IN THE ROYAL CHAMBERS OF THE NOBLE HIPPOLYTE...
IT ISN'T FAIR, I TELL YOU!
I AM QUEEN OF THE AMAZONS, NOT MY DAUGHTER!
IF THERE IS A CHALLENGE TO BE MET, THEN I SHOULD BE THE ONE TO MEET IT!
WE RETREATED TO THIS ISLAND BECAUSE I ONCE ALLOWED A BRUTISH DEMIGOD TO TREAT ME LIKE A DOG!
MUST WE ALL NOW SUFFER FOR REFUSING TO ALLOW IT AGAIN?!
PLEASE, MOTHER--IT IS MORE THAN THAT! THIS IS AN OPPORTUNITY TO FINALLY LEARN MY TRUE DESTINY!
DEFEATING ARES WAS BUT THE FIRST STEP IN MY ULTIMATE AWAKENING!
ONLY BY ANSWERING THIS CHALLENGE SHALL I EVER FEEL TRULY WHOLE!
AND TO COMPLETE YOUR SPIRITUAL BIRTH, YOU MUST RISK PROBABLE DEATH ONCE MORE--WITHOUT QUESTION?
IT IS THE WILL OF THE GODS, MOTHER!
THEN HOW CAN I BELIEVE WE WILL EVER TRULY BE FREE--WHEN THE GODDESSES WHO BORE US SURRENDER TO ZEUS' EVERY WHIM!
SOMETIMES I BELIEVE THAT WE ARE ALL MERELY PAWNS IN SOME INCOMPREHENSIBLE CELESTIAL GAME--
--AND FRANKLY, DAUGHTER, I HAVE BEGUN TO TIRE OF IT!
MOTHER...?
DO NOT FRET, DIANA--YOUR MOTHER'S BITTERNESS WILL PASS.
WE OWE OUR VERY EXISTENCE TO THE WILL OF THE GODS--AND WE MUST SERVE THEM NOBLY.
YOU HAVE BEEN CHOSEN FOR A GREAT AND AWESOME MISSION, PRINCESS.
DO NOT SHIRK YOUR RESPONSIBILITY, DIANA...
...AND YOU MAY WELL BECOME OUR SAVIOR!
15

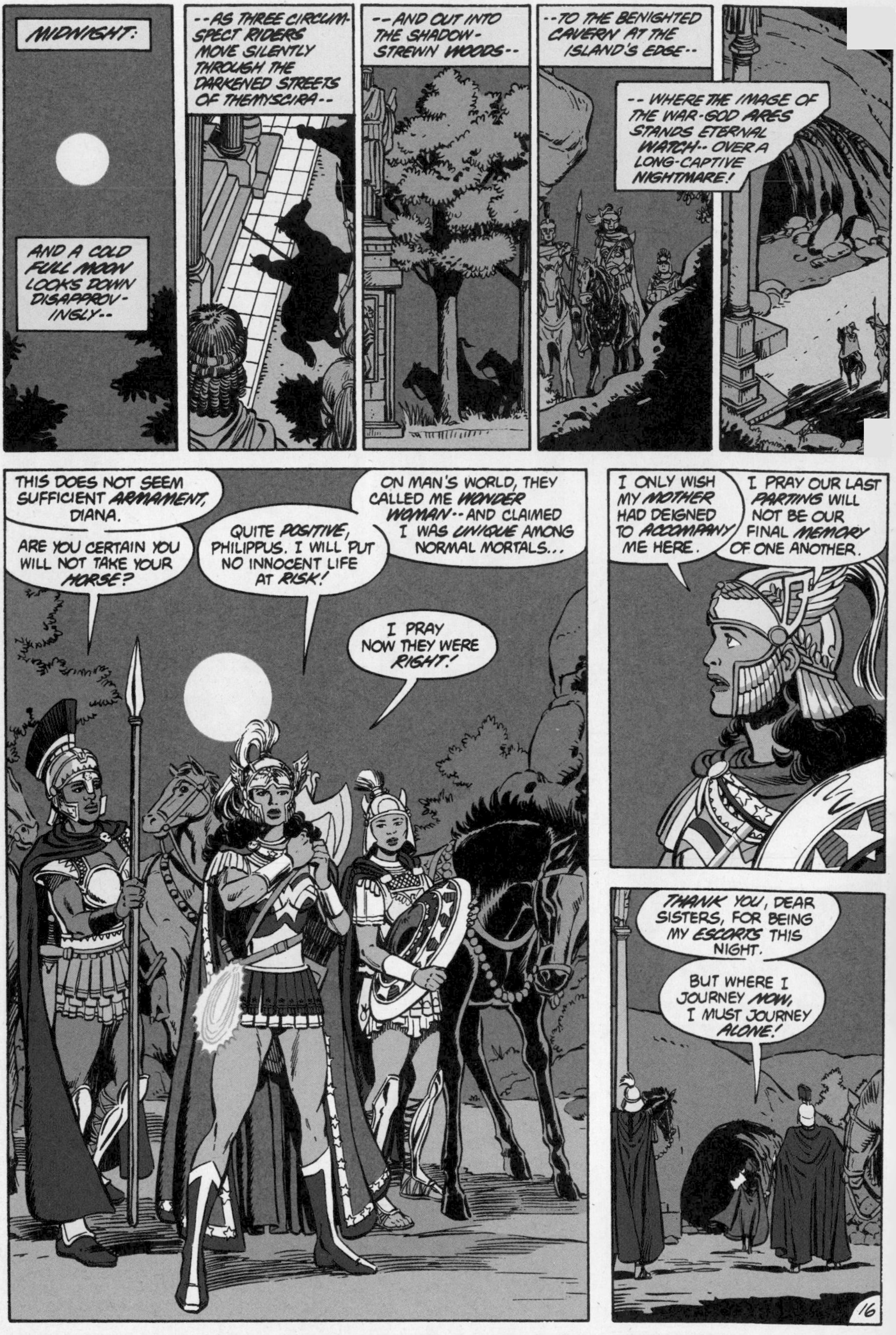
MIDNIGHT:
AND A COLD FULL MOON LOOKS DOWN DISAPPROV-INGLY--
--AS THREE CIRCUM-SPECT RIDERS MOVE SILENTLY THROUGH THE DARKENED STREETS OF THEMYSCIRA--
--AND OUT INTO THE SHADOW-STREWN WOODS--
--TO THE BENIGHTED CAVERN AT THE ISLAND'S EDGE--
--WHERE THE IMAGE OF THE WAR-GOD ARES STANDS ETERNAL WATCH--OVER A LONG-CAPTIVE NIGHTMARE!
THIS DOES NOT SEEM SUFFICIENT ARMAMENT, DIANA.
ARE YOU CERTAIN YOU WILL NOT TAKE YOUR HORSE?
QUITE POSITIVE, PHILIPPUS. I WILL PUT NO INNOCENT LIFE AT RISK!
ON MAN'S WORLD, THEY CALLED ME WONDER WOMAN--AND CLAIMED I WAS UNIQUE AMONG NORMAL MORTALS...
I PRAY NOW THEY WERE RIGHT!
I ONLY WISH MY MOTHER HAD DEIGNED TO ACCOMPANY ME HERE.
I PRAY OUR LAST PARTING WILL NOT BE OUR FINAL MEMORY OF ONE ANOTHER.
THANK YOU, DEAR SISTERS, FOR BEING MY ESCORTS THIS NIGHT.
BUT WHERE I JOURNEY NOW, I MUST JOURNEY ALONE!
16

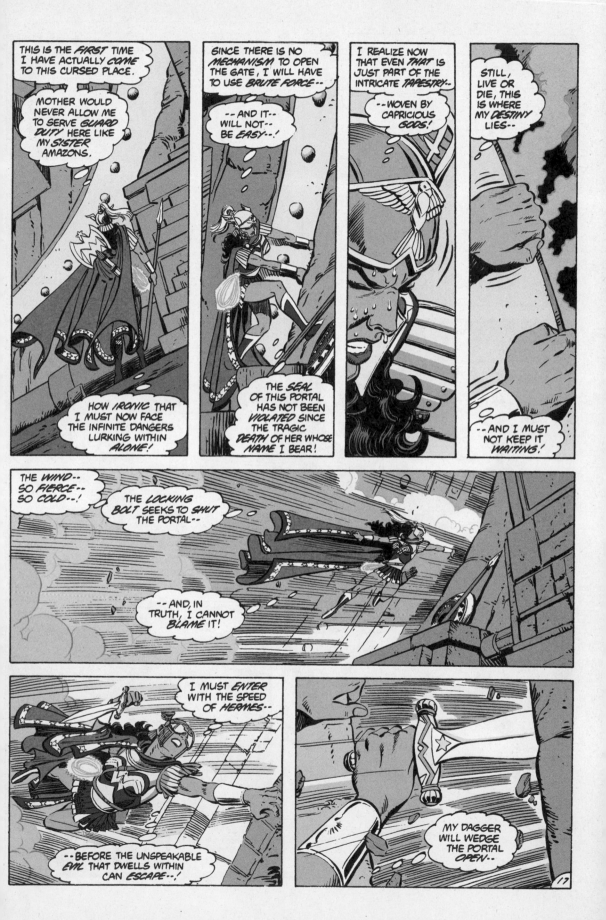

THIS IS THE *FIRST* TIME I HAVE ACTUALLY *COME* TO THIS CURSED PLACE.

MOTHER WOULD NEVER ALLOW ME TO SERVE *GUARD DUTY* HERE LIKE MY *SISTER* AMAZONS.

HOW *IRONIC* THAT I MUST NOW FACE THE INFINITE DANGERS LURKING WITHIN *ALONE!*

SINCE THERE IS NO *MECHANISM* TO OPEN THE GATE, I WILL HAVE TO USE *BRUTE FORCE*--

--AND IT-- WILL NOT-- BE *EASY*--!

THE *SEAL* OF THIS PORTAL HAS NOT BEEN *VIOLATED* SINCE THE TRAGIC *DEATH* OF HER WHOSE *NAME* I BEAR!

I REALIZE NOW THAT EVEN *THAT* IS JUST PART OF THE INTRICATE *TAPESTRY*--

--WOVEN BY CAPRICIOUS *GODS!*

STILL, LIVE OR DIE, THIS IS WHERE MY *DESTINY* LIES--

--AND I MUST NOT KEEP IT *WAITING!*

THE *WIND*-- SO FIERCE-- SO COLD--!

THE *LOCKING BOLT* SEEKS TO *SHUT* THE PORTAL--

--AND, IN TRUTH, I CANNOT *BLAME* IT!

I MUST *ENTER* WITH THE SPEED OF *HERMES*--

--BEFORE THE UNSPEAKABLE *EVIL* THAT DWELLS WITHIN CAN *ESCAPE*--!

MY DAGGER WILL WEDGE THE PORTAL *OPEN*--

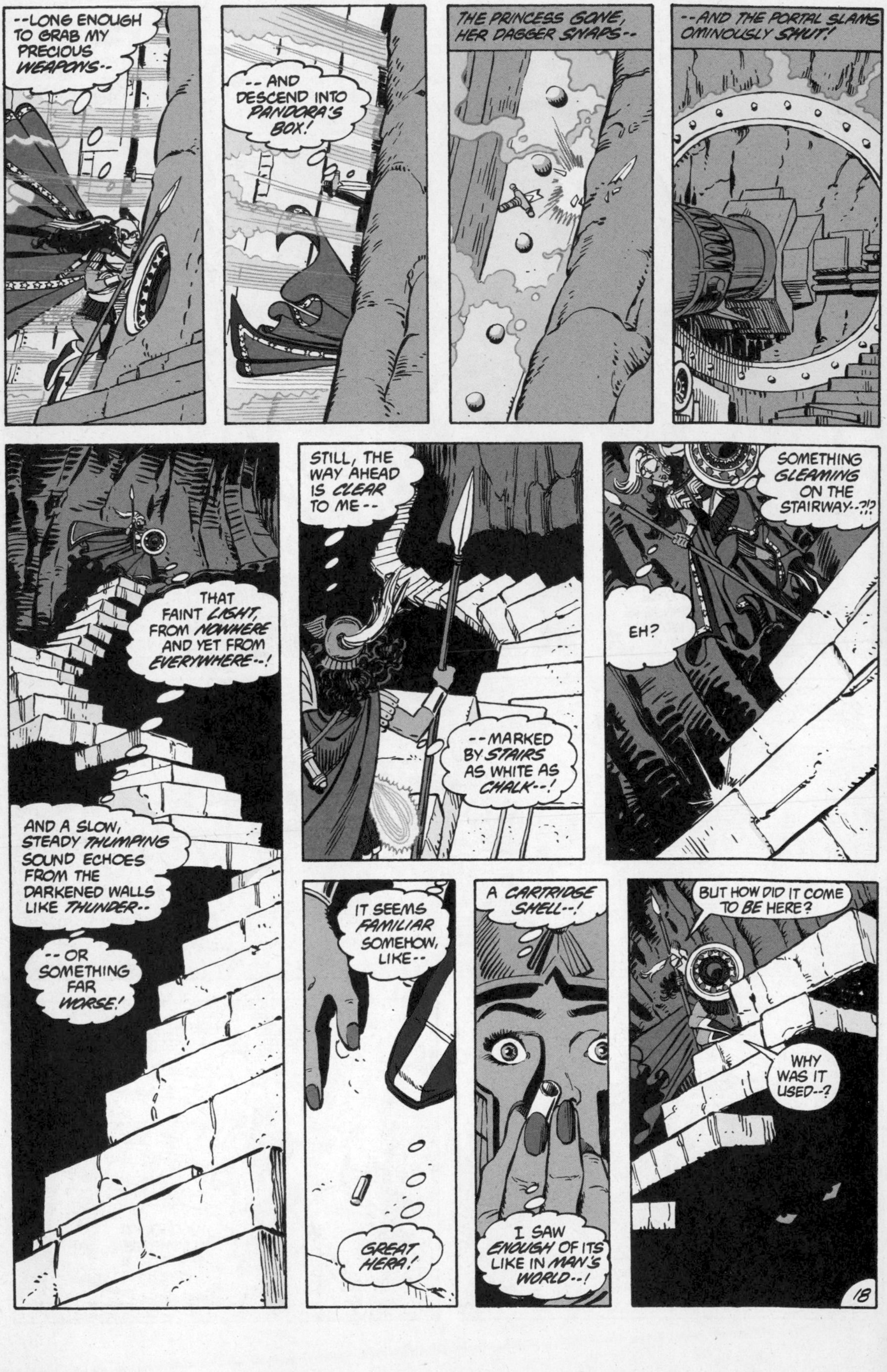
--LONG ENOUGH TO GRAB MY PRECIOUS WEAPONS--
--AND DESCEND INTO PANDORA'S BOX!
THE PRINCESS GONE, HER DAGGER SNAPS--
--AND THE PORTAL SLAMS OMINOUSLY SHUT!
THAT FAINT LIGHT, FROM NOWHERE AND YET FROM EVERYWHERE--!
AND A SLOW, STEADY THUMPING SOUND ECHOES FROM THE DARKENED WALLS LIKE THUNDER--
--OR SOMETHING FAR WORSE!
STILL, THE WAY AHEAD IS CLEAR TO ME--
--MARKED BY STAIRS AS WHITE AS CHALK--!
SOMETHING GLEAMING ON THE STAIRWAY--?!?
EH?
IT SEEMS FAMILIAR SOMEHOW, LIKE--
GREAT HERA!
A CARTRIDGE SHELL--!
I SAW ENOUGH OF ITS LIKE IN MAN'S WORLD--!
BUT HOW DID IT COME TO BE HERE?
WHY WAS IT USED--?
18

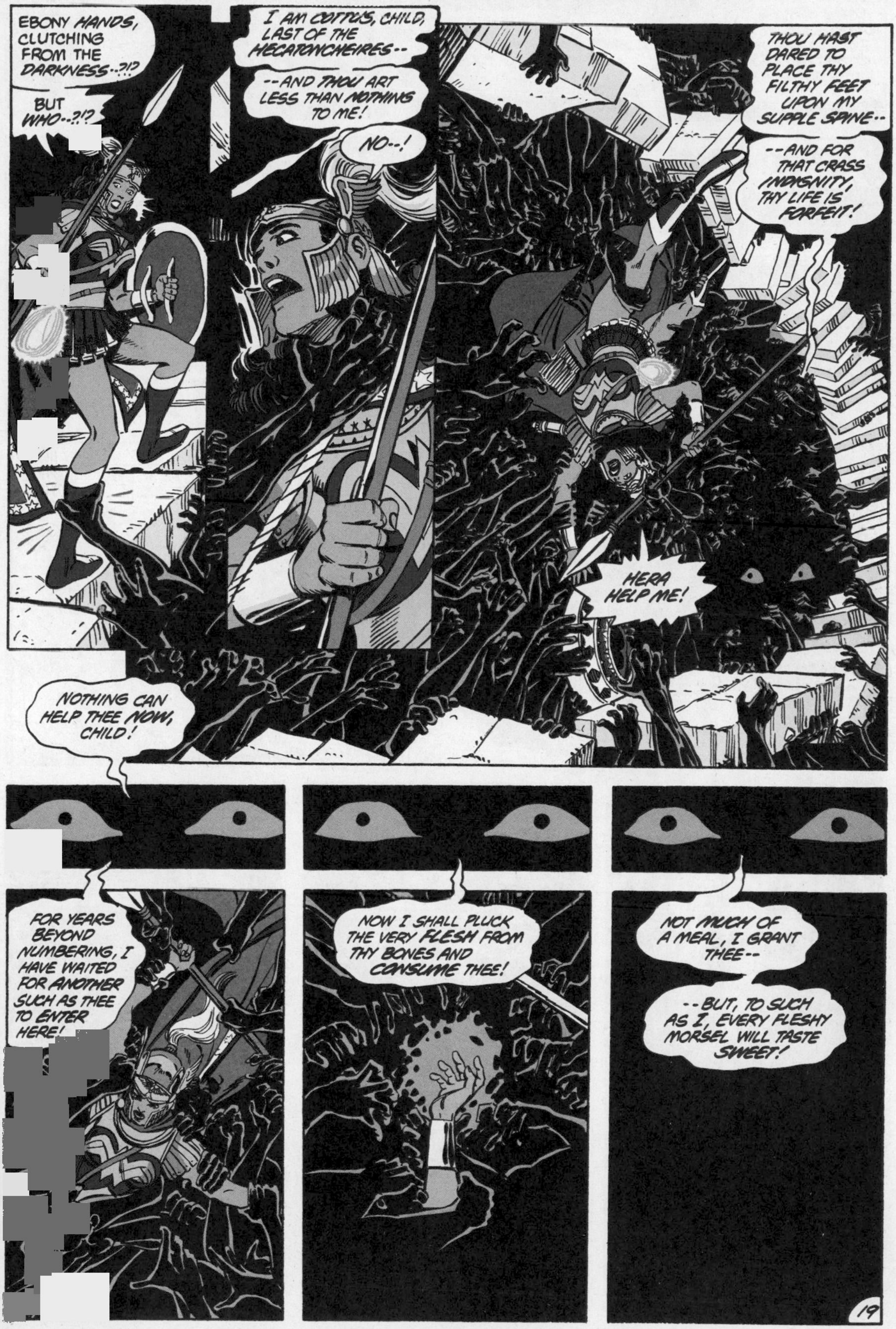
EBONY HANDS, CLUTCHING FROM THE DARKNESS..?!?
BUT WHO--?!?
I AM COTTUS, CHILD, LAST OF THE HECATONCHEIRES--
--AND THOU ART LESS THAN NOTHING TO ME!
NO--!
THOU HAST DARED TO PLACE THY FILTHY FEET UPON MY SUPPLE SPINE..
--AND FOR THAT CRASS INDIGNITY, THY LIFE IS FORFEIT!
HERA HELP ME!
NOTHING CAN HELP THEE NOW, CHILD!
FOR YEARS BEYOND NUMBERING, I HAVE WAITED FOR ANOTHER SUCH AS THEE TO ENTER HERE!
NOW I SHALL PLUCK THE VERY FLESH FROM THY BONES AND CONSUME THEE!
NOT MUCH OF A MEAL, I GRANT THEE--
--BUT, TO SUCH AS I, EVERY FLESHY MORSEL WILL TASTE SWEET!
19

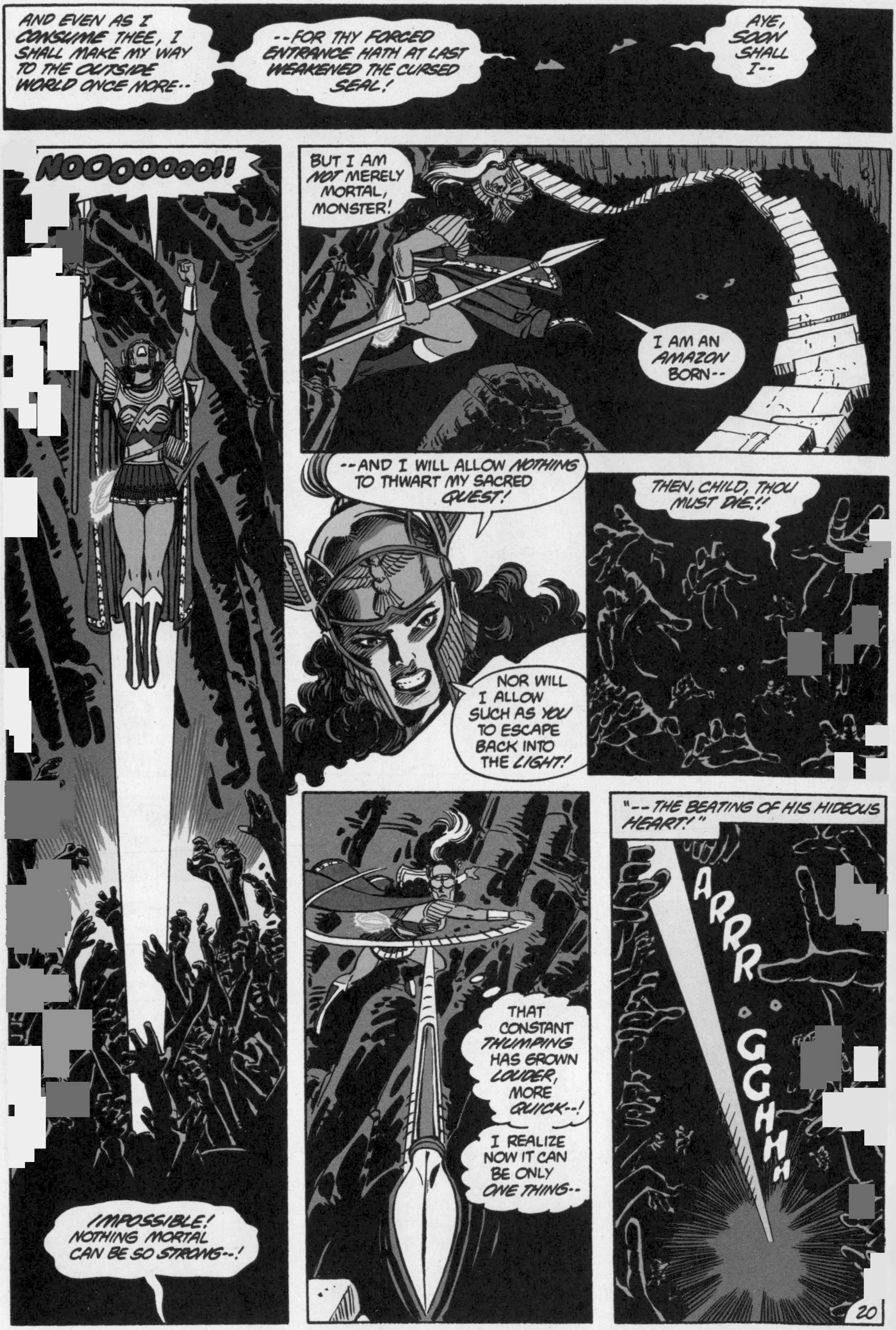
AND EVEN AS I CONSUME THEE, I SHALL MAKE MY WAY TO THE OUTSIDE WORLD ONCE MORE--
--FOR THY FORCED ENTRANCE HATH AT LAST WEAKENED THE CURSED SEAL!
AYE, SOON SHALL I--
NOOOOOOOO!!
IMPOSSIBLE! NOTHING MORTAL CAN BE SO STRONG--!
BUT I AM NOT MERELY MORTAL, MONSTER!
I AM AN AMAZON BORN--
--AND I WILL ALLOW NOTHING TO THWART MY SACRED QUEST!
NOR WILL I ALLOW SUCH AS YOU TO ESCAPE BACK INTO THE LIGHT!
THEN, CHILD, THOU MUST DIE!!
THAT CONSTANT THUMPING HAS GROWN LOUDER, MORE QUICK--!
I REALIZE NOW IT CAN BE ONLY ONE THING--
"--THE BEATING OF HIS HIDEOUS HEART!"
ARRR GGHHH
20

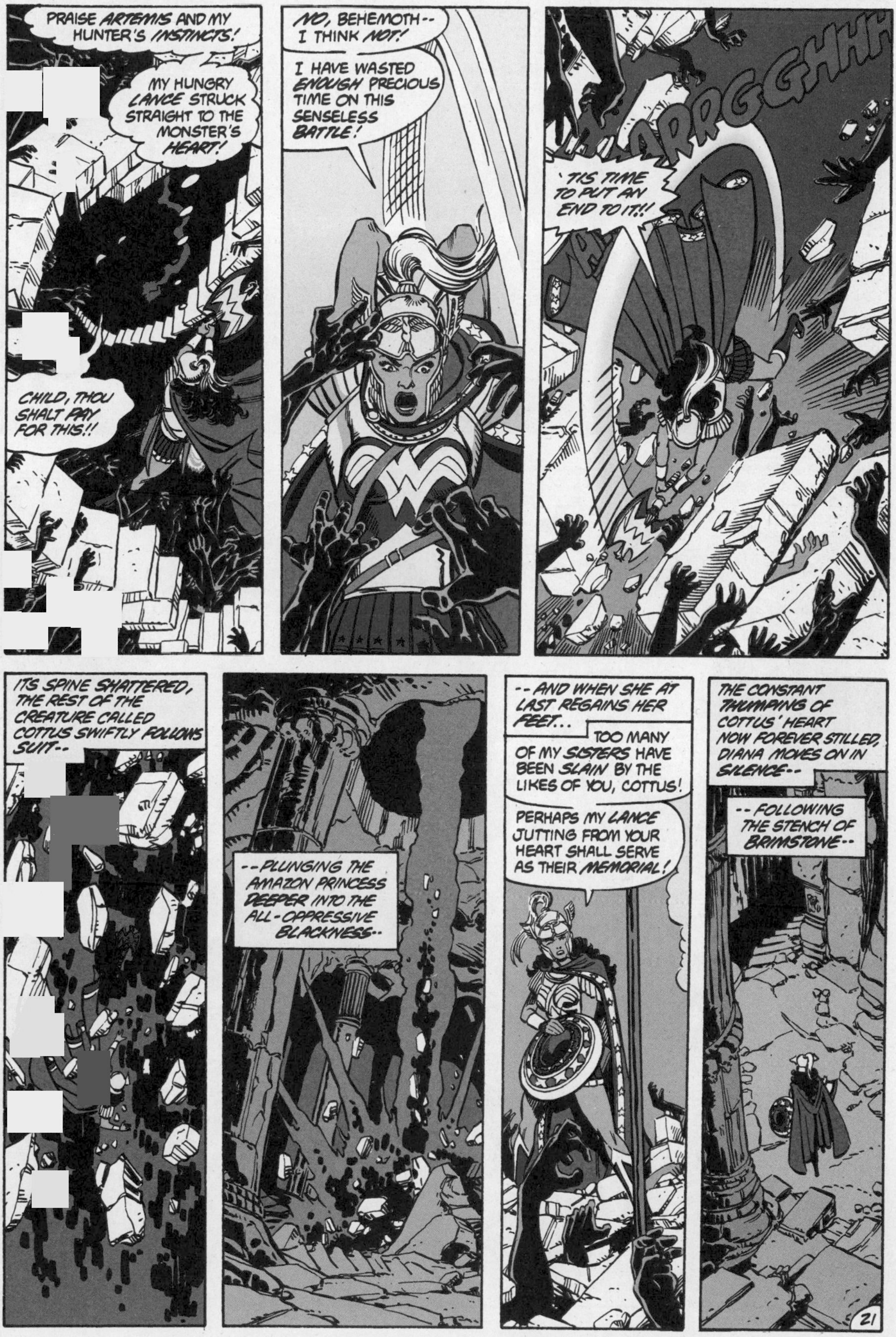
PRAISE ARTEMIS AND MY HUNTER'S INSTINCTS!
MY HUNGRY LANCE STRUCK STRAIGHT TO THE MONSTER'S HEART!
CHILD, THOU SHALT PAY FOR THIS!!
NO, BEHEMOTH-- I THINK NOT!
I HAVE WASTED ENOUGH PRECIOUS TIME ON THIS SENSELESS BATTLE!
ARRGGHHH
'TIS TIME TO PUT AN END TO IT!!
ITS SPINE SHATTERED, THE REST OF THE CREATURE CALLED COTTUS SWIFTLY FOLLOWS SUIT--
--PLUNGING THE AMAZON PRINCESS DEEPER INTO THE ALL-OPPRESSIVE BLACKNESS--
--AND WHEN SHE AT LAST REGAINS HER FEET...
TOO MANY OF MY SISTERS HAVE BEEN SLAIN BY THE LIKES OF YOU, COTTUS!
PERHAPS MY LANCE JUTTING FROM YOUR HEART SHALL SERVE AS THEIR MEMORIAL!
THE CONSTANT THUMPING OF COTTUS' HEART NOW FOREVER STILLED, DIANA MOVES ON IN SILENCE--
--FOLLOWING THE STENCH OF BRIMSTONE--
21

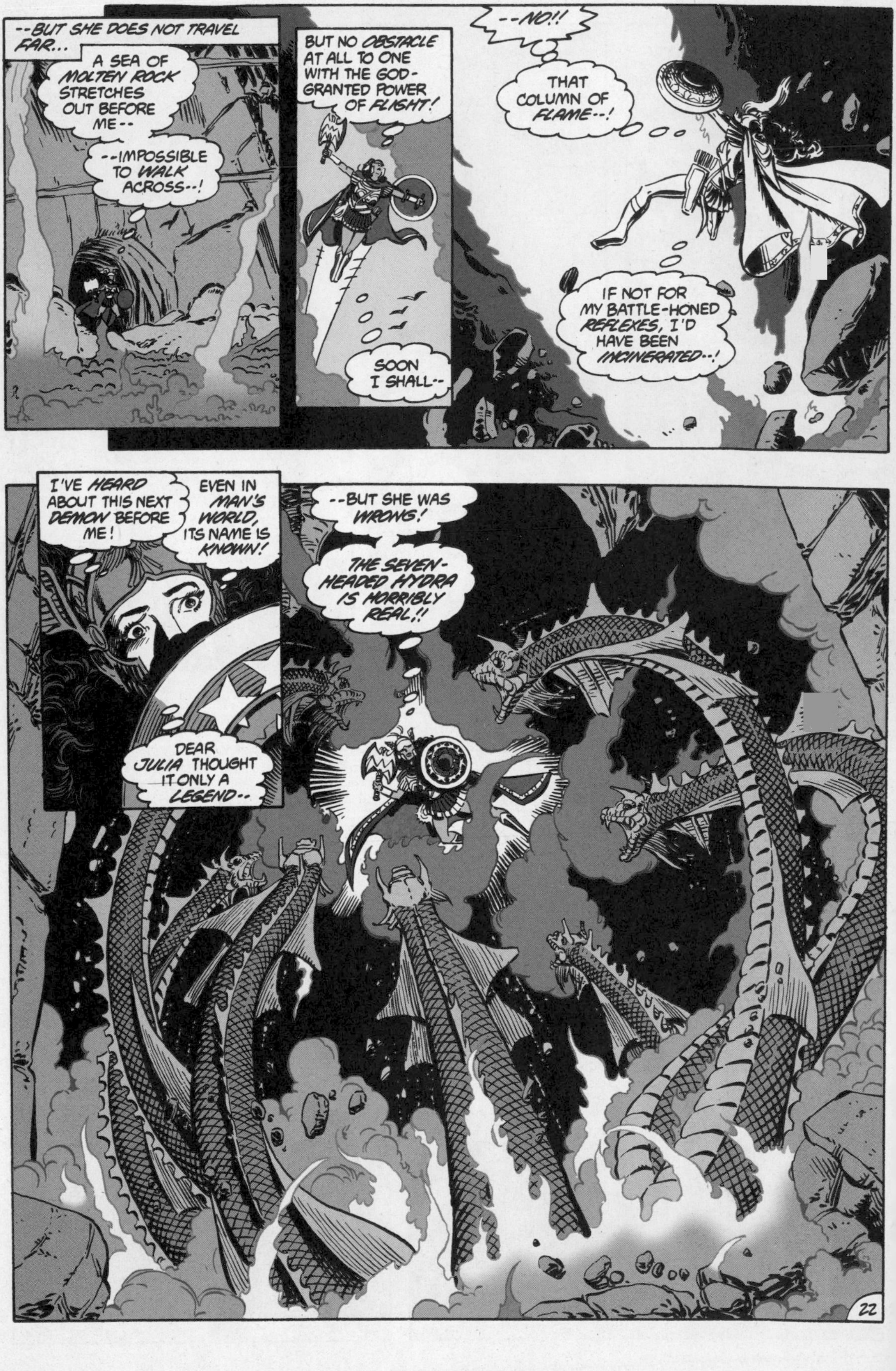
--BUT SHE DOES NOT TRAVEL FAR...
A SEA OF MOLTEN ROCK STRETCHES OUT BEFORE ME--
--IMPOSSIBLE TO WALK ACROSS--!
BUT NO OBSTACLE AT ALL TO ONE WITH THE GOD-GRANTED POWER OF FLIGHT!
SOON I SHALL--
--NO!!
THAT COLUMN OF FLAME--!
IF NOT FOR MY BATTLE-HONED REFLEXES, I'D HAVE BEEN INCINERATED--!
I'VE HEARD ABOUT THIS NEXT DEMON BEFORE ME!
EVEN IN MAN'S WORLD, ITS NAME IS KNOWN!
DEAR JULIA THOUGHT IT ONLY A LEGEND--
--BUT SHE WAS WRONG!
THE SEVEN-HEADED HYDRA IS HORRIBLY REAL!!
22

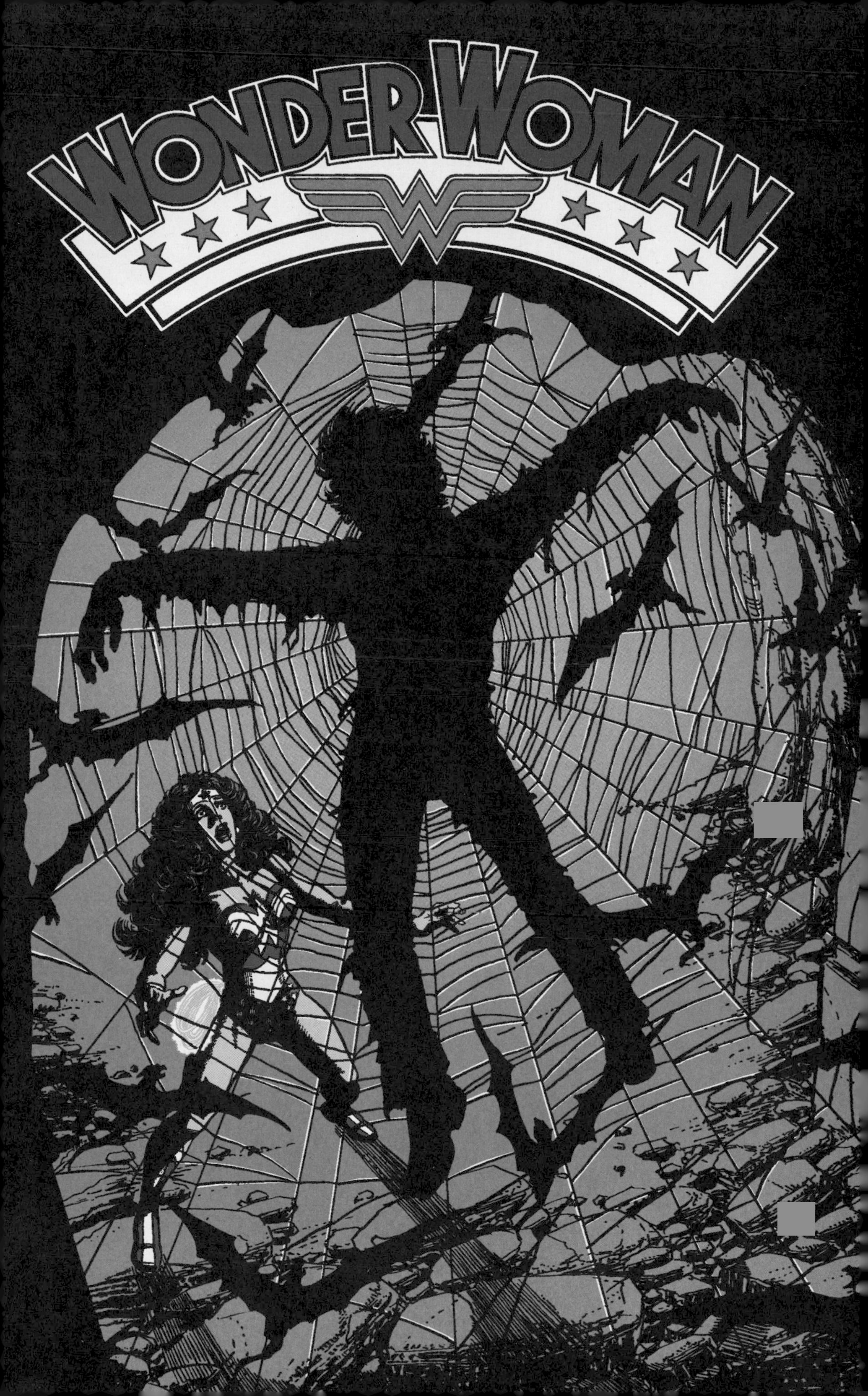
WONDER WOMAN

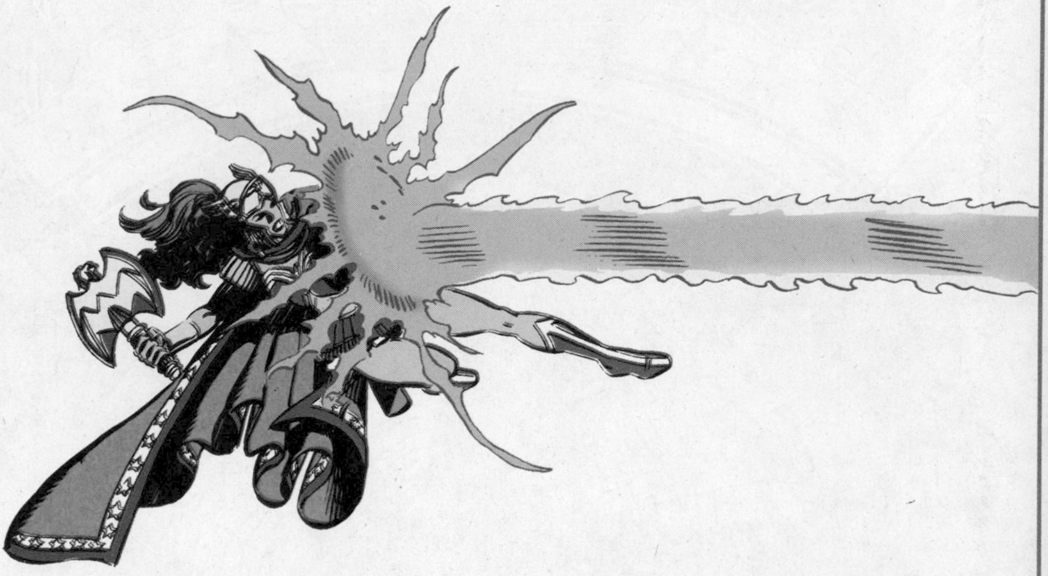

WONDER WOMAN

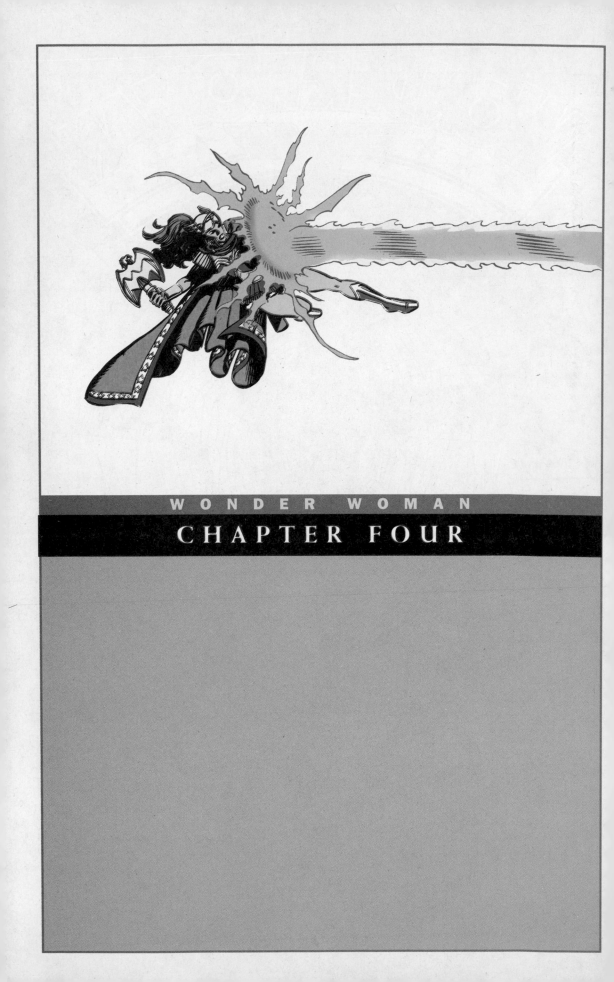

CHAPTER FOUR

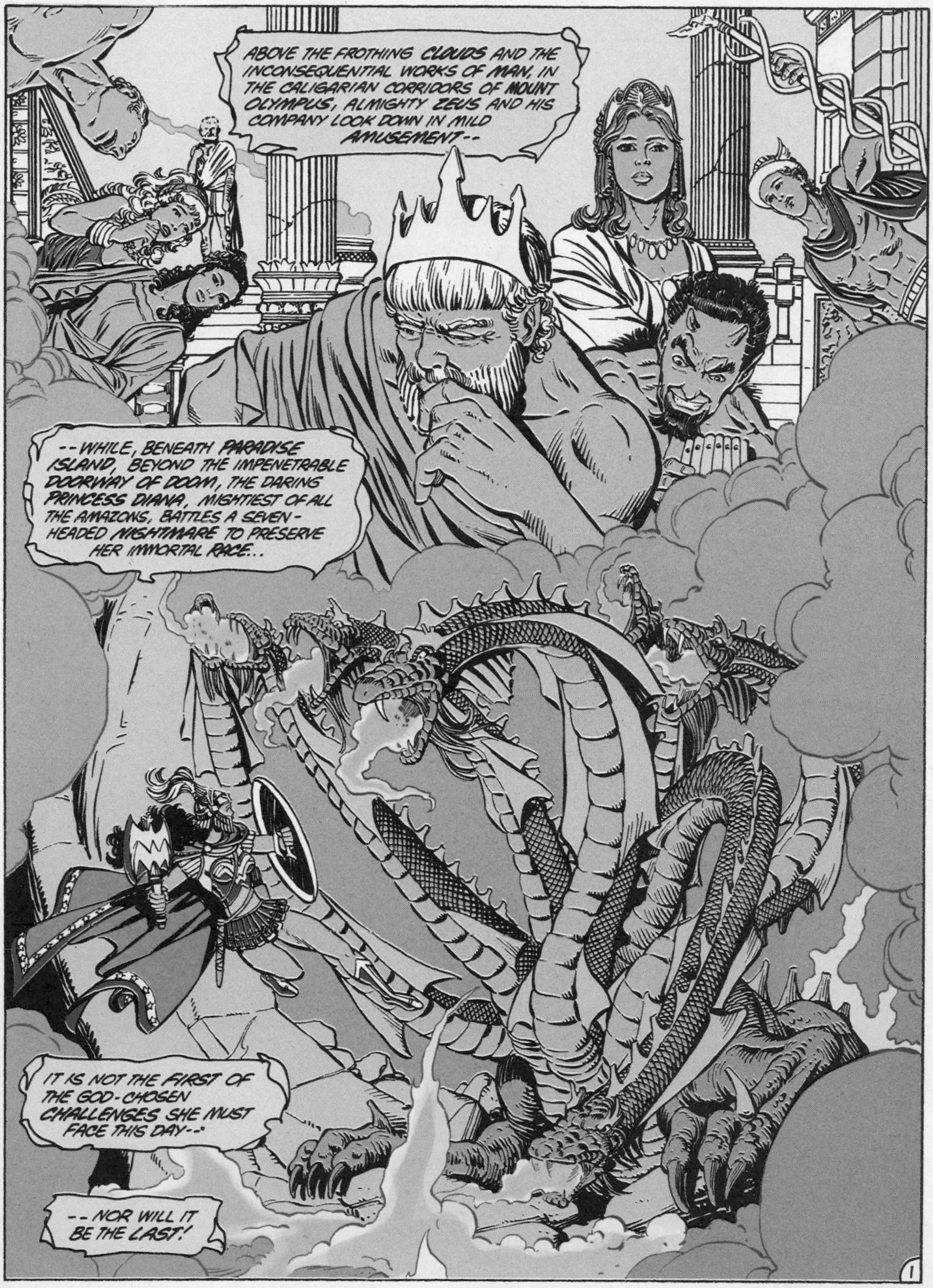
ABOVE THE FROTHING CLOUDS AND THE INCONSEQUENTIAL WORKS OF MAN, IN THE CALIGARIAN CORRIDORS OF MOUNT OLYMPUS, ALMIGHTY ZEUS AND HIS COMPANY LOOK DOWN IN MILD AMUSEMENT--
--WHILE, BENEATH PARADISE ISLAND, BEYOND THE IMPENETRABLE DOORWAY OF DOOM, THE DARING PRINCESS DIANA, MIGHTIEST OF ALL THE AMAZONS, BATTLES A SEVEN-HEADED NIGHTMARE TO PRESERVE HER IMMORTAL RACE...
IT IS NOT THE FIRST OF THE GOD-CHOSEN CHALLENGES SHE MUST FACE THIS DAY--
--NOR WILL IT BE THE LAST!
1

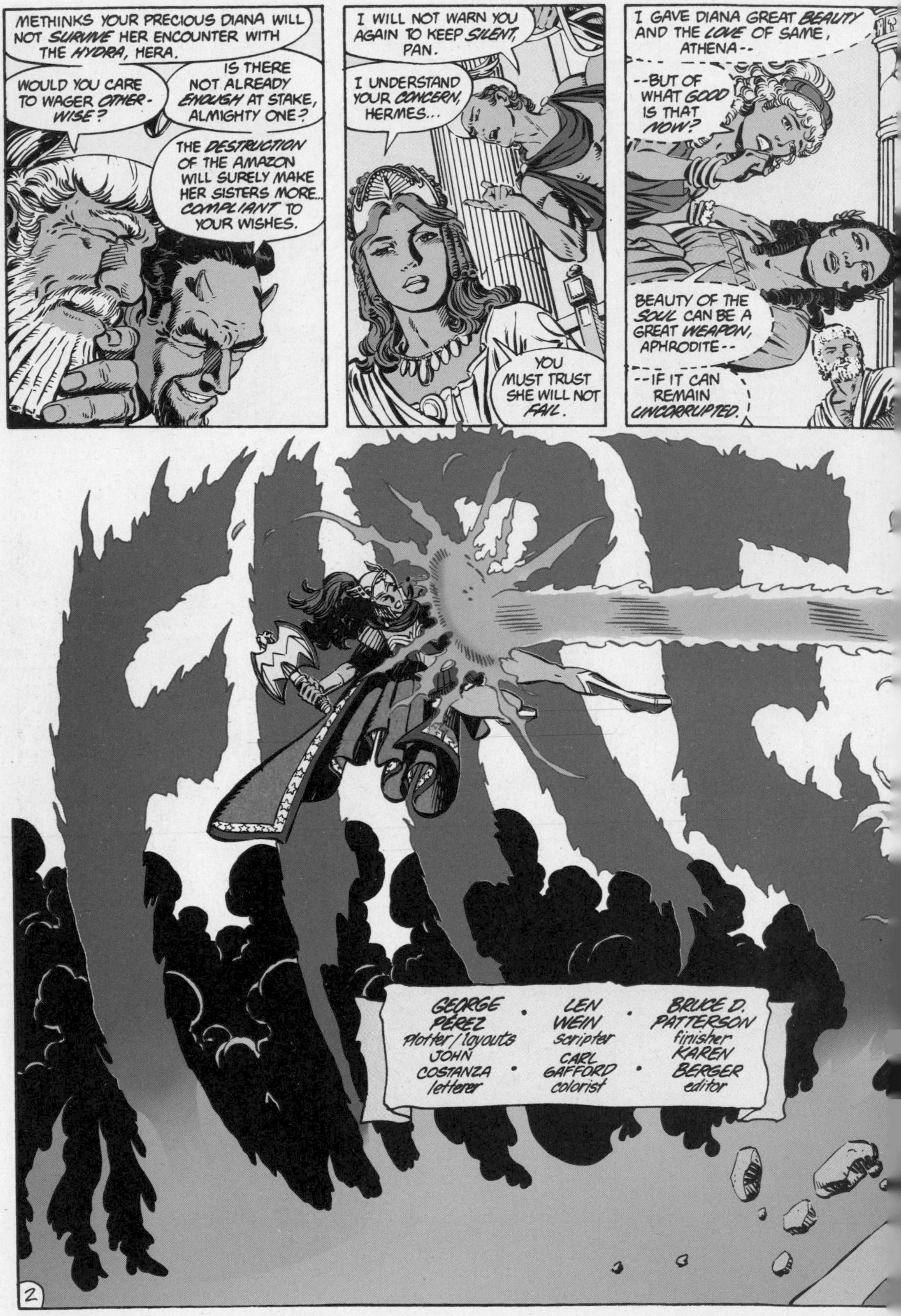
METHINKS YOUR PRECIOUS DIANA WILL NOT SURVIVE HER ENCOUNTER WITH THE HYDRA, HERA.
WOULD YOU CARE TO WAGER OTHER-WISE?
IS THERE NOT ALREADY ENOUGH AT STAKE, ALMIGHTY ONE?
THE DESTRUCTION OF THE AMAZON WILL SURELY MAKE HER SISTERS MORE... COMPLIANT TO YOUR WISHES.
I WILL NOT WARN YOU AGAIN TO KEEP SILENT, PAN.
I UNDERSTAND YOUR CONCERN, HERMES...
YOU MUST TRUST SHE WILL NOT FAIL.
I GAVE DIANA GREAT BEAUTY AND THE LOVE OF SAME, ATHENA--
--BUT OF WHAT GOOD IS THAT NOW?
BEAUTY OF THE SOUL CAN BE A GREAT WEAPON, APHRODITE--
--IF IT CAN REMAIN UNCORRUPTED.
GEORGE PÉREZ plotter/layouts · LEN WEIN scripter · BRUCE D. PATTERSON finisher
JOHN COSTANZA letterer · CARL GAFFORD colorist · KAREN BERGER editor
2

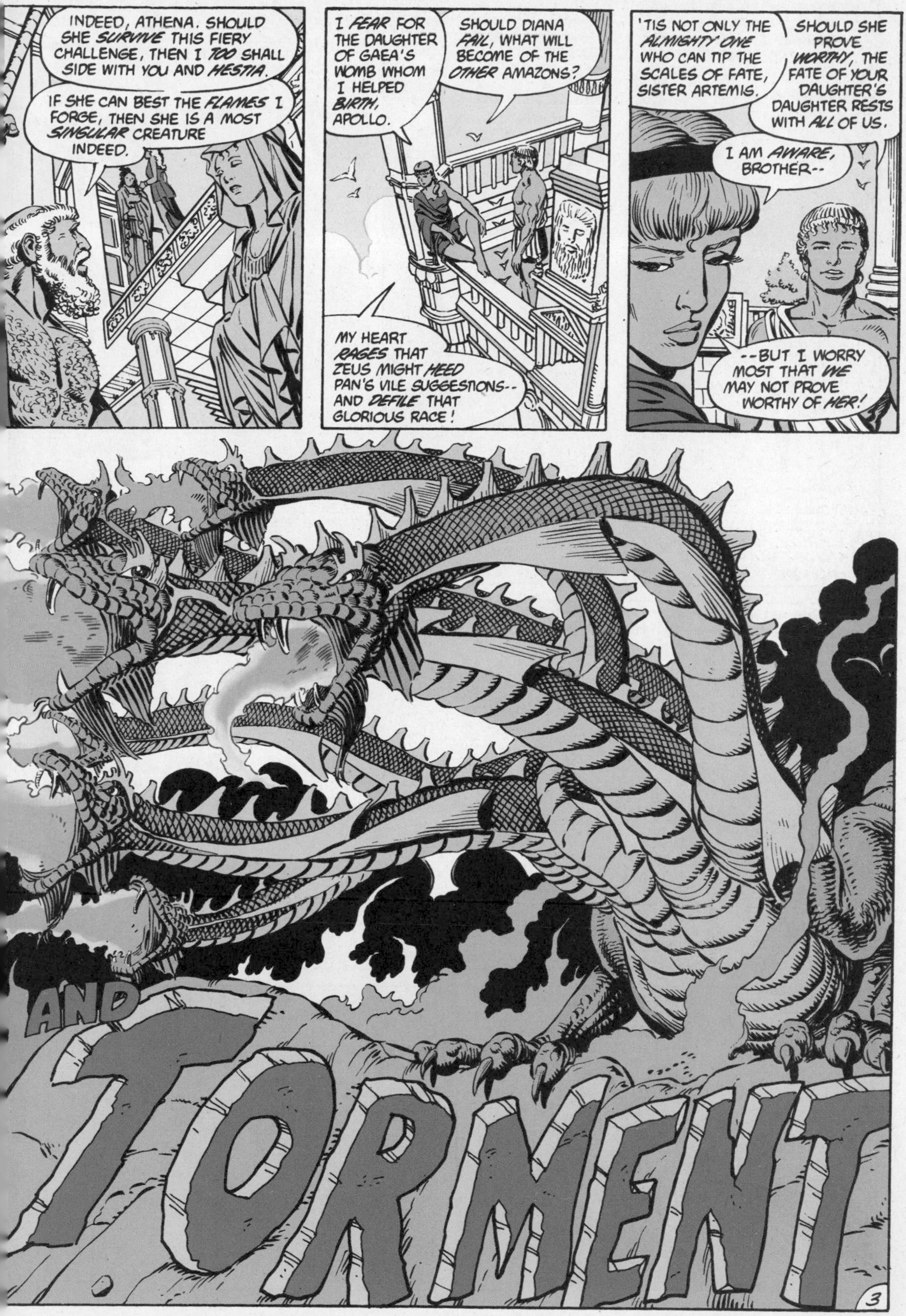
INDEED, ATHENA. SHOULD SHE SURVIVE THIS FIERY CHALLENGE, THEN I TOO SHALL SIDE WITH YOU AND HESTIA.
IF SHE CAN BEST THE FLAMES I FORGE, THEN SHE IS A MOST SINGULAR CREATURE INDEED.
I FEAR FOR THE DAUGHTER OF GAEA'S WOMB WHOM I HELPED BIRTH, APOLLO.
SHOULD DIANA FAIL, WHAT WILL BECOME OF THE OTHER AMAZONS?
MY HEART RAGES THAT ZEUS MIGHT HEED PAN'S VILE SUGGESTIONS--AND DEFILE THAT GLORIOUS RACE!
'TIS NOT ONLY THE ALMIGHTY ONE WHO CAN TIP THE SCALES OF FATE, SISTER ARTEMIS.
SHOULD SHE PROVE WORTHY, THE FATE OF YOUR DAUGHTER'S DAUGHTER RESTS WITH ALL OF US.
I AM AWARE, BROTHER--
--BUT I WORRY MOST THAT WE MAY NOT PROVE WORTHY OF HER!
AND
TORMENT
3

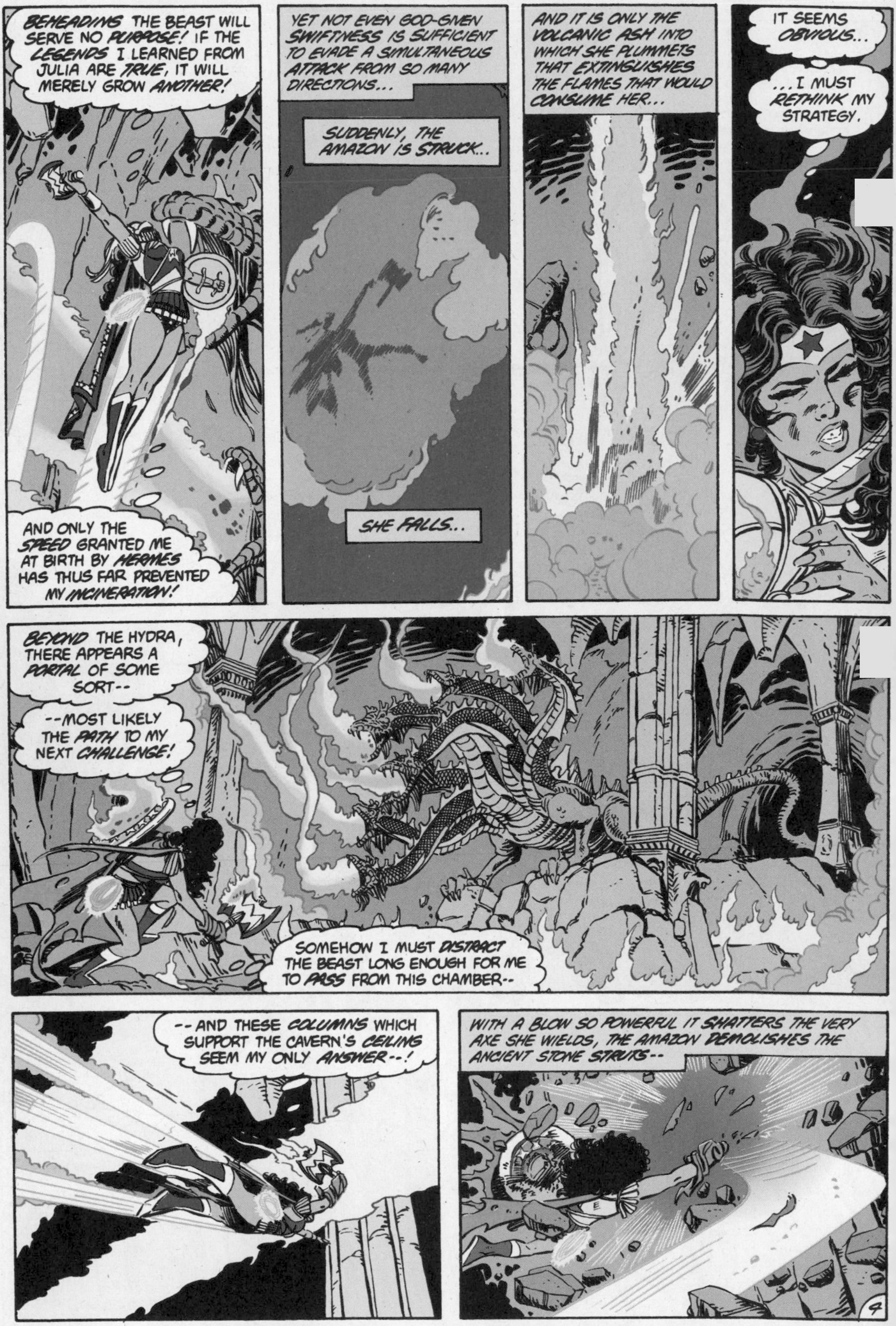
BEHEADING THE BEAST WILL SERVE NO PURPOSE! IF THE LEGENDS I LEARNED FROM JULIA ARE TRUE, IT WILL MERELY GROW ANOTHER!
AND ONLY THE SPEED GRANTED ME AT BIRTH BY HERMES HAS THUS FAR PREVENTED MY INCINERATION!
YET NOT EVEN GOD-GIVEN SWIFTNESS IS SUFFICIENT TO EVADE A SIMULTANEOUS ATTACK FROM SO MANY DIRECTIONS...
SUDDENLY, THE AMAZON IS STRUCK...
SHE FALLS...
AND IT IS ONLY THE VOLCANIC ASH INTO WHICH SHE PLUMMETS THAT EXTINGUISHES THE FLAMES THAT WOULD CONSUME HER...
IT SEEMS OBVIOUS...
...I MUST RETHINK MY STRATEGY.
BEYOND THE HYDRA, THERE APPEARS A PORTAL OF SOME SORT--
--MOST LIKELY THE PATH TO MY NEXT CHALLENGE!
SOMEHOW I MUST DISTRACT THE BEAST LONG ENOUGH FOR ME TO PASS FROM THIS CHAMBER--
--AND THESE COLUMNS WHICH SUPPORT THE CAVERN'S CEILING SEEM MY ONLY ANSWER--!
WITH A BLOW SO POWERFUL IT SHATTERS THE VERY AXE SHE WIELDS, THE AMAZON DEMOLISHES THE ANCIENT STONE STRUTS--
4

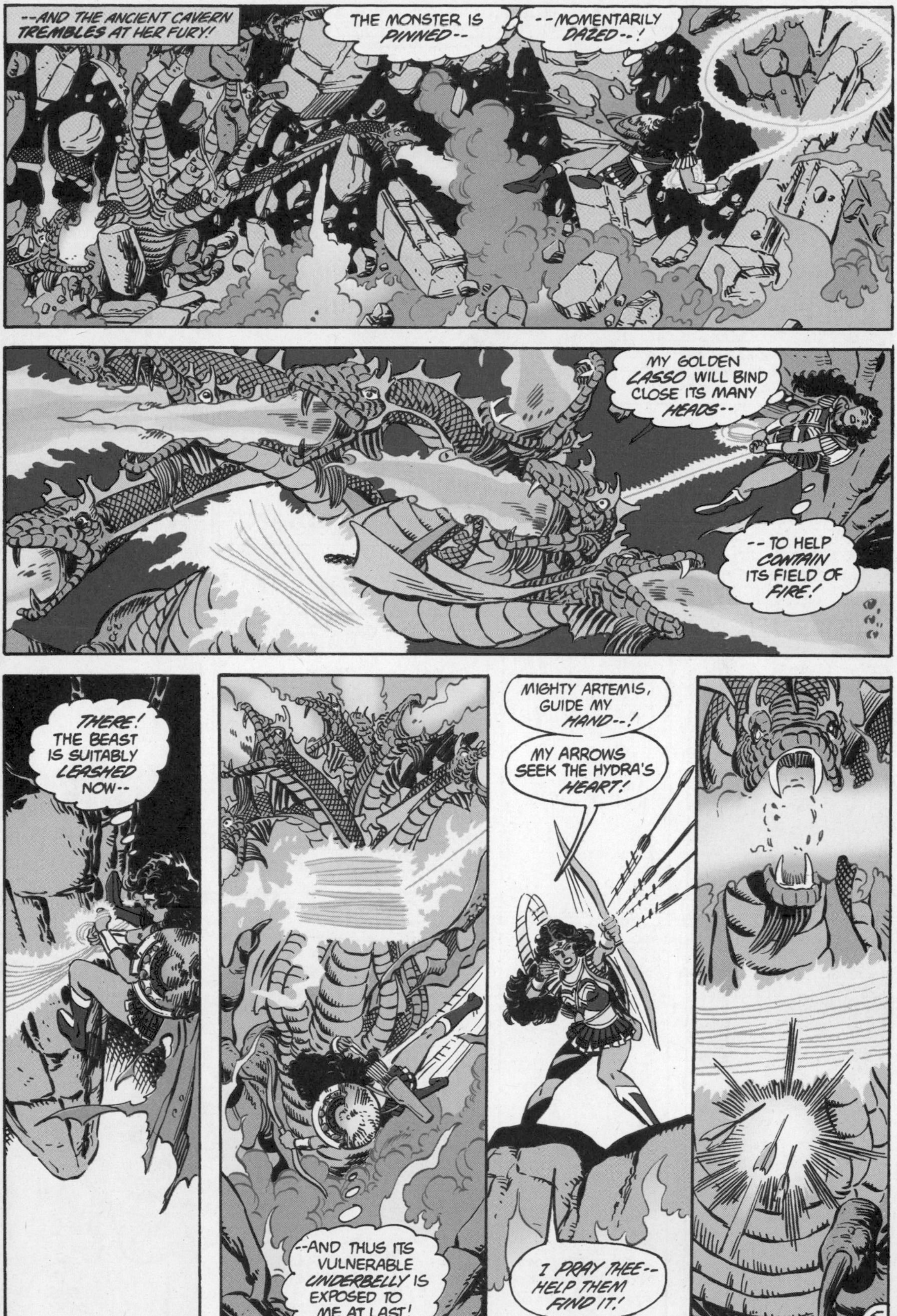
--AND THE ANCIENT CAVERN TREMBLES AT HER FURY!
THE MONSTER IS PINNED--
--MOMENTARILY DAZED--!
MY GOLDEN LASSO WILL BIND CLOSE ITS MANY HEADS--
--TO HELP CONTAIN ITS FIELD OF FIRE!
THERE! THE BEAST IS SUITABLY LEASHED NOW--
--AND THUS ITS VULNERABLE UNDERBELLY IS EXPOSED TO ME AT LAST!
MIGHTY ARTEMIS, GUIDE MY HAND--!
MY ARROWS SEEK THE HYDRA'S HEART!
I PRAY THEE-- HELP THEM FIND IT!
5

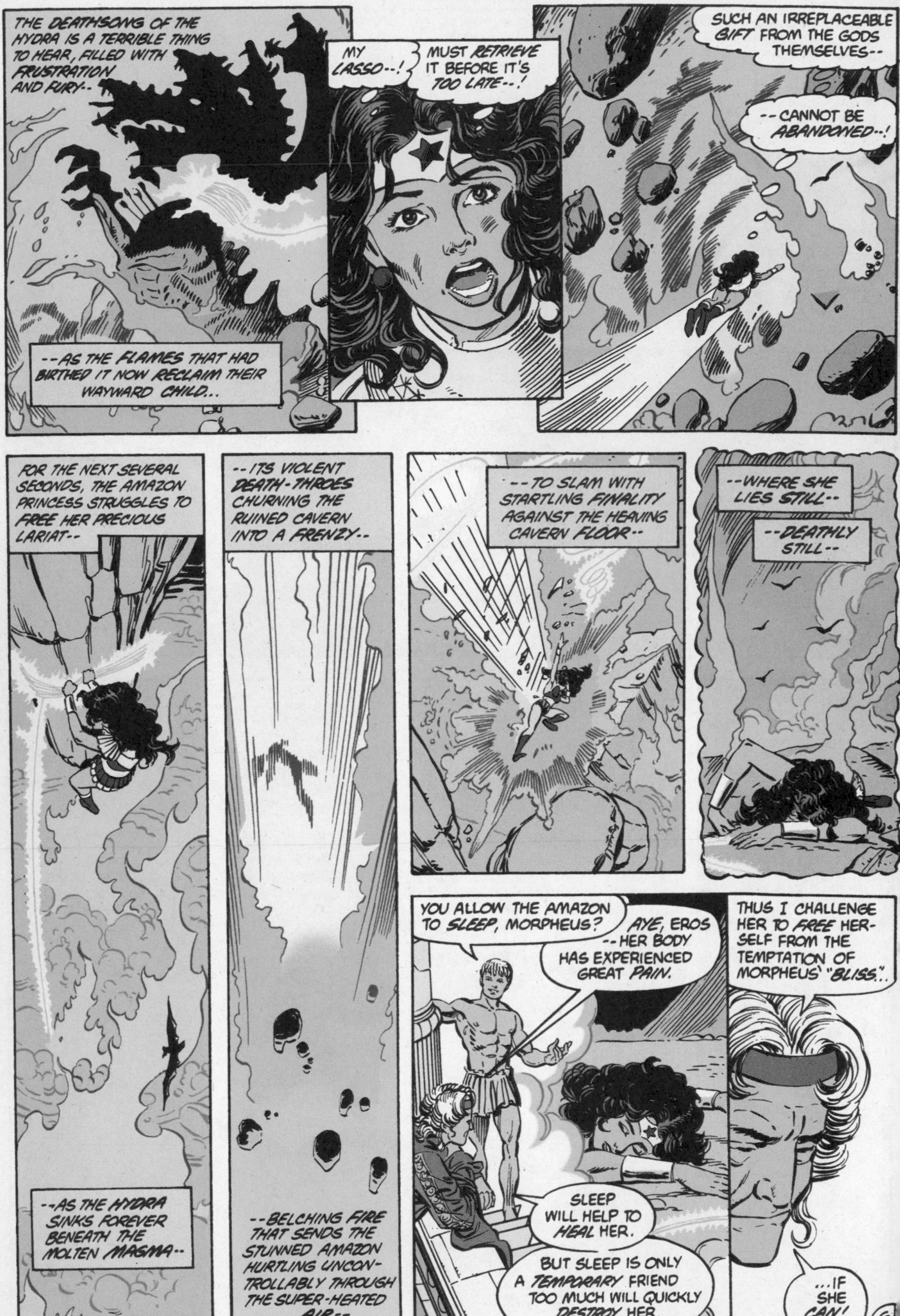
THE DEATHSONG OF THE HYDRA IS A TERRIBLE THING TO HEAR, FILLED WITH FRUSTRATION AND FURY--
--AS THE FLAMES THAT HAD BIRTHED IT NOW RECLAIM THEIR WAYWARD CHILD...
MY LASSO--!
MUST RETRIEVE IT BEFORE IT'S TOO LATE--!
SUCH AN IRREPLACEABLE GIFT FROM THE GODS THEMSELVES--
--CANNOT BE ABANDONED--!
FOR THE NEXT SEVERAL SECONDS, THE AMAZON PRINCESS STRUGGLES TO FREE HER PRECIOUS LARIAT--
--AS THE HYDRA SINKS FOREVER BENEATH THE MOLTEN MAGMA--
--ITS VIOLENT DEATH-THROES CHURNING THE RUINED CAVERN INTO A FRENZY--
--BELCHING FIRE THAT SENDS THE STUNNED AMAZON HURTLING UNCONTROLLABLY THROUGH THE SUPER-HEATED AIR--
--TO SLAM WITH STARTLING FINALITY AGAINST THE HEAVING CAVERN FLOOR--
--WHERE SHE LIES STILL--
--DEATHLY STILL--
YOU ALLOW THE AMAZON TO SLEEP, MORPHEUS?
AYE, EROS --HER BODY HAS EXPERIENCED GREAT PAIN.
SLEEP WILL HELP TO HEAL HER.
BUT SLEEP IS ONLY A TEMPORARY FRIEND TOO MUCH WILL QUICKLY DESTROY HER.
THUS I CHALLENGE HER TO FREE HERSELF FROM THE TEMPTATION OF MORPHEUS' "BLISS"...
...IF SHE CAN!
6

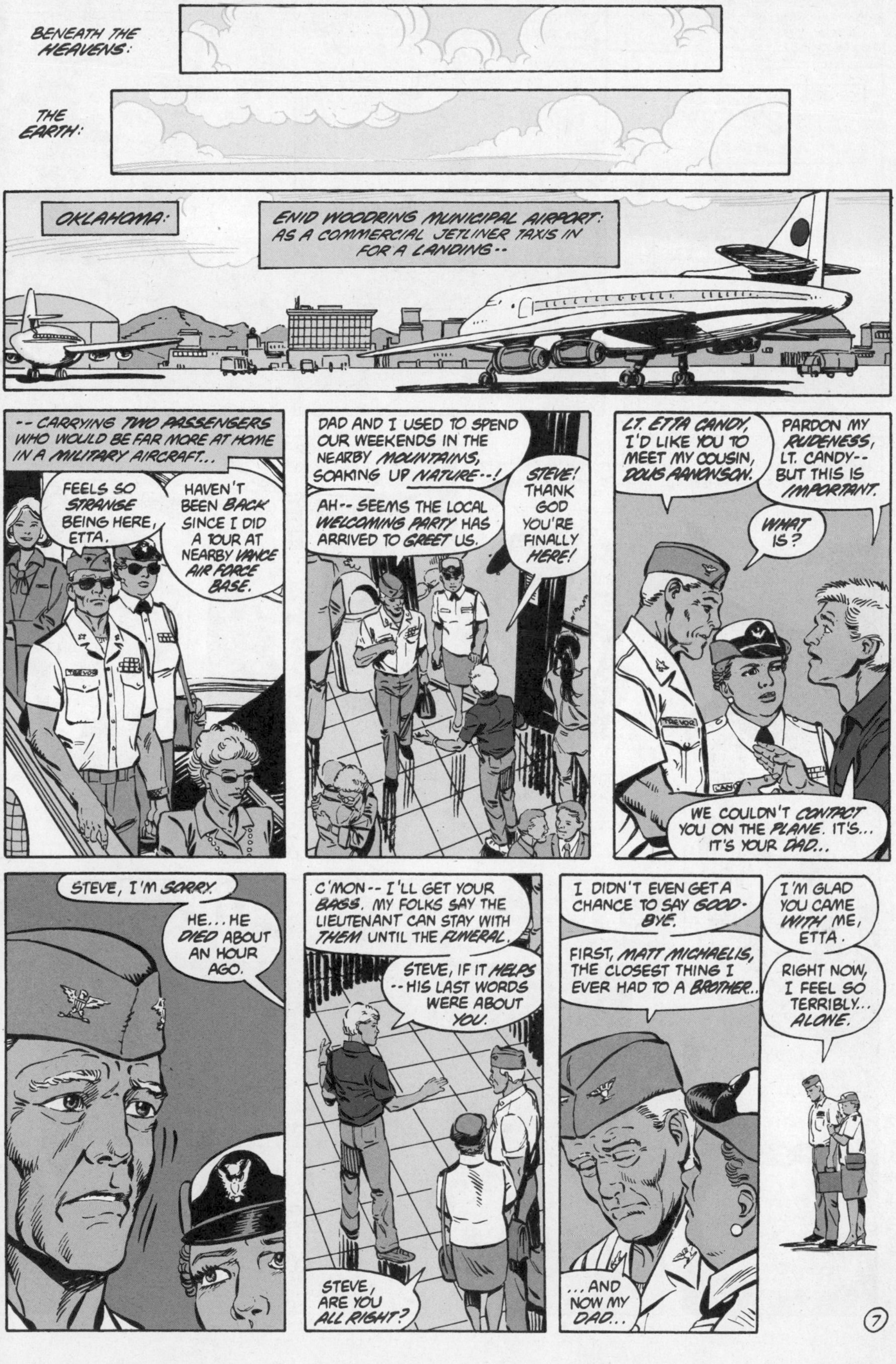
BENEATH THE HEAVENS:
THE EARTH:
OKLAHOMA:
ENID WOODRING MUNICIPAL AIRPORT: AS A COMMERCIAL JETLINER TAXIS IN FOR A LANDING--
--CARRYING TWO PASSENGERS WHO WOULD BE FAR MORE AT HOME IN A MILITARY AIRCRAFT...
FEELS SO STRANGE BEING HERE, ETTA.
HAVEN'T BEEN BACK SINCE I DID A TOUR AT NEARBY VANCE AIR FORCE BASE.
DAD AND I USED TO SPEND OUR WEEKENDS IN THE NEARBY MOUNTAINS, SOAKING UP NATURE--!
AH-- SEEMS THE LOCAL WELCOMING PARTY HAS ARRIVED TO GREET US.
STEVE! THANK GOD YOU'RE FINALLY HERE!
LT. ETTA CANDY, I'D LIKE YOU TO MEET MY COUSIN, DOUG AANONSON.
PARDON MY RUDENESS, LT. CANDY-- BUT THIS IS IMPORTANT.
WHAT IS?
WE COULDN'T CONTACT YOU ON THE PLANE. IT'S... IT'S YOUR DAD...
STEVE, I'M SORRY.
HE... HE DIED ABOUT AN HOUR AGO.
C'MON-- I'LL GET YOUR BAGS. MY FOLKS SAY THE LIEUTENANT CAN STAY WITH THEM UNTIL THE FUNERAL.
STEVE, IF IT HELPS --HIS LAST WORDS WERE ABOUT YOU.
STEVE, ARE YOU ALL RIGHT?
I DIDN'T EVEN GET A CHANCE TO SAY GOOD-BYE.
FIRST, MATT MICHAELIS, THE CLOSEST THING I EVER HAD TO A BROTHER...
...AND NOW MY DAD...
I'M GLAD YOU CAME WITH ME, ETTA.
RIGHT NOW, I FEEL SO TERRIBLY... ALONE.
7

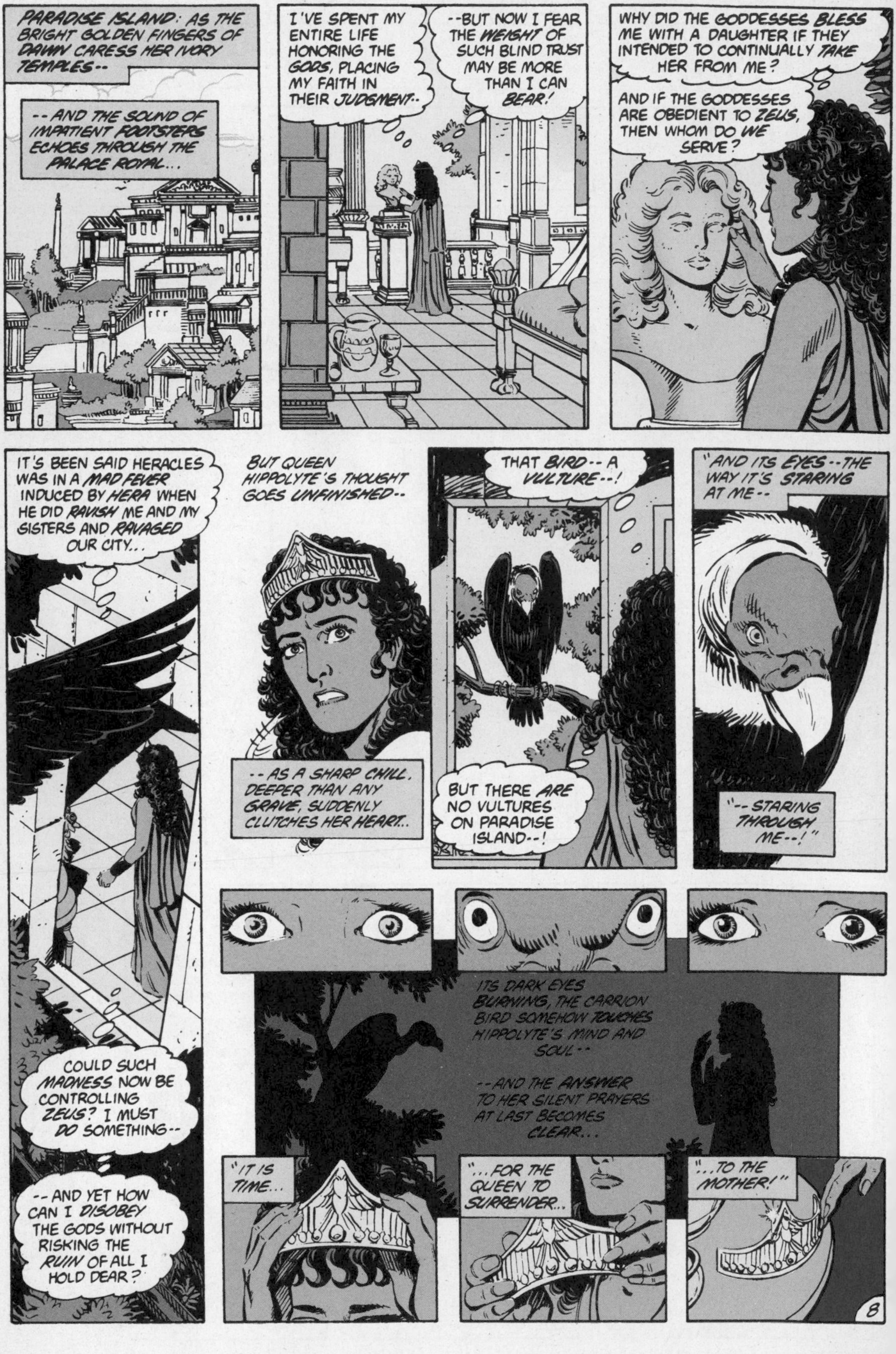

PARADISE ISLAND: AS THE BRIGHT GOLDEN FINGERS OF DAWN CARESS HER IVORY TEMPLES--
--AND THE SOUND OF IMPATIENT FOOTSTEPS ECHOES THROUGH THE PALACE ROYAL...
I'VE SPENT MY ENTIRE LIFE HONORING THE GODS, PLACING MY FAITH IN THEIR JUDGMENT..
--BUT NOW I FEAR THE WEIGHT OF SUCH BLIND TRUST MAY BE MORE THAN I CAN BEAR!
WHY DID THE GODDESSES BLESS ME WITH A DAUGHTER IF THEY INTENDED TO CONTINUALLY TAKE HER FROM ME?
AND IF THE GODDESSES ARE OBEDIENT TO ZEUS, THEN WHOM DO WE SERVE?
IT'S BEEN SAID HERACLES WAS IN A MAD FEVER INDUCED BY HERA WHEN HE DID RAVISH ME AND MY SISTERS AND RAVAGED OUR CITY...
COULD SUCH MADNESS NOW BE CONTROLLING ZEUS? I MUST DO SOMETHING--
--AND YET HOW CAN I DISOBEY THE GODS WITHOUT RISKING THE RUIN OF ALL I HOLD DEAR?
BUT QUEEN HIPPOLYTE'S THOUGHT GOES UNFINISHED--
--AS A SHARP CHILL, DEEPER THAN ANY GRAVE, SUDDENLY CLUTCHES HER HEART...
THAT BIRD-- A VULTURE--!
BUT THERE ARE NO VULTURES ON PARADISE ISLAND--!
"AND ITS EYES--THE WAY IT'S STARING AT ME--
"--STARING THROUGH ME--!"
ITS DARK EYES BURNING, THE CARRION BIRD SOMEHOW TOUCHES HIPPOLYTE'S MIND AND SOUL--
--AND THE ANSWER TO HER SILENT PRAYERS AT LAST BECOMES CLEAR...
"IT IS TIME...
"...FOR THE QUEEN TO SURRENDER...
"...TO THE MOTHER!"
8

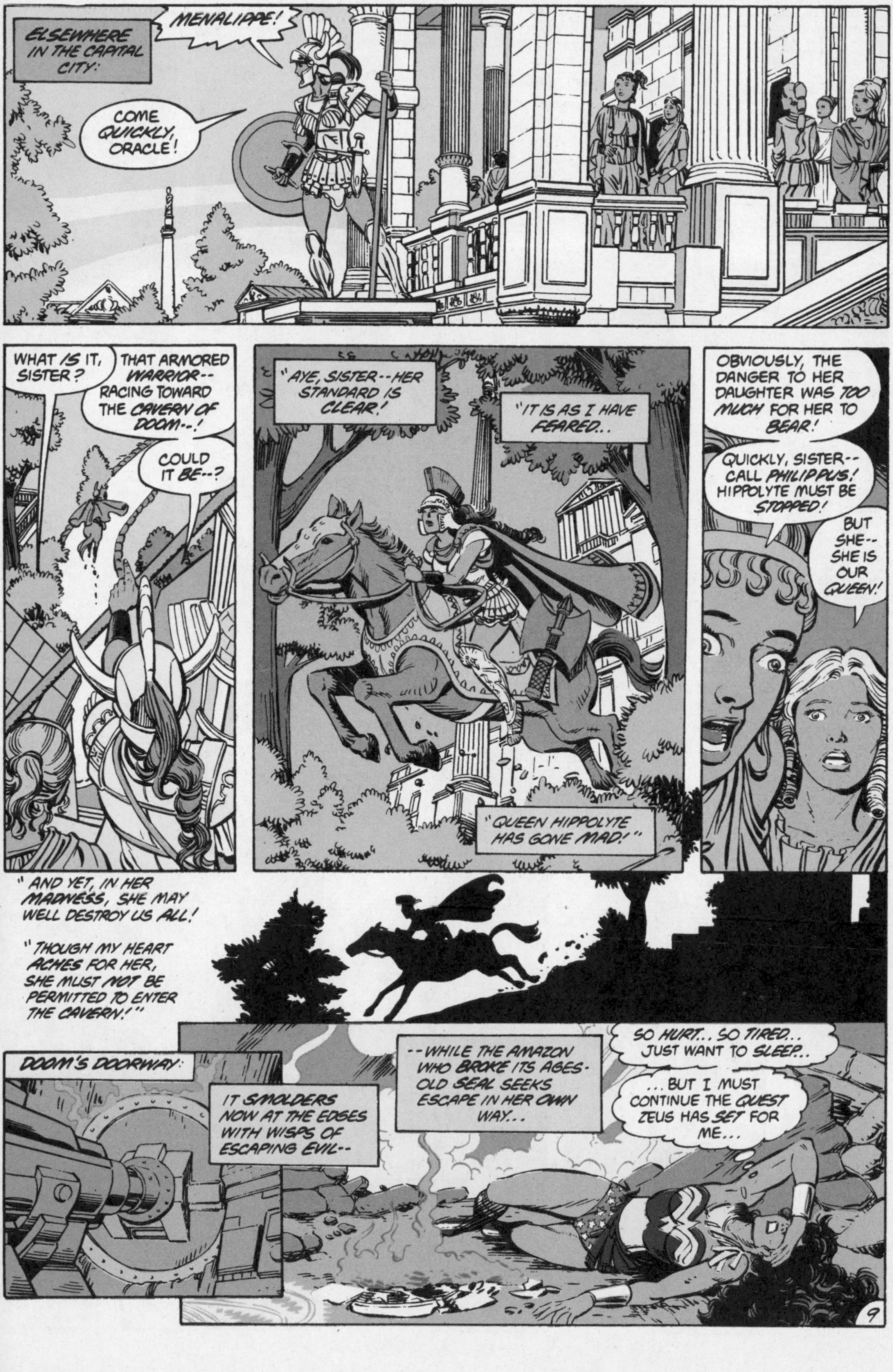

ELSEWHERE IN THE CAPITAL CITY:
MENALIPPE!
COME QUICKLY, ORACLE!
WHAT IS IT, SISTER?
THAT ARMORED WARRIOR-- RACING TOWARD THE CAVERN OF DOOM--!
COULD IT BE--?
"AYE, SISTER--HER STANDARD IS CLEAR!
"IT IS AS I HAVE FEARED...
"QUEEN HIPPOLYTE HAS GONE MAD!"
OBVIOUSLY, THE DANGER TO HER DAUGHTER WAS TOO MUCH FOR HER TO BEAR!
QUICKLY, SISTER-- CALL PHILIPPUS! HIPPOLYTE MUST BE STOPPED!
BUT SHE-- SHE IS OUR QUEEN!
"AND YET, IN HER MADNESS, SHE MAY WELL DESTROY US ALL!
"THOUGH MY HEART ACHES FOR HER, SHE MUST NOT BE PERMITTED TO ENTER THE CAVERN!"
DOOM'S DOORWAY:
IT SMOLDERS NOW AT THE EDGES WITH WISPS OF ESCAPING EVIL--
--WHILE THE AMAZON WHO BROKE ITS AGES-OLD SEAL SEEKS ESCAPE IN HER OWN WAY...
SO HURT... SO TIRED... JUST WANT TO SLEEP...
...BUT I MUST CONTINUE THE QUEST ZEUS HAS SET FOR ME...
9

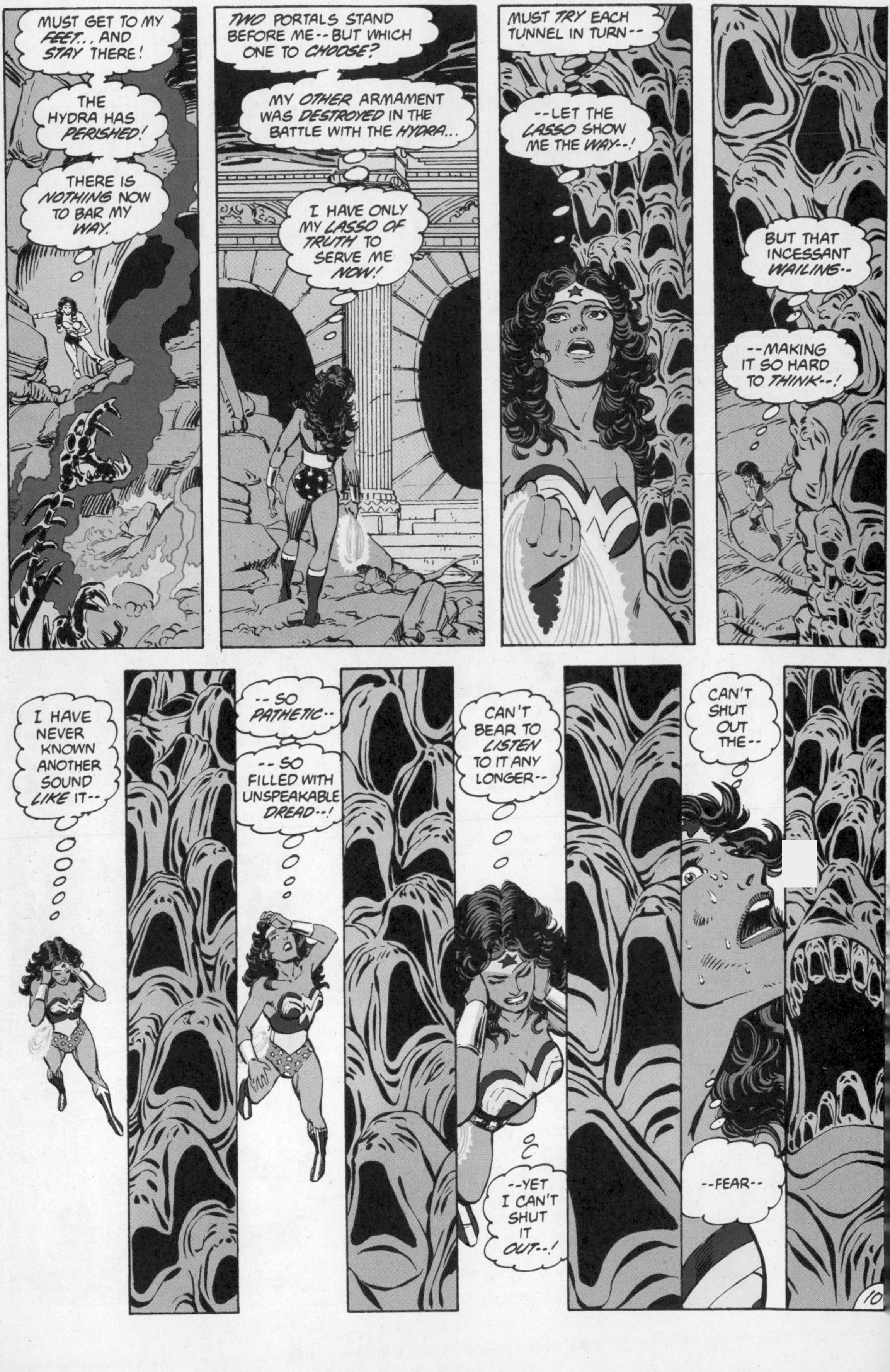
MUST GET TO MY FEET.., AND STAY THERE!
THE HYDRA HAS PERISHED!
THERE IS NOTHING NOW TO BAR MY WAY.
TWO PORTALS STAND BEFORE ME--BUT WHICH ONE TO CHOOSE?
MY OTHER ARMAMENT WAS DESTROYED IN THE BATTLE WITH THE HYDRA...
I HAVE ONLY MY LASSO OF TRUTH TO SERVE ME NOW!
MUST TRY EACH TUNNEL IN TURN--
--LET THE LASSO SHOW ME THE WAY--!
BUT THAT INCESSANT WAILING--
--MAKING IT SO HARD TO THINK--!
I HAVE NEVER KNOWN ANOTHER SOUND LIKE IT--
--SO PATHETIC--
--SO FILLED WITH UNSPEAKABLE DREAD--!
CAN'T BEAR TO LISTEN TO IT ANY LONGER--
--YET I CAN'T SHUT IT OUT--!
CAN'T SHUT OUT THE--
--FEAR--
10

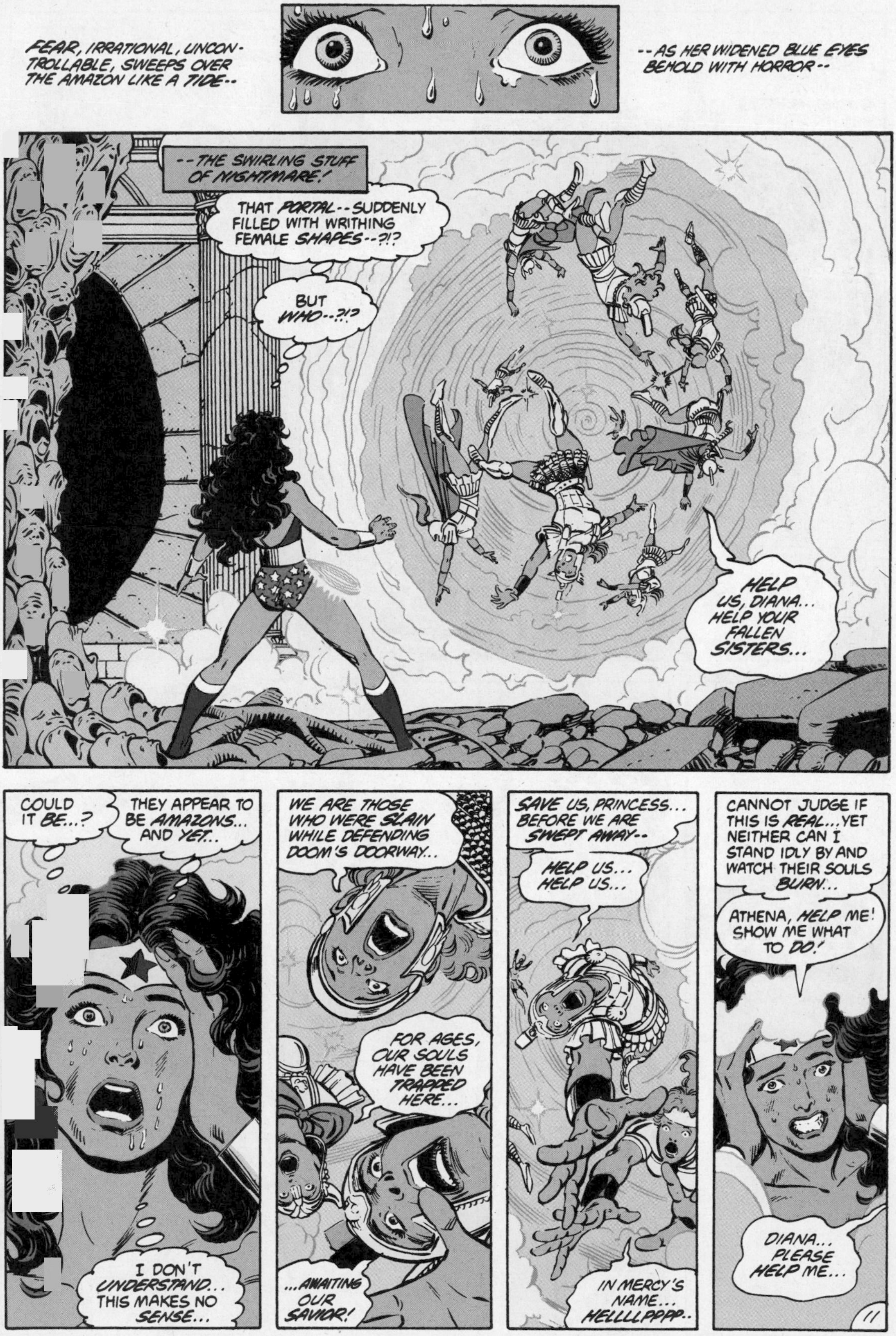

FEAR, IRRATIONAL, UNCONTROLLABLE, SWEEPS OVER THE AMAZON LIKE A TIDE--
--AS HER WIDENED BLUE EYES BEHOLD WITH HORROR--
--THE SWIRLING STUFF OF NIGHTMARE!
THAT PORTAL--SUDDENLY FILLED WITH WRITHING FEMALE SHAPES--?!?
BUT WHO--?!?
HELP US, DIANA... HELP YOUR FALLEN SISTERS...
COULD IT BE...?
THEY APPEAR TO BE AMAZONS... AND YET...
I DON'T UNDERSTAND... THIS MAKES NO SENSE...
WE ARE THOSE WHO WERE SLAIN WHILE DEFENDING DOOM'S DOORWAY...
FOR AGES, OUR SOULS HAVE BEEN TRAPPED HERE...
...AWAITING OUR SAVIOR!
SAVE US, PRINCESS... BEFORE WE ARE SWEPT AWAY--
HELP US... HELP US...
IN MERCY'S NAME... HELLLLPPPP..
CANNOT JUDGE IF THIS IS REAL... YET NEITHER CAN I STAND IDLY BY AND WATCH THEIR SOULS BURN...
ATHENA, HELP ME! SHOW ME WHAT TO DO!
DIANA... PLEASE HELP ME...
11

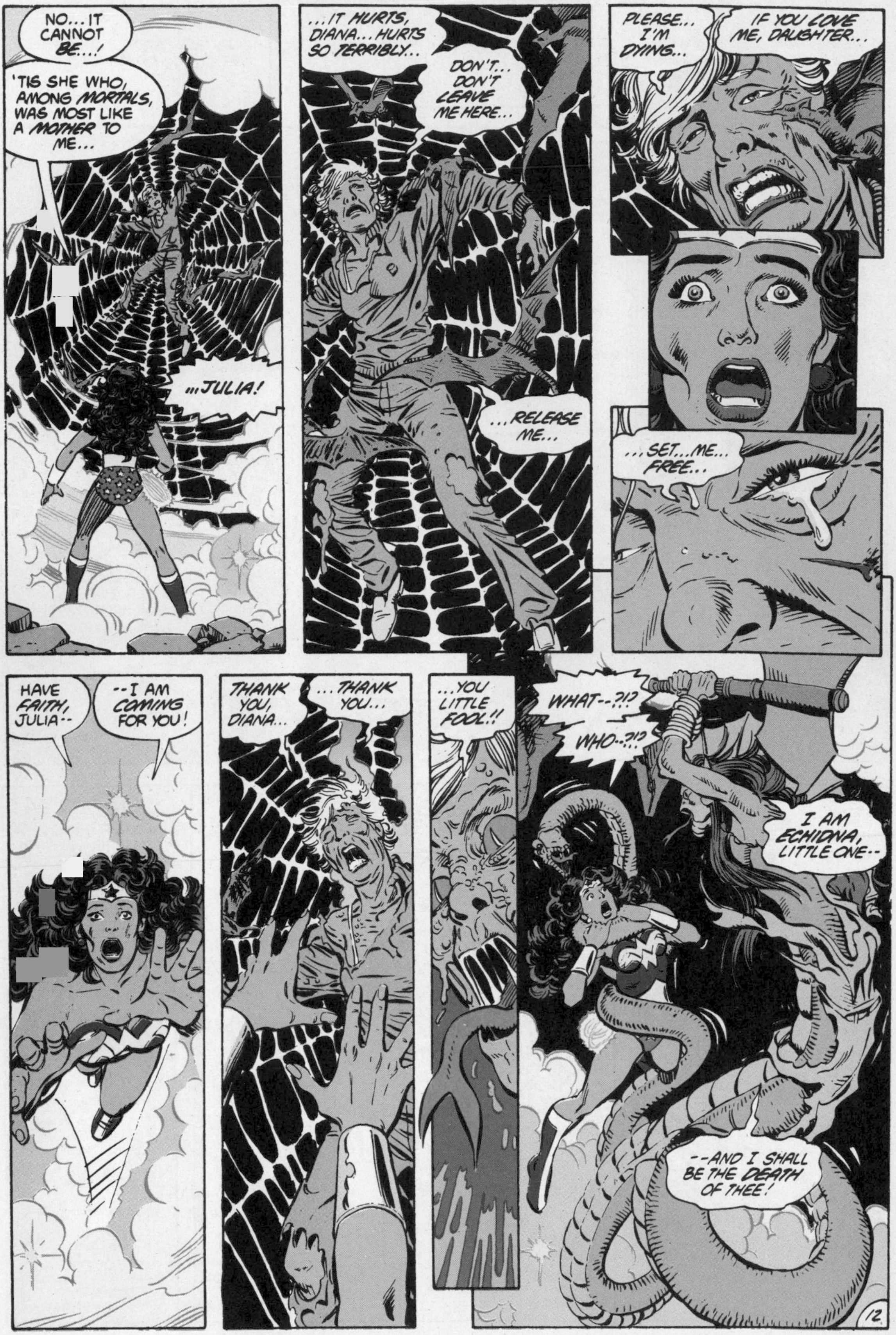
NO... IT CANNOT BE...!
'TIS SHE WHO, AMONG MORTALS, WAS MOST LIKE A MOTHER TO ME...
...JULIA!
...IT HURTS, DIANA... HURTS SO TERRIBLY...
DON'T... DON'T LEAVE ME HERE...
...RELEASE ME...
PLEASE... I'M DYING...
IF YOU LOVE ME, DAUGHTER...
...SET...ME... FREE...
HAVE FAITH, JULIA--
--I AM COMING FOR YOU!
THANK YOU, DIANA...
...THANK YOU...
...YOU LITTLE FOOL!!
WHAT--?!?
WHO--?!?
I AM ECHIDNA, LITTLE ONE--
--AND I SHALL BE THE DEATH OF THEE!
12

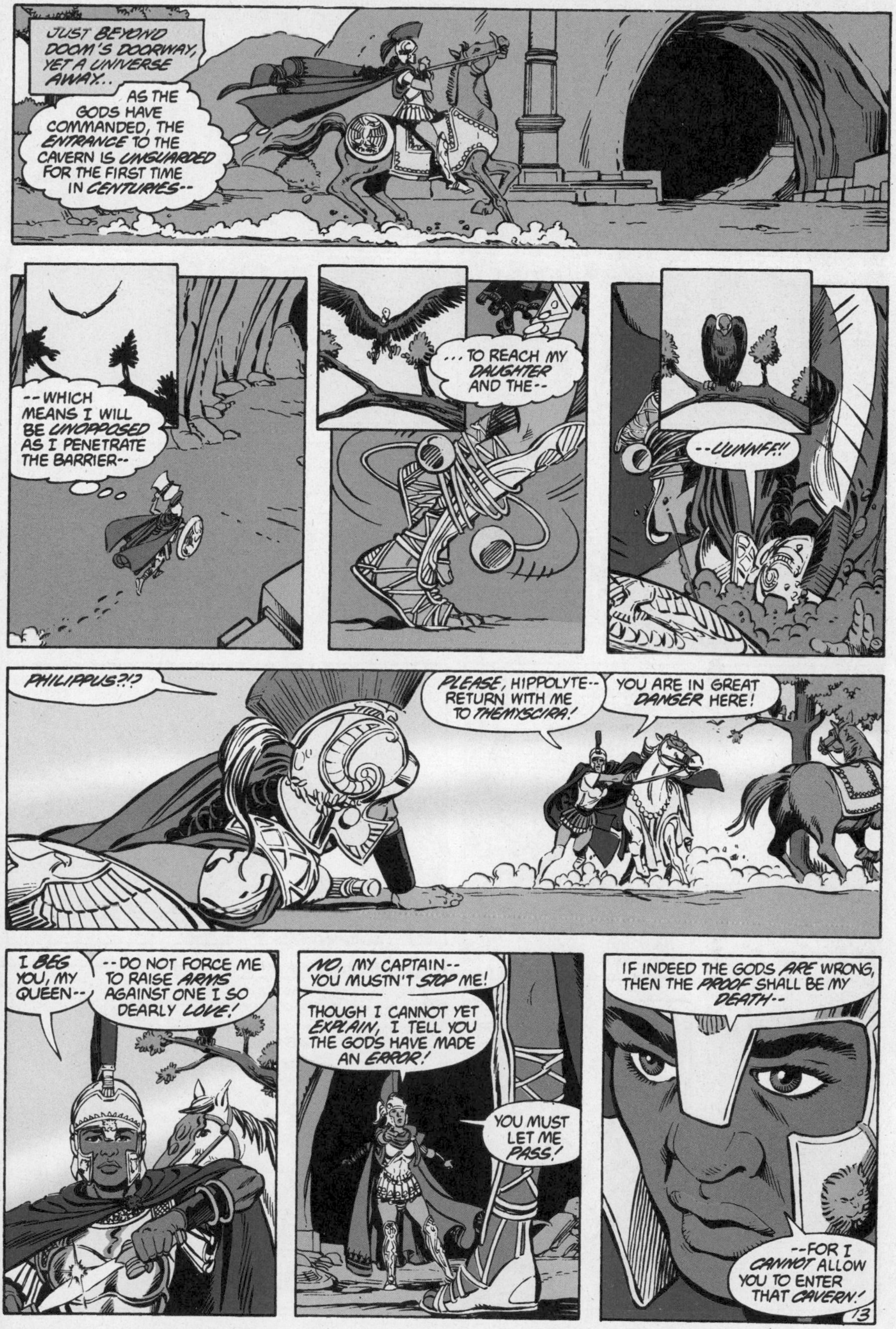
JUST BEYOND DOOM'S DOORWAY, YET A UNIVERSE AWAY...
AS THE GODS HAVE COMMANDED, THE ENTRANCE TO THE CAVERN IS UNGUARDED FOR THE FIRST TIME IN CENTURIES--
--WHICH MEANS I WILL BE UNOPPOSED AS I PENETRATE THE BARRIER--
...TO REACH MY DAUGHTER AND THE--
--UUNNFF!!
PHILIPPUS?!?
PLEASE, HIPPOLYTE-- RETURN WITH ME TO THEMYSCIRA!
YOU ARE IN GREAT DANGER HERE!
I BEG YOU, MY QUEEN--
--DO NOT FORCE ME TO RAISE ARMS AGAINST ONE I SO DEARLY LOVE!
NO, MY CAPTAIN-- YOU MUSTN'T STOP ME!
THOUGH I CANNOT YET EXPLAIN, I TELL YOU THE GODS HAVE MADE AN ERROR!
YOU MUST LET ME PASS!
IF INDEED THE GODS ARE WRONG, THEN THE PROOF SHALL BE MY DEATH--
--FOR I CANNOT ALLOW YOU TO ENTER THAT CAVERN!
13

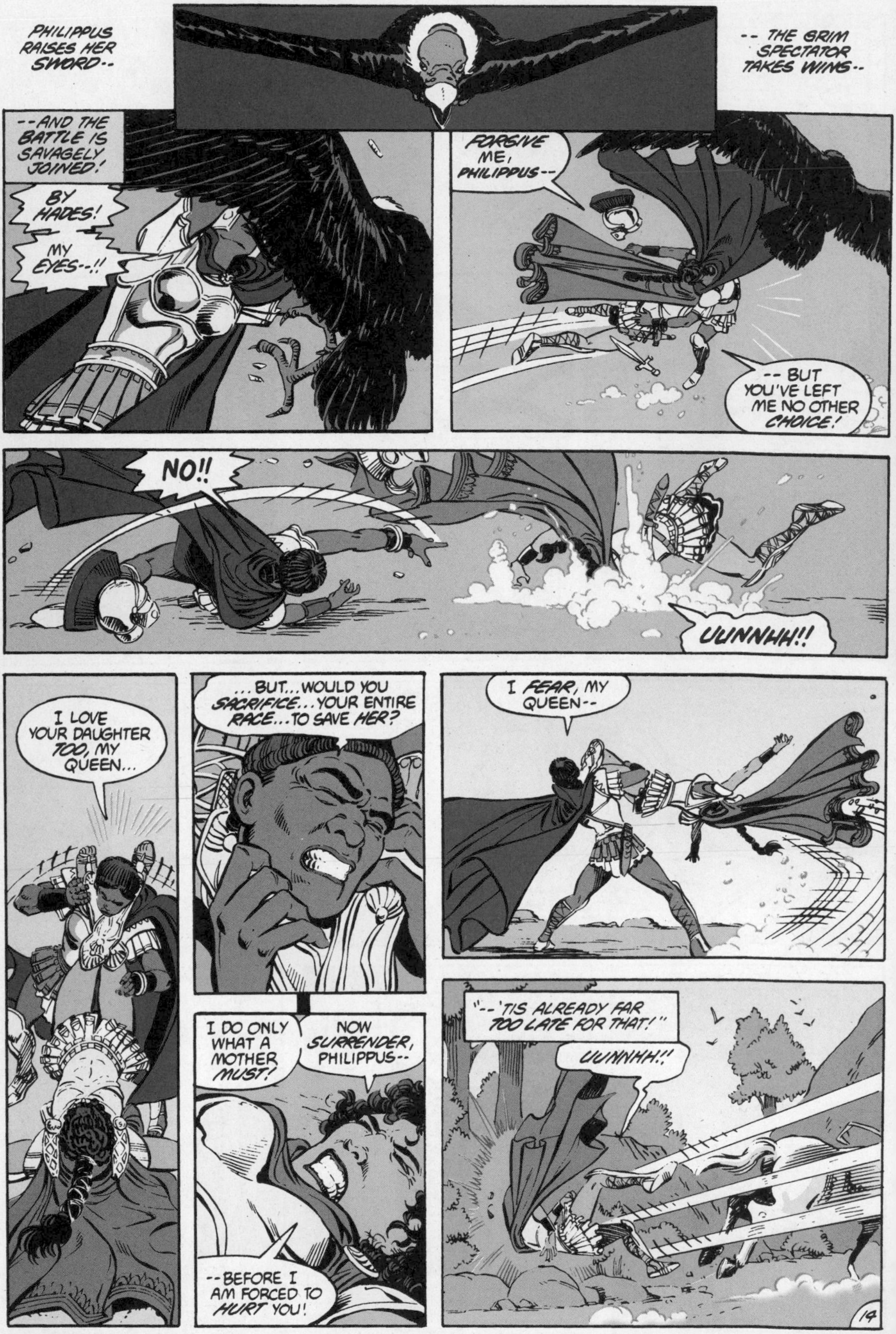
PHILIPPUS RAISES HER SWORD--
-- THE GRIM SPECTATOR TAKES WING--
--AND THE BATTLE IS SAVAGELY JOINED!
BY HADES!
MY EYES--!!
FORGIVE ME, PHILIPPUS--
-- BUT YOU'VE LEFT ME NO OTHER CHOICE!
NO!!
UUNNHH!!
I LOVE YOUR DAUGHTER TOO, MY QUEEN...
...BUT...WOULD YOU SACRIFICE...YOUR ENTIRE RACE...TO SAVE HER?
I DO ONLY WHAT A MOTHER MUST!
NOW SURRENDER, PHILIPPUS--
--BEFORE I AM FORCED TO HURT YOU!
I FEAR, MY QUEEN--
"--'TIS ALREADY FAR TOO LATE FOR THAT!"
UUNNHH!!
14

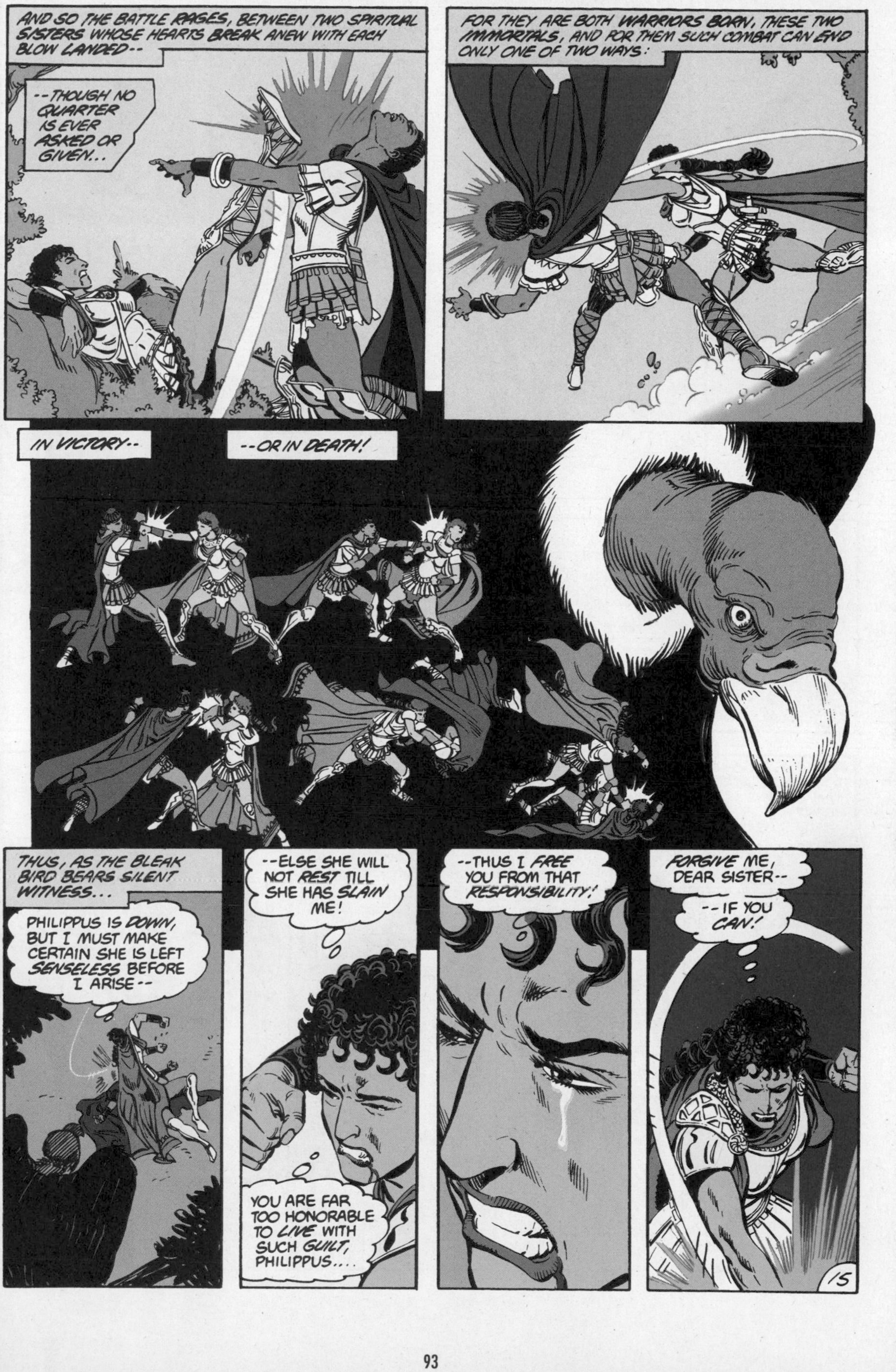
AND SO THE BATTLE RAGES, BETWEEN TWO SPIRITUAL SISTERS WHOSE HEARTS BREAK ANEW WITH EACH BLOW LANDED--
--THOUGH NO QUARTER IS EVER ASKED OR GIVEN...
FOR THEY ARE BOTH WARRIORS BORN, THESE TWO IMMORTALS, AND FOR THEM SUCH COMBAT CAN END ONLY ONE OF TWO WAYS:
IN VICTORY--
--OR IN DEATH!
THUS, AS THE BLEAK BIRD BEARS SILENT WITNESS...
PHILIPPUS IS DOWN, BUT I MUST MAKE CERTAIN SHE IS LEFT SENSELESS BEFORE I ARISE--
--ELSE SHE WILL NOT REST TILL SHE HAS SLAIN ME!
YOU ARE FAR TOO HONORABLE TO LIVE WITH SUCH GUILT, PHILIPPUS...
--THUS I FREE YOU FROM THAT RESPONSIBILITY!
FORGIVE ME, DEAR SISTER--
--IF YOU CAN!
15

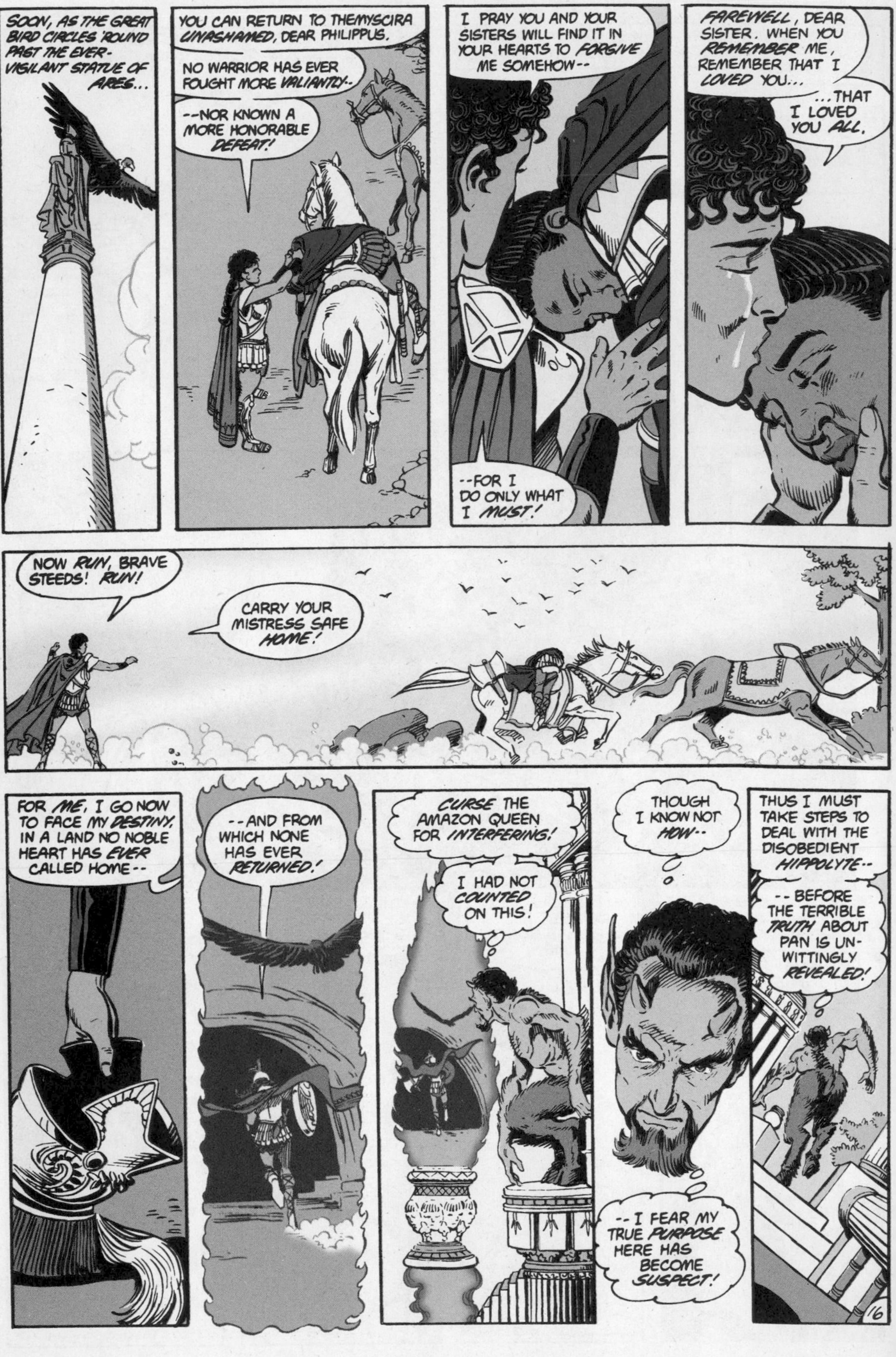
SOON, AS THE GREAT BIRD CIRCLES 'ROUND PAST THE EVER-VIGILANT STATUE OF ARES...
YOU CAN RETURN TO THEMYSCIRA UNASHAMED, DEAR PHILIPPUS.
NO WARRIOR HAS EVER FOUGHT MORE VALIANTLY--
--NOR KNOWN A MORE HONORABLE DEFEAT!
I PRAY YOU AND YOUR SISTERS WILL FIND IT IN YOUR HEARTS TO FORGIVE ME SOMEHOW--
--FOR I DO ONLY WHAT I MUST!
FAREWELL, DEAR SISTER. WHEN YOU REMEMBER ME, REMEMBER THAT I LOVED YOU...
...THAT I LOVED YOU ALL.
NOW RUN, BRAVE STEEDS! RUN!
CARRY YOUR MISTRESS SAFE HOME!
FOR ME, I GO NOW TO FACE MY DESTINY, IN A LAND NO NOBLE HEART HAS EVER CALLED HOME--
--AND FROM WHICH NONE HAS EVER RETURNED!
CURSE THE AMAZON QUEEN FOR INTERFERING!
I HAD NOT COUNTED ON THIS!
THOUGH I KNOW NOT HOW--
--I FEAR MY TRUE PURPOSE HERE HAS BECOME SUSPECT!
THUS I MUST TAKE STEPS TO DEAL WITH THE DISOBEDIENT HIPPOLYTE--
--BEFORE THE TERRIBLE TRUTH ABOUT PAN IS UNWITTINGLY REVEALED!
16

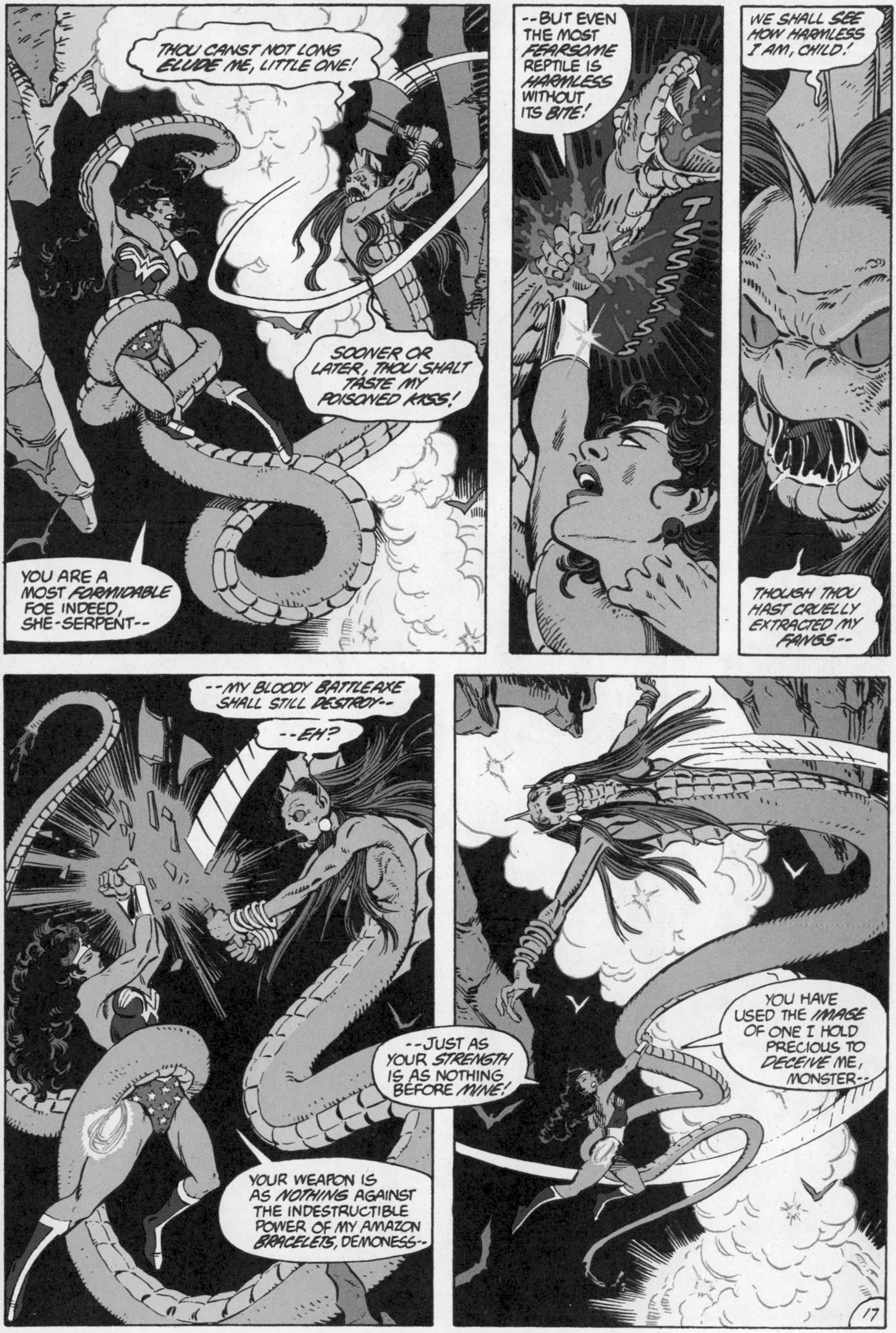
THOU CANST NOT LONG ELUDE ME, LITTLE ONE!
SOONER OR LATER, THOU SHALT TASTE MY POISONED KISS!
YOU ARE A MOST FORMIDABLE FOE INDEED, SHE-SERPENT--
--BUT EVEN THE MOST FEARSOME REPTILE IS HARMLESS WITHOUT ITS BITE!
TSSSSSSSS
WE SHALL SEE HOW HARMLESS I AM, CHILD!
THOUGH THOU HAST CRUELLY EXTRACTED MY FANGS--
--MY BLOODY BATTLEAXE SHALL STILL DESTROY--
--EH?
YOUR WEAPON IS AS NOTHING AGAINST THE INDESTRUCTIBLE POWER OF MY AMAZON BRACELETS, DEMONESS--
--JUST AS YOUR STRENGTH IS AS NOTHING BEFORE MINE!
YOU HAVE USED THE IMAGE OF ONE I HOLD PRECIOUS TO DECEIVE ME, MONSTER--
17

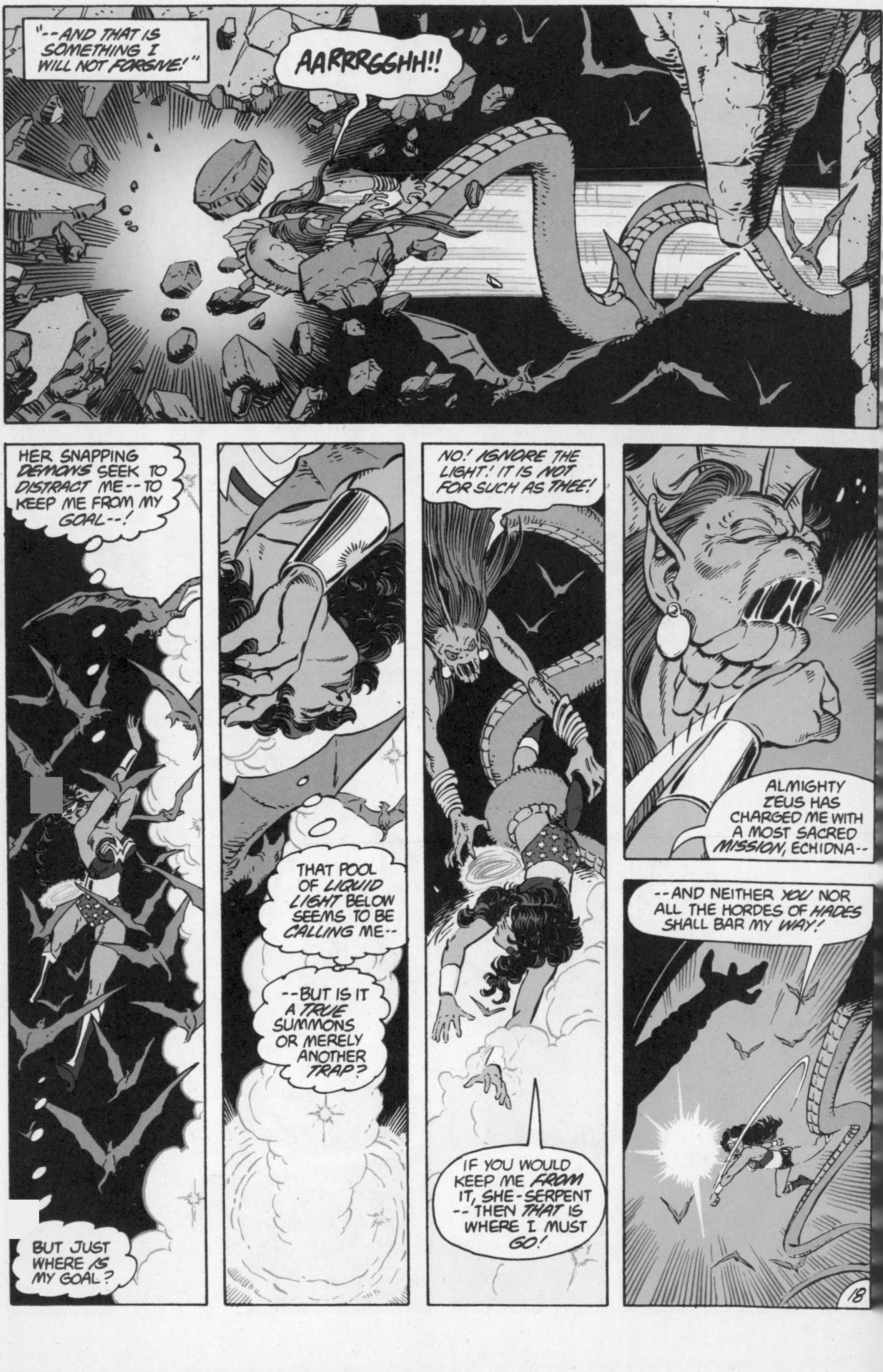
"--AND THAT IS SOMETHING I WILL NOT FORGIVE!"
AARRRGGHH!!
HER SNAPPING DEMONS SEEK TO DISTRACT ME--TO KEEP ME FROM MY GOAL--!
BUT JUST WHERE IS MY GOAL?
THAT POOL OF LIQUID LIGHT BELOW SEEMS TO BE CALLING ME--
--BUT IS IT A TRUE SUMMONS OR MERELY ANOTHER TRAP?
NO! IGNORE THE LIGHT! IT IS NOT FOR SUCH AS THEE!
IF YOU WOULD KEEP ME FROM IT, SHE-SERPENT --THEN THAT IS WHERE I MUST GO!
ALMIGHTY ZEUS HAS CHARGED ME WITH A MOST SACRED MISSION, ECHIDNA--
--AND NEITHER YOU NOR ALL THE HORDES OF HADES SHALL BAR MY WAY!
18

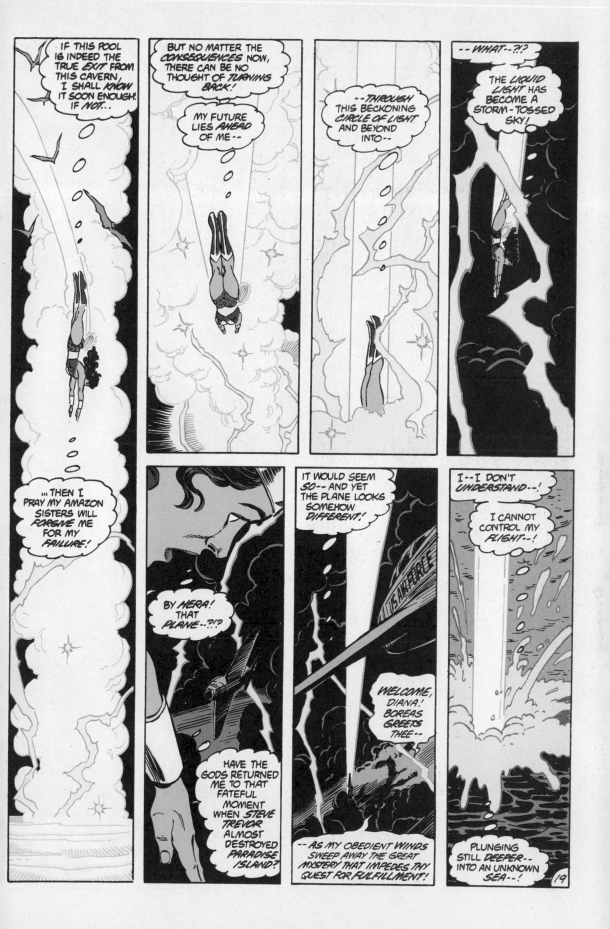

IF THIS POOL IS INDEED THE TRUE *EXIT* FROM THIS CAVERN, I SHALL *KNOW* IT SOON ENOUGH! IF *NOT*...

BUT NO MATTER THE *CONSEQUENCES* NOW, THERE CAN BE NO THOUGHT OF *TURNING BACK*!

MY FUTURE LIES *AHEAD* OF ME--

--THROUGH THIS BECKONING *CIRCLE OF LIGHT* AND BEYOND INTO--

-- *WHAT*--?!?

THE *LIQUID LIGHT* HAS BECOME A STORM-TOSSED SKY!

...THEN I PRAY MY AMAZON SISTERS WILL *FORGIVE* ME FOR MY *FAILURE*!

BY *HERA!* THAT *PLANE*--?!?

HAVE THE GODS RETURNED ME TO THAT FATEFUL MOMENT WHEN *STEVE TREVOR* ALMOST DESTROYED *PARADISE ISLAND*?

IT WOULD SEEM *SO*-- AND YET THE PLANE LOOKS SOMEHOW *DIFFERENT*!

WELCOME, DIANA! *BOREAS* GREETS THEE--

-- AS MY OBEDIENT WINDS SWEEP AWAY THE GREAT MYSTERY THAT IMPEDES THY QUEST FOR FULFILLMENT!

I--I DON'T *UNDERSTAND*--!

I CANNOT CONTROL MY *FLIGHT*--!

PLUNGING STILL *DEEPER*-- INTO AN UNKNOWN *SEA*--!

19

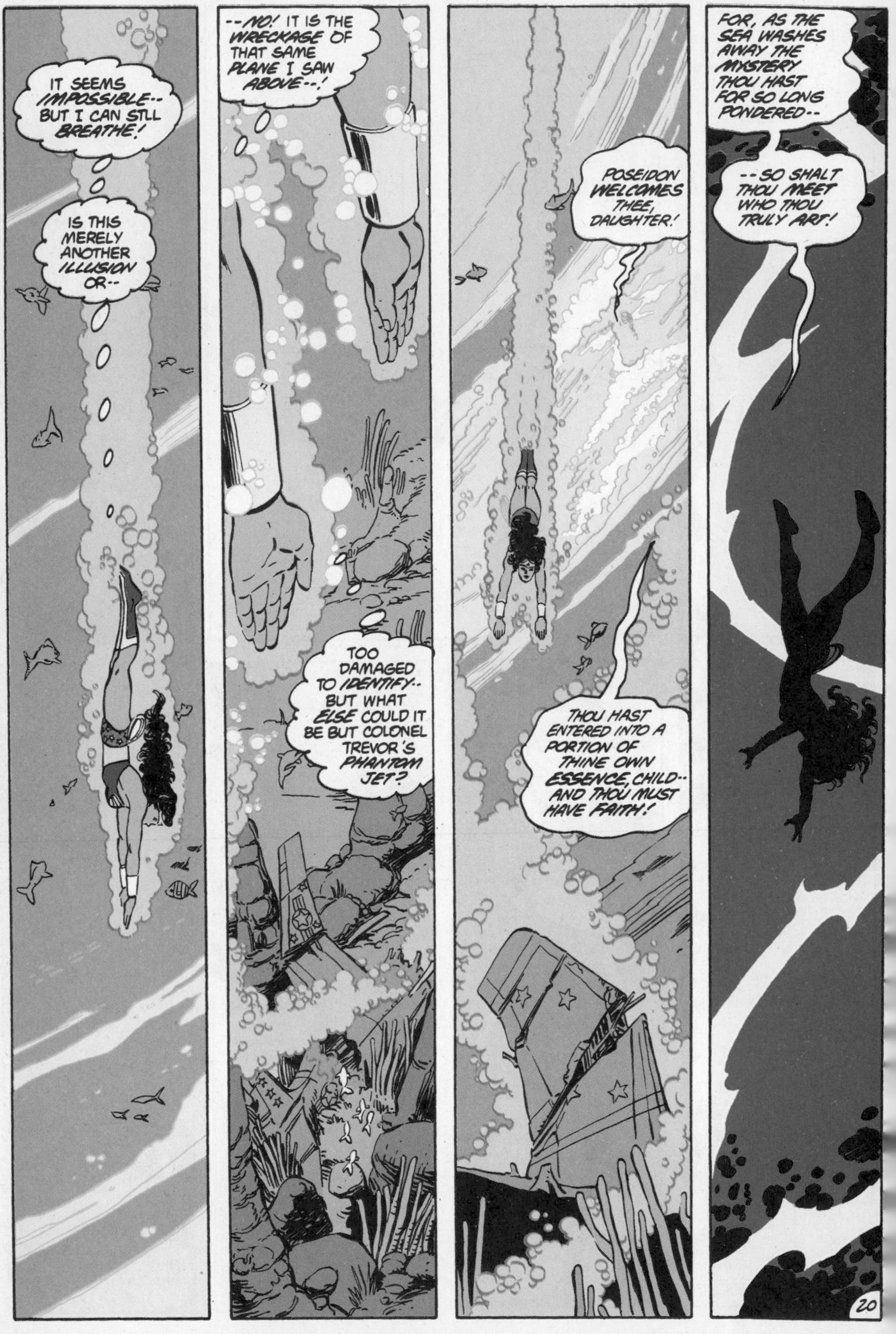

IT SEEMS IMPOSSIBLE-- BUT I CAN STILL BREATHE!
IS THIS MERELY ANOTHER ILLUSION OR--
--NO! IT IS THE WRECKAGE OF THAT SAME PLANE I SAW ABOVE--!
TOO DAMAGED TO IDENTIFY-- BUT WHAT ELSE COULD IT BE BUT COLONEL TREVOR'S PHANTOM JET?
POSEIDON WELCOMES THEE, DAUGHTER!
THOU HAST ENTERED INTO A PORTION OF THINE OWN ESSENCE, CHILD-- AND THOU MUST HAVE FAITH!
FOR, AS THE SEA WASHES AWAY THE MYSTERY THOU HAST FOR SO LONG PONDERED--
--SO SHALT THOU MEET WHO THOU TRULY ART!
20

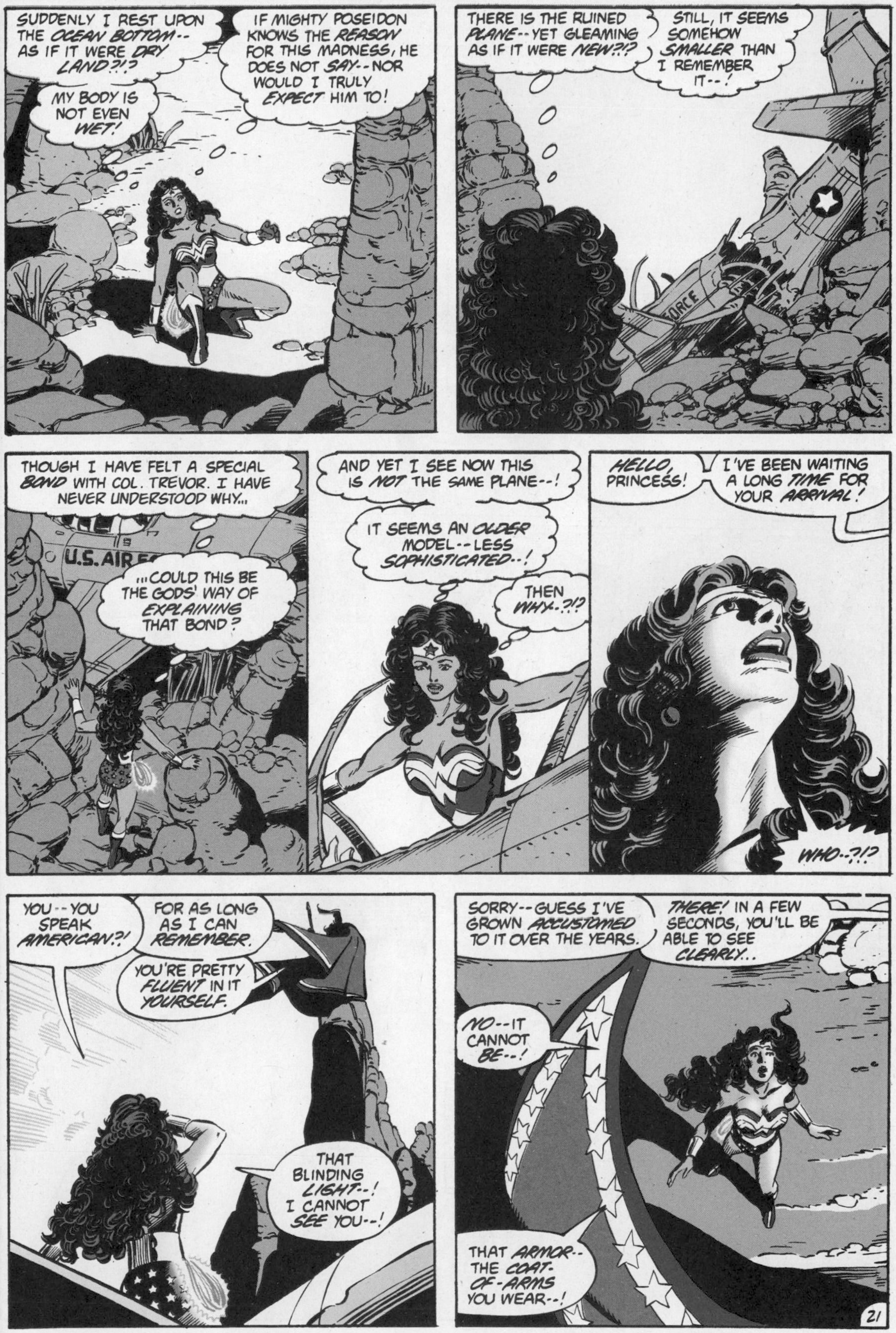
SUDDENLY I REST UPON THE OCEAN BOTTOM-- AS IF IT WERE DRY LAND?!?
MY BODY IS NOT EVEN WET!
IF MIGHTY POSEIDON KNOWS THE REASON FOR THIS MADNESS, HE DOES NOT SAY--NOR WOULD I TRULY EXPECT HIM TO!
THERE IS THE RUINED PLANE--YET GLEAMING AS IF IT WERE NEW?!?
STILL, IT SEEMS SOMEHOW SMALLER THAN I REMEMBER IT--!
THOUGH I HAVE FELT A SPECIAL BOND WITH COL. TREVOR, I HAVE NEVER UNDERSTOOD WHY...
U.S. AIR F
...COULD THIS BE THE GODS' WAY OF EXPLAINING THAT BOND?
AND YET I SEE NOW THIS IS NOT THE SAME PLANE--!
IT SEEMS AN OLDER MODEL--LESS SOPHISTICATED--!
THEN WHY--?!?
HELLO, PRINCESS!
I'VE BEEN WAITING A LONG TIME FOR YOUR ARRIVAL!
WHO--?!?
YOU--YOU SPEAK AMERICAN?!
FOR AS LONG AS I CAN REMEMBER.
YOU'RE PRETTY FLUENT IN IT YOURSELF.
THAT BLINDING LIGHT--! I CANNOT SEE YOU--!
SORRY--GUESS I'VE GROWN ACCUSTOMED TO IT OVER THE YEARS.
THERE! IN A FEW SECONDS, YOU'LL BE ABLE TO SEE CLEARLY...
NO--IT CANNOT BE--!
THAT ARMOR-- THE COAT-OF-ARMS YOU WEAR--!
21

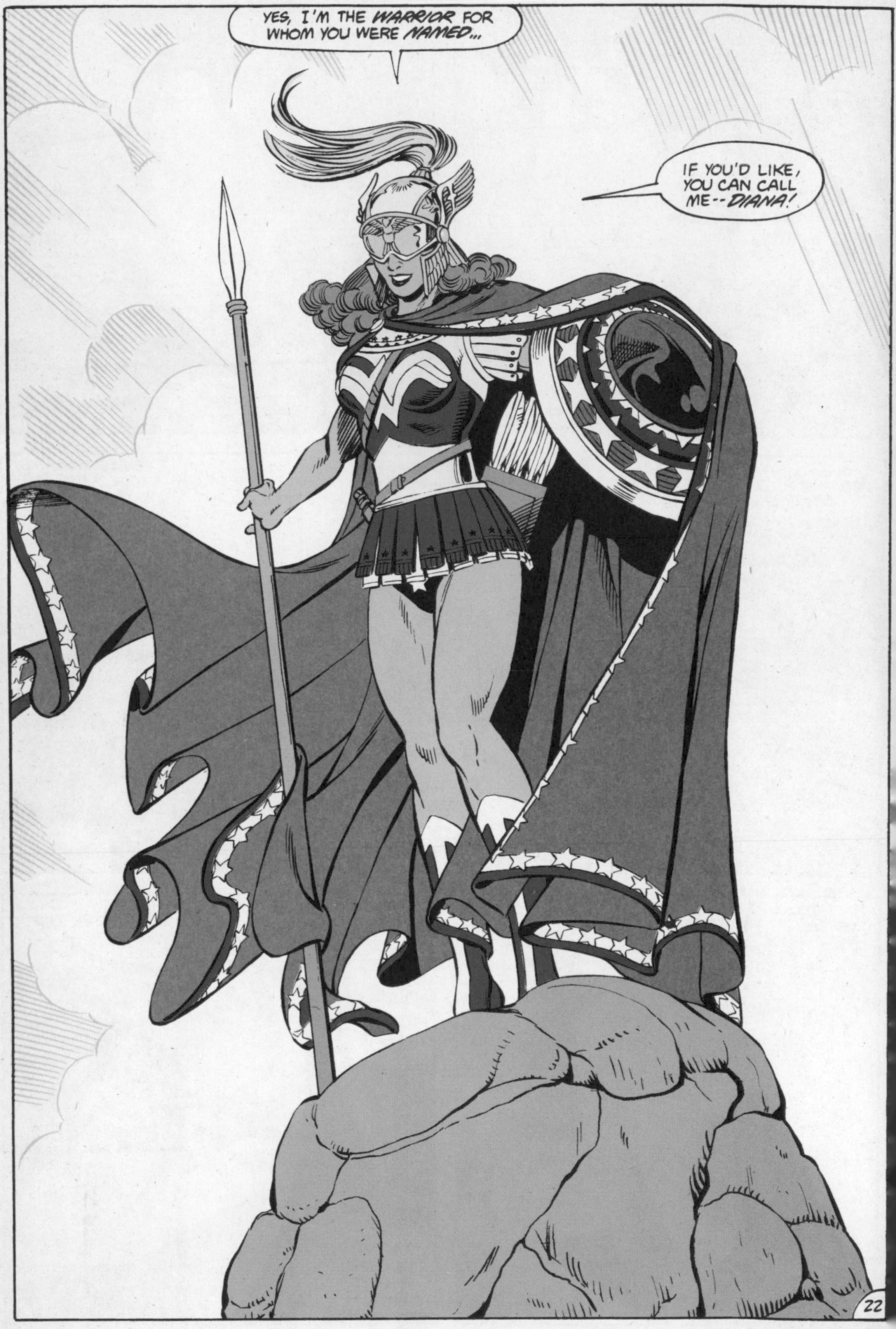
YES, I'M THE WARRIOR FOR WHOM YOU WERE NAMED...
IF YOU'D LIKE, YOU CAN CALL ME--DIANA!
22

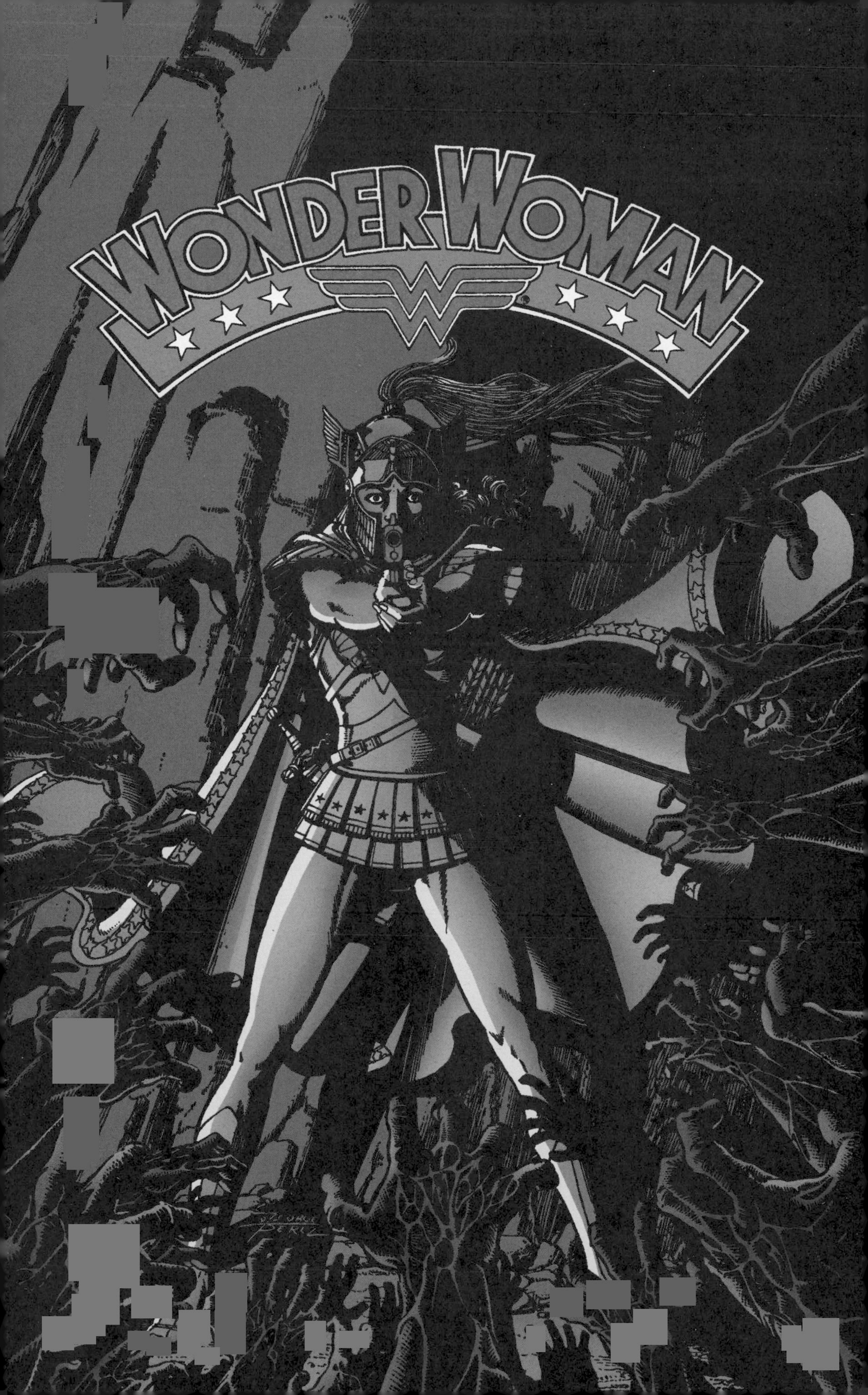
WONDER WOMAN

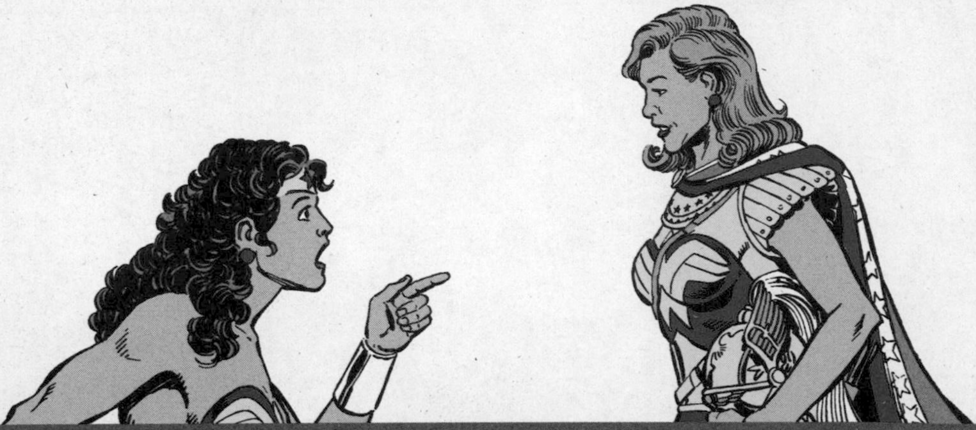

WONDER WOMAN

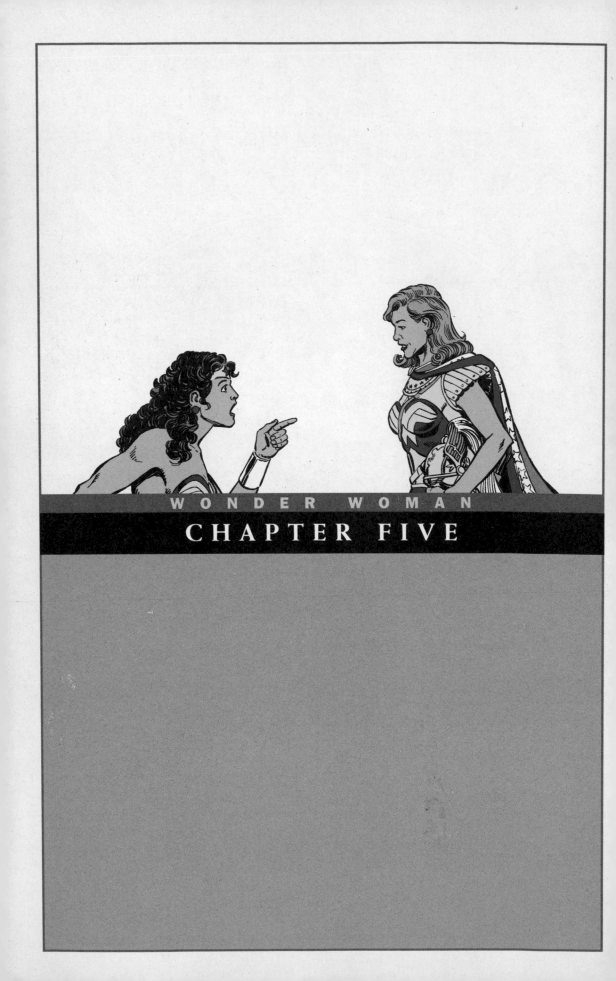

CHAPTER FIVE

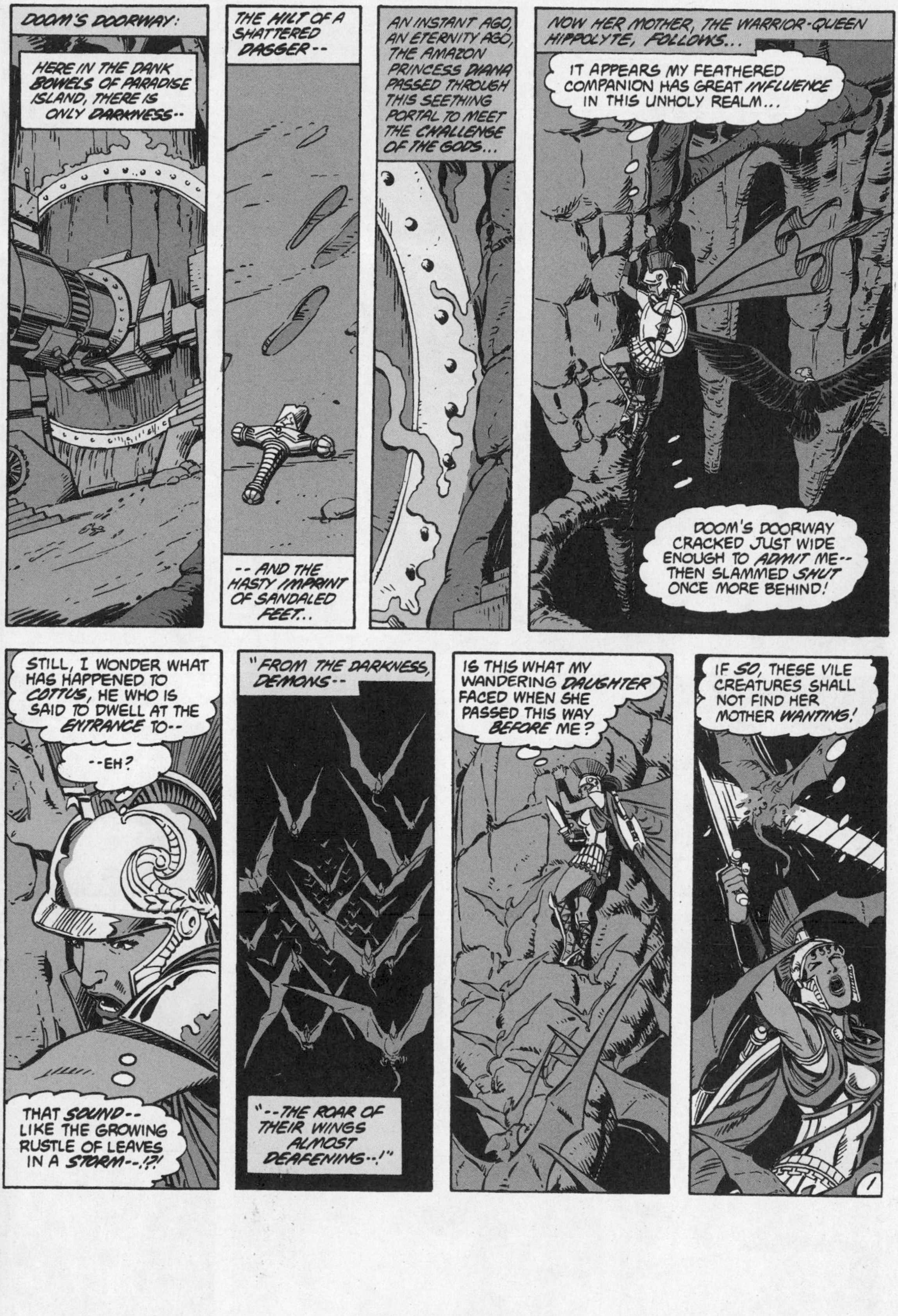
DOOM'S DOORWAY:
HERE IN THE DANK BOWELS OF PARADISE ISLAND, THERE IS ONLY DARKNESS--
THE HILT OF A SHATTERED DAGGER--
--AND THE HASTY IMPRINT OF SANDALED FEET...
AN INSTANT AGO, AN ETERNITY AGO, THE AMAZON PRINCESS DIANA PASSED THROUGH THIS SEETHING PORTAL TO MEET THE CHALLENGE OF THE GODS...
NOW HER MOTHER, THE WARRIOR-QUEEN HIPPOLYTE, FOLLOWS...
IT APPEARS MY FEATHERED COMPANION HAS GREAT INFLUENCE IN THIS UNHOLY REALM...
DOOM'S DOORWAY CRACKED JUST WIDE ENOUGH TO ADMIT ME--THEN SLAMMED SHUT ONCE MORE BEHIND!
STILL, I WONDER WHAT HAS HAPPENED TO COTTUS, HE WHO IS SAID TO DWELL AT THE ENTRANCE TO--
--EH?
THAT SOUND--LIKE THE GROWING RUSTLE OF LEAVES IN A STORM--.!?!
"FROM THE DARKNESS, DEMONS--
"--THE ROAR OF THEIR WINGS ALMOST DEAFENING--!"
IS THIS WHAT MY WANDERING DAUGHTER FACED WHEN SHE PASSED THIS WAY BEFORE ME?
IF SO, THESE VILE CREATURES SHALL NOT FIND HER MOTHER WANTING!
1

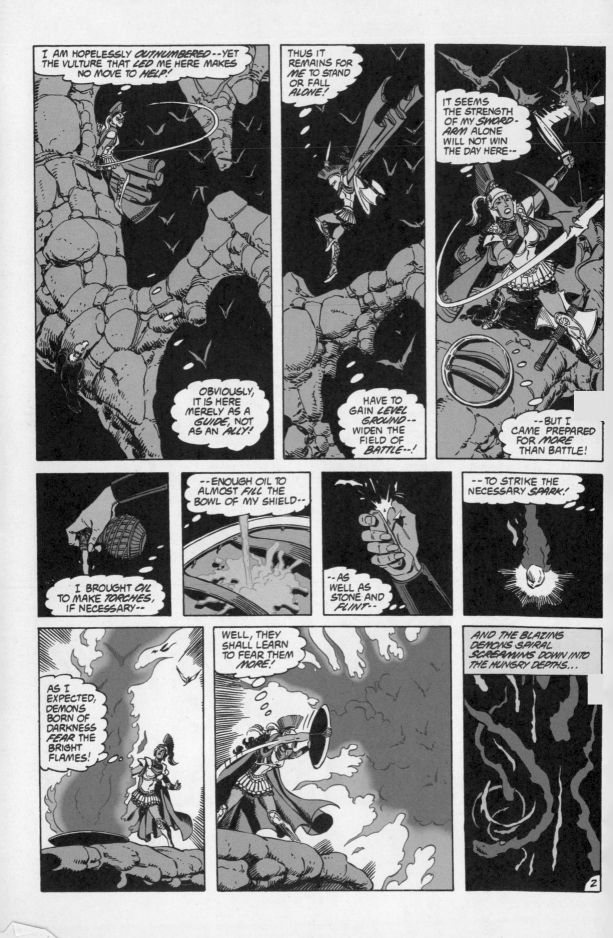

I AM HOPELESSLY *OUTNUMBERED*--YET THE VULTURE THAT *LED* ME HERE MAKES NO MOVE TO *HELP!*

OBVIOUSLY, IT IS HERE MERELY AS A *GUIDE*, NOT AS AN *ALLY!*

THUS IT REMAINS FOR *ME* TO STAND OR FALL *ALONE!*

HAVE TO GAIN *LEVEL GROUND*-- WIDEN THE FIELD OF *BATTLE*--!

IT SEEMS THE STRENGTH OF MY *SWORD-ARM* ALONE WILL NOT WIN THE DAY HERE--

--BUT I CAME PREPARED FOR *MORE* THAN BATTLE!

I BROUGHT *OIL* TO MAKE *TORCHES*, IF NECESSARY--

--ENOUGH OIL TO ALMOST *FILL* THE BOWL OF MY SHIELD--

--AS WELL AS STONE AND *FLINT*--

--TO STRIKE THE NECESSARY *SPARK!*

AS I EXPECTED, DEMONS BORN OF DARKNESS *FEAR* THE BRIGHT FLAMES!

WELL, THEY SHALL LEARN TO FEAR THEM *MORE!*

AND THE BLAZING DEMONS SPIRAL SCREAMING DOWN INTO THE HUNGRY DEPTHS...

2

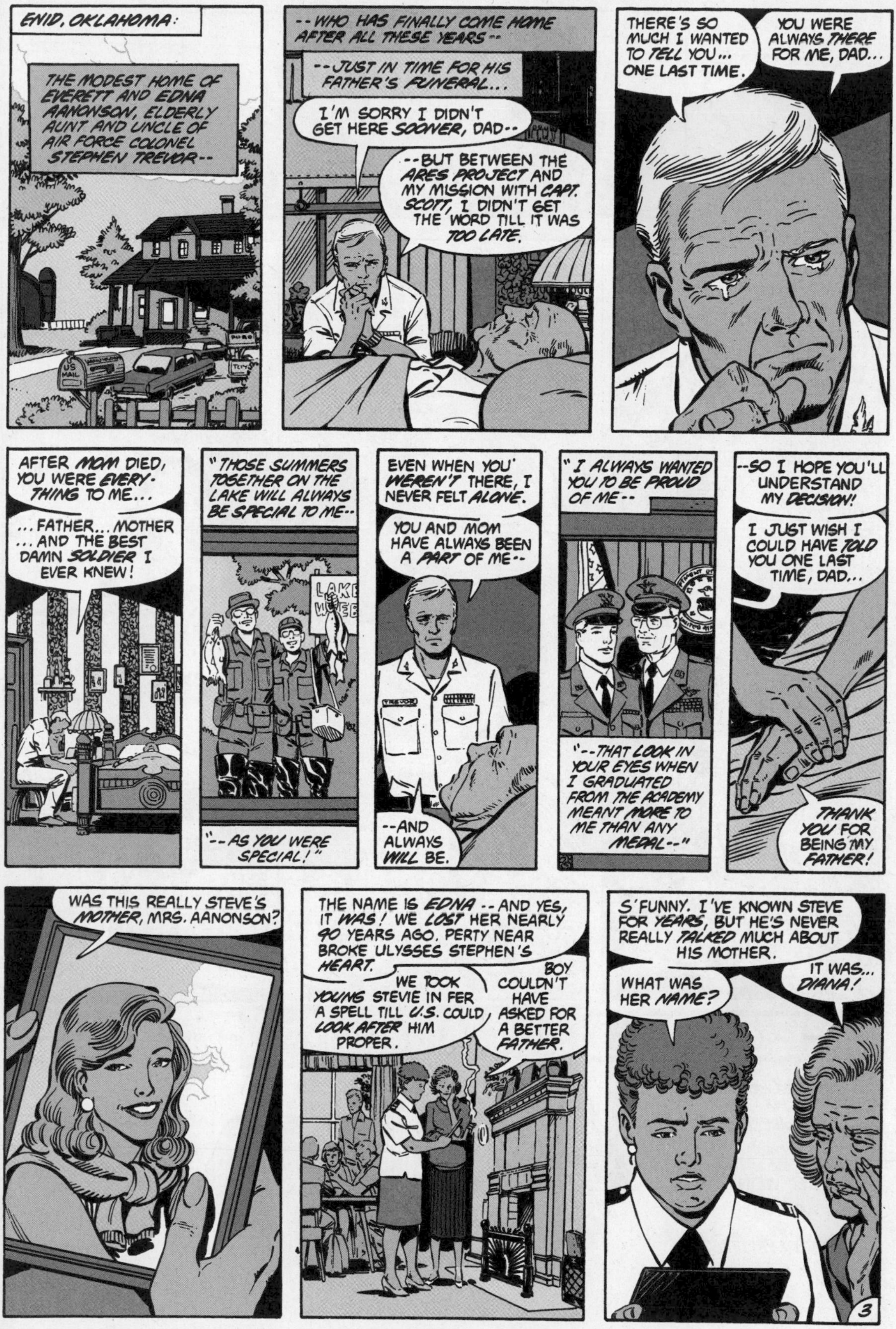
ENID, OKLAHOMA:
THE MODEST HOME OF EVERETT AND EDNA AANONSON, ELDERLY AUNT AND UNCLE OF AIR FORCE COLONEL STEPHEN TREVOR--
US MAIL
--WHO HAS FINALLY COME HOME AFTER ALL THESE YEARS--
--JUST IN TIME FOR HIS FATHER'S FUNERAL...
I'M SORRY I DIDN'T GET HERE SOONER, DAD--
--BUT BETWEEN THE ARES PROJECT AND MY MISSION WITH CAPT. SCOTT, I DIDN'T GET THE WORD TILL IT WAS TOO LATE.
THERE'S SO MUCH I WANTED TO TELL YOU... ONE LAST TIME.
YOU WERE ALWAYS THERE FOR ME, DAD...
AFTER MOM DIED, YOU WERE EVERYTHING TO ME...
...FATHER... MOTHER ...AND THE BEST DAMN SOLDIER I EVER KNEW!
"THOSE SUMMERS TOGETHER ON THE LAKE WILL ALWAYS BE SPECIAL TO ME--
"--AS YOU WERE SPECIAL!"
EVEN WHEN YOU WEREN'T THERE, I NEVER FELT ALONE.
YOU AND MOM HAVE ALWAYS BEEN A PART OF ME--
TREVOR
--AND ALWAYS WILL BE.
"I ALWAYS WANTED YOU TO BE PROUD OF ME--
"--THAT LOOK IN YOUR EYES WHEN I GRADUATED FROM THE ACADEMY MEANT MORE TO ME THAN ANY MEDAL--"
--SO I HOPE YOU'LL UNDERSTAND MY DECISION!
I JUST WISH I COULD HAVE TOLD YOU ONE LAST TIME, DAD...
THANK YOU FOR BEING MY FATHER!
WAS THIS REALLY STEVE'S MOTHER, MRS. AANONSON?
THE NAME IS EDNA--AND YES, IT WAS! WE LOST HER NEARLY 40 YEARS AGO. PERTY NEAR BROKE ULYSSES STEPHEN'S HEART.
WE TOOK YOUNG STEVIE IN FER A SPELL TILL U.S. COULD LOOK AFTER HIM PROPER.
BOY COULDN'T HAVE ASKED FOR A BETTER FATHER.
S'FUNNY. I'VE KNOWN STEVE FOR YEARS, BUT HE'S NEVER REALLY TALKED MUCH ABOUT HIS MOTHER.
WHAT WAS HER NAME?
IT WAS... DIANA!
3

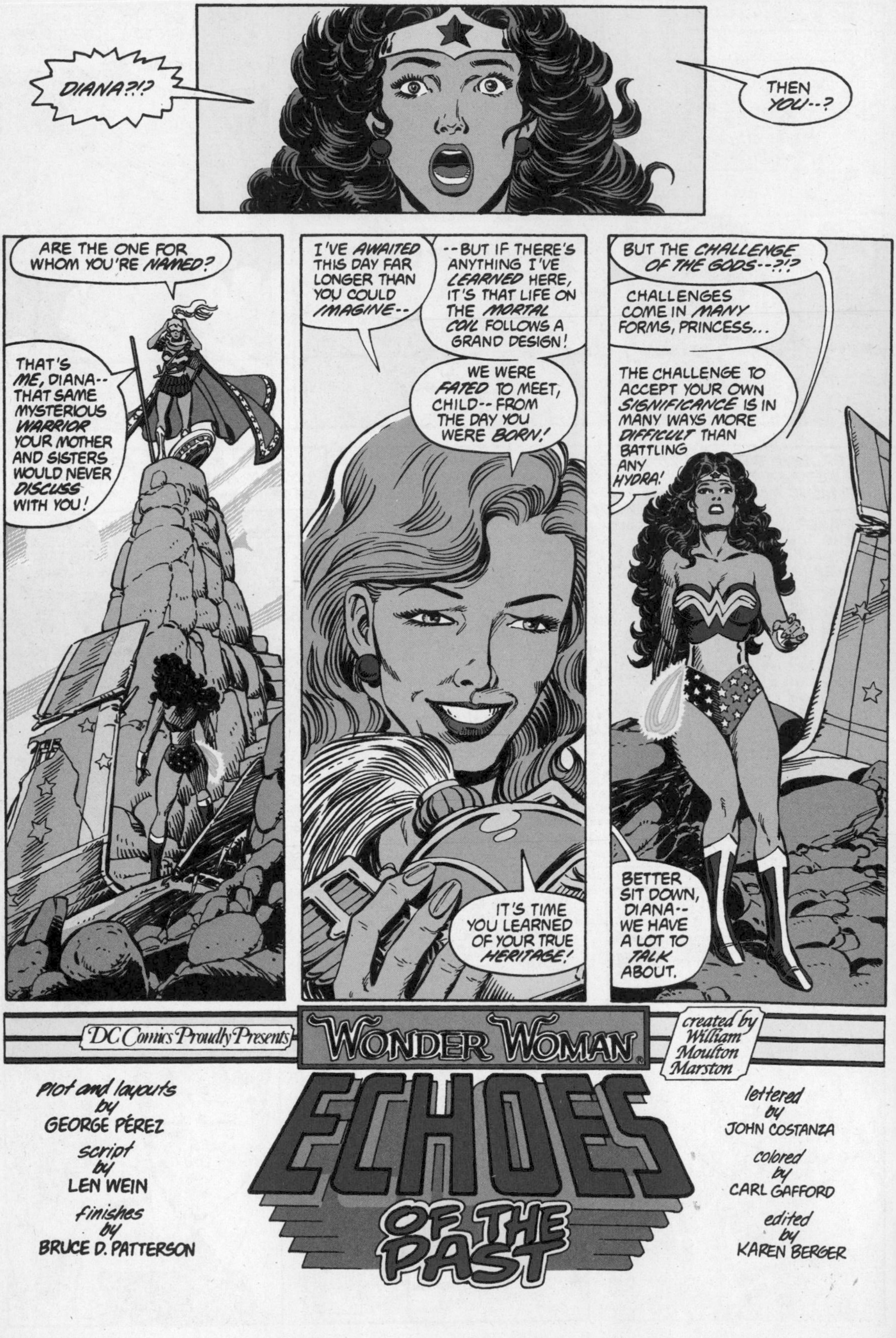
DIANA?!?
THEN YOU--?
ARE THE ONE FOR WHOM YOU'RE NAMED?
THAT'S ME, DIANA-- THAT SAME MYSTERIOUS WARRIOR YOUR MOTHER AND SISTERS WOULD NEVER DISCUSS WITH YOU!
I'VE AWAITED THIS DAY FAR LONGER THAN YOU COULD IMAGINE--
--BUT IF THERE'S ANYTHING I'VE LEARNED HERE, IT'S THAT LIFE ON THE MORTAL COIL FOLLOWS A GRAND DESIGN!
WE WERE FATED TO MEET, CHILD-- FROM THE DAY YOU WERE BORN!
IT'S TIME YOU LEARNED OF YOUR TRUE HERITAGE!
BUT THE CHALLENGE OF THE GODS--?!?
CHALLENGES COME IN MANY FORMS, PRINCESS...
THE CHALLENGE TO ACCEPT YOUR OWN SIGNIFICANCE IS IN MANY WAYS MORE DIFFICULT THAN BATTLING ANY HYDRA!
BETTER SIT DOWN, DIANA-- WE HAVE A LOT TO TALK ABOUT.
DC Comics Proudly Presents
WONDER WOMAN
created by William Moulton Marston
ECHOES OF THE PAST
plot and layouts by GEORGE PÉREZ
script by LEN WEIN
finishes by BRUCE D. PATTERSON
lettered by JOHN COSTANZA
colored by CARL GAFFORD
edited by KAREN BERGER

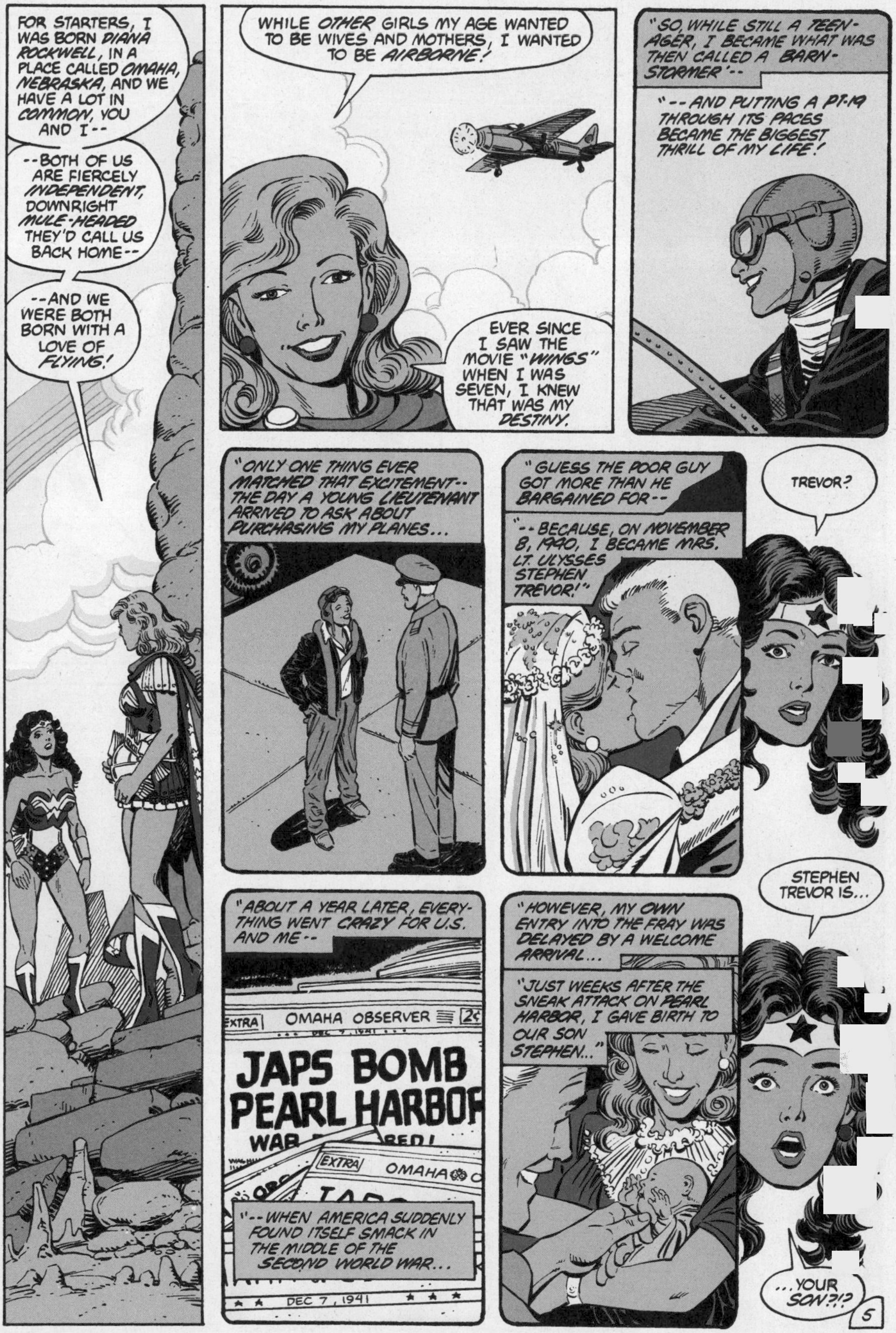
FOR STARTERS, I WAS BORN DIANA ROCKWELL, IN A PLACE CALLED OMAHA, NEBRASKA, AND WE HAVE A LOT IN COMMON, YOU AND I--
--BOTH OF US ARE FIERCELY INDEPENDENT, DOWNRIGHT MULE-HEADED THEY'D CALL US BACK HOME--
--AND WE WERE BOTH BORN WITH A LOVE OF FLYING!
WHILE OTHER GIRLS MY AGE WANTED TO BE WIVES AND MOTHERS, I WANTED TO BE AIRBORNE!
EVER SINCE I SAW THE MOVIE "WINGS" WHEN I WAS SEVEN, I KNEW THAT WAS MY DESTINY.
"SO, WHILE STILL A TEEN-AGER, I BECAME WHAT WAS THEN CALLED A BARN-STORMER'--
"--AND PUTTING A PT-19 THROUGH ITS PACES BECAME THE BIGGEST THRILL OF MY LIFE!
"ONLY ONE THING EVER MATCHED THAT EXCITEMENT--THE DAY A YOUNG LIEUTENANT ARRIVED TO ASK ABOUT PURCHASING MY PLANES...
"GUESS THE POOR GUY GOT MORE THAN HE BARGAINED FOR--
"--BECAUSE, ON NOVEMBER 8, 1940, I BECAME MRS. LT. ULYSSES STEPHEN TREVOR!"
TREVOR?
"ABOUT A YEAR LATER, EVERY-THING WENT CRAZY FOR U.S. AND ME--
EXTRA OMAHA OBSERVER 2¢
DEC 7, 1941
JAPS BOMB PEARL HARBOR
EXTRA OMAHA
"--WHEN AMERICA SUDDENLY FOUND ITSELF SMACK IN THE MIDDLE OF THE SECOND WORLD WAR...
DEC 7, 1941
"HOWEVER, MY OWN ENTRY INTO THE FRAY WAS DELAYED BY A WELCOME ARRIVAL...
"JUST WEEKS AFTER THE SNEAK ATTACK ON PEARL HARBOR, I GAVE BIRTH TO OUR SON STEPHEN..."
STEPHEN TREVOR IS...
...YOUR SON?!?
5

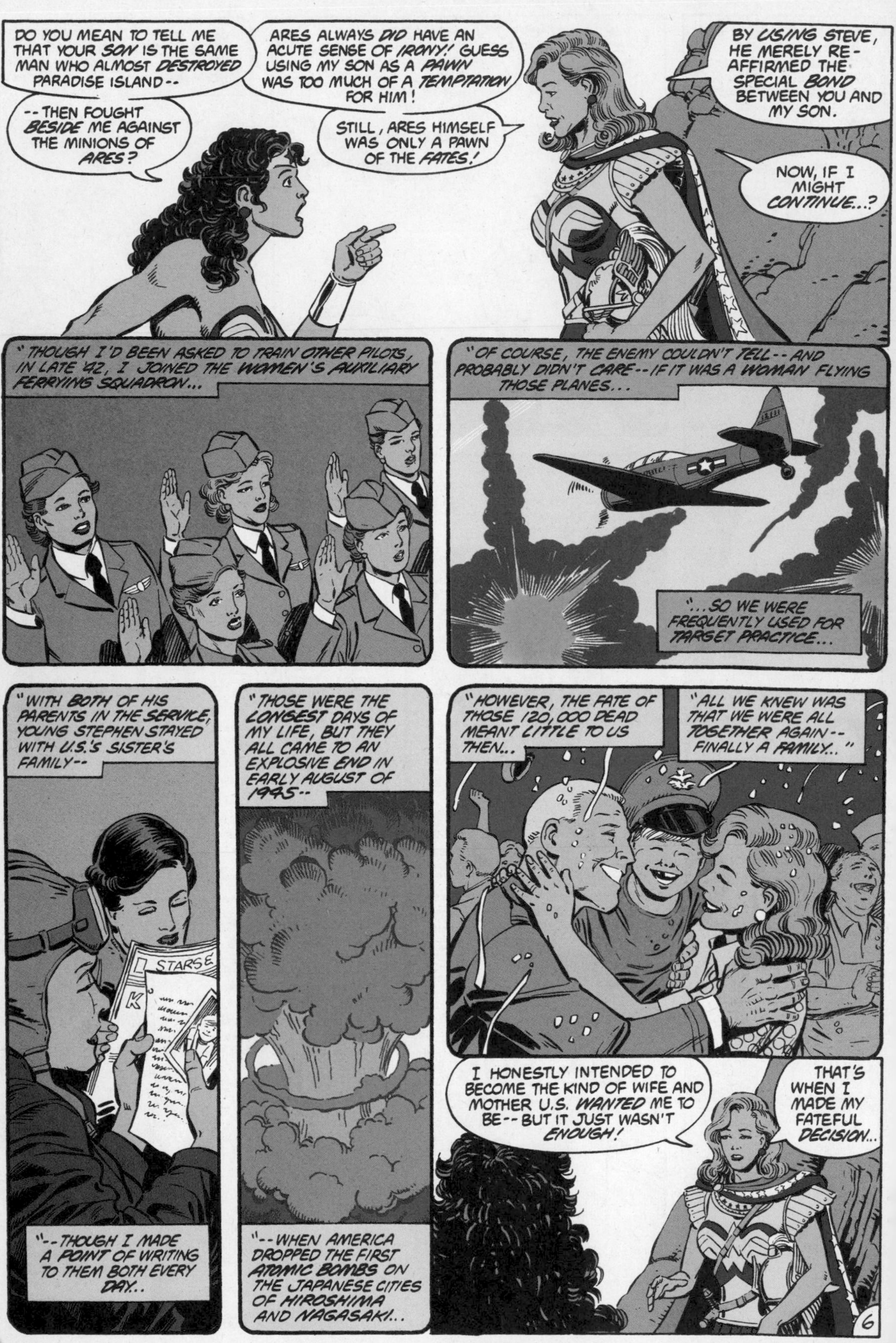
DO YOU MEAN TO TELL ME THAT YOUR SON IS THE SAME MAN WHO ALMOST DESTROYED PARADISE ISLAND--
--THEN FOUGHT BESIDE ME AGAINST THE MINIONS OF ARES?
ARES ALWAYS DID HAVE AN ACUTE SENSE OF IRONY! GUESS USING MY SON AS A PAWN WAS TOO MUCH OF A TEMPTATION FOR HIM!
STILL, ARES HIMSELF WAS ONLY A PAWN OF THE FATES!
BY USING STEVE, HE MERELY RE-AFFIRMED THE SPECIAL BOND BETWEEN YOU AND MY SON.
NOW, IF I MIGHT CONTINUE...?
"THOUGH I'D BEEN ASKED TO TRAIN OTHER PILOTS, IN LATE '42, I JOINED THE WOMEN'S AUXILIARY FERRYING SQUADRON...
"OF COURSE, THE ENEMY COULDN'T TELL--AND PROBABLY DIDN'T CARE--IF IT WAS A WOMAN FLYING THOSE PLANES...
"...SO WE WERE FREQUENTLY USED FOR TARGET PRACTICE...
"WITH BOTH OF HIS PARENTS IN THE SERVICE, YOUNG STEPHEN STAYED WITH U.S.'S SISTER'S FAMILY--
"--THOUGH I MADE A POINT OF WRITING TO THEM BOTH EVERY DAY..
"THOSE WERE THE LONGEST DAYS OF MY LIFE, BUT THEY ALL CAME TO AN EXPLOSIVE END IN EARLY AUGUST OF 1945--
"--WHEN AMERICA DROPPED THE FIRST ATOMIC BOMBS ON THE JAPANESE CITIES OF HIROSHIMA AND NAGASAKI...
"HOWEVER, THE FATE OF THOSE 120,000 DEAD MEANT LITTLE TO US THEN...
"ALL WE KNEW WAS THAT WE WERE ALL TOGETHER AGAIN--FINALLY A FAMILY..."
I HONESTLY INTENDED TO BECOME THE KIND OF WIFE AND MOTHER U.S. WANTED ME TO BE--BUT IT JUST WASN'T ENOUGH!
THAT'S WHEN I MADE MY FATEFUL DECISION...
6

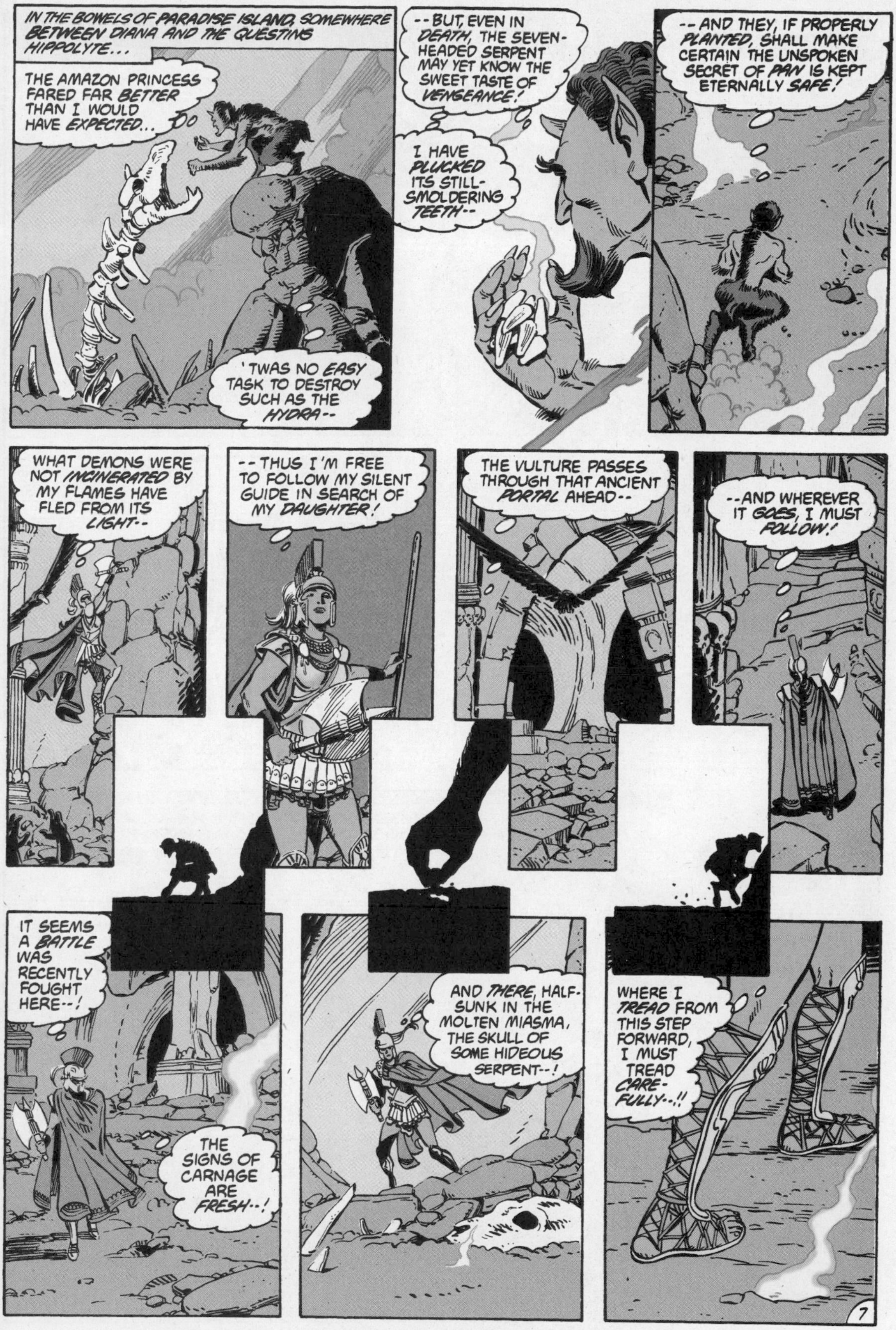
IN THE BOWELS OF PARADISE ISLAND, SOMEWHERE BETWEEN DIANA AND THE QUESTING HIPPOLYTE...
THE AMAZON PRINCESS FARED FAR BETTER THAN I WOULD HAVE EXPECTED...
'TWAS NO EASY TASK TO DESTROY SUCH AS THE HYDRA--
--BUT, EVEN IN DEATH, THE SEVEN-HEADED SERPENT MAY YET KNOW THE SWEET TASTE OF VENGEANCE!
I HAVE PLUCKED ITS STILL-SMOLDERING TEETH--
--AND THEY, IF PROPERLY PLANTED, SHALL MAKE CERTAIN THE UNSPOKEN SECRET OF PAN IS KEPT ETERNALLY SAFE!
WHAT DEMONS WERE NOT INCINERATED BY MY FLAMES HAVE FLED FROM ITS LIGHT--
--THUS I'M FREE TO FOLLOW MY SILENT GUIDE IN SEARCH OF MY DAUGHTER!
THE VULTURE PASSES THROUGH THAT ANCIENT PORTAL AHEAD--
--AND WHEREVER IT GOES, I MUST FOLLOW!
IT SEEMS A BATTLE WAS RECENTLY FOUGHT HERE--!
THE SIGNS OF CARNAGE ARE FRESH--!
AND THERE, HALF-SUNK IN THE MOLTEN MIASMA, THE SKULL OF SOME HIDEOUS SERPENT--!
WHERE I TREAD FROM THIS STEP FORWARD, I MUST TREAD CARE-FULLY--!!
7

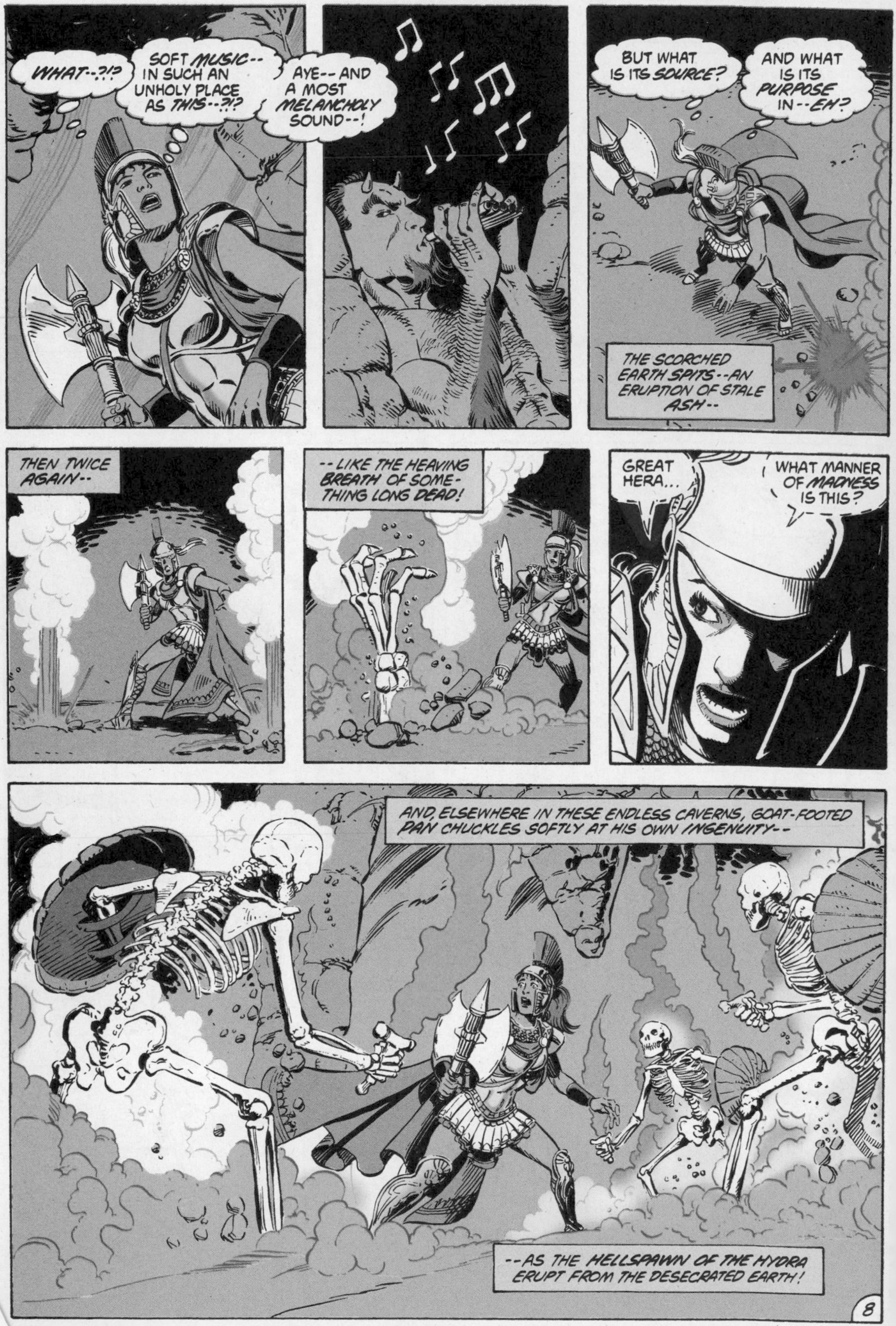
WHAT--?!?
SOFT MUSIC-- IN SUCH AN UNHOLY PLACE AS THIS--?!?
AYE-- AND A MOST MELANCHOLY SOUND--!
BUT WHAT IS ITS SOURCE?
AND WHAT IS ITS PURPOSE IN--EN?
THE SCORCHED EARTH SPITS--AN ERUPTION OF STALE ASH--
THEN TWICE AGAIN--
--LIKE THE HEAVING BREATH OF SOME-THING LONG DEAD!
GREAT HERA...
WHAT MANNER OF MADNESS IS THIS?
AND, ELSEWHERE IN THESE ENDLESS CAVERNS, GOAT-FOOTED PAN CHUCKLES SOFTLY AT HIS OWN INGENUITY--
--AS THE HELLSPAWN OF THE HYDRA ERUPT FROM THE DESECRATED EARTH!
8

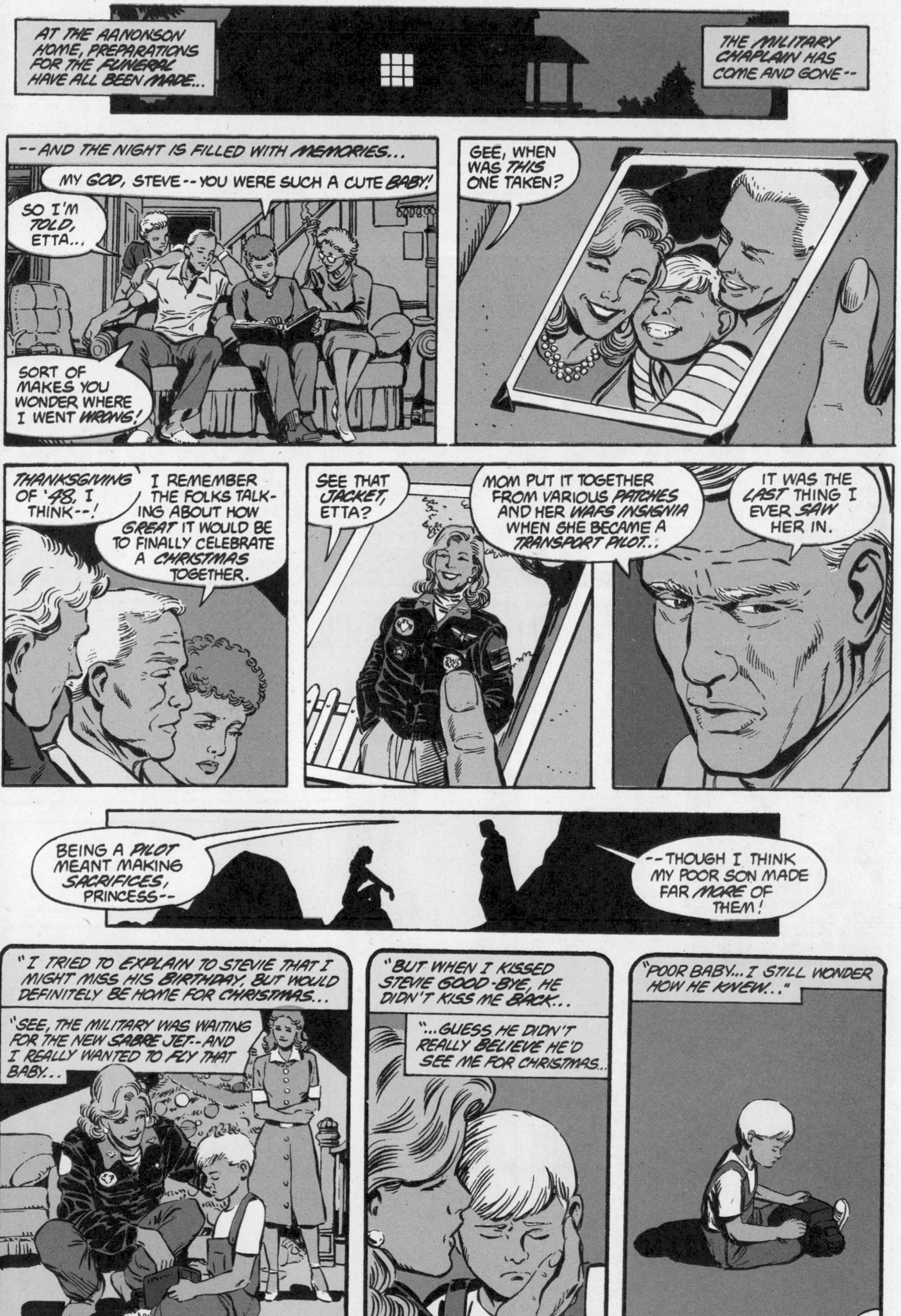
AT THE AANONSON HOME, PREPARATIONS FOR THE FUNERAL HAVE ALL BEEN MADE...
THE MILITARY CHAPLAIN HAS COME AND GONE--
--AND THE NIGHT IS FILLED WITH MEMORIES...
MY GOD, STEVE--YOU WERE SUCH A CUTE BABY!
SO I'M TOLD, ETTA...
SORT OF MAKES YOU WONDER WHERE I WENT WRONG!
GEE, WHEN WAS THIS ONE TAKEN?
THANKSGIVING OF '48, I THINK--!
I REMEMBER THE FOLKS TALKING ABOUT HOW GREAT IT WOULD BE TO FINALLY CELEBRATE A CHRISTMAS TOGETHER.
SEE THAT JACKET, ETTA?
MOM PUT IT TOGETHER FROM VARIOUS PATCHES AND HER WAFS INSIGNIA WHEN SHE BECAME A TRANSPORT PILOT...
IT WAS THE LAST THING I EVER SAW HER IN.
BEING A PILOT MEANT MAKING SACRIFICES, PRINCESS--
--THOUGH I THINK MY POOR SON MADE FAR MORE OF THEM!
"I TRIED TO EXPLAIN TO STEVIE THAT I MIGHT MISS HIS BIRTHDAY, BUT WOULD DEFINITELY BE HOME FOR CHRISTMAS...
"SEE, THE MILITARY WAS WAITING FOR THE NEW SABRE JET--AND I REALLY WANTED TO FLY THAT BABY...
"BUT WHEN I KISSED STEVIE GOOD-BYE, HE DIDN'T KISS ME BACK...
"...GUESS HE DIDN'T REALLY BELIEVE HE'D SEE ME FOR CHRISTMAS...
"POOR BABY...I STILL WONDER HOW HE KNEW..."
9

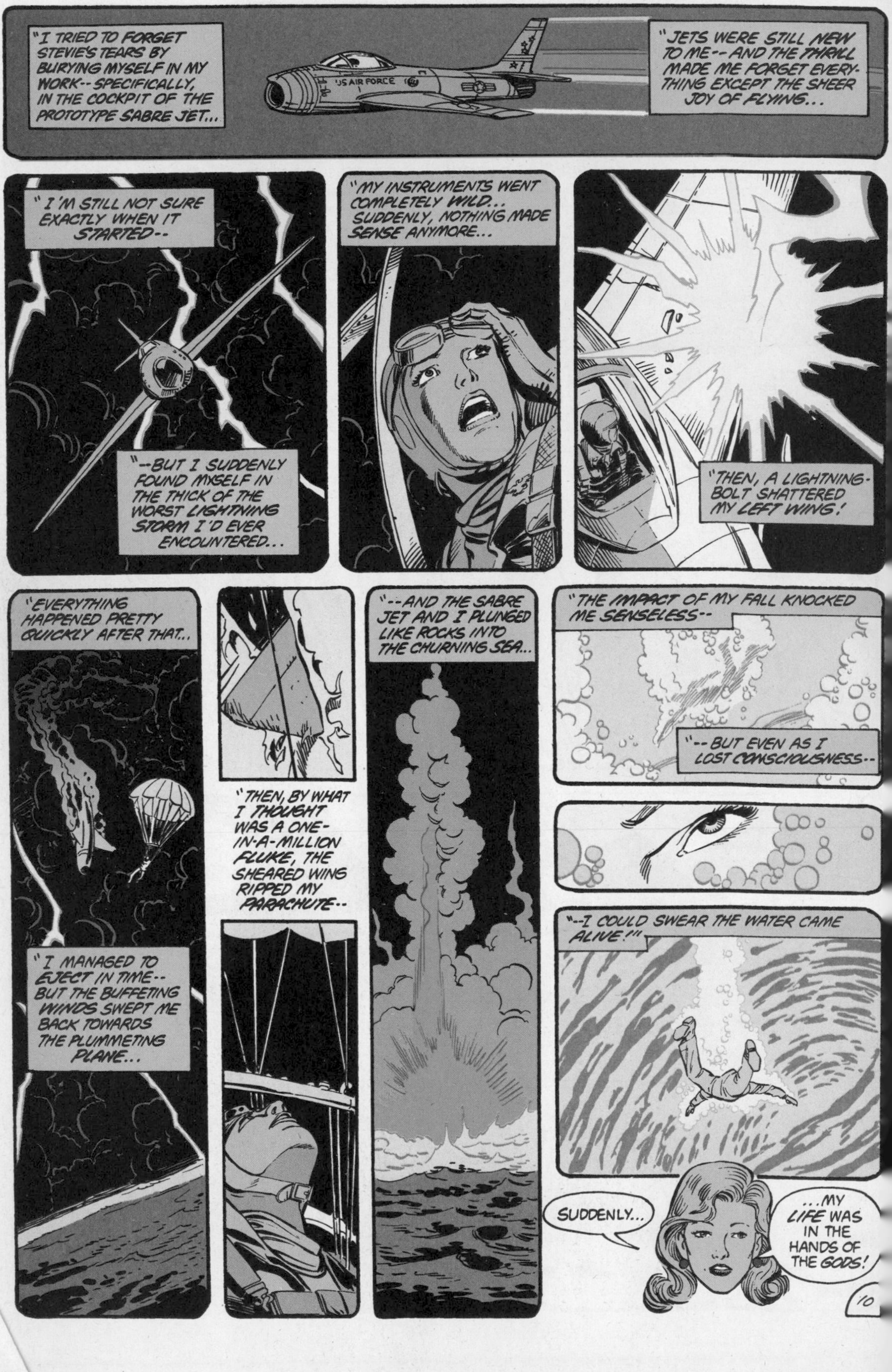
"I TRIED TO FORGET STEVIE'S TEARS BY BURYING MYSELF IN MY WORK--SPECIFICALLY, IN THE COCKPIT OF THE PROTOTYPE SABRE JET...
US AIR FORCE
"JETS WERE STILL NEW TO ME--AND THE THRILL MADE ME FORGET EVERYTHING EXCEPT THE SHEER JOY OF FLYING...
"I'M STILL NOT SURE EXACTLY WHEN IT STARTED--
"--BUT I SUDDENLY FOUND MYSELF IN THE THICK OF THE WORST LIGHTNING STORM I'D EVER ENCOUNTERED...
"MY INSTRUMENTS WENT COMPLETELY WILD... SUDDENLY, NOTHING MADE SENSE ANYMORE...
"THEN, A LIGHTNING-BOLT SHATTERED MY LEFT WING!
"EVERYTHING HAPPENED PRETTY QUICKLY AFTER THAT...
"I MANAGED TO EJECT IN TIME--BUT THE BUFFETING WINDS SWEPT ME BACK TOWARDS THE PLUMMETING PLANE...
"THEN, BY WHAT I THOUGHT WAS A ONE-IN-A-MILLION FLUKE, THE SHEARED WING RIPPED MY PARACHUTE--
"--AND THE SABRE JET AND I PLUNGED LIKE ROCKS INTO THE CHURNING SEA...
"THE IMPACT OF MY FALL KNOCKED ME SENSELESS--
"--BUT EVEN AS I LOST CONSCIOUSNESS--
"--I COULD SWEAR THE WATER CAME ALIVE!"
SUDDENLY...
...MY LIFE WAS IN THE HANDS OF THE GODS!
10

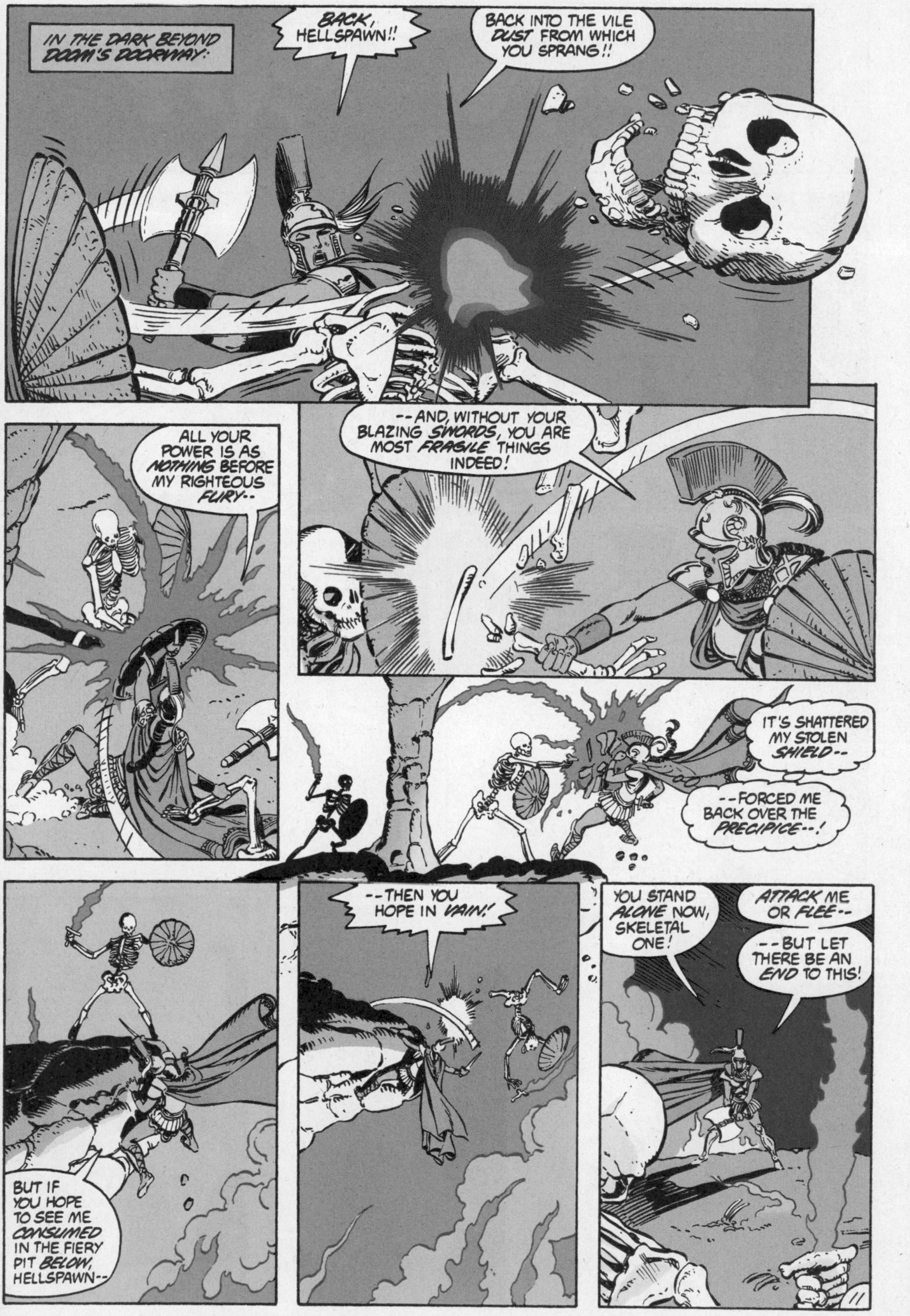
IN THE DARK BEYOND DOOM'S DOORWAY:
BACK, HELLSPAWN!!
BACK INTO THE VILE DUST FROM WHICH YOU SPRANG!!
ALL YOUR POWER IS AS NOTHING BEFORE MY RIGHTEOUS FURY--
--AND, WITHOUT YOUR BLAZING SWORDS, YOU ARE MOST FRAGILE THINGS INDEED!
IT'S SHATTERED MY STOLEN SHIELD--
--FORCED ME BACK OVER THE PRECIPICE--!
BUT IF YOU HOPE TO SEE ME CONSUMED IN THE FIERY PIT BELOW, HELLSPAWN--
--THEN YOU HOPE IN VAIN!
YOU STAND ALONE NOW, SKELETAL ONE!
ATTACK ME OR FLEE--
--BUT LET THERE BE AN END TO THIS!

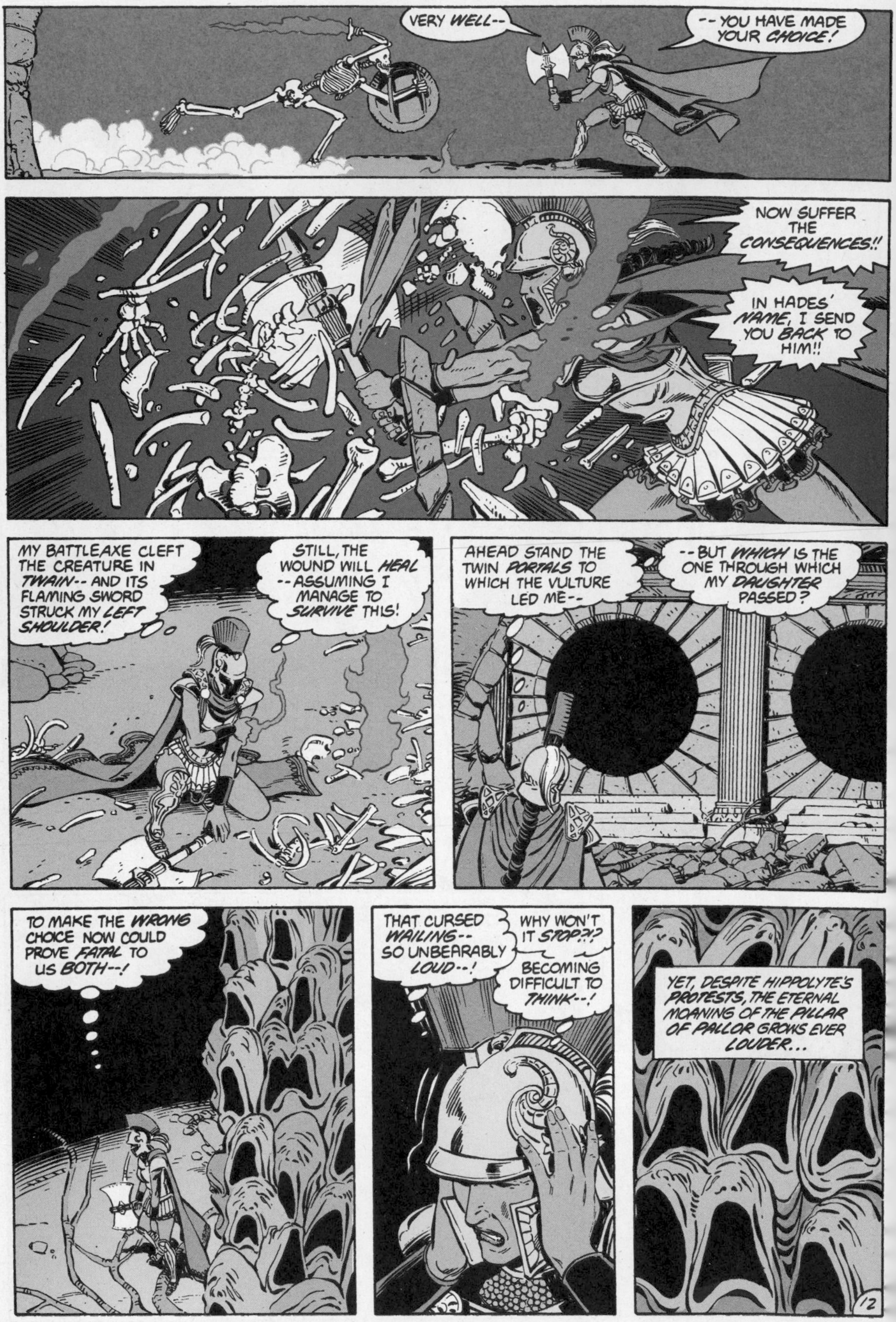
VERY WELL--
--YOU HAVE MADE YOUR CHOICE!
NOW SUFFER THE CONSEQUENCES!!
IN HADES' NAME, I SEND YOU BACK TO HIM!!
MY BATTLEAXE CLEFT THE CREATURE IN TWAIN-- AND ITS FLAMING SWORD STRUCK MY LEFT SHOULDER!
STILL, THE WOUND WILL HEAL --ASSUMING I MANAGE TO SURVIVE THIS!
AHEAD STAND THE TWIN PORTALS TO WHICH THE VULTURE LED ME--
--BUT WHICH IS THE ONE THROUGH WHICH MY DAUGHTER PASSED?
TO MAKE THE WRONG CHOICE NOW COULD PROVE FATAL TO US BOTH--!
THAT CURSED WAILING-- SO UNBEARABLY LOUD--!
WHY WON'T IT STOP?!?
BECOMING DIFFICULT TO THINK--!
YET, DESPITE HIPPOLYTE'S PROTESTS, THE ETERNAL MOANING OF THE PILLAR OF PALLOR GROWS EVER LOUDER...
12

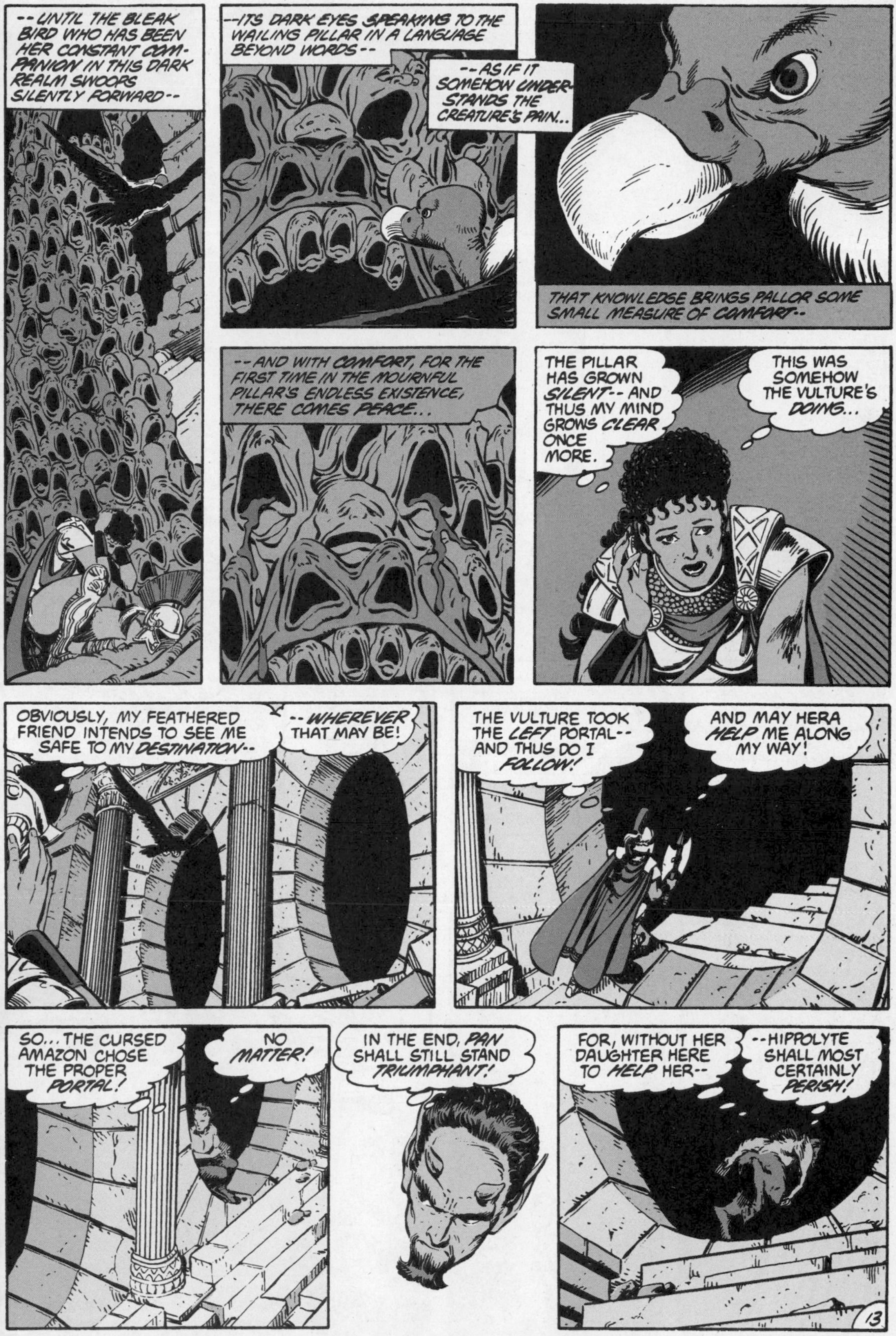
--UNTIL THE BLEAK BIRD WHO HAS BEEN HER CONSTANT COMPANION IN THIS DARK REALM SWOOPS SILENTLY FORWARD--
--ITS DARK EYES SPEAKING TO THE WAILING PILLAR IN A LANGUAGE BEYOND WORDS--
--AS IF IT SOMEHOW UNDERSTANDS THE CREATURE'S PAIN...
THAT KNOWLEDGE BRINGS PALLOR SOME SMALL MEASURE OF COMFORT--
--AND WITH COMFORT, FOR THE FIRST TIME IN THE MOURNFUL PILLAR'S ENDLESS EXISTENCE, THERE COMES PEACE...
THE PILLAR HAS GROWN SILENT--AND THUS MY MIND GROWS CLEAR ONCE MORE.
THIS WAS SOMEHOW THE VULTURE'S DOING...
OBVIOUSLY, MY FEATHERED FRIEND INTENDS TO SEE ME SAFE TO MY DESTINATION--
--WHEREVER THAT MAY BE!
THE VULTURE TOOK THE LEFT PORTAL--AND THUS DO I FOLLOW!
AND MAY HERA HELP ME ALONG MY WAY!
SO... THE CURSED AMAZON CHOSE THE PROPER PORTAL!
NO MATTER!
IN THE END, PAN SHALL STILL STAND TRIUMPHANT!
FOR, WITHOUT HER DAUGHTER HERE TO HELP HER--
--HIPPOLYTE SHALL MOST CERTAINLY PERISH!
13

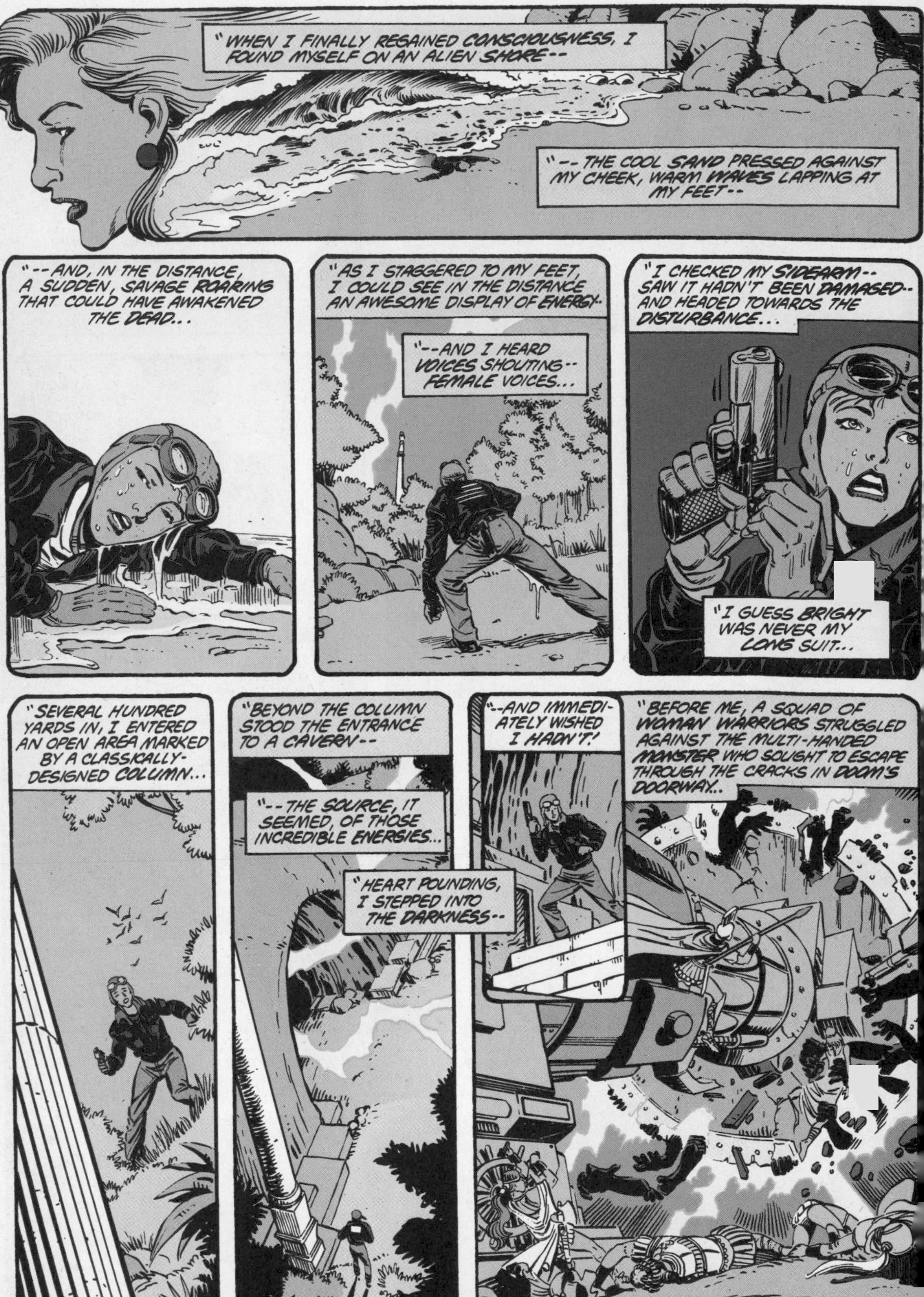
"WHEN I FINALLY REGAINED CONSCIOUSNESS, I FOUND MYSELF ON AN ALIEN SHORE--
"--THE COOL SAND PRESSED AGAINST MY CHEEK, WARM WAVES LAPPING AT MY FEET--
"--AND, IN THE DISTANCE, A SUDDEN, SAVAGE ROARING THAT COULD HAVE AWAKENED THE DEAD...
"AS I STAGGERED TO MY FEET, I COULD SEE IN THE DISTANCE AN AWESOME DISPLAY OF ENERGY.
"--AND I HEARD VOICES SHOUTING-- FEMALE VOICES...
"I CHECKED MY SIDEARM-- SAW IT HADN'T BEEN DAMAGED-- AND HEADED TOWARDS THE DISTURBANCE...
"I GUESS BRIGHT WAS NEVER MY LONG SUIT...
"SEVERAL HUNDRED YARDS IN, I ENTERED AN OPEN AREA MARKED BY A CLASSICALLY-DESIGNED COLUMN...
"BEYOND THE COLUMN STOOD THE ENTRANCE TO A CAVERN--
"--THE SOURCE, IT SEEMED, OF THOSE INCREDIBLE ENERGIES...
"HEART POUNDING, I STEPPED INTO THE DARKNESS--
"--AND IMMEDIATELY WISHED I HADN'T!
"BEFORE ME, A SQUAD OF WOMAN WARRIORS STRUGGLED AGAINST THE MULTI-HANDED MONSTER WHO SOUGHT TO ESCAPE THROUGH THE CRACKS IN DOOM'S DOORWAY...
"I LATER LEARNED THE MONSTER'S NAME WAS COTTUS...
14

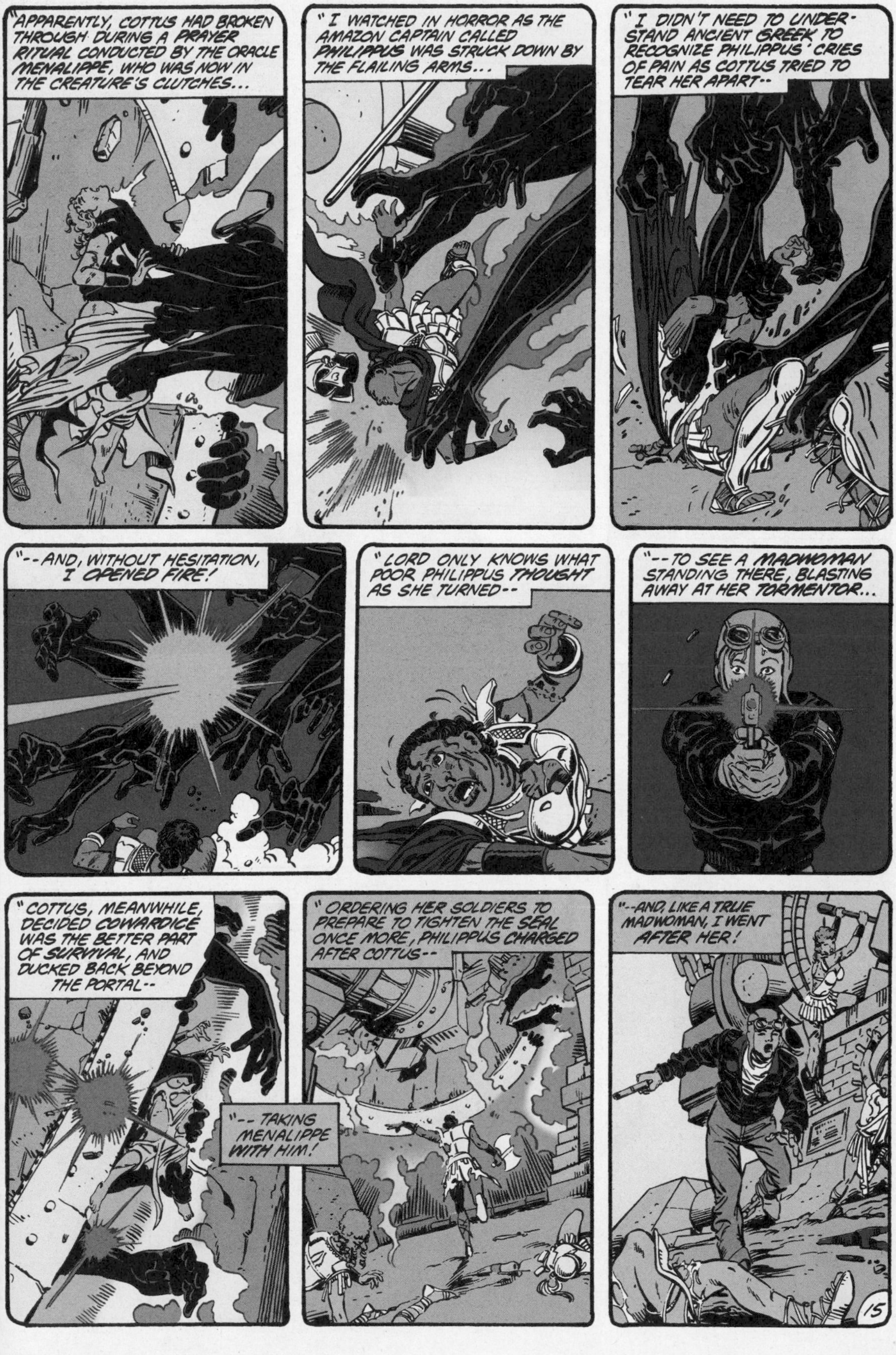
"APPARENTLY, COTTUS HAD BROKEN THROUGH DURING A PRAYER RITUAL CONDUCTED BY THE ORACLE MENALIPPE, WHO WAS NOW IN THE CREATURE'S CLUTCHES...
"I WATCHED IN HORROR AS THE AMAZON CAPTAIN CALLED PHILIPPUS WAS STRUCK DOWN BY THE FLAILING ARMS...
"I DIDN'T NEED TO UNDERSTAND ANCIENT GREEK TO RECOGNIZE PHILIPPUS' CRIES OF PAIN AS COTTUS TRIED TO TEAR HER APART--
"--AND, WITHOUT HESITATION, I OPENED FIRE!
"LORD ONLY KNOWS WHAT POOR PHILIPPUS THOUGHT AS SHE TURNED--
"--TO SEE A MADWOMAN STANDING THERE, BLASTING AWAY AT HER TORMENTOR...
"COTTUS, MEANWHILE, DECIDED COWARDICE WAS THE BETTER PART OF SURVIVAL, AND DUCKED BACK BEYOND THE PORTAL--
"--TAKING MENALIPPE WITH HIM!
"ORDERING HER SOLDIERS TO PREPARE TO TIGHTEN THE SEAL ONCE MORE, PHILIPPUS CHARGED AFTER COTTUS--
"--AND, LIKE A TRUE MADWOMAN, I WENT AFTER HER!
15

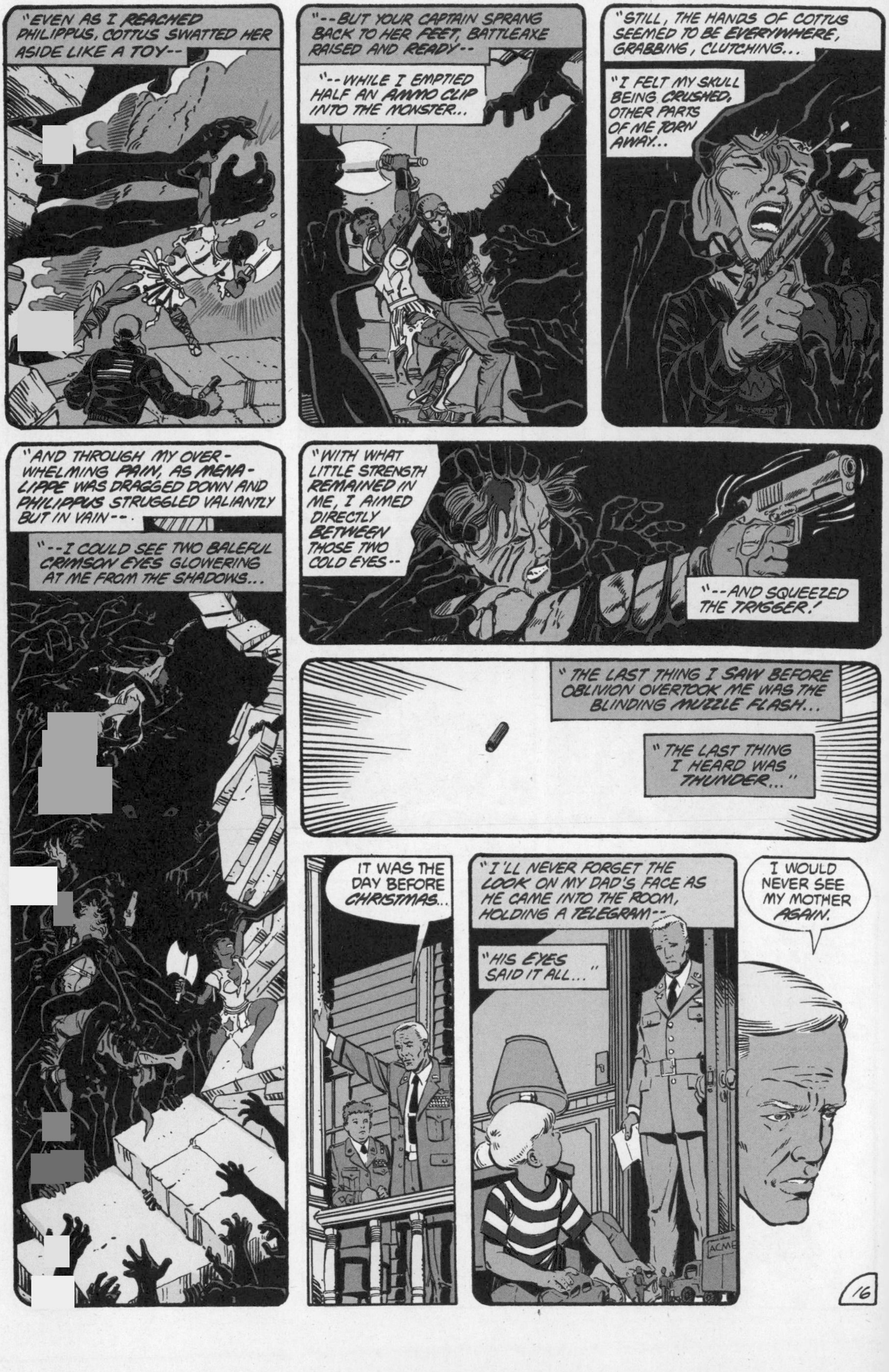
"EVEN AS I REACHED PHILIPPUS, COTTUS SWATTED HER ASIDE LIKE A TOY--
"--BUT YOUR CAPTAIN SPRANG BACK TO HER FEET, BATTLEAXE RAISED AND READY--
"--WHILE I EMPTIED HALF AN AMMO CLIP INTO THE MONSTER...
"STILL, THE HANDS OF COTTUS SEEMED TO BE EVERYWHERE, GRABBING, CLUTCHING...
"I FELT MY SKULL BEING CRUSHED, OTHER PARTS OF ME TORN AWAY...
"AND THROUGH MY OVER-WHELMING PAIN, AS MENA-LIPPE WAS DRAGGED DOWN AND PHILIPPUS STRUGGLED VALIANTLY BUT IN VAIN--.
"--I COULD SEE TWO BALEFUL CRIMSON EYES GLOWERING AT ME FROM THE SHADOWS...
"WITH WHAT LITTLE STRENGTH REMAINED IN ME, I AIMED DIRECTLY BETWEEN THOSE TWO COLD EYES--
"--AND SQUEEZED THE TRIGGER!
"THE LAST THING I SAW BEFORE OBLIVION OVERTOOK ME WAS THE BLINDING MUZZLE FLASH...
"THE LAST THING I HEARD WAS THUNDER..."
IT WAS THE DAY BEFORE CHRISTMAS...
"I'LL NEVER FORGET THE LOOK ON MY DAD'S FACE AS HE CAME INTO THE ROOM, HOLDING A TELEGRAM--
"HIS EYES SAID IT ALL..."
I WOULD NEVER SEE MY MOTHER AGAIN.
ACME
16

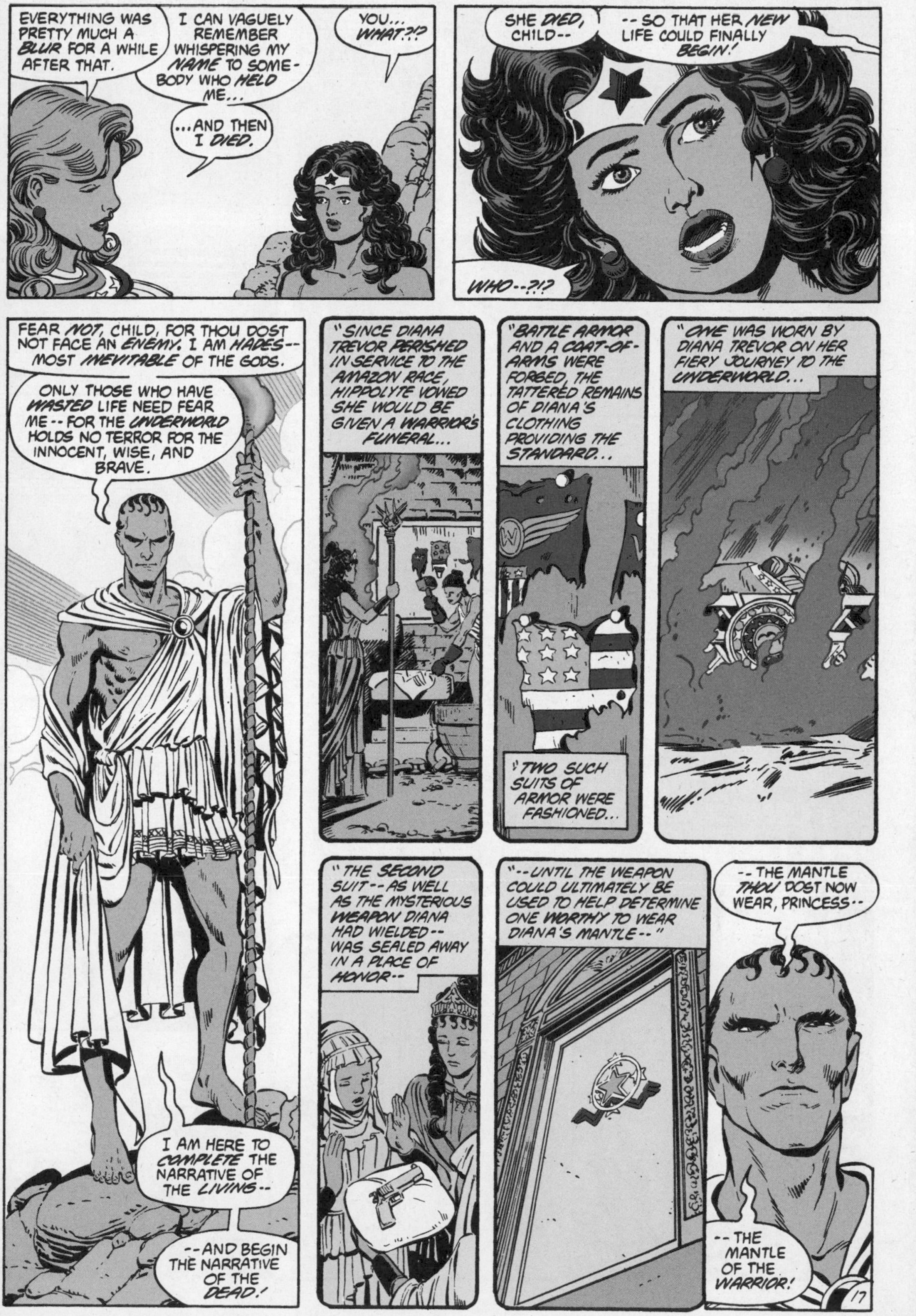
EVERYTHING WAS PRETTY MUCH A BLUR FOR A WHILE AFTER THAT.
I CAN VAGUELY REMEMBER WHISPERING MY NAME TO SOMEBODY WHO HELD ME...
...AND THEN I DIED.
YOU... WHAT?!?
SHE DIED, CHILD--
-- SO THAT HER NEW LIFE COULD FINALLY BEGIN!
WHO--?!?
FEAR NOT, CHILD, FOR THOU DOST NOT FACE AN ENEMY. I AM HADES-- MOST INEVITABLE OF THE GODS.
ONLY THOSE WHO HAVE WASTED LIFE NEED FEAR ME -- FOR THE UNDERWORLD HOLDS NO TERROR FOR THE INNOCENT, WISE, AND BRAVE.
I AM HERE TO COMPLETE THE NARRATIVE OF THE LIVING--
--AND BEGIN THE NARRATIVE OF THE DEAD!
"SINCE DIANA TREVOR PERISHED IN SERVICE TO THE AMAZON RACE, HIPPOLYTE VOWED SHE WOULD BE GIVEN A WARRIOR'S FUNERAL...
"BATTLE ARMOR AND A COAT-OF-ARMS WERE FORGED, THE TATTERED REMAINS OF DIANA'S CLOTHING PROVIDING THE STANDARD...
"TWO SUCH SUITS OF ARMOR WERE FASHIONED...
"ONE WAS WORN BY DIANA TREVOR ON HER FIERY JOURNEY TO THE UNDERWORLD...
"THE SECOND SUIT--AS WELL AS THE MYSTERIOUS WEAPON DIANA HAD WIELDED--WAS SEALED AWAY IN A PLACE OF HONOR--
"--UNTIL THE WEAPON COULD ULTIMATELY BE USED TO HELP DETERMINE ONE WORTHY TO WEAR DIANA'S MANTLE--"
--THE MANTLE THOU DOST NOW WEAR, PRINCESS--
--THE MANTLE OF THE WARRIOR!
17

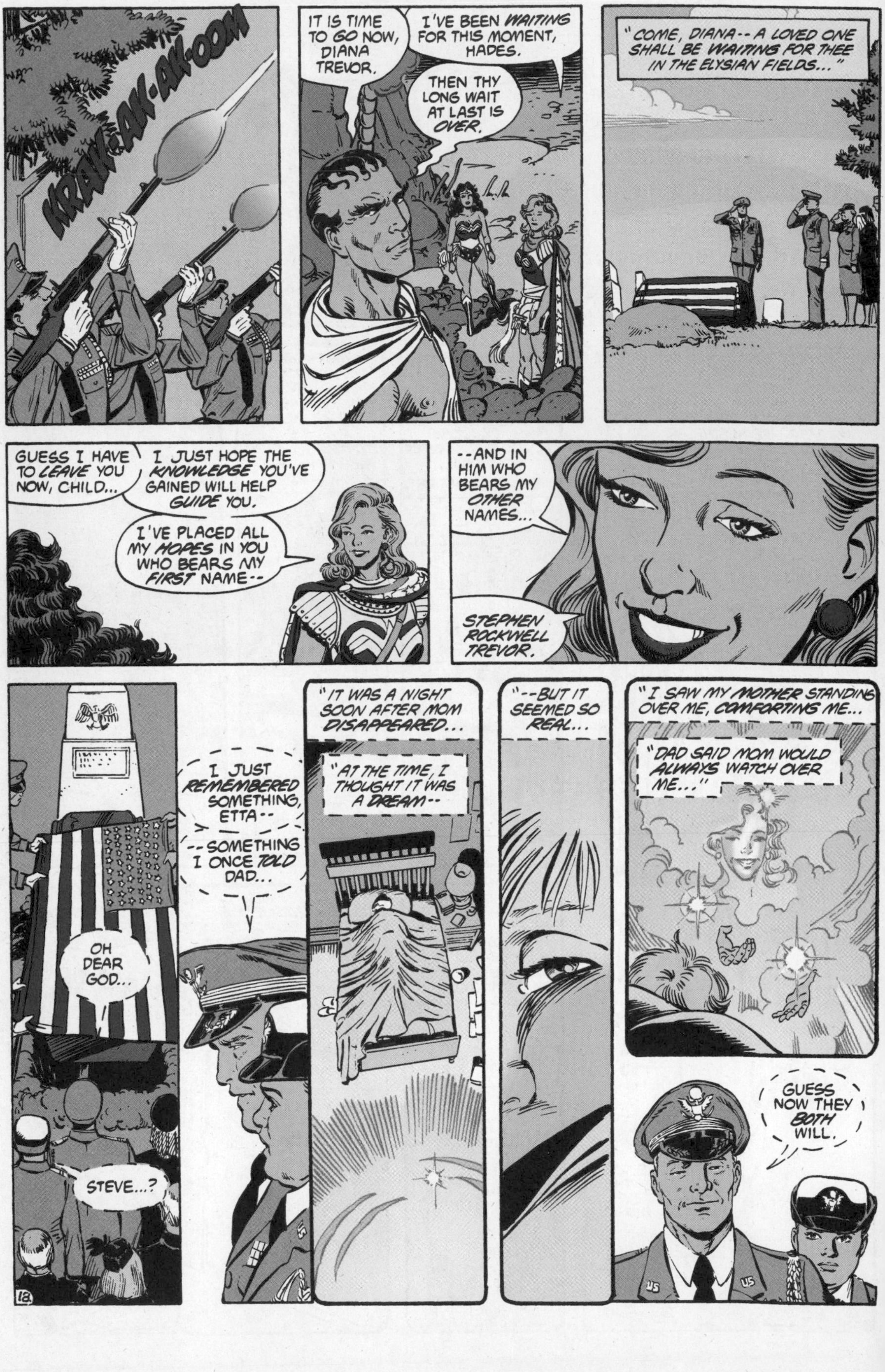
KRAK-AK-AK-OOM
IT IS TIME TO GO NOW, DIANA TREVOR.
I'VE BEEN WAITING FOR THIS MOMENT, HADES.
THEN THY LONG WAIT AT LAST IS OVER.
"COME, DIANA-- A LOVED ONE SHALL BE WAITING FOR THEE IN THE ELYSIAN FIELDS..."
GUESS I HAVE TO LEAVE YOU NOW, CHILD...
I JUST HOPE THE KNOWLEDGE YOU'VE GAINED WILL HELP GUIDE YOU.
I'VE PLACED ALL MY HOPES IN YOU WHO BEARS MY FIRST NAME--
--AND IN HIM WHO BEARS MY OTHER NAMES...
STEPHEN ROCKWELL TREVOR.
OH DEAR GOD...
STEVE...?
I JUST REMEMBERED SOMETHING, ETTA--
--SOMETHING I ONCE TOLD DAD...
"IT WAS A NIGHT SOON AFTER MOM DISAPPEARED...
"AT THE TIME, I THOUGHT IT WAS A DREAM--
"--BUT IT SEEMED SO REAL...
"I SAW MY MOTHER STANDING OVER ME, COMFORTING ME...
"DAD SAID MOM WOULD ALWAYS WATCH OVER ME..."
GUESS NOW THEY BOTH WILL.
18

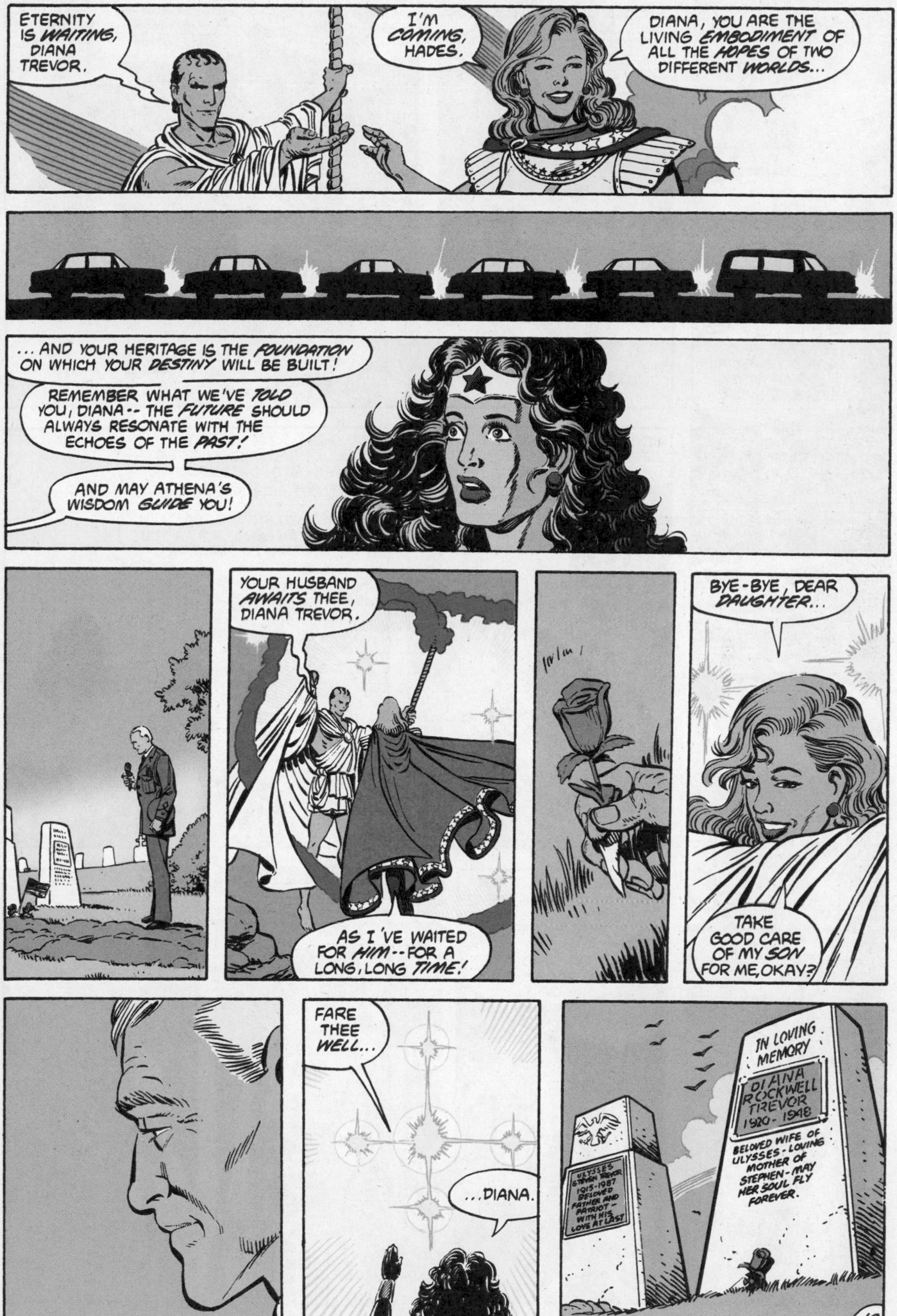
ETERNITY IS WAITING, DIANA TREVOR.
I'M COMING, HADES.
DIANA, YOU ARE THE LIVING EMBODIMENT OF ALL THE HOPES OF TWO DIFFERENT WORLDS...
... AND YOUR HERITAGE IS THE FOUNDATION ON WHICH YOUR DESTINY WILL BE BUILT!
REMEMBER WHAT WE'VE TOLD YOU, DIANA -- THE FUTURE SHOULD ALWAYS RESONATE WITH THE ECHOES OF THE PAST!
AND MAY ATHENA'S WISDOM GUIDE YOU!
YOUR HUSBAND AWAITS THEE, DIANA TREVOR.
AS I'VE WAITED FOR HIM -- FOR A LONG, LONG TIME!
BYE-BYE, DEAR DAUGHTER...
TAKE GOOD CARE OF MY SON FOR ME, OKAY?
FARE THEE WELL...
...DIANA.
ULYSSES STEVEN TREVOR 1915-1987 BELOVED FATHER AND PATRIOT - WITH HIS LOVE AT LAST
IN LOVING MEMORY
DIANA ROCKWELL TREVOR 1920 - 1948
BELOVED WIFE OF ULYSSES - LOVING MOTHER OF STEPHEN - MAY HER SOUL FLY FOREVER.
19

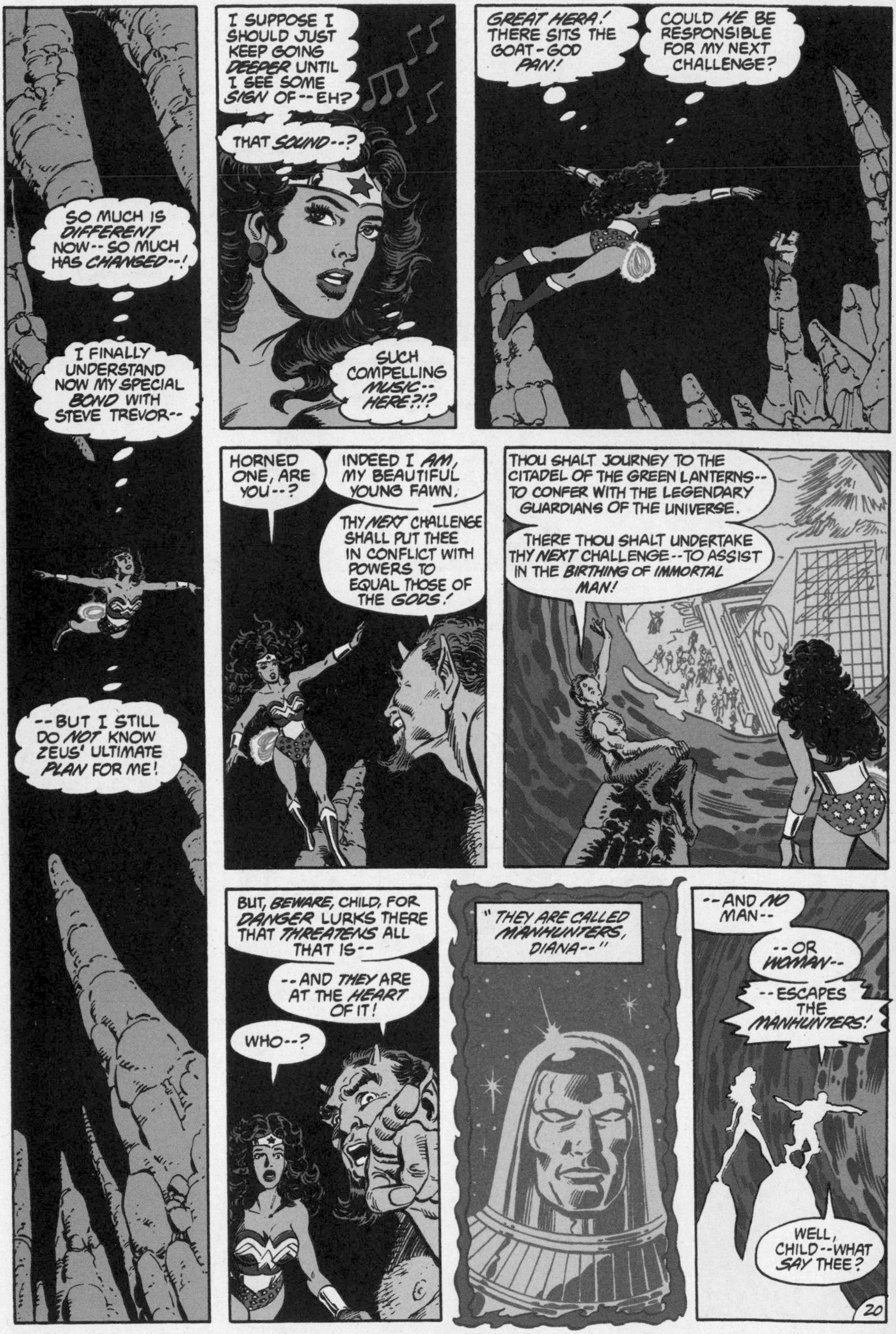
SO MUCH IS DIFFERENT NOW-- SO MUCH HAS CHANGED--!
I FINALLY UNDERSTAND NOW MY SPECIAL BOND WITH STEVE TREVOR--
--BUT I STILL DO NOT KNOW ZEUS' ULTIMATE PLAN FOR ME!
I SUPPOSE I SHOULD JUST KEEP GOING DEEPER UNTIL I SEE SOME SIGN OF--EH?
THAT SOUND--?
SUCH COMPELLING MUSIC-- HERE?!?
GREAT HERA! THERE SITS THE GOAT-GOD PAN!
COULD HE BE RESPONSIBLE FOR MY NEXT CHALLENGE?
HORNED ONE, ARE YOU--?
INDEED I AM, MY BEAUTIFUL YOUNG FAWN.
THY NEXT CHALLENGE SHALL PUT THEE IN CONFLICT WITH POWERS TO EQUAL THOSE OF THE GODS!
THOU SHALT JOURNEY TO THE CITADEL OF THE GREEN LANTERNS-- TO CONFER WITH THE LEGENDARY GUARDIANS OF THE UNIVERSE.
THERE THOU SHALT UNDERTAKE THY NEXT CHALLENGE--TO ASSIST IN THE BIRTHING OF IMMORTAL MAN!
BUT, BEWARE, CHILD, FOR DANGER LURKS THERE THAT THREATENS ALL THAT IS--
--AND THEY ARE AT THE HEART OF IT!
WHO--?
"THEY ARE CALLED MANHUNTERS, DIANA--"
--AND NO MAN--
--OR WOMAN--
--ESCAPES THE MANHUNTERS!
WELL, CHILD--WHAT SAY THEE?
20

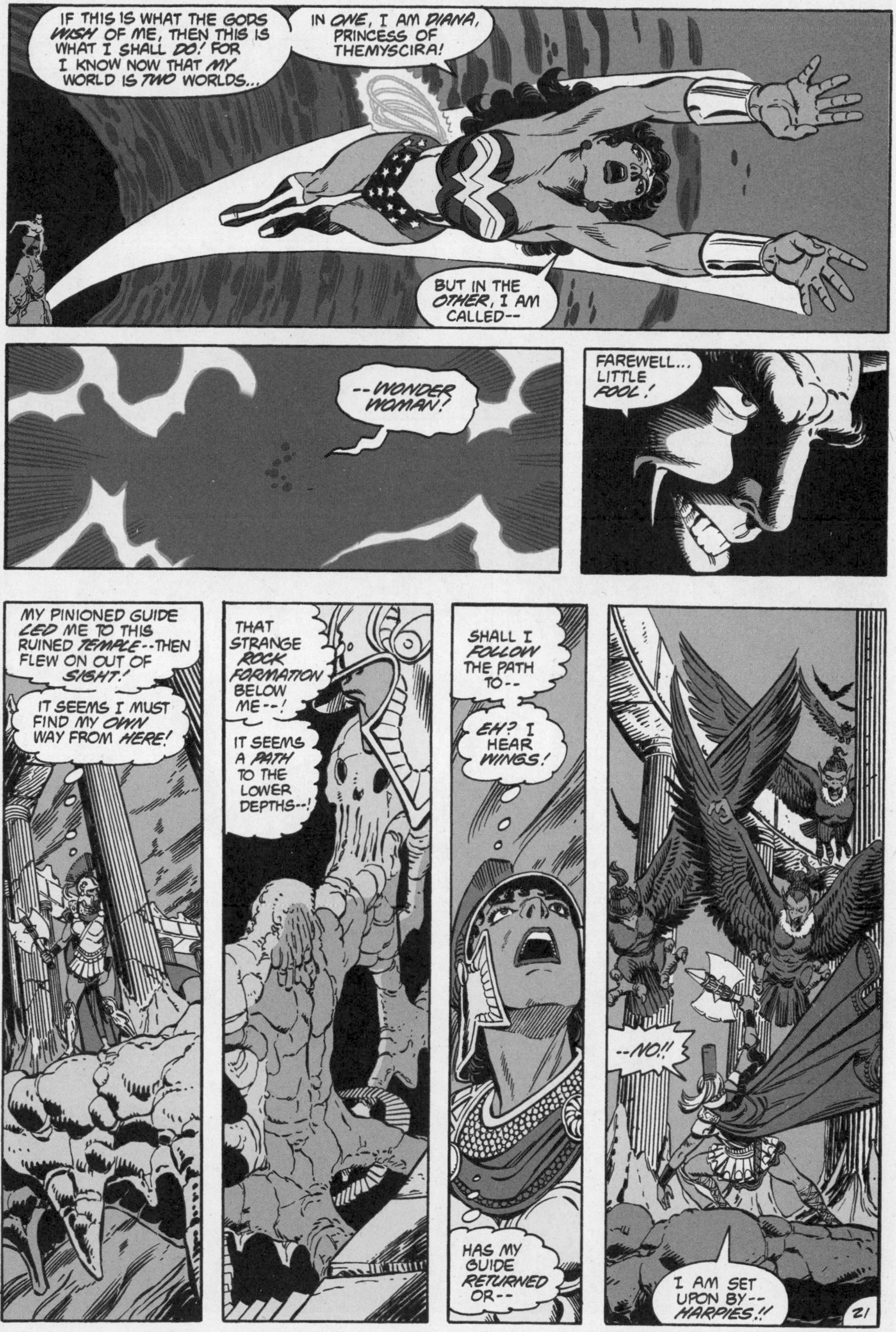
IF THIS IS WHAT THE GODS WISH OF ME, THEN THIS IS WHAT I SHALL DO! FOR I KNOW NOW THAT MY WORLD IS TWO WORLDS...
IN ONE, I AM DIANA, PRINCESS OF THEMYSCIRA!
BUT IN THE OTHER, I AM CALLED--
--WONDER WOMAN!
FAREWELL... LITTLE FOOL!
MY PINIONED GUIDE LED ME TO THIS RUINED TEMPLE--THEN FLEW ON OUT OF SIGHT!
IT SEEMS I MUST FIND MY OWN WAY FROM HERE!
THAT STRANGE ROCK FORMATION BELOW ME--!
IT SEEMS A PATH TO THE LOWER DEPTHS--!
SHALL I FOLLOW THE PATH TO--
EH? I HEAR WINGS!
HAS MY GUIDE RETURNED OR--
--NO!!
I AM SET UPON BY-- HARPIES!!
21

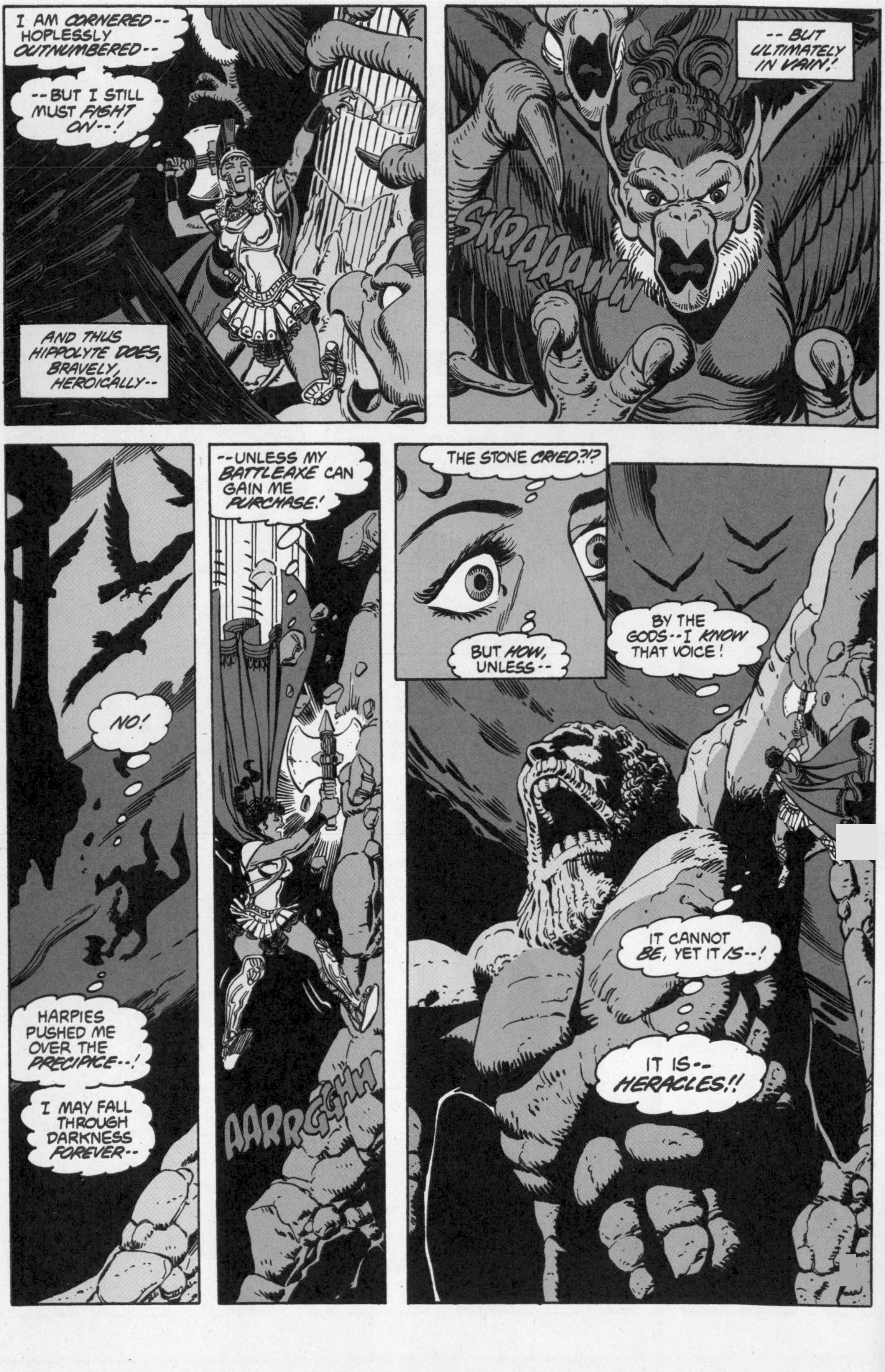
I AM CORNERED-- HOPLESSLY OUTNUMBERED--
--BUT I STILL MUST FIGHT ON--!
AND THUS HIPPOLYTE DOES, BRAVELY, HEROICALLY--
--BUT ULTIMATELY IN VAIN!
SKRAAAAWWW
NO!
HARPIES PUSHED ME OVER THE PRECIPICE--!
I MAY FALL THROUGH DARKNESS FOREVER--
--UNLESS MY BATTLEAXE CAN GAIN ME PURCHASE!
AARRGGHH
THE STONE CRIED?!?
BUT HOW, UNLESS--
BY THE GODS--I KNOW THAT VOICE!
IT CANNOT BE, YET IT IS--!
IT IS-- HERACLES!!

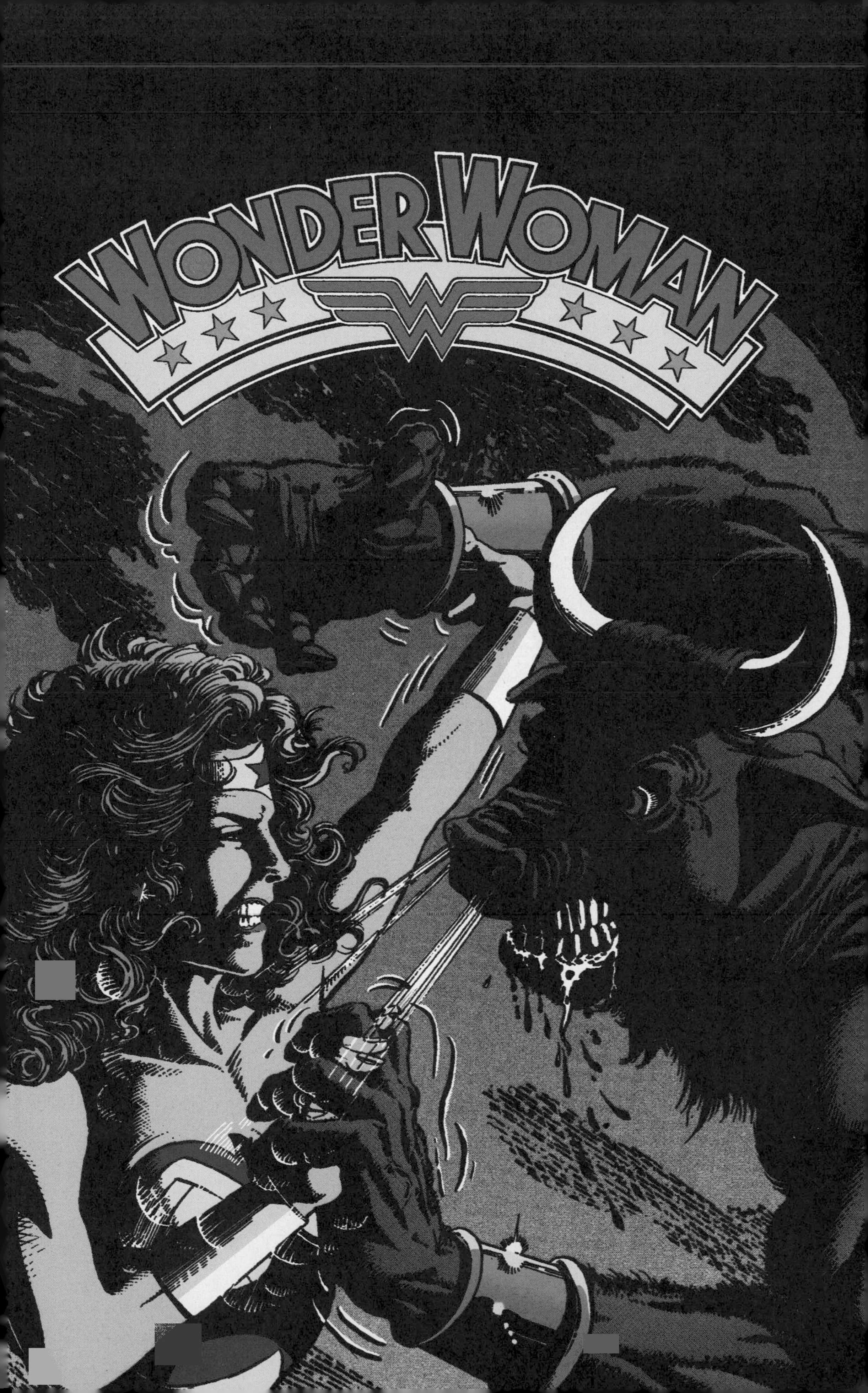
WONDER WOMAN

WONDER WOMAN
CHAPTER SIX

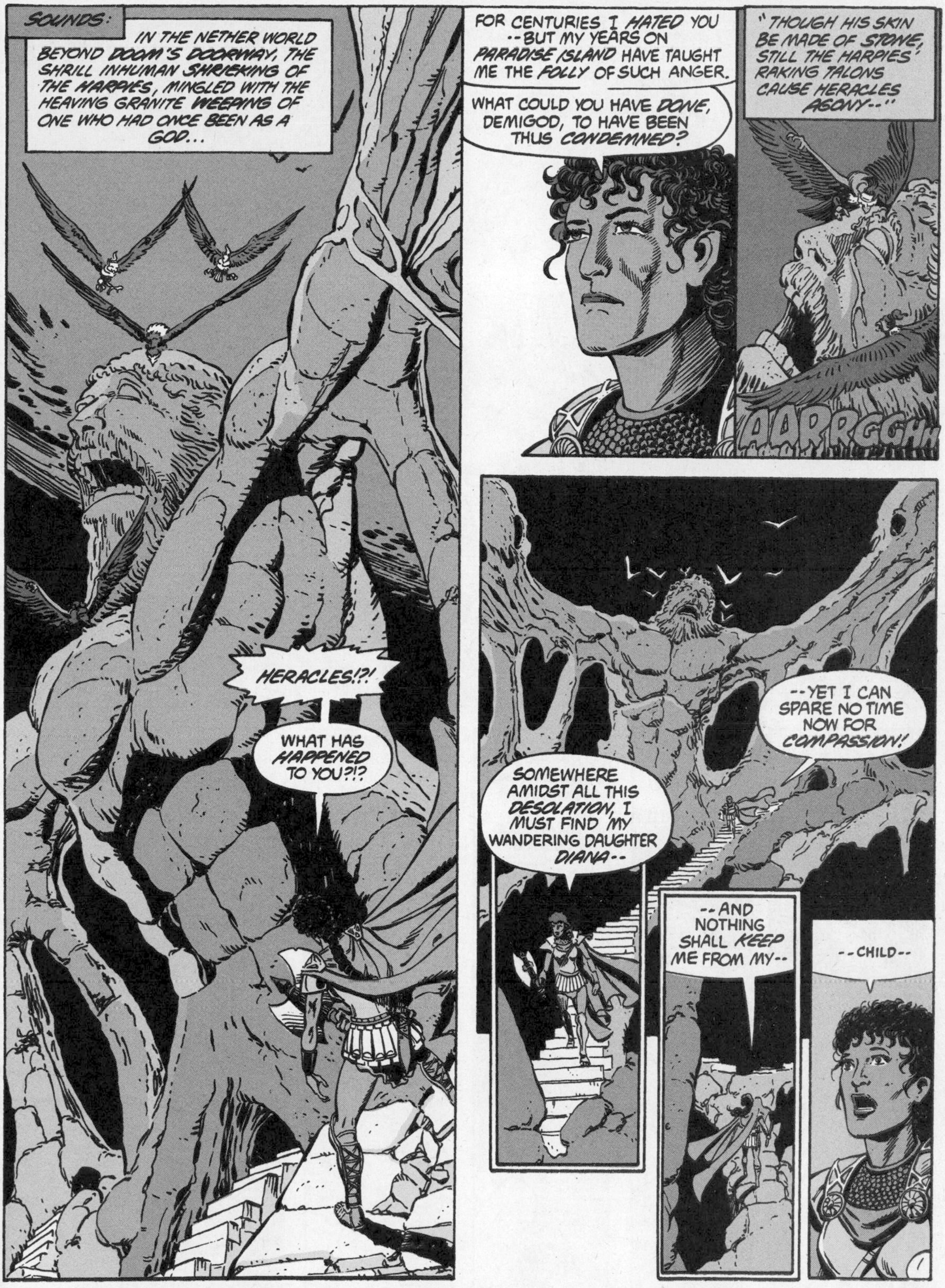
SOUNDS:
IN THE NETHER WORLD BEYOND DOOM'S DOORWAY, THE SHRILL INHUMAN SHRIEKING OF THE HARPIES, MINGLED WITH THE HEAVING GRANITE WEEPING OF ONE WHO HAD ONCE BEEN AS A GOD...
HERACLES!?!
WHAT HAS HAPPENED TO YOU?!?
FOR CENTURIES I HATED YOU --BUT MY YEARS ON PARADISE ISLAND HAVE TAUGHT ME THE FOLLY OF SUCH ANGER.
WHAT COULD YOU HAVE DONE, DEMIGOD, TO HAVE BEEN THUS CONDEMNED?
"THOUGH HIS SKIN BE MADE OF STONE, STILL THE HARPIES' RAKING TALONS CAUSE HERACLES AGONY--"
AARRGGHH
--YET I CAN SPARE NO TIME NOW FOR COMPASSION!
SOMEWHERE AMIDST ALL THIS DESOLATION, I MUST FIND MY WANDERING DAUGHTER DIANA--
--AND NOTHING SHALL KEEP ME FROM MY--
--CHILD--

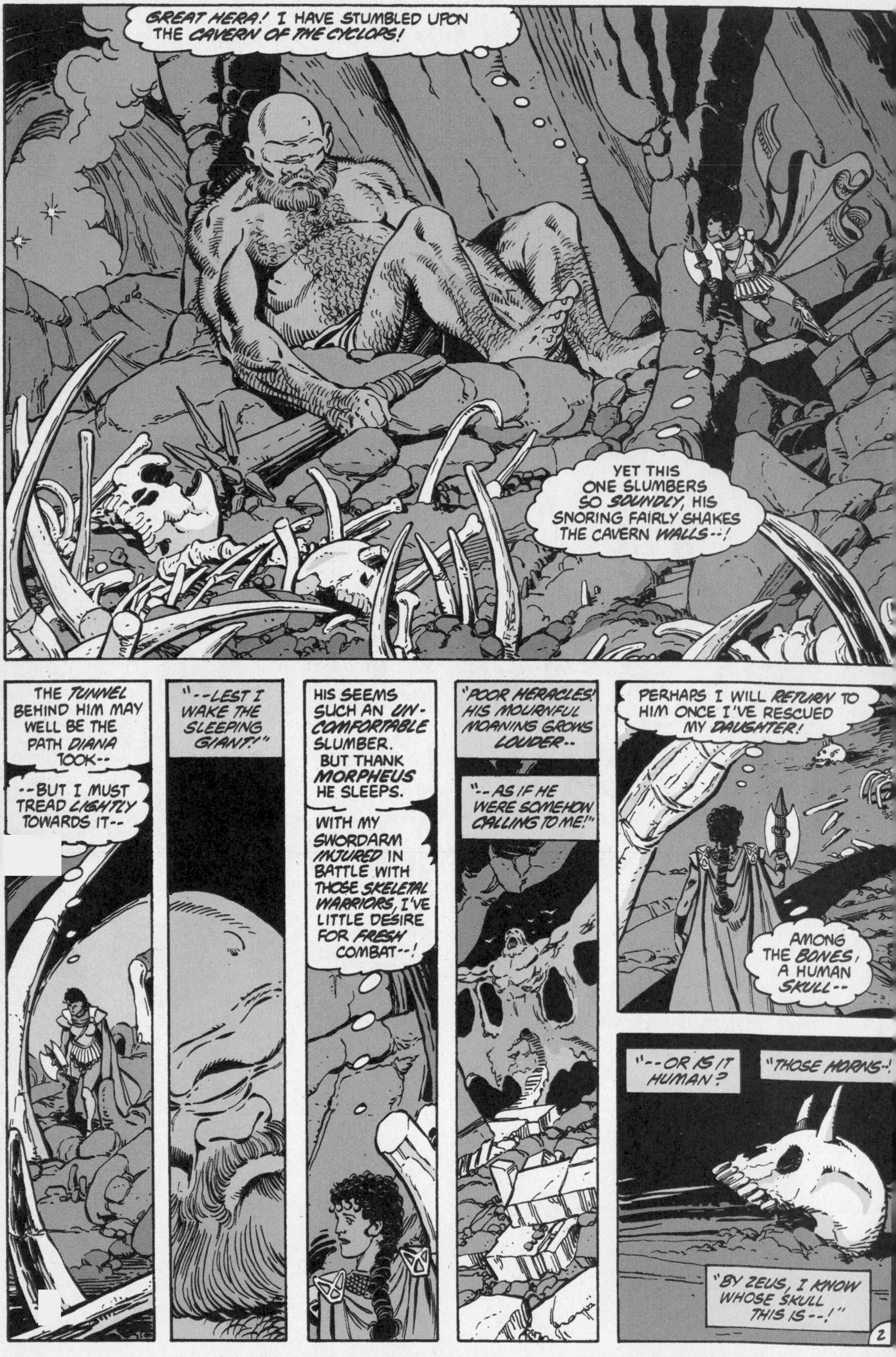
GREAT HERA! I HAVE STUMBLED UPON THE CAVERN OF THE CYCLOPS!
YET THIS ONE SLUMBERS SO SOUNDLY, HIS SNORING FAIRLY SHAKES THE CAVERN WALLS--!
THE TUNNEL BEHIND HIM MAY WELL BE THE PATH DIANA TOOK--
--BUT I MUST TREAD LIGHTLY TOWARDS IT--
"--LEST I WAKE THE SLEEPING GIANT!"
HIS SEEMS SUCH AN UN-COMFORTABLE SLUMBER. BUT THANK MORPHEUS HE SLEEPS.
WITH MY SWORDARM INJURED IN BATTLE WITH THOSE SKELETAL WARRIORS, I'VE LITTLE DESIRE FOR FRESH COMBAT--!
"POOR HERACLES! HIS MOURNFUL MOANING GROWS LOUDER--
"--AS IF HE WERE SOMEHOW CALLING TO ME!"
PERHAPS I WILL RETURN TO HIM ONCE I'VE RESCUED MY DAUGHTER!
AMONG THE BONES, A HUMAN SKULL--
"--OR IS IT HUMAN?
"THOSE HORNS--!
"BY ZEUS, I KNOW WHOSE SKULL THIS IS--!"
2

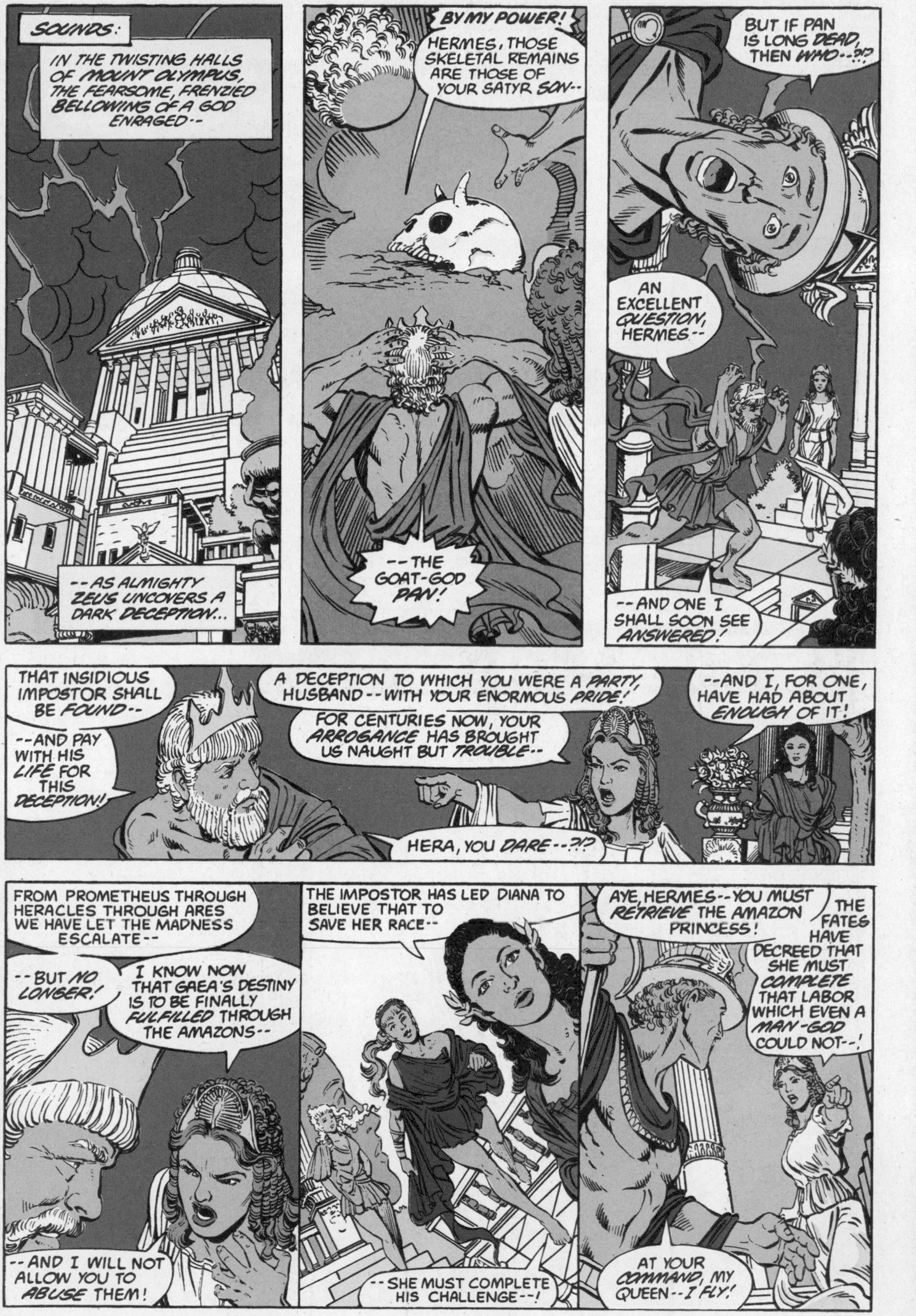
SOUNDS:
IN THE TWISTING HALLS OF MOUNT OLYMPUS, THE FEARSOME, FRENZIED BELLOWING OF A GOD ENRAGED--
--AS ALMIGHTY ZEUS UNCOVERS A DARK DECEPTION...
BY MY POWER!
HERMES, THOSE SKELETAL REMAINS ARE THOSE OF YOUR SATYR SON--
--THE GOAT-GOD PAN!
BUT IF PAN IS LONG DEAD, THEN WHO--?!?
AN EXCELLENT QUESTION, HERMES--
--AND ONE I SHALL SOON SEE ANSWERED!
THAT INSIDIOUS IMPOSTOR SHALL BE FOUND--
--AND PAY WITH HIS LIFE FOR THIS DECEPTION!
A DECEPTION TO WHICH YOU WERE A PARTY, HUSBAND--WITH YOUR ENORMOUS PRIDE!
FOR CENTURIES NOW, YOUR ARROGANCE HAS BROUGHT US NAUGHT BUT TROUBLE--
HERA, YOU DARE--?!?
--AND I, FOR ONE, HAVE HAD ABOUT ENOUGH OF IT!
FROM PROMETHEUS THROUGH HERACLES THROUGH ARES WE HAVE LET THE MADNESS ESCALATE--
--BUT NO LONGER!
I KNOW NOW THAT GAEA'S DESTINY IS TO BE FINALLY FULFILLED THROUGH THE AMAZONS--
--AND I WILL NOT ALLOW YOU TO ABUSE THEM!
THE IMPOSTOR HAS LED DIANA TO BELIEVE THAT TO SAVE HER RACE--
--SHE MUST COMPLETE HIS CHALLENGE--!
AYE, HERMES--YOU MUST RETRIEVE THE AMAZON PRINCESS!
THE FATES HAVE DECREED THAT SHE MUST COMPLETE THAT LABOR WHICH EVEN A MAN-GOD COULD NOT--!
AT YOUR COMMAND, MY QUEEN--I FLY!

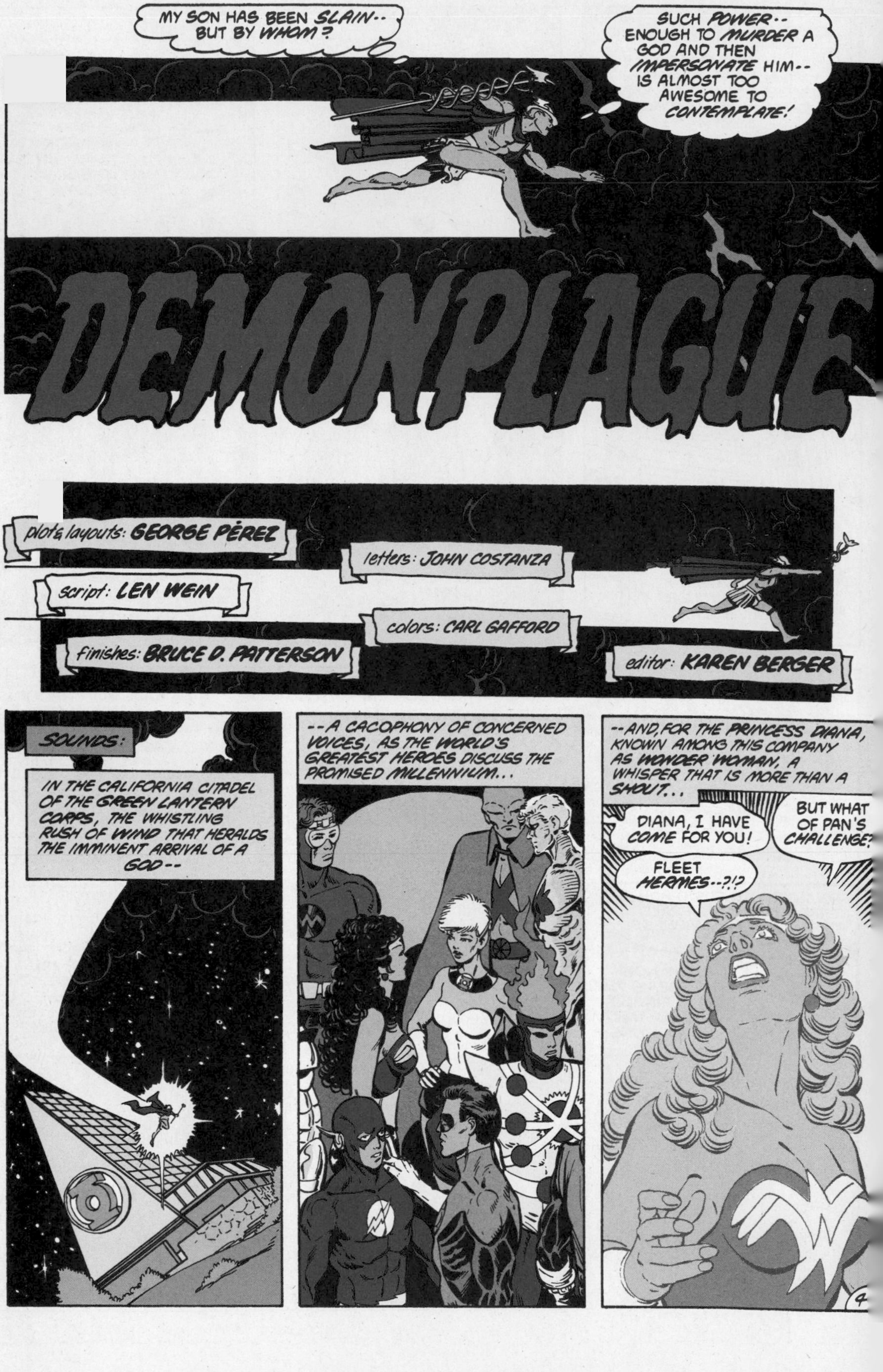

MY SON HAS BEEN SLAIN-- BUT BY WHOM?
SUCH POWER-- ENOUGH TO MURDER A GOD AND THEN IMPERSONATE HIM-- IS ALMOST TOO AWESOME TO CONTEMPLATE!
DEMONPLAGUE
plot & layouts: GEORGE PÉREZ
script: LEN WEIN
finishes: BRUCE D. PATTERSON
letters: JOHN COSTANZA
colors: CARL GAFFORD
editor: KAREN BERGER
SOUNDS:
IN THE CALIFORNIA CITADEL OF THE GREEN LANTERN CORPS, THE WHISTLING RUSH OF WIND THAT HERALDS THE IMMINENT ARRIVAL OF A GOD--
--A CACOPHONY OF CONCERNED VOICES, AS THE WORLD'S GREATEST HEROES DISCUSS THE PROMISED MILLENNIUM...
--AND, FOR THE PRINCESS DIANA, KNOWN AMONG THIS COMPANY AS WONDER WOMAN, A WHISPER THAT IS MORE THAN A SHOUT...
DIANA, I HAVE COME FOR YOU!
BUT WHAT OF PAN'S CHALLENGE?
FLEET HERMES--?!?
4

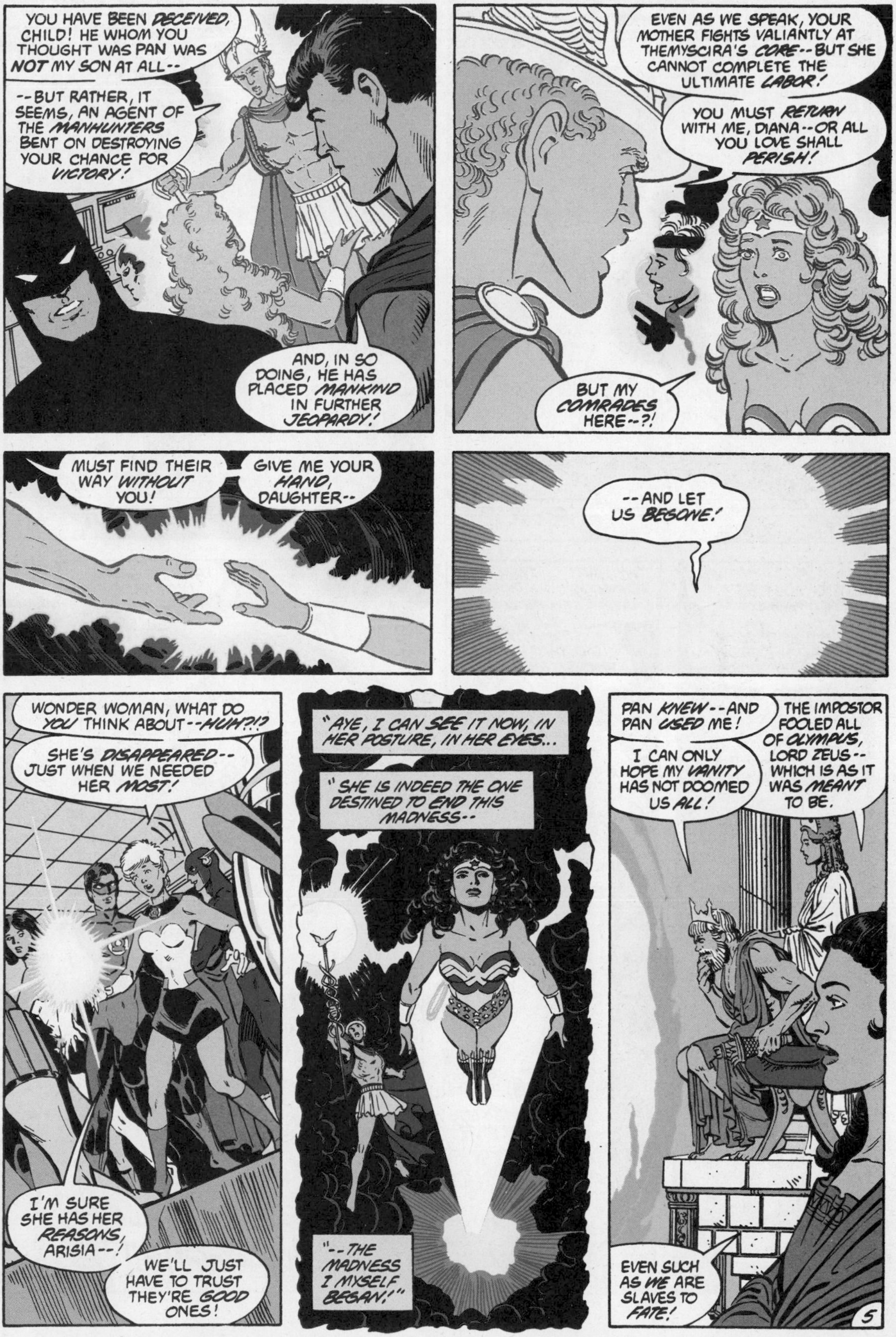

YOU HAVE BEEN DECEIVED, CHILD! HE WHOM YOU THOUGHT WAS PAN WAS NOT MY SON AT ALL--
--BUT RATHER, IT SEEMS, AN AGENT OF THE MANHUNTERS BENT ON DESTROYING YOUR CHANCE FOR VICTORY!
AND, IN SO DOING, HE HAS PLACED MANKIND IN FURTHER JEOPARDY!
EVEN AS WE SPEAK, YOUR MOTHER FIGHTS VALIANTLY AT THEMYSCIRA'S CORE--BUT SHE CANNOT COMPLETE THE ULTIMATE LABOR!
YOU MUST RETURN WITH ME, DIANA--OR ALL YOU LOVE SHALL PERISH!
BUT MY COMRADES HERE--?!
MUST FIND THEIR WAY WITHOUT YOU!
GIVE ME YOUR HAND, DAUGHTER--
--AND LET US BEGONE!
WONDER WOMAN, WHAT DO YOU THINK ABOUT--HUH?!?
SHE'S DISAPPEARED--JUST WHEN WE NEEDED HER MOST!
I'M SURE SHE HAS HER REASONS, ARISIA--!
WE'LL JUST HAVE TO TRUST THEY'RE GOOD ONES!
"AYE, I CAN SEE IT NOW, IN HER POSTURE, IN HER EYES...
"SHE IS INDEED THE ONE DESTINED TO END THIS MADNESS--
"--THE MADNESS I MYSELF BEGAN!"
PAN KNEW--AND PAN USED ME!
I CAN ONLY HOPE MY VANITY HAS NOT DOOMED US ALL!
THE IMPOSTOR FOOLED ALL OF OLYMPUS, LORD ZEUS--WHICH IS AS IT WAS MEANT TO BE.
EVEN SUCH AS WE ARE SLAVES TO FATE!
5

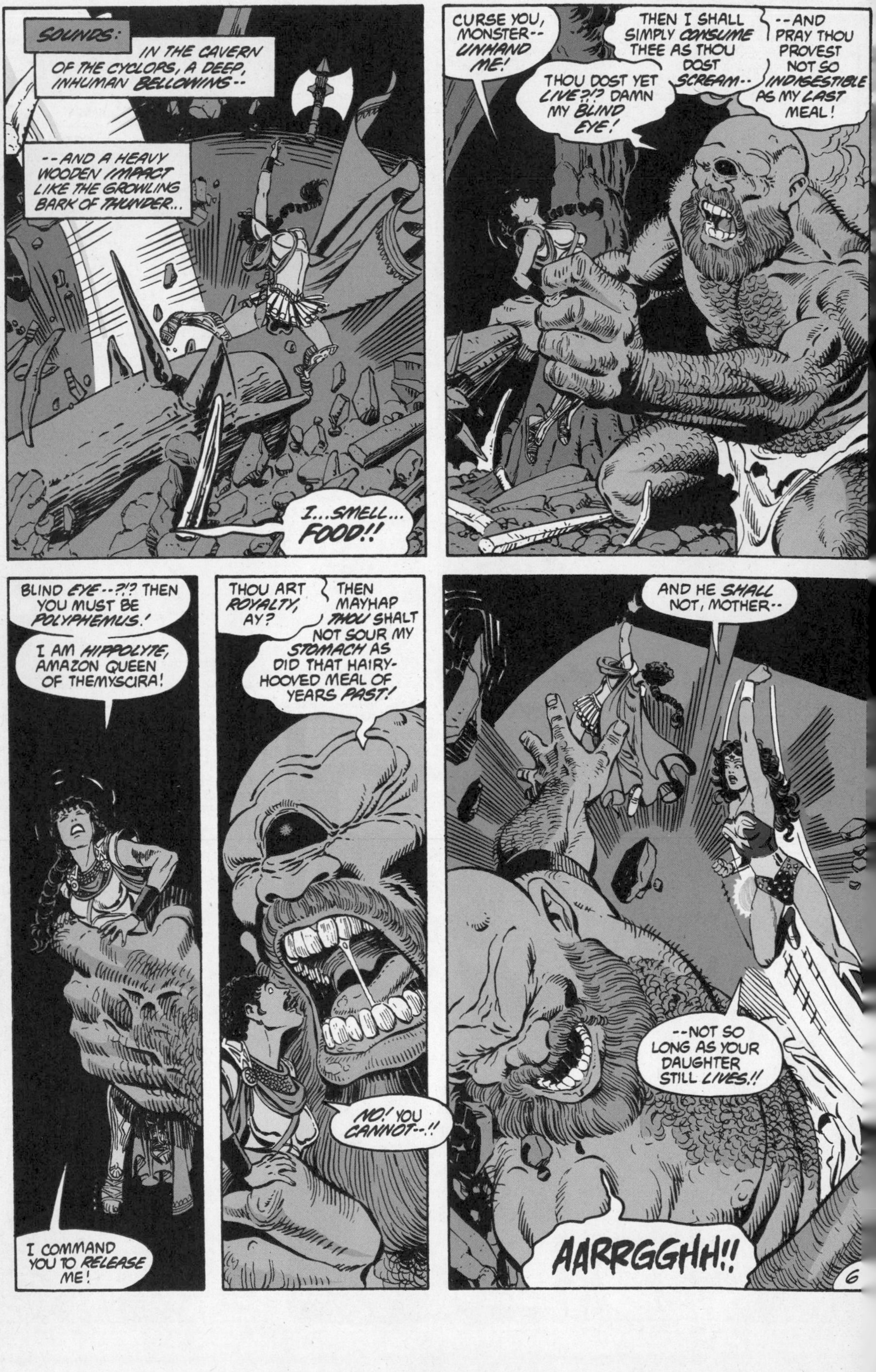
SOUNDS:
IN THE CAVERN OF THE CYCLOPS, A DEEP, INHUMAN BELLOWING--
--AND A HEAVY WOODEN IMPACT LIKE THE GROWLING BARK OF THUNDER...
I...SMELL... FOOD!!
CURSE YOU, MONSTER-- UNHAND ME!
THOU DOST YET LIVE?!? DAMN MY BLIND EYE!
THEN I SHALL SIMPLY CONSUME THEE AS THOU DOST SCREAM--
--AND PRAY THOU PROVEST NOT SO INDIGESTIBLE AS MY LAST MEAL!
BLIND EYE--?!? THEN YOU MUST BE POLYPHEMUS!
I AM HIPPOLYTE, AMAZON QUEEN OF THEMYSCIRA!
I COMMAND YOU TO RELEASE ME!
THOU ART ROYALTY, AY?
THEN MAYHAP THOU SHALT NOT SOUR MY STOMACH AS DID THAT HAIRY-HOOVED MEAL OF YEARS PAST!
NO! YOU CANNOT--!!
AND HE SHALL NOT, MOTHER--
--NOT SO LONG AS YOUR DAUGHTER STILL LIVES!!
AARRGGHH!!
6

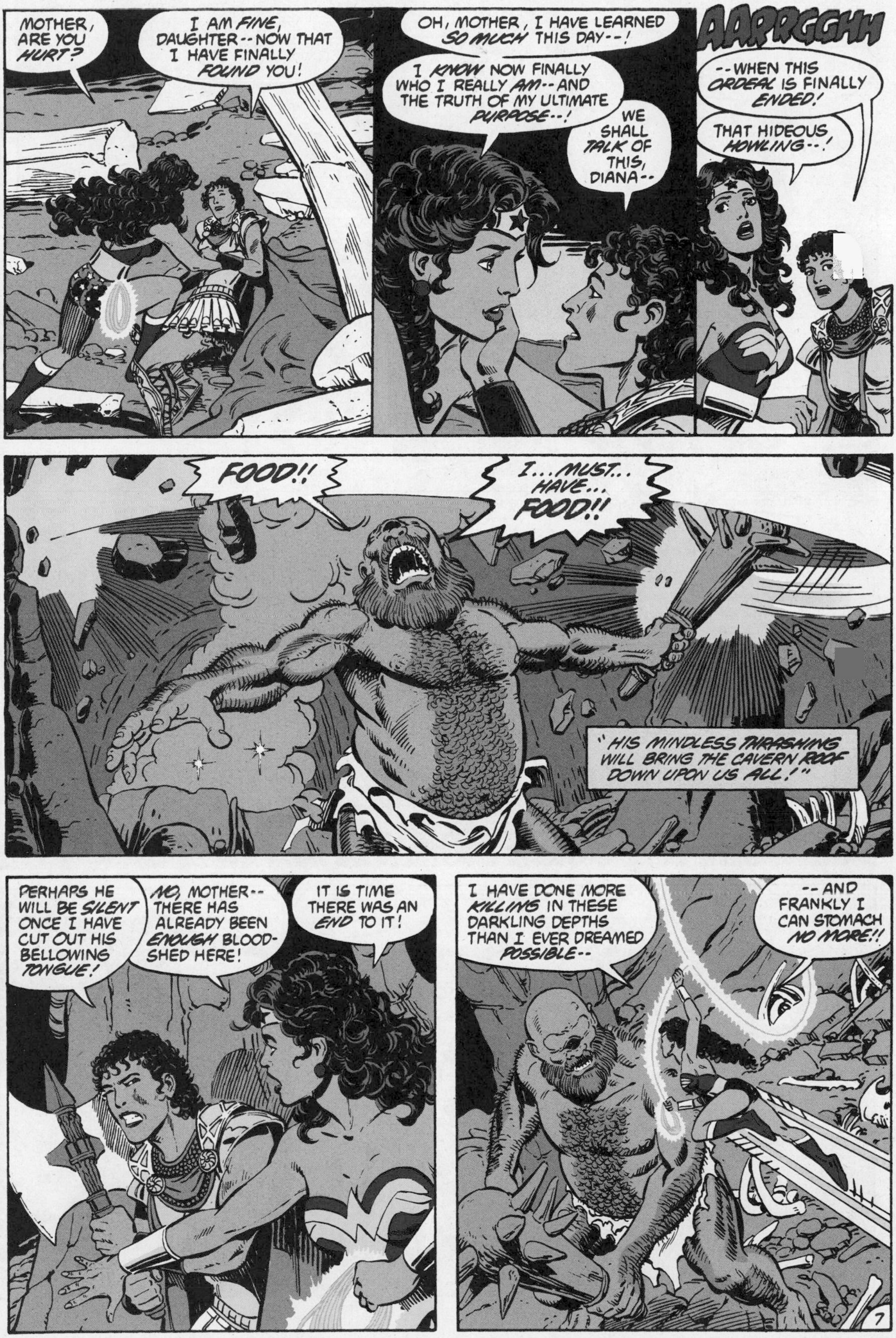
MOTHER, ARE YOU HURT?
I AM FINE, DAUGHTER--NOW THAT I HAVE FINALLY FOUND YOU!
OH, MOTHER, I HAVE LEARNED SO MUCH THIS DAY--!
I KNOW NOW FINALLY WHO I REALLY AM--AND THE TRUTH OF MY ULTIMATE PURPOSE--!
WE SHALL TALK OF THIS, DIANA--
AARRGGHH
--WHEN THIS ORDEAL IS FINALLY ENDED!
THAT HIDEOUS HOWLING--!
FOOD!!
I...MUST... HAVE... FOOD!!
"HIS MINDLESS THRASHING WILL BRING THE CAVERN ROOF DOWN UPON US ALL!"
PERHAPS HE WILL BE SILENT ONCE I HAVE CUT OUT HIS BELLOWING TONGUE!
NO, MOTHER--THERE HAS ALREADY BEEN ENOUGH BLOODSHED HERE!
IT IS TIME THERE WAS AN END TO IT!
I HAVE DONE MORE KILLING IN THESE DARKLING DEPTHS THAN I EVER DREAMED POSSIBLE--
--AND FRANKLY I CAN STOMACH NO MORE!!
7

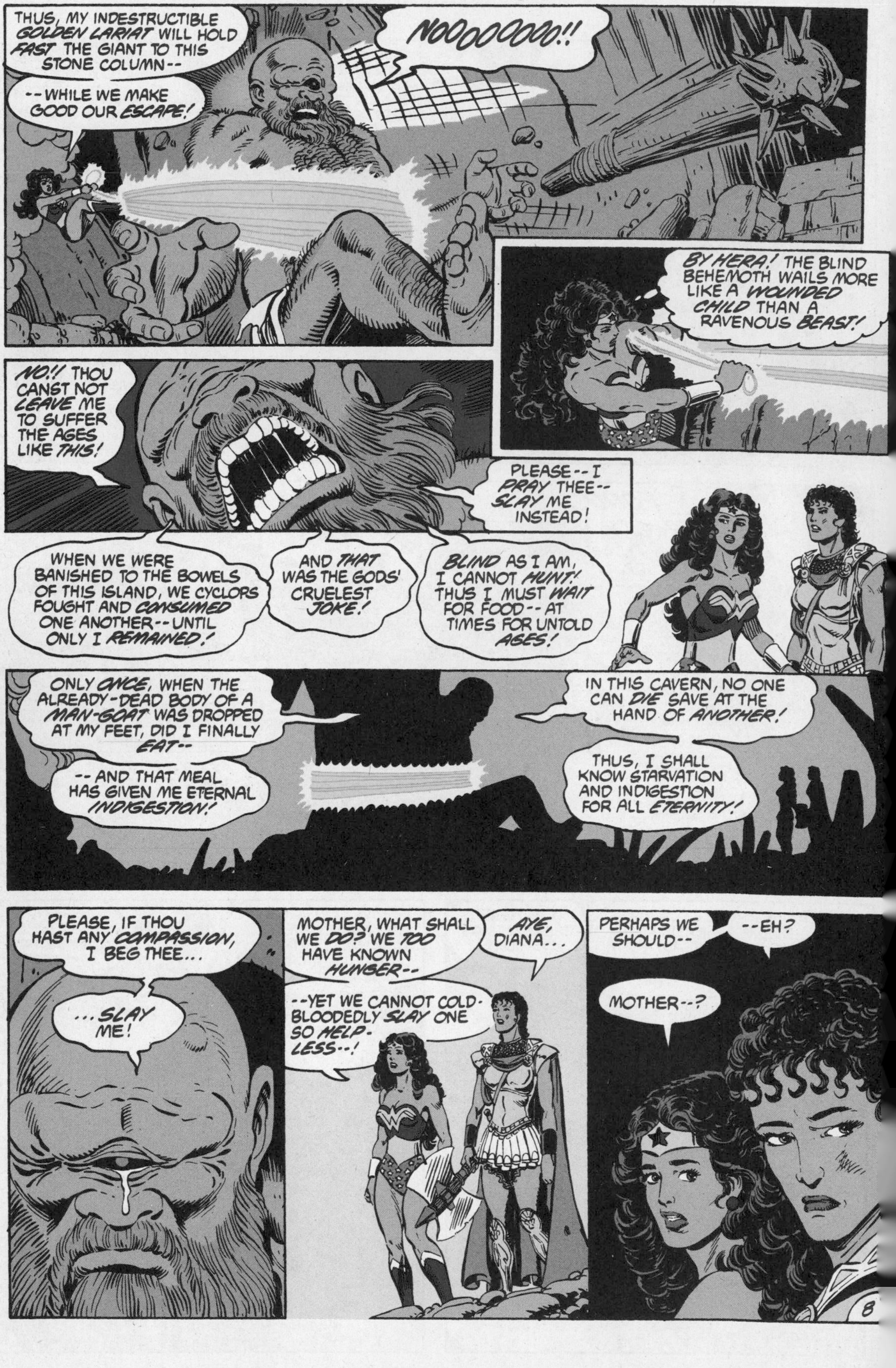
THUS, MY INDESTRUCTIBLE GOLDEN LARIAT WILL HOLD FAST THE GIANT TO THIS STONE COLUMN--
--WHILE WE MAKE GOOD OUR ESCAPE!
NOOOOOOOO!!
BY HERA! THE BLIND BEHEMOTH WAILS MORE LIKE A WOUNDED CHILD THAN A RAVENOUS BEAST!
NO!! THOU CANST NOT LEAVE ME TO SUFFER THE AGES LIKE THIS!
PLEASE--I PRAY THEE--SLAY ME INSTEAD!
WHEN WE WERE BANISHED TO THE BOWELS OF THIS ISLAND, WE CYCLOPS FOUGHT AND CONSUMED ONE ANOTHER--UNTIL ONLY I REMAINED!
AND THAT WAS THE GODS' CRUELEST JOKE!
BLIND AS I AM, I CANNOT HUNT! THUS I MUST WAIT FOR FOOD--AT TIMES FOR UNTOLD AGES!
ONLY ONCE, WHEN THE ALREADY-DEAD BODY OF A MAN-GOAT WAS DROPPED AT MY FEET, DID I FINALLY EAT--
--AND THAT MEAL HAS GIVEN ME ETERNAL INDIGESTION!
IN THIS CAVERN, NO ONE CAN DIE SAVE AT THE HAND OF ANOTHER!
THUS, I SHALL KNOW STARVATION AND INDIGESTION FOR ALL ETERNITY!
PLEASE, IF THOU HAST ANY COMPASSION, I BEG THEE...
...SLAY ME!
MOTHER, WHAT SHALL WE DO? WE TOO HAVE KNOWN HUNGER--
AYE, DIANA...
--YET WE CANNOT COLD-BLOODEDLY SLAY ONE SO HELP-LESS--!
PERHAPS WE SHOULD--
--EH?
MOTHER--?
8

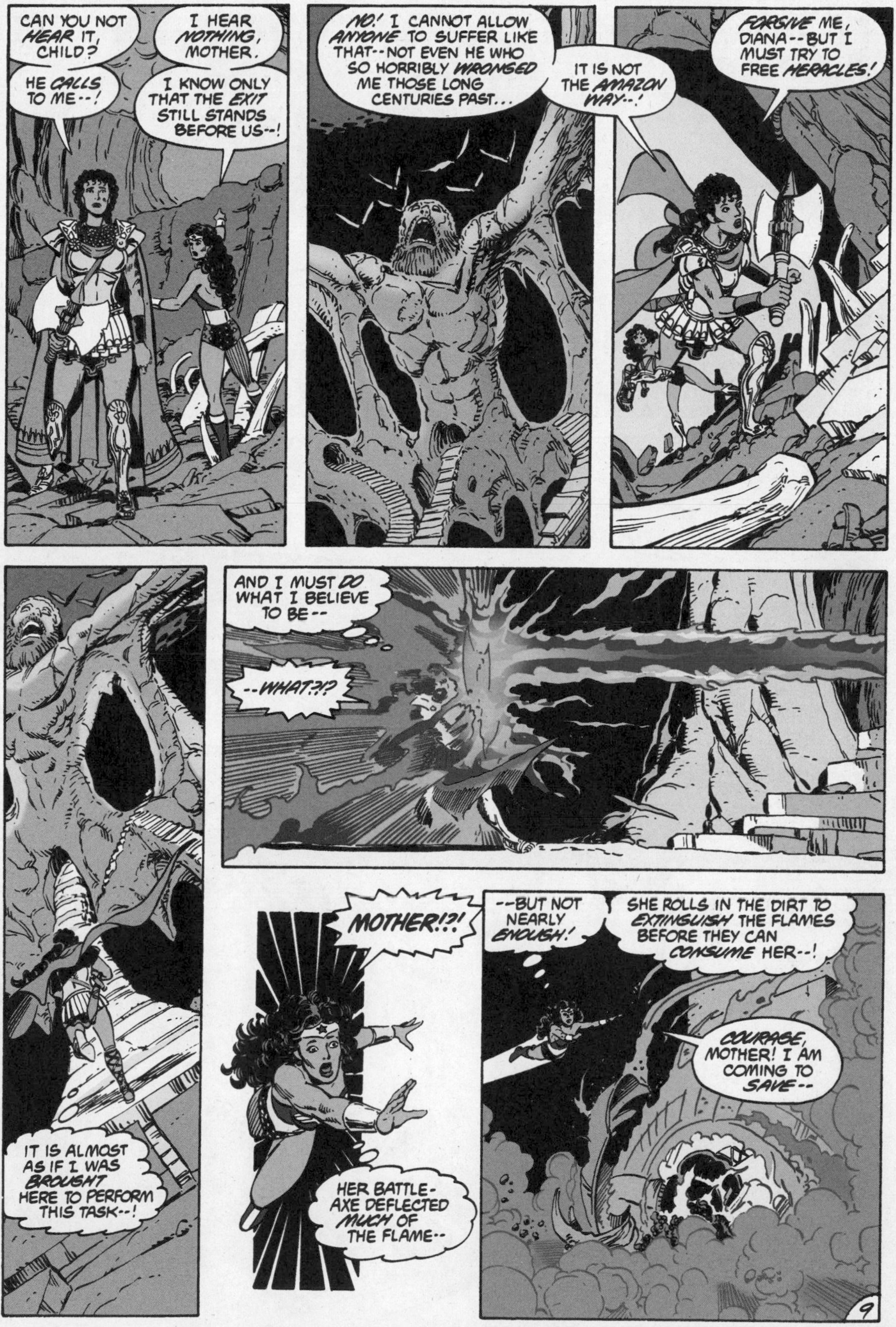
CAN YOU NOT HEAR IT, CHILD?
HE CALLS TO ME--!
I HEAR NOTHING, MOTHER.
I KNOW ONLY THAT THE EXIT STILL STANDS BEFORE US--!
NO! I CANNOT ALLOW ANYONE TO SUFFER LIKE THAT--NOT EVEN HE WHO SO HORRIBLY WRONGED ME THOSE LONG CENTURIES PAST...
IT IS NOT THE AMAZON WAY--!
FORGIVE ME, DIANA--BUT I MUST TRY TO FREE HERACLES!
IT IS ALMOST AS IF I WAS BROUGHT HERE TO PERFORM THIS TASK--!
AND I MUST DO WHAT I BELIEVE TO BE--
--WHAT?!?
MOTHER!?!
HER BATTLE-AXE DEFLECTED MUCH OF THE FLAME--
--BUT NOT NEARLY ENOUGH!
SHE ROLLS IN THE DIRT TO EXTINGUISH THE FLAMES BEFORE THEY CAN CONSUME HER--!
COURAGE, MOTHER! I AM COMING TO SAVE--
9

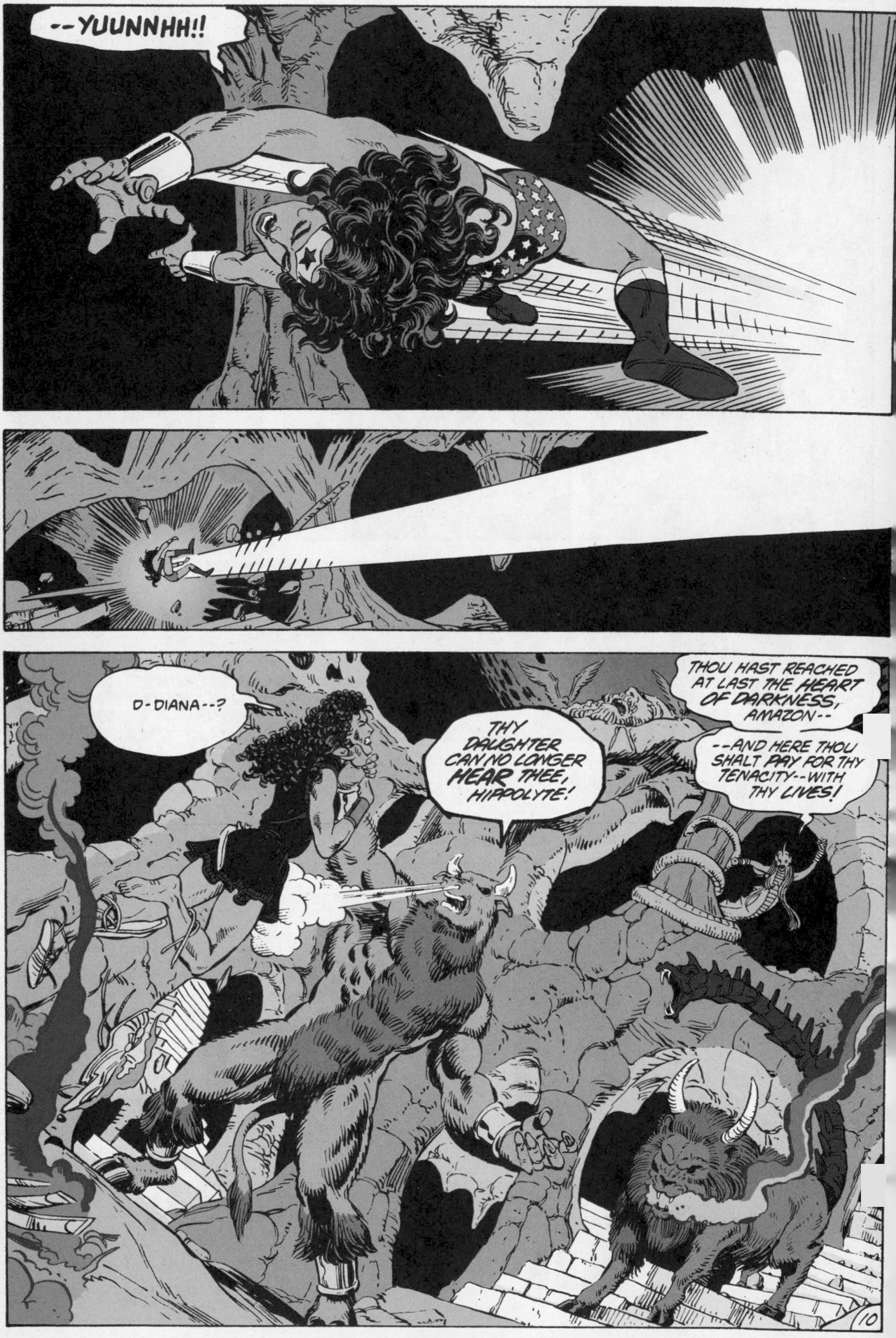
--YUUNNHH!!
D-DIANA--?
THY DAUGHTER CAN NO LONGER HEAR THEE, HIPPOLYTE!
THOU HAST REACHED AT LAST THE HEART OF DARKNESS, AMAZON--
--AND HERE THOU SHALT PAY FOR THY TENACITY--WITH THY LIVES!
10

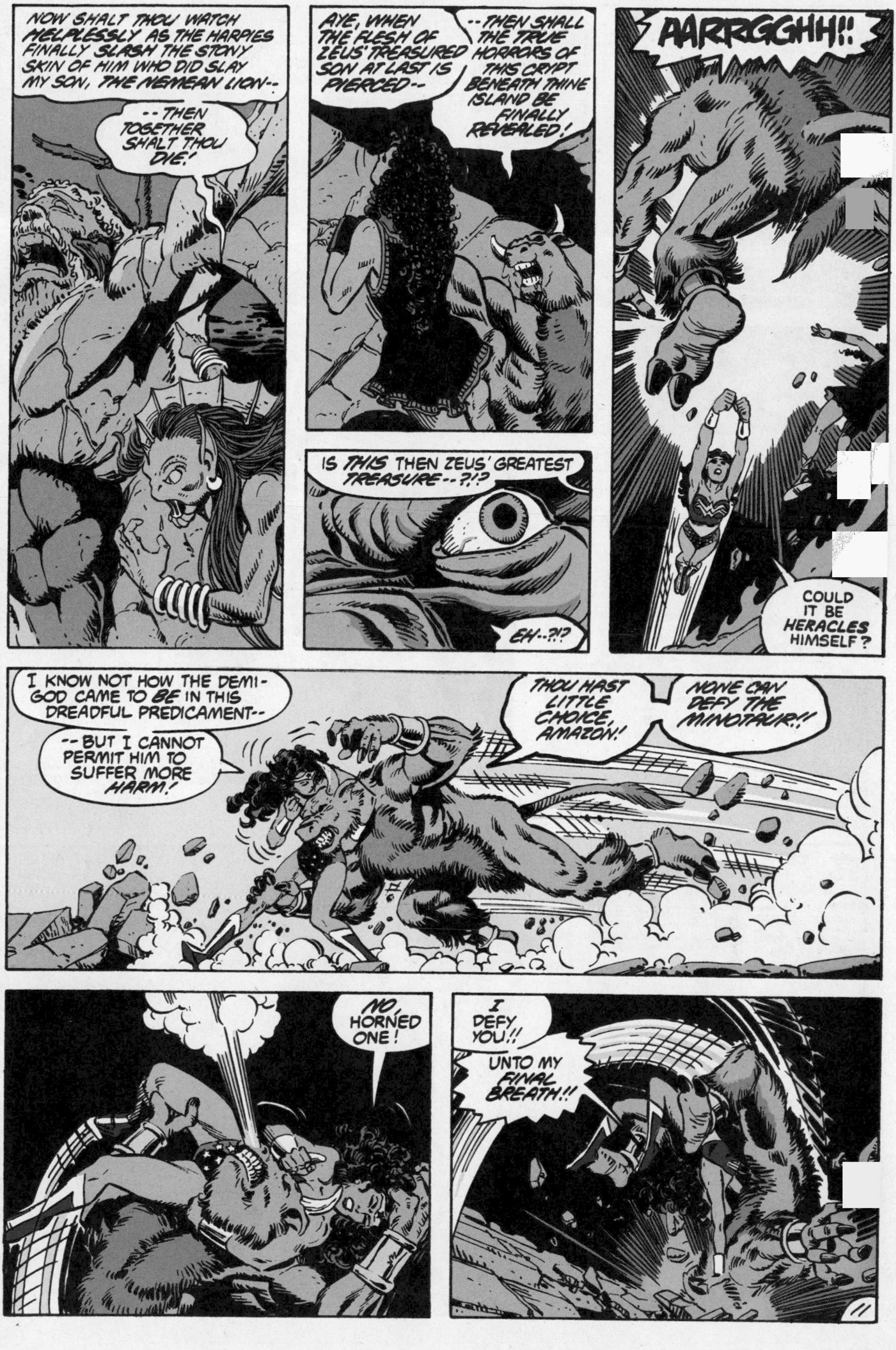
NOW SHALT THOU WATCH HELPLESSLY AS THE HARPIES FINALLY SLASH THE STONY SKIN OF HIM WHO DID SLAY MY SON, THE NEMEAN LION--
--THEN TOGETHER SHALT THOU DIE!
AYE, WHEN THE FLESH OF ZEUS' TREASURED SON AT LAST IS PIERCED--
--THEN SHALL THE TRUE HORRORS OF THIS CRYPT BENEATH THINE ISLAND BE FINALLY REVEALED!
IS THIS THEN ZEUS' GREATEST TREASURE--?!?
EH--?!?
AARRGGHH!!
COULD IT BE HERACLES HIMSELF?
I KNOW NOT HOW THE DEMI-GOD CAME TO BE IN THIS DREADFUL PREDICAMENT--
--BUT I CANNOT PERMIT HIM TO SUFFER MORE HARM!
THOU HAST LITTLE CHOICE, AMAZON!
NONE CAN DEFY THE MINOTAUR!!
NO, HORNED ONE!
I DEFY YOU!!
UNTO MY FINAL BREATH!!
11

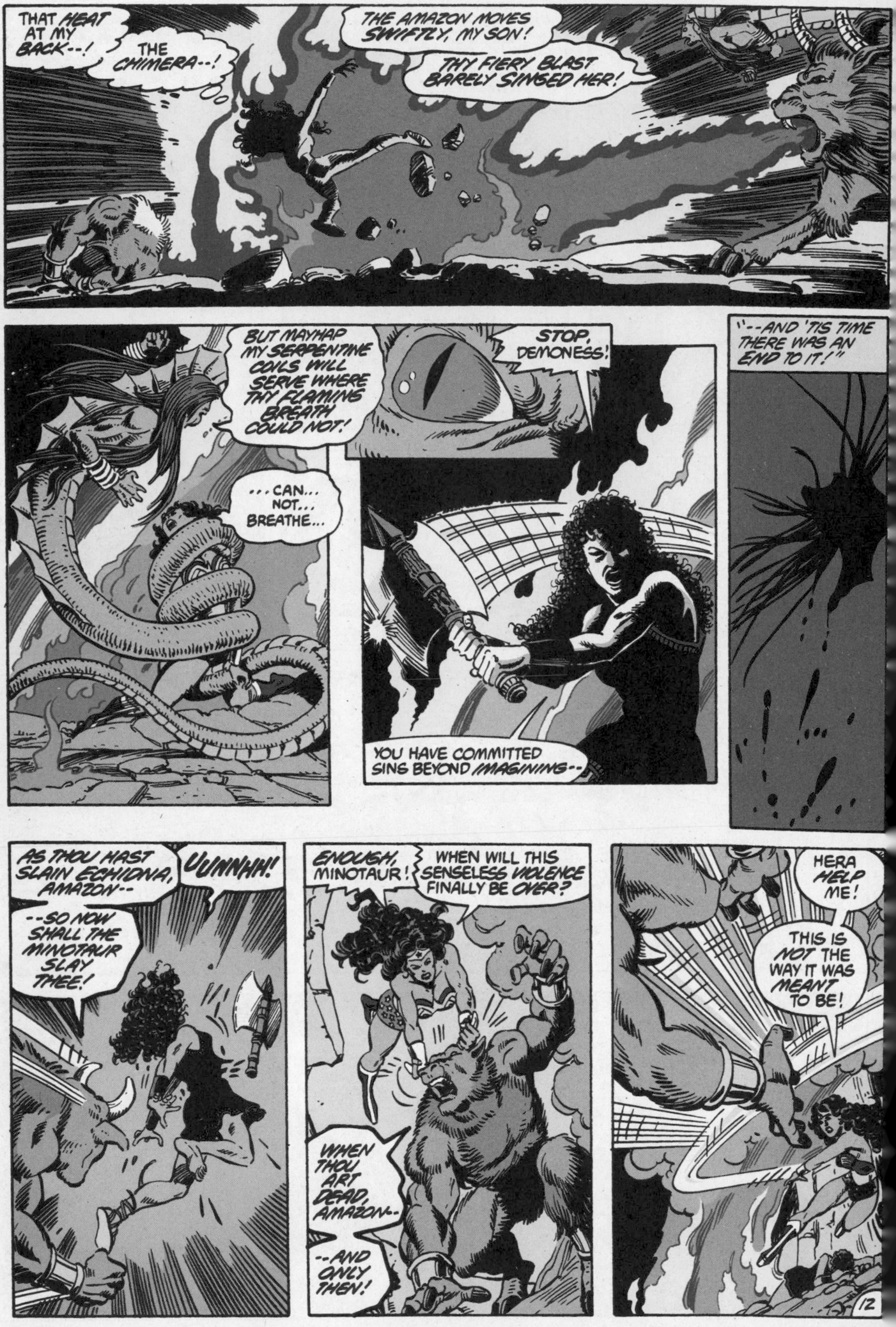
THAT HEAT AT MY BACK--!
THE CHIMERA--!
THE AMAZON MOVES SWIFTLY, MY SON!
THY FIERY BLAST BARELY SINSED HER!
BUT MAYHAP MY SERPENTINE COILS WILL SERVE WHERE THY FLAMING BREATH COULD NOT!
...CAN... NOT... BREATHE...
STOP, DEMONESS!
YOU HAVE COMMITTED SINS BEYOND IMAGINING--
"--AND 'TIS TIME THERE WAS AN END TO IT!"
AS THOU HAST SLAIN ECHIDNA, AMAZON--
UUNNHH!
--SO NOW SHALL THE MINOTAUR SLAY THEE!
ENOUGH, MINOTAUR!
WHEN WILL THIS SENSELESS VIOLENCE FINALLY BE OVER?
WHEN THOU ART DEAD, AMAZON--
--AND ONLY THEN!
HERA HELP ME!
THIS IS NOT THE WAY IT WAS MEANT TO BE!
12

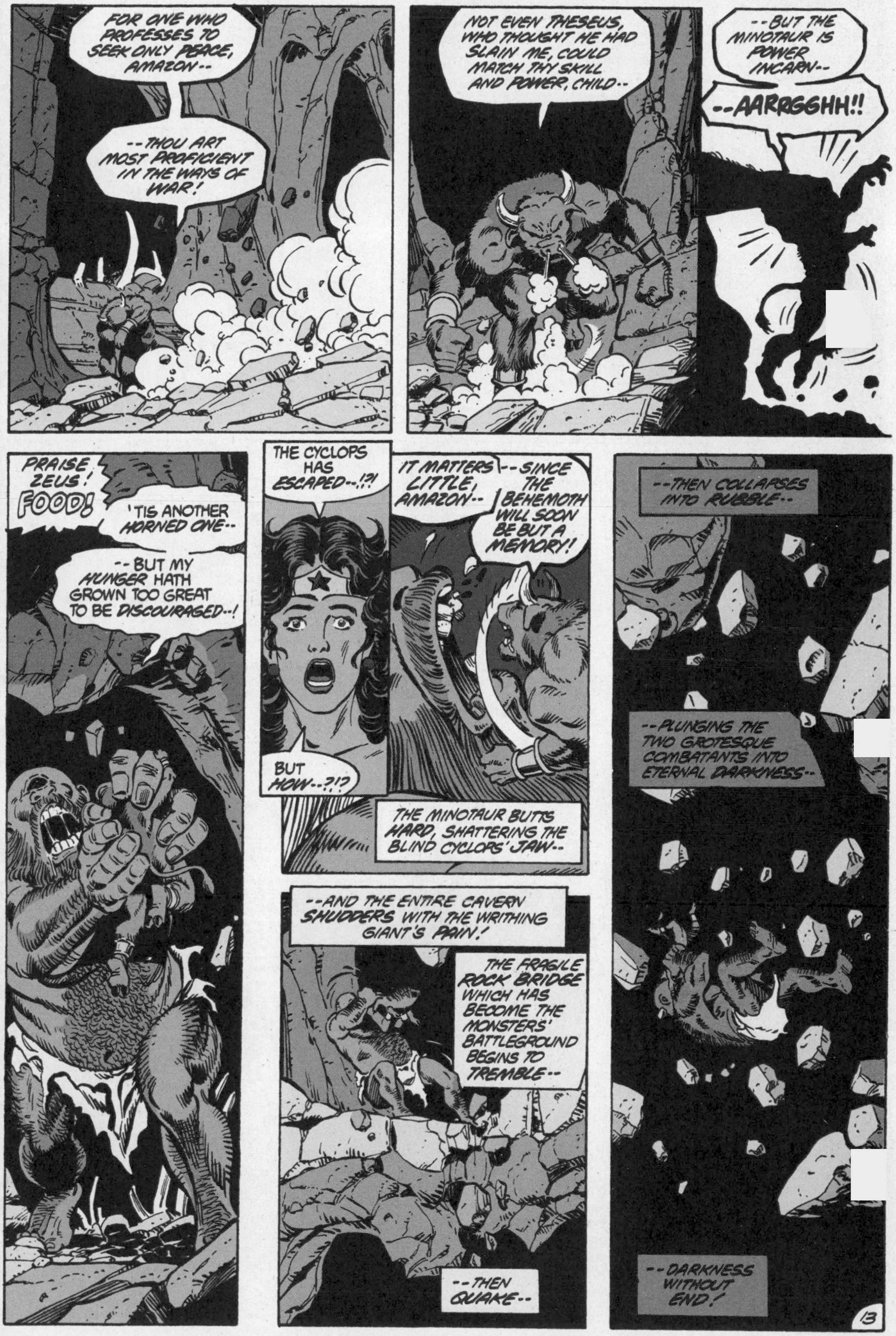
FOR ONE WHO PROFESSES TO SEEK ONLY PEACE, AMAZON--
--THOU ART MOST PROFICIENT IN THE WAYS OF WAR!
NOT EVEN THESEUS, WHO THOUGHT HE HAD SLAIN ME, COULD MATCH THY SKILL AND POWER, CHILD--
--BUT THE MINOTAUR IS POWER INCARN--
--AARRGGHH!!
PRAISE ZEUS! FOOD!
'TIS ANOTHER HORNED ONE--
--BUT MY HUNGER HATH GROWN TOO GREAT TO BE DISCOURAGED--!
THE CYCLOPS HAS ESCAPED--!?!
BUT HOW--?!?
IT MATTERS LITTLE, AMAZON--
--SINCE THE BEHEMOTH WILL SOON BE BUT A MEMORY!
THE MINOTAUR BUTTS HARD, SHATTERING THE BLIND CYCLOPS' JAW--
--AND THE ENTIRE CAVERN SHUDDERS WITH THE WRITHING GIANT'S PAIN!
THE FRAGILE ROCK BRIDGE WHICH HAS BECOME THE MONSTERS' BATTLEGROUND BEGINS TO TREMBLE--
--THEN QUAKE--
--THEN COLLAPSES INTO RUBBLE--
--PLUNGING THE TWO GROTESQUE COMBATANTS INTO ETERNAL DARKNESS--
--DARKNESS WITHOUT END!
13

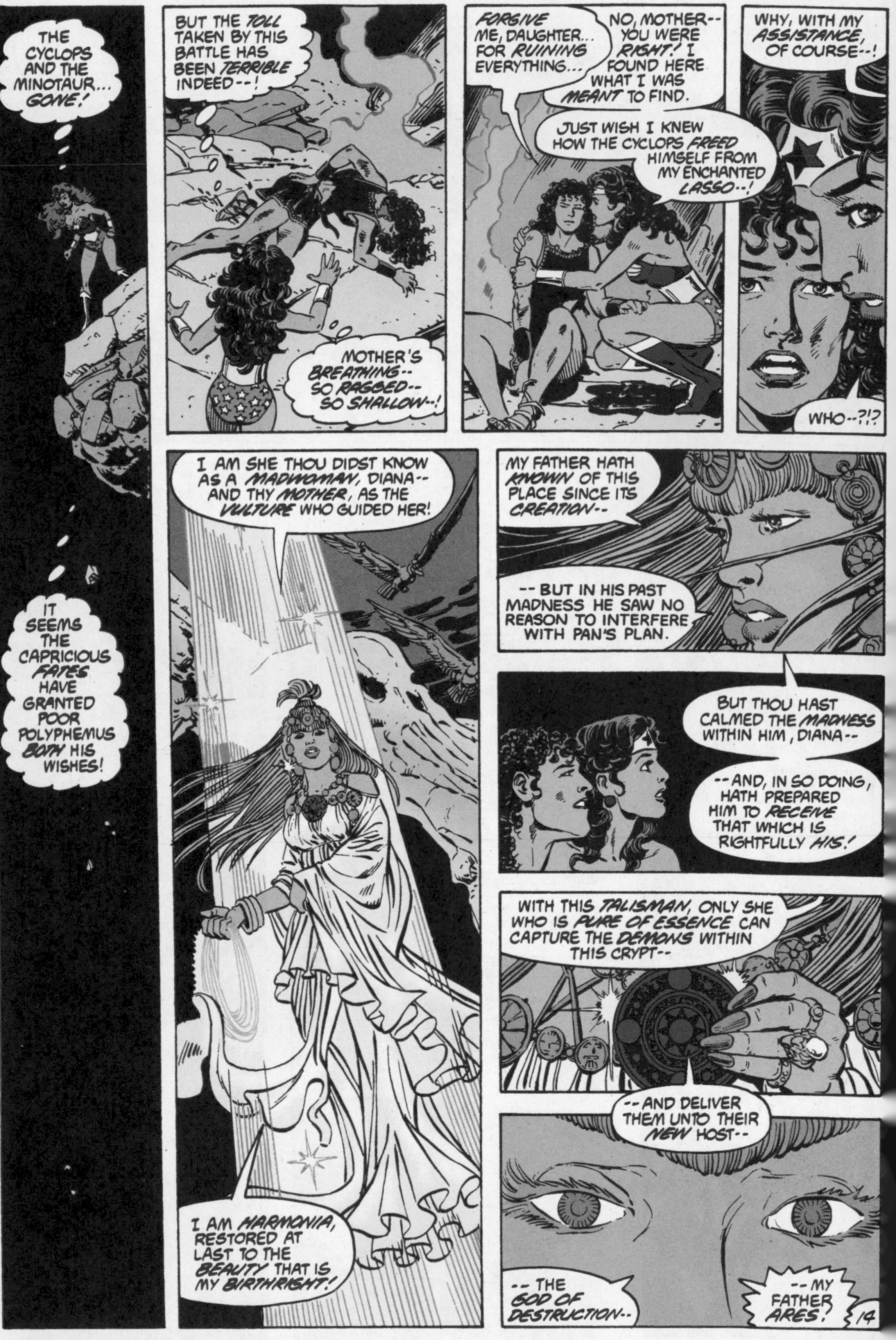
THE CYCLOPS AND THE MINOTAUR... GONE!
IT SEEMS THE CAPRICIOUS FATES HAVE GRANTED POOR POLYPHEMUS BOTH HIS WISHES!
BUT THE TOLL TAKEN BY THIS BATTLE HAS BEEN TERRIBLE INDEED--!
MOTHER'S BREATHING-- SO RAGGED-- SO SHALLOW--!
FORGIVE ME, DAUGHTER... FOR RUINING EVERYTHING...
NO, MOTHER-- YOU WERE RIGHT! I FOUND HERE WHAT I WAS MEANT TO FIND.
JUST WISH I KNEW HOW THE CYCLOPS FREED HIMSELF FROM MY ENCHANTED LASSO--!
WHY, WITH MY ASSISTANCE, OF COURSE--!
WHO--?!?
I AM SHE THOU DIDST KNOW AS A MADWOMAN, DIANA-- AND THY MOTHER, AS THE VULTURE WHO GUIDED HER!
I AM HARMONIA, RESTORED AT LAST TO THE BEAUTY THAT IS MY BIRTHRIGHT!
MY FATHER HATH KNOWN OF THIS PLACE SINCE ITS CREATION--
-- BUT IN HIS PAST MADNESS HE SAW NO REASON TO INTERFERE WITH PAN'S PLAN.
BUT THOU HAST CALMED THE MADNESS WITHIN HIM, DIANA--
--AND, IN SO DOING, HATH PREPARED HIM TO RECEIVE THAT WHICH IS RIGHTFULLY HIS!
WITH THIS TALISMAN, ONLY SHE WHO IS PURE OF ESSENCE CAN CAPTURE THE DEMONS WITHIN THIS CRYPT--
--AND DELIVER THEM UNTO THEIR NEW HOST--
-- THE GOD OF DESTRUCTION--
--MY FATHER ARES!
14

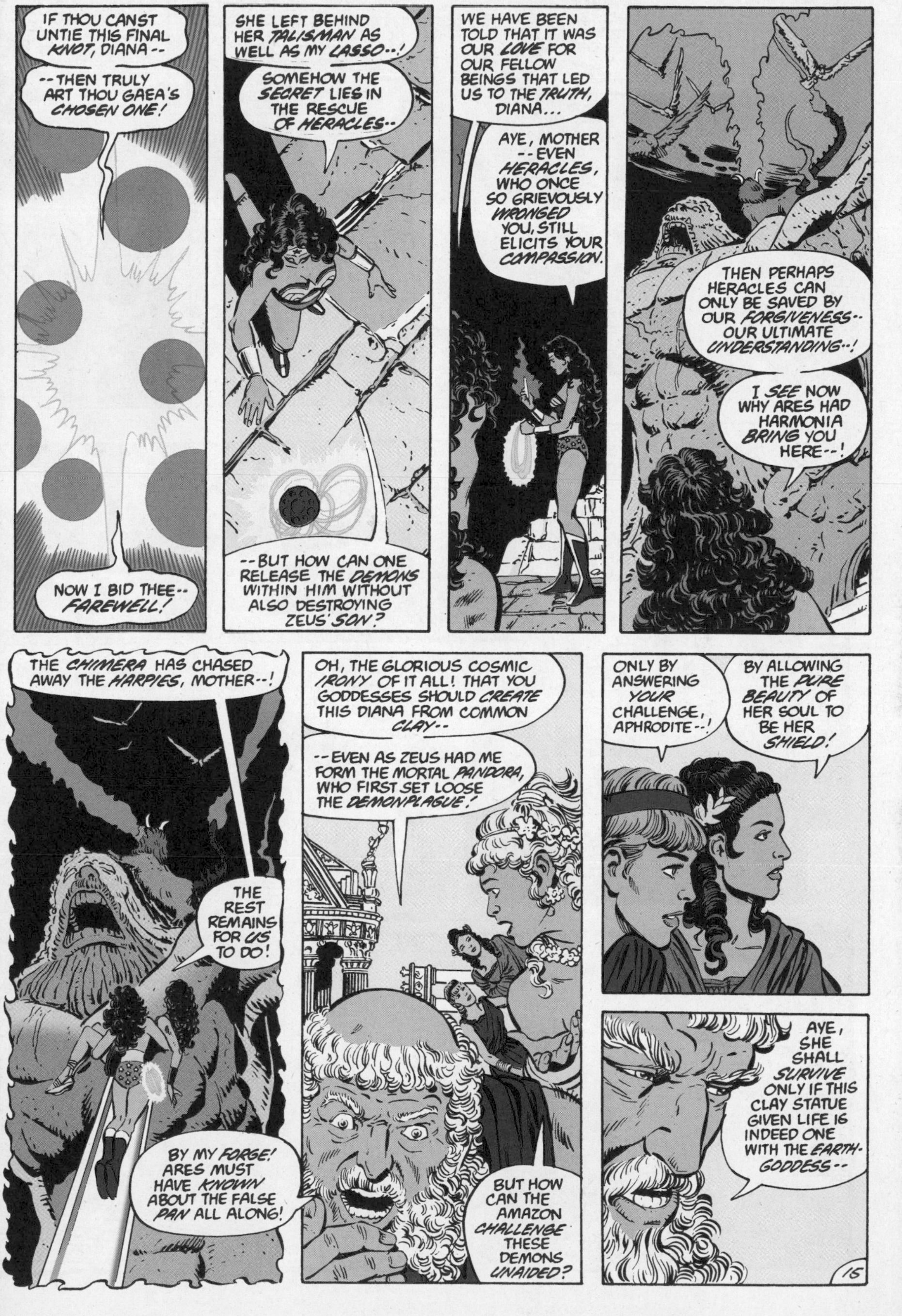

IF THOU CANST UNTIE THIS FINAL KNOT, DIANA --
-- THEN TRULY ART THOU GAEA'S CHOSEN ONE!
NOW I BID THEE-- FAREWELL!
SHE LEFT BEHIND HER TALISMAN AS WELL AS MY LASSO--!
SOMEHOW THE SECRET LIES IN THE RESCUE OF HERACLES--
--BUT HOW CAN ONE RELEASE THE DEMONS WITHIN HIM WITHOUT ALSO DESTROYING ZEUS' SON?
WE HAVE BEEN TOLD THAT IT WAS OUR LOVE FOR OUR FELLOW BEINGS THAT LED US TO THE TRUTH, DIANA...
AYE, MOTHER --EVEN HERACLES, WHO ONCE SO GRIEVOUSLY WRONGED YOU, STILL ELICITS YOUR COMPASSION.
THEN PERHAPS HERACLES CAN ONLY BE SAVED BY OUR FORGIVENESS-- OUR ULTIMATE UNDERSTANDING--!
I SEE NOW WHY ARES HAD HARMONIA BRING YOU HERE--!
THE CHIMERA HAS CHASED AWAY THE HARPIES, MOTHER--!
THE REST REMAINS FOR US TO DO!
BY MY FORGE! ARES MUST HAVE KNOWN ABOUT THE FALSE PAN ALL ALONG!
OH, THE GLORIOUS COSMIC IRONY OF IT ALL! THAT YOU GODDESSES SHOULD CREATE THIS DIANA FROM COMMON CLAY--
--EVEN AS ZEUS HAD ME FORM THE MORTAL PANDORA, WHO FIRST SET LOOSE THE DEMONPLAGUE!
BUT HOW CAN THE AMAZON CHALLENGE THESE DEMONS UNAIDED?
ONLY BY ANSWERING YOUR CHALLENGE, APHRODITE--!
BY ALLOWING THE PURE BEAUTY OF HER SOUL TO BE HER SHIELD!
AYE, SHE SHALL SURVIVE ONLY IF THIS CLAY STATUE GIVEN LIFE IS INDEED ONE WITH THE EARTH-GODDESS--
15

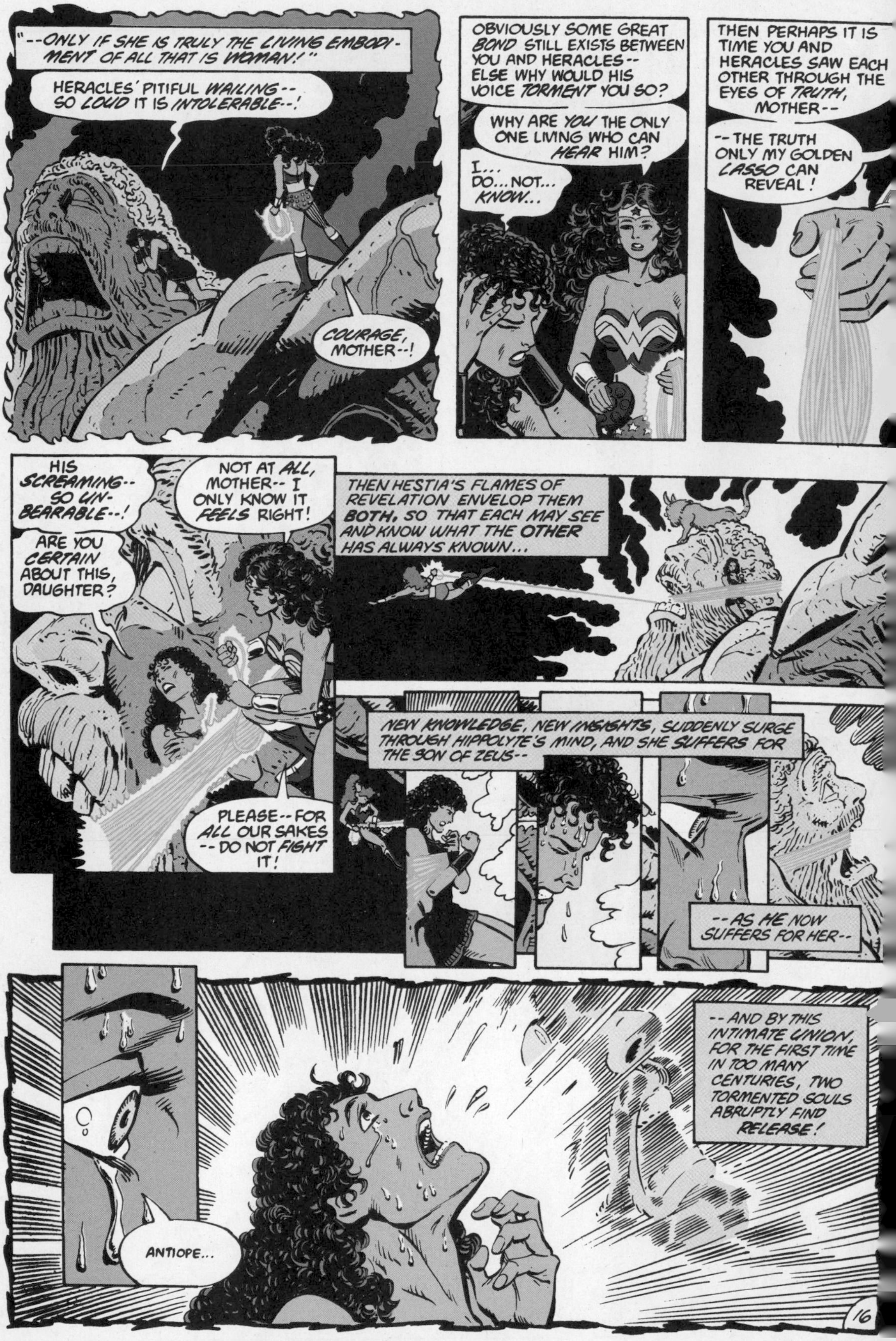
"--ONLY IF SHE IS TRULY THE LIVING EMBODIMENT OF ALL THAT IS WOMAN!"
HERACLES' PITIFUL WAILING-- SO LOUD IT IS INTOLERABLE--!
COURAGE, MOTHER--!
OBVIOUSLY SOME GREAT BOND STILL EXISTS BETWEEN YOU AND HERACLES-- ELSE WHY WOULD HIS VOICE TORMENT YOU SO?
WHY ARE YOU THE ONLY ONE LIVING WHO CAN HEAR HIM?
I... DO... NOT... KNOW...
THEN PERHAPS IT IS TIME YOU AND HERACLES SAW EACH OTHER THROUGH THE EYES OF TRUTH, MOTHER--
--THE TRUTH ONLY MY GOLDEN LASSO CAN REVEAL!
HIS SCREAMING-- SO UNBEARABLE--!
NOT AT ALL, MOTHER-- I ONLY KNOW IT FEELS RIGHT!
ARE YOU CERTAIN ABOUT THIS, DAUGHTER?
PLEASE--FOR ALL OUR SAKES --DO NOT FIGHT IT!
THEN HESTIA'S FLAMES OF REVELATION ENVELOP THEM BOTH, SO THAT EACH MAY SEE AND KNOW WHAT THE OTHER HAS ALWAYS KNOWN...
NEW KNOWLEDGE, NEW INSIGHTS, SUDDENLY SURGE THROUGH HIPPOLYTE'S MIND, AND SHE SUFFERS FOR THE SON OF ZEUS--
--AS HE NOW SUFFERS FOR HER--
ANTIOPE...
--AND BY THIS INTIMATE UNION, FOR THE FIRST TIME IN TOO MANY CENTURIES, TWO TORMENTED SOULS ABRUPTLY FIND RELEASE!
16

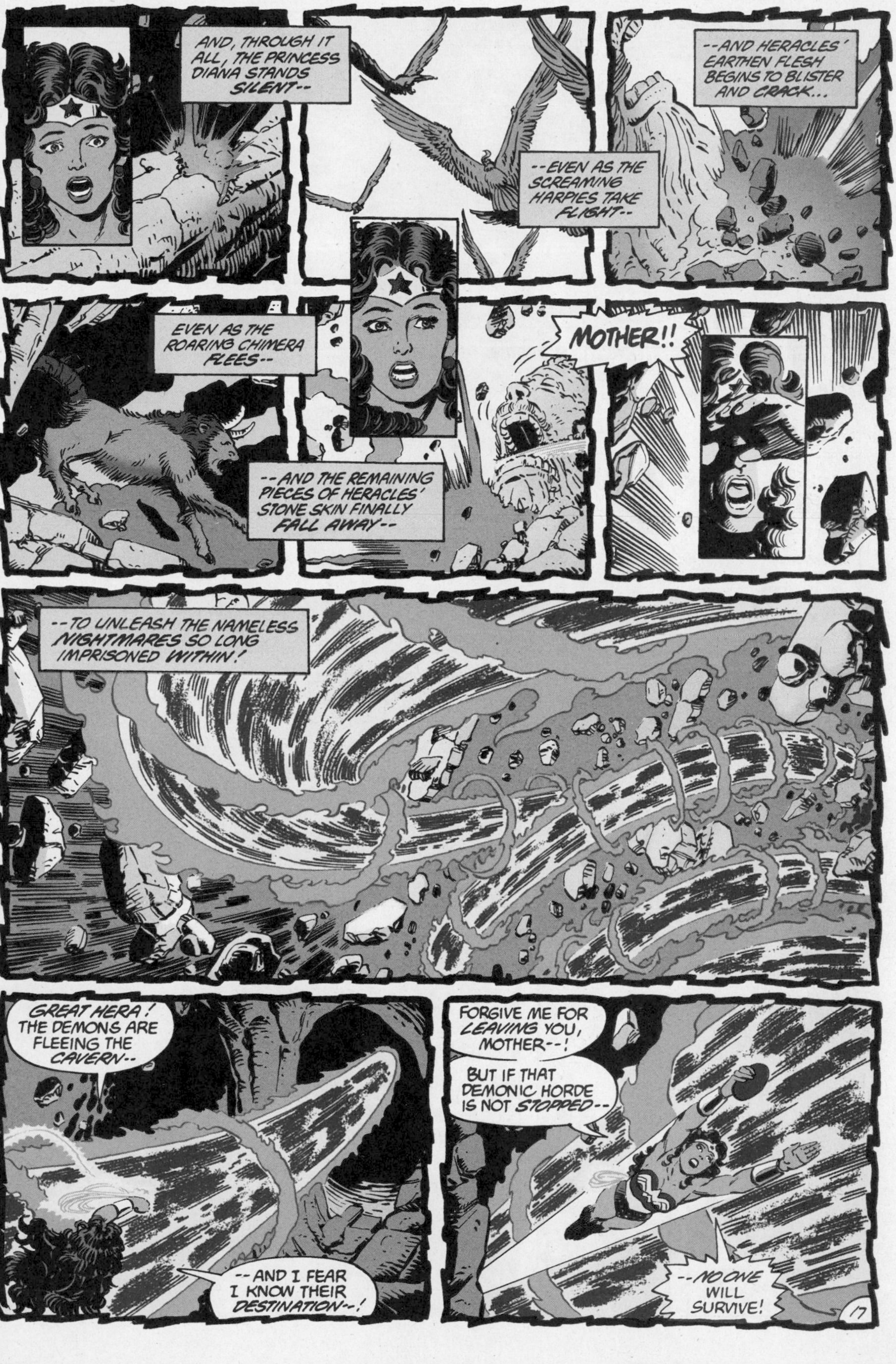

AND, THROUGH IT ALL, THE PRINCESS DIANA STANDS SILENT--
--EVEN AS THE SCREAMING HARPIES TAKE FLIGHT--
--AND HERACLES' EARTHEN FLESH BEGINS TO BLISTER AND CRACK...
EVEN AS THE ROARING CHIMERA FLEES--
--AND THE REMAINING PIECES OF HERACLES' STONE SKIN FINALLY FALL AWAY--
MOTHER!!
--TO UNLEASH THE NAMELESS NIGHTMARES SO LONG IMPRISONED WITHIN!
GREAT HERA! THE DEMONS ARE FLEEING THE CAVERN--
--AND I FEAR I KNOW THEIR DESTINATION--!
FORGIVE ME FOR LEAVING YOU, MOTHER--!
BUT IF THAT DEMONIC HORDE IS NOT STOPPED--
--NO ONE WILL SURVIVE!
17

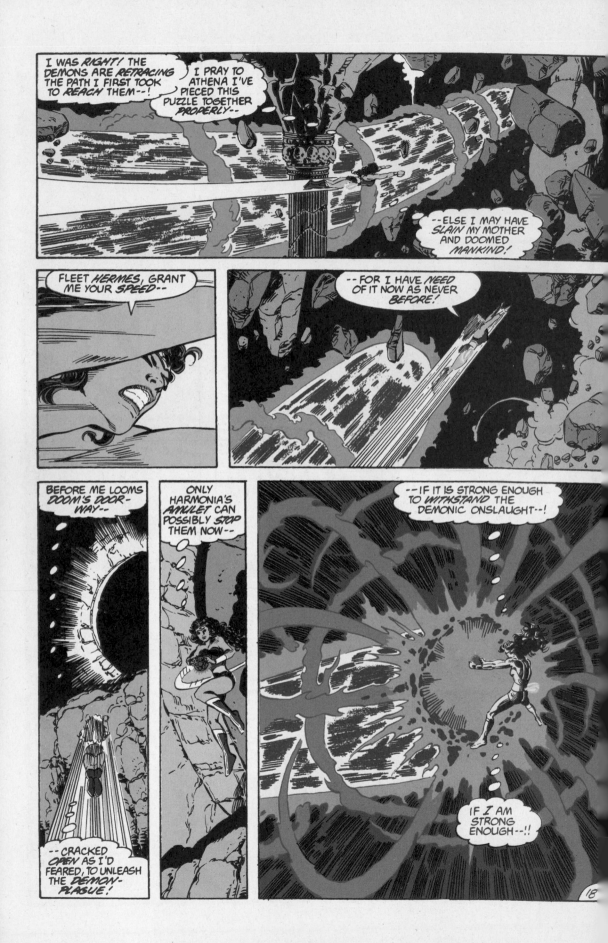

I WAS *RIGHT!* THE DEMONS ARE *RETRACING* THE PATH I FIRST TOOK TO *REACH* THEM--!

I PRAY TO ATHENA I'VE PIECED THIS PUZZLE TOGETHER *PROPERLY*--

--ELSE I MAY HAVE *SLAIN* MY MOTHER AND DOOMED MANKIND!

FLEET *HERMES,* GRANT ME YOUR *SPEED*--

--FOR I HAVE *NEED* OF IT NOW AS NEVER *BEFORE!*

BEFORE ME LOOMS *DOOM'S* DOOR-WAY--

--CRACKED *OPEN* AS I'D FEARED, TO UNLEASH THE *DEMON-PLAGUE!*

ONLY *HARMONIA'S* *AMULET* CAN POSSIBLY *STOP* THEM NOW--

--IF IT IS STRONG ENOUGH TO *WITHSTAND* THE DEMONIC ONSLAUGHT--!

IF *I* AM STRONG ENOUGH--!!

18

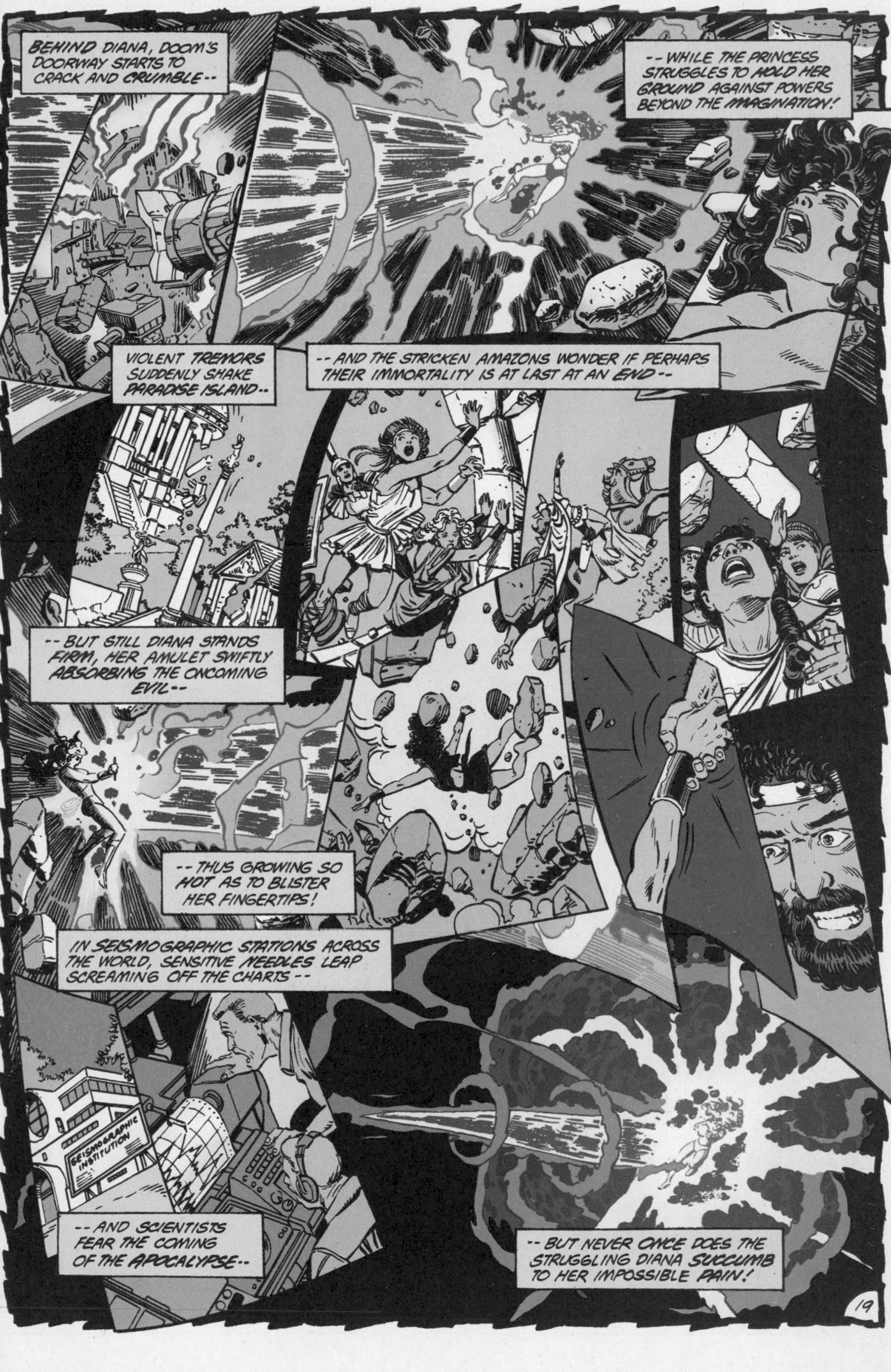
BEHIND DIANA, DOOM'S DOORWAY STARTS TO CRACK AND CRUMBLE--
--WHILE THE PRINCESS STRUGGLES TO HOLD HER GROUND AGAINST POWERS BEYOND THE IMAGINATION!
VIOLENT TREMORS SUDDENLY SHAKE PARADISE ISLAND..
--AND THE STRICKEN AMAZONS WONDER IF PERHAPS THEIR IMMORTALITY IS AT LAST AT AN END--
--BUT STILL DIANA STANDS FIRM, HER AMULET SWIFTLY ABSORBING THE ONCOMING EVIL--
--THUS GROWING SO HOT AS TO BLISTER HER FINGERTIPS!
IN SEISMOGRAPHIC STATIONS ACROSS THE WORLD, SENSITIVE NEEDLES LEAP SCREAMING OFF THE CHARTS--
SEISMOGRAPHIC INSTITUTION
--AND SCIENTISTS FEAR THE COMING OF THE APOCALYPSE..
--BUT NEVER ONCE DOES THE STRUGGLING DIANA SUCCUMB TO HER IMPOSSIBLE PAIN!
19

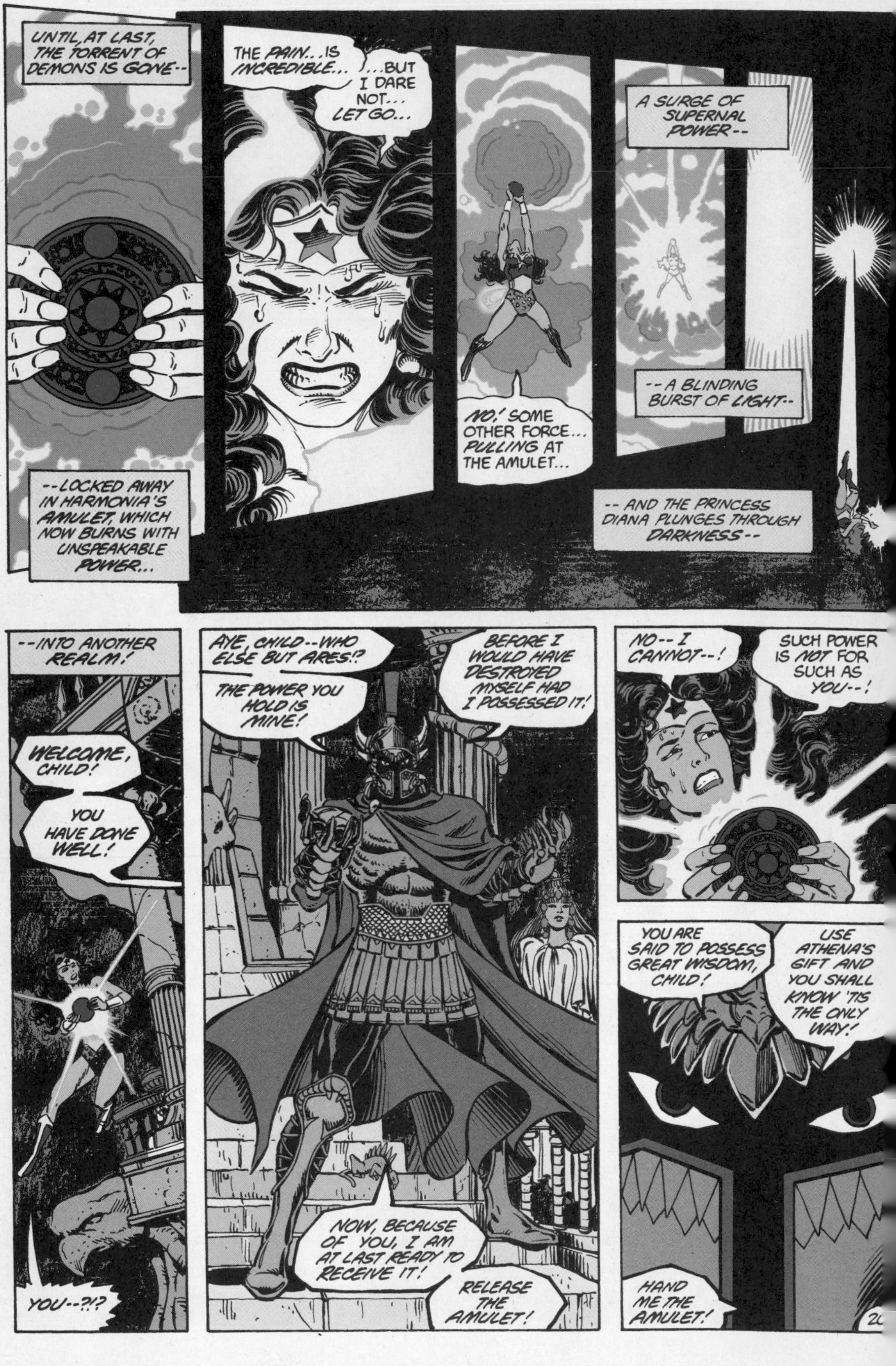
UNTIL, AT LAST, THE TORRENT OF DEMONS IS GONE--
--LOCKED AWAY IN HARMONIA'S AMULET, WHICH NOW BURNS WITH UNSPEAKABLE POWER...
THE PAIN...IS INCREDIBLE...
...BUT I DARE NOT... LET GO...
NO! SOME OTHER FORCE... PULLING AT THE AMULET...
A SURGE OF SUPERNAL POWER--
--A BLINDING BURST OF LIGHT--
-- AND THE PRINCESS DIANA PLUNGES THROUGH DARKNESS--
--INTO ANOTHER REALM!
WELCOME, CHILD!
YOU HAVE DONE WELL!
YOU--?!?
AYE, CHILD--WHO ELSE BUT ARES!?
THE POWER YOU HOLD IS MINE!
BEFORE I WOULD HAVE DESTROYED MYSELF HAD I POSSESSED IT!
NOW, BECAUSE OF YOU, I AM AT LAST READY TO RECEIVE IT!
RELEASE THE AMULET!
NO-- I CANNOT--!
SUCH POWER IS NOT FOR SUCH AS YOU--!
YOU ARE SAID TO POSSESS GREAT WISDOM, CHILD!
USE ATHENIA'S GIFT AND YOU SHALL KNOW 'TIS THE ONLY WAY!
HAND ME THE AMULET!

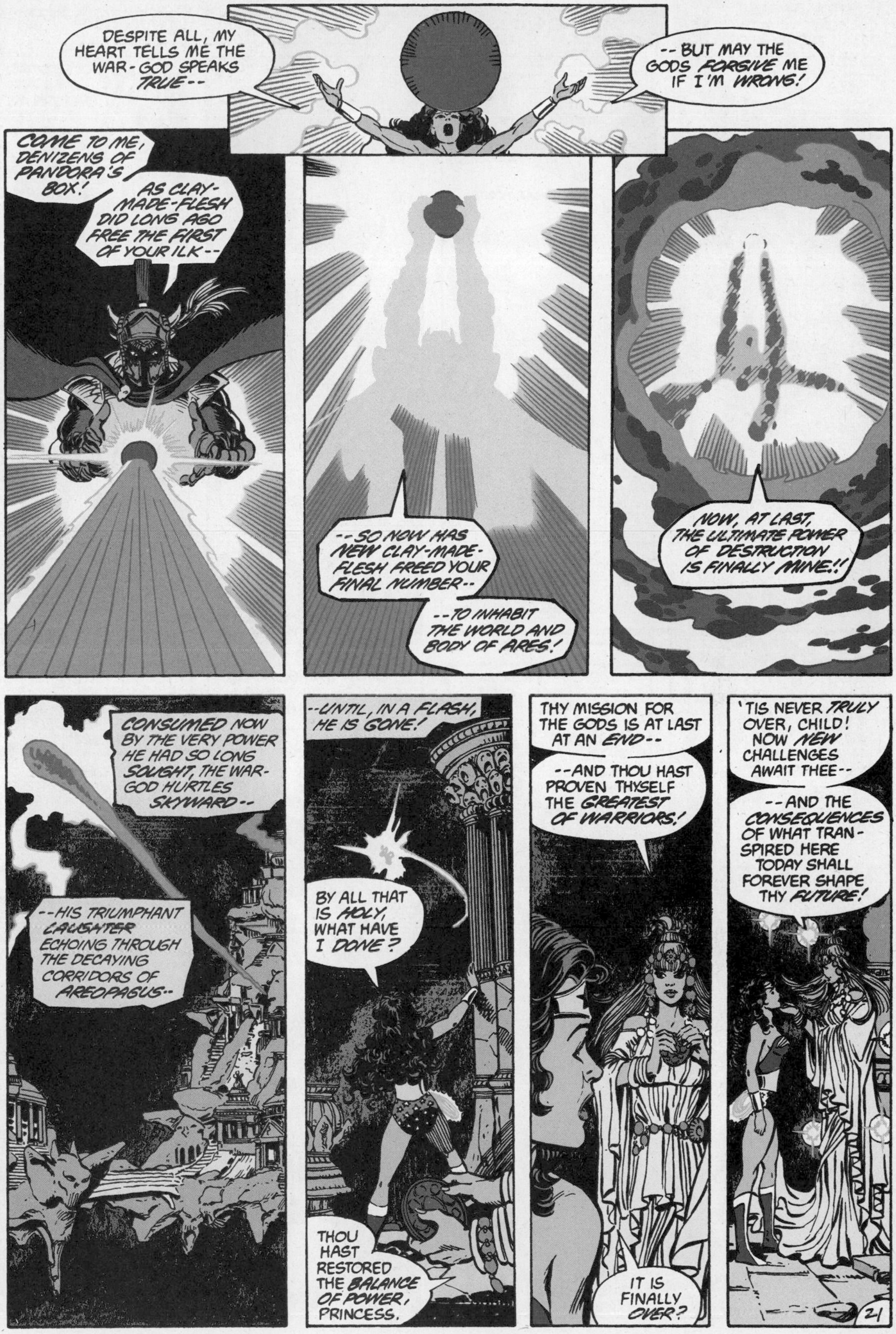

DESPITE ALL, MY HEART TELLS ME THE WAR-GOD SPEAKS TRUE--
--BUT MAY THE GODS FORGIVE ME IF I'M WRONG!
COME TO ME, DENIZENS OF PANDORA'S BOX!
AS CLAY-MADE-FLESH DID LONG AGO FREE THE FIRST OF YOUR ILK--
--SO NOW HAS NEW CLAY-MADE-FLESH FREED YOUR FINAL NUMBER--
--TO INHABIT THE WORLD AND BODY OF ARES!
NOW, AT LAST, THE ULTIMATE POWER OF DESTRUCTION IS FINALLY MINE!!
CONSUMED NOW BY THE VERY POWER HE HAD SO LONG SOUGHT, THE WAR-GOD HURTLES SKYWARD--
--HIS TRIUMPHANT LAUGHTER ECHOING THROUGH THE DECAYING CORRIDORS OF AREOPAGUS--
--UNTIL, IN A FLASH, HE IS GONE!
BY ALL THAT IS HOLY, WHAT HAVE I DONE?
THOU HAST RESTORED THE BALANCE OF POWER, PRINCESS.
THY MISSION FOR THE GODS IS AT LAST AT AN END--
--AND THOU HAST PROVEN THYSELF THE GREATEST OF WARRIORS!
IT IS FINALLY OVER?
'TIS NEVER TRULY OVER, CHILD! NOW NEW CHALLENGES AWAIT THEE--
--AND THE CONSEQUENCES OF WHAT TRANSPIRED HERE TODAY SHALL FOREVER SHAPE THY FUTURE!
21

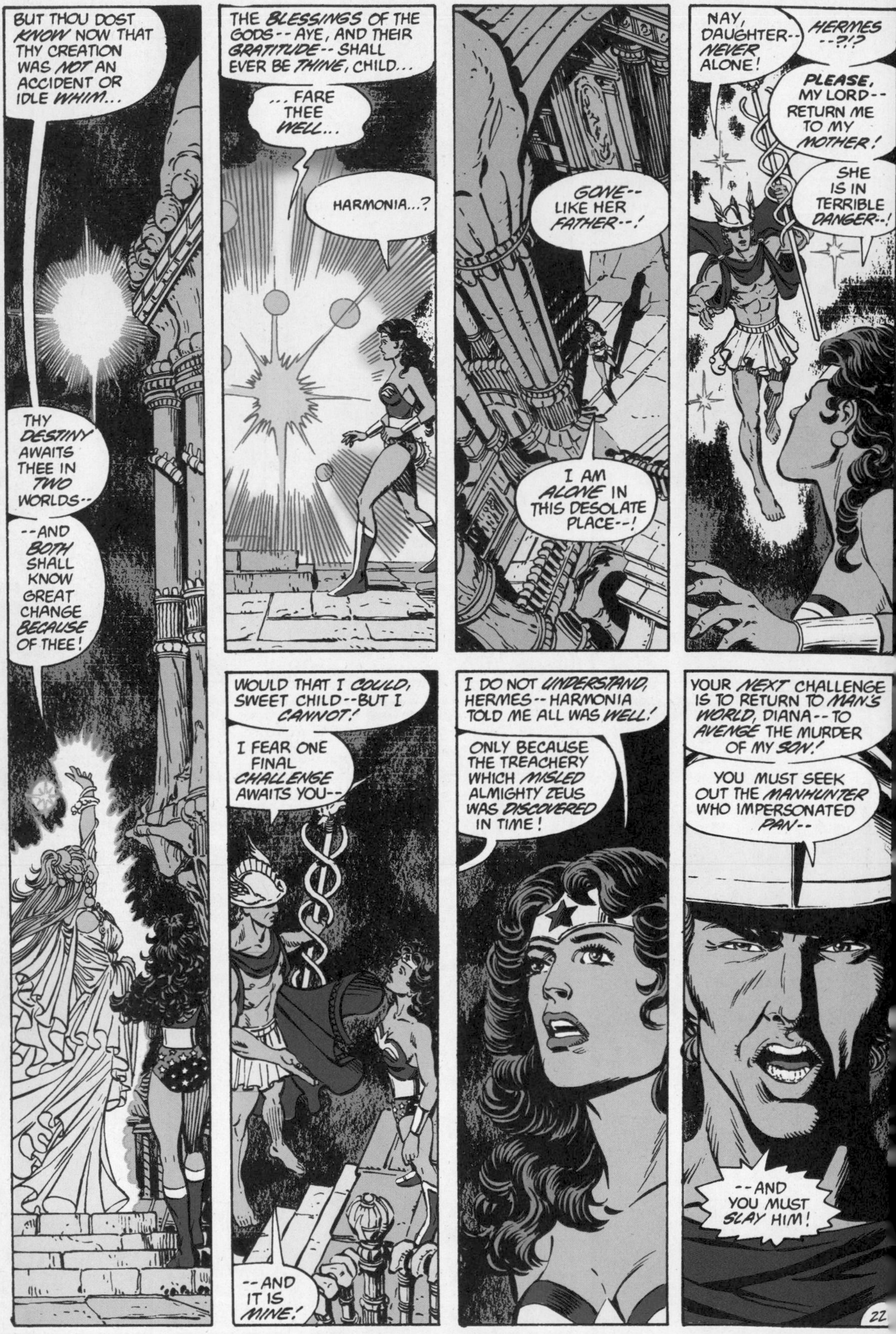
BUT THOU DOST KNOW NOW THAT THY CREATION WAS NOT AN ACCIDENT OR IDLE WHIM...
THY DESTINY AWAITS THEE IN TWO WORLDS--
--AND BOTH SHALL KNOW GREAT CHANGE BECAUSE OF THEE!
THE BLESSINGS OF THE GODS--AYE, AND THEIR GRATITUDE--SHALL EVER BE THINE, CHILD...
...FARE THEE WELL...
HARMONIA...?
GONE--LIKE HER FATHER--!
I AM ALONE IN THIS DESOLATE PLACE--!
NAY, DAUGHTER--NEVER ALONE!
HERMES--?!?
PLEASE, MY LORD--RETURN ME TO MY MOTHER!
SHE IS IN TERRIBLE DANGER--!
WOULD THAT I COULD, SWEET CHILD--BUT I CANNOT!
I FEAR ONE FINAL CHALLENGE AWAITS YOU--
--AND IT IS MINE!
I DO NOT UNDERSTAND, HERMES--HARMONIA TOLD ME ALL WAS WELL!
ONLY BECAUSE THE TREACHERY WHICH MISLED ALMIGHTY ZEUS WAS DISCOVERED IN TIME!
YOUR NEXT CHALLENGE IS TO RETURN TO MAN'S WORLD, DIANA--TO AVENGE THE MURDER OF MY SON!
YOU MUST SEEK OUT THE MANHUNTER WHO IMPERSONATED PAN--
--AND YOU MUST SLAY HIM!
22

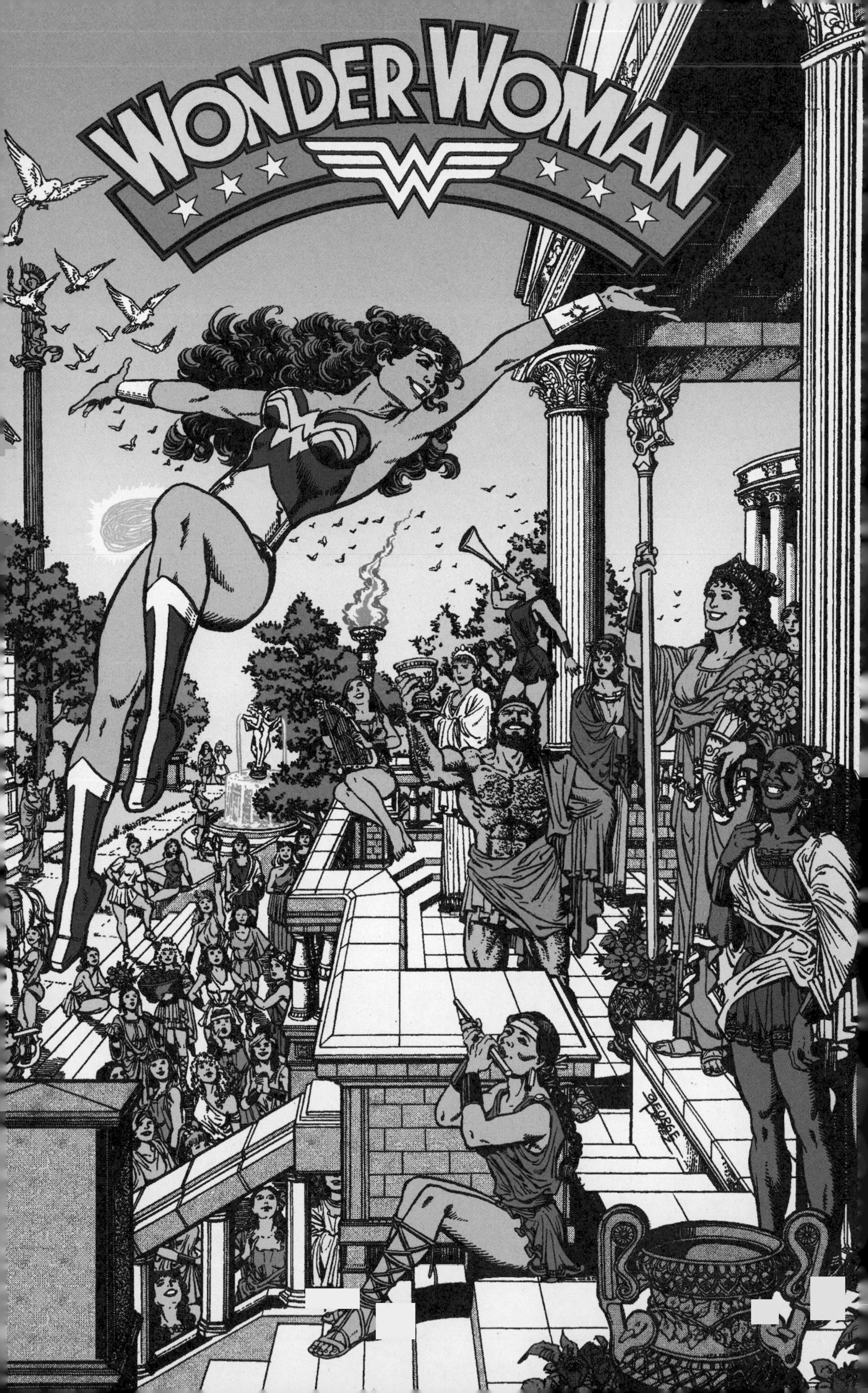
WONDER WOMAN
GEORGE PÉREZ

WONDER WOMAN

CHAPTER SEVEN

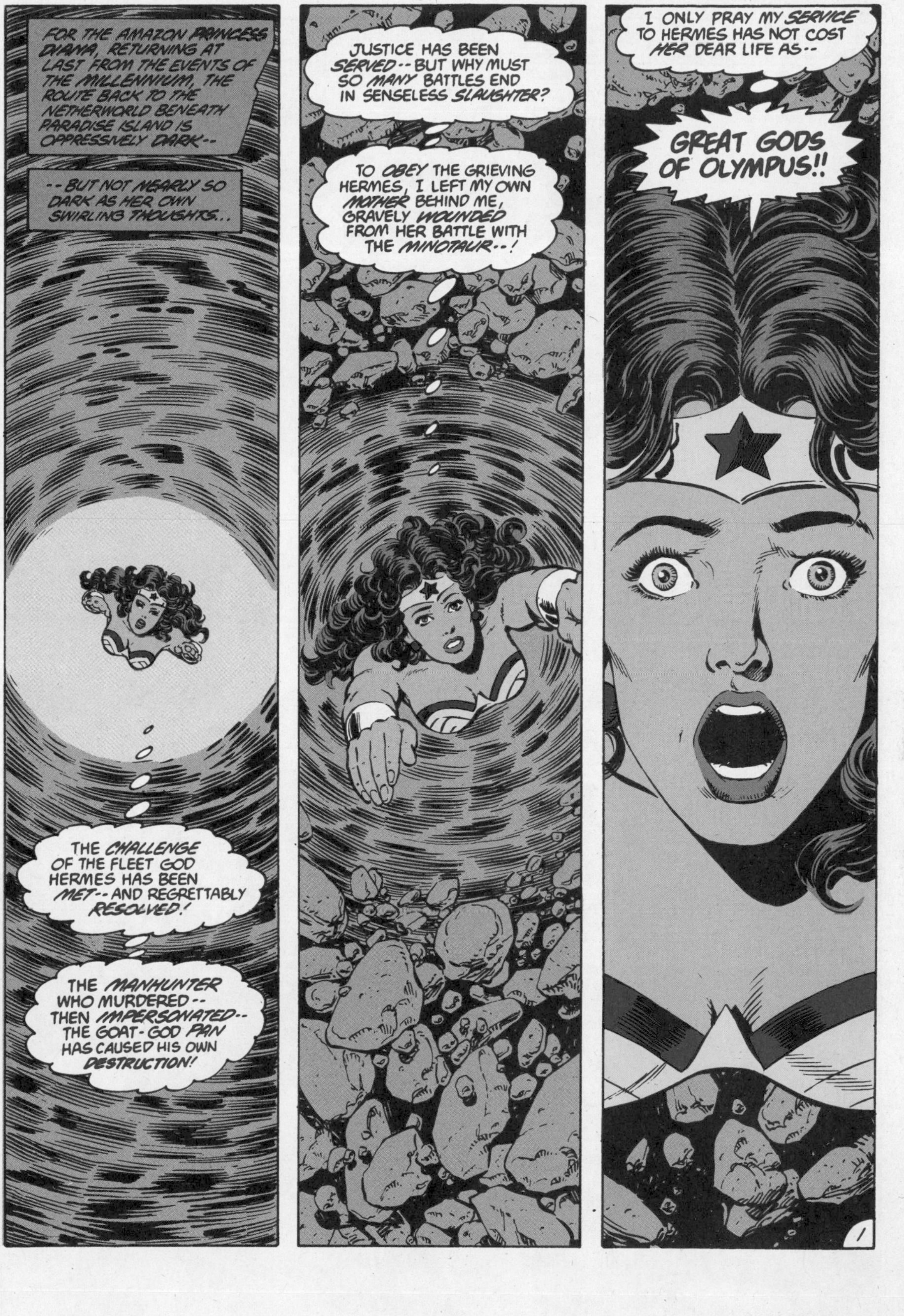
FOR THE AMAZON PRINCESS DIANA, RETURNING AT LAST FROM THE EVENTS OF THE MILLENNIUM, THE ROUTE BACK TO THE NETHERWORLD BENEATH PARADISE ISLAND IS OPPRESSIVELY DARK--
--BUT NOT NEARLY SO DARK AS HER OWN SWIRLING THOUGHTS...
THE CHALLENGE OF THE FLEET GOD HERMES HAS BEEN MET--AND REGRETTABLY RESOLVED!
THE MANHUNTER WHO MURDERED--THEN IMPERSONATED--THE GOAT-GOD PAN HAS CAUSED HIS OWN DESTRUCTION!
JUSTICE HAS BEEN SERVED--BUT WHY MUST SO MANY BATTLES END IN SENSELESS SLAUGHTER?
TO OBEY THE GRIEVING HERMES, I LEFT MY OWN MOTHER BEHIND ME, GRAVELY WOUNDED FROM HER BATTLE WITH THE MINOTAUR--!
I ONLY PRAY MY SERVICE TO HERMES HAS NOT COST HER DEAR LIFE AS--
GREAT GODS OF OLYMPUS!!
1

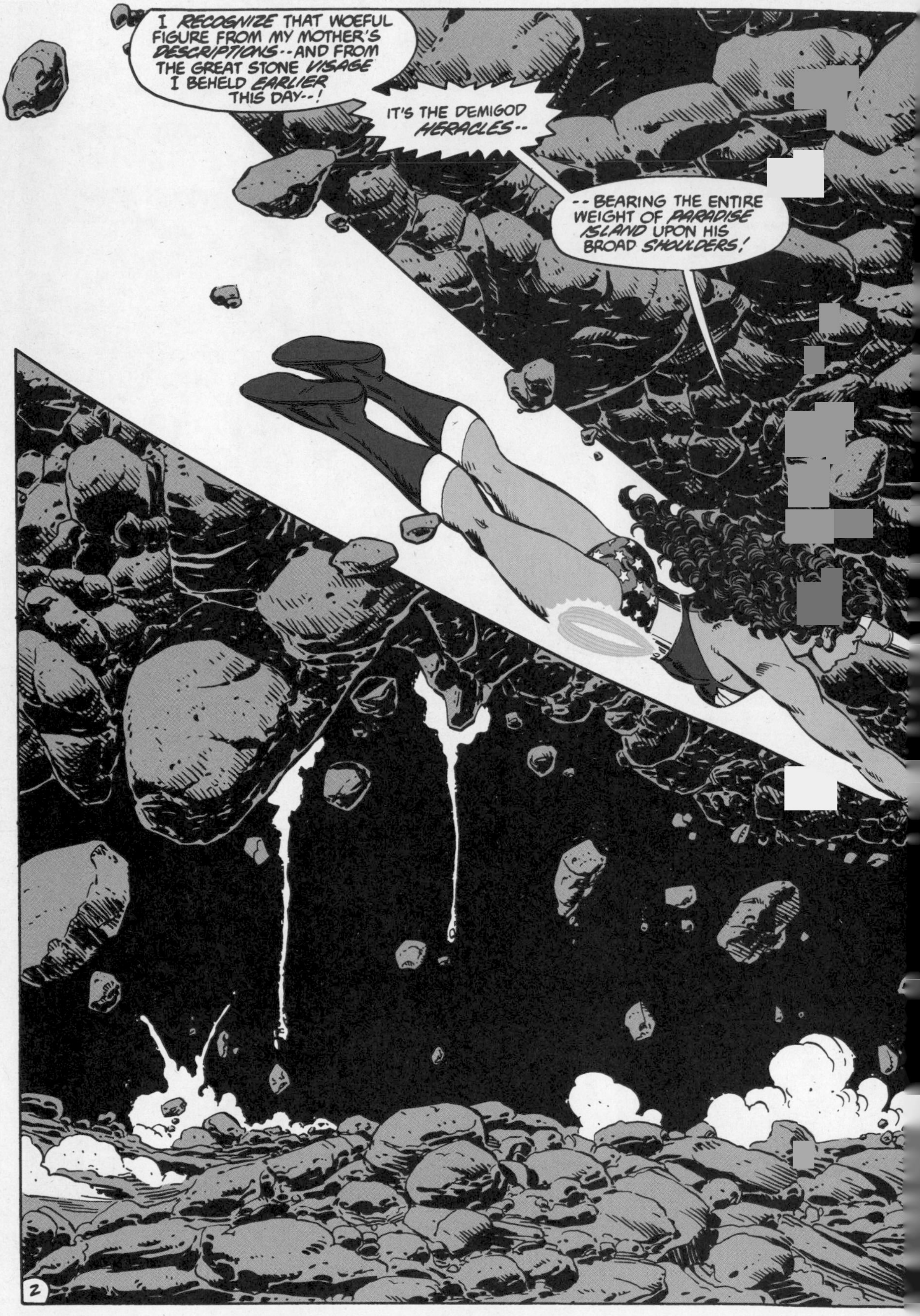
I RECOGNIZE THAT WOEFUL FIGURE FROM MY MOTHER'S DESCRIPTIONS--AND FROM THE GREAT STONE VISAGE I BEHELD EARLIER THIS DAY--!
IT'S THE DEMIGOD HERACLES--
--BEARING THE ENTIRE WEIGHT OF PARADISE ISLAND UPON HIS BROAD SHOULDERS!
2

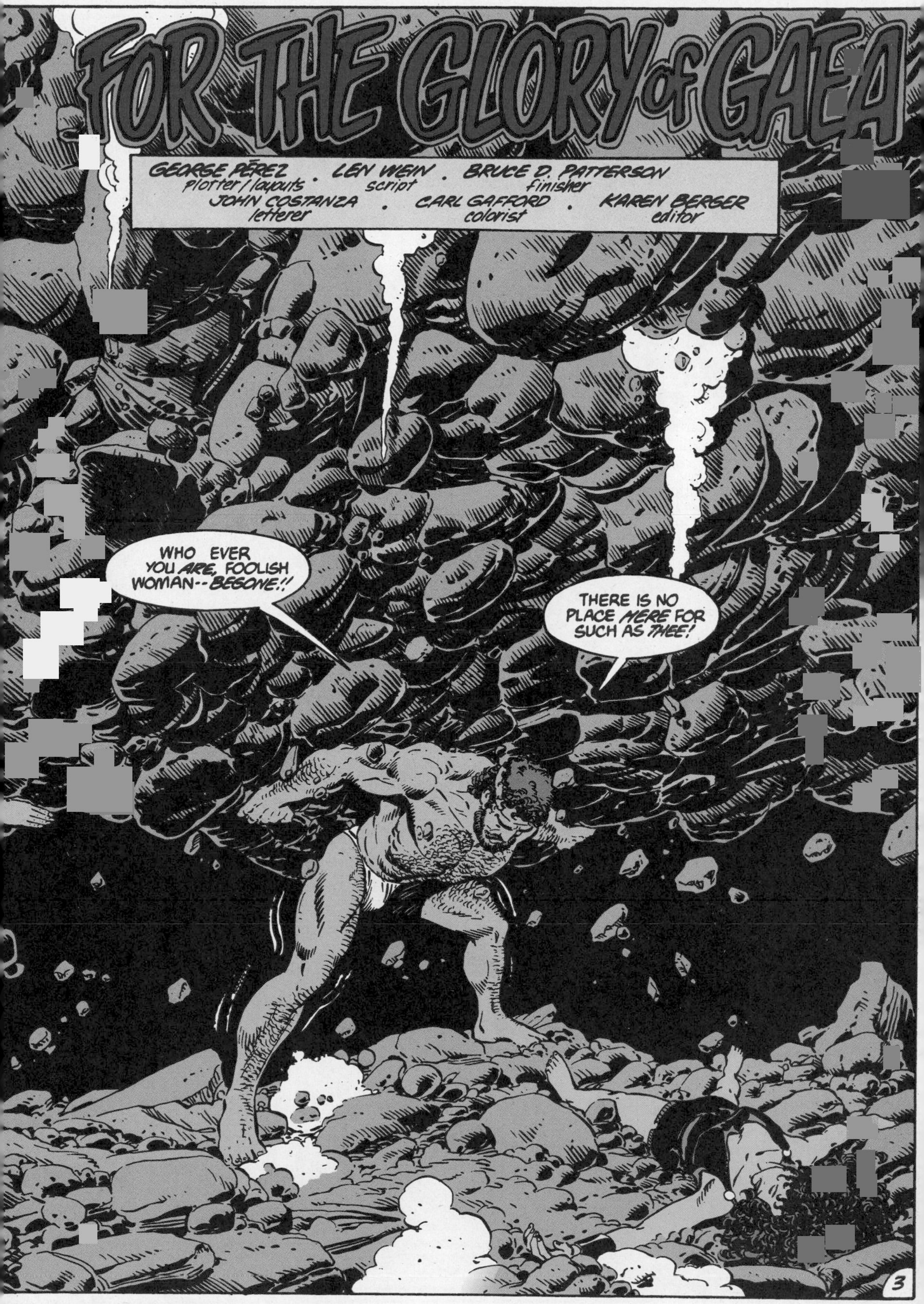
FOR THE GLORY of GAEA
GEORGE PÉREZ plotter/layouts . LEN WEIN script . BRUCE D. PATTERSON finisher
JOHN COSTANZA letterer . CARL GAFFORD colorist . KAREN BERGER editor
WHO EVER YOU ARE, FOOLISH WOMAN--BEGONE!!
THERE IS NO PLACE HERE FOR SUCH AS THEE!
3

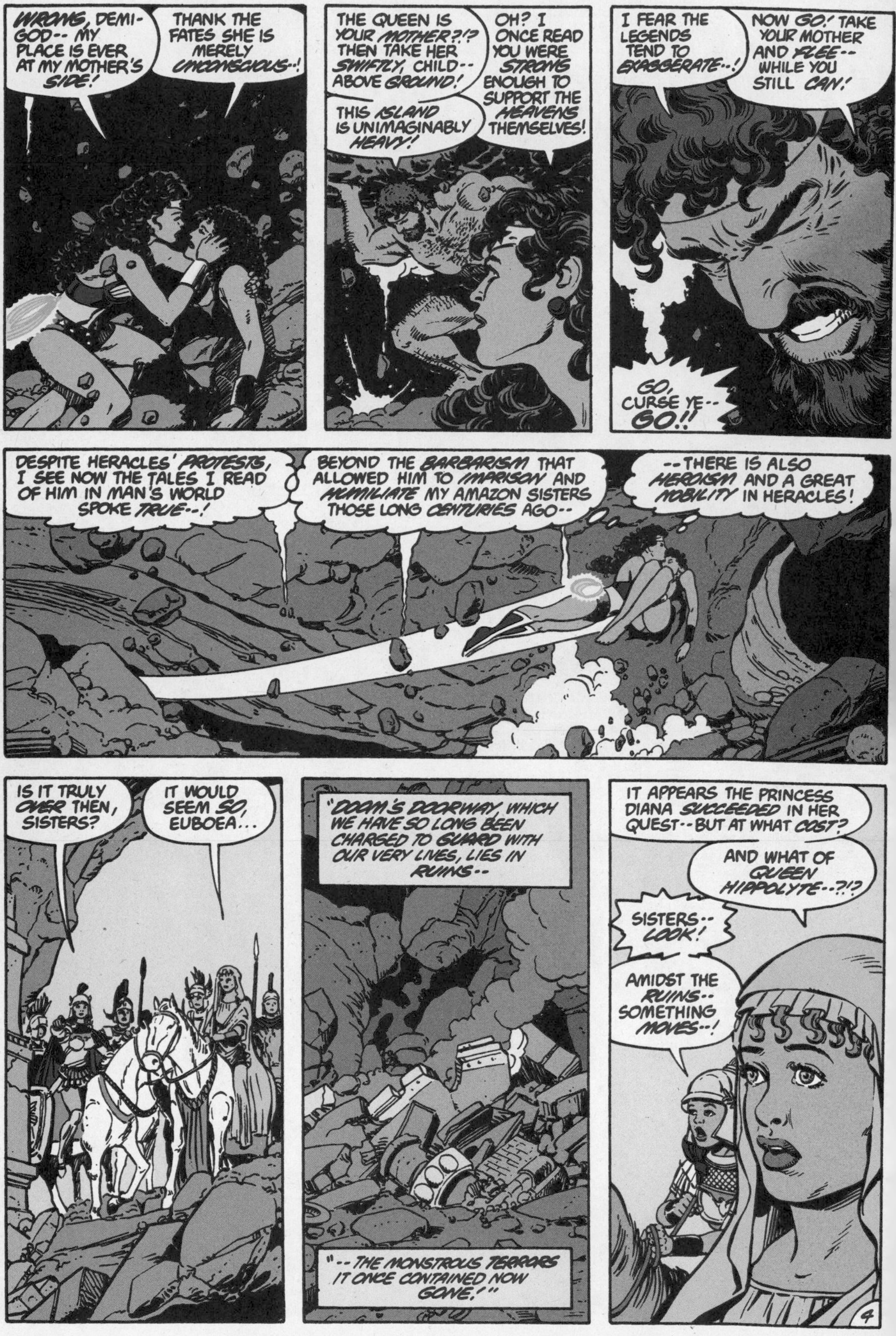
WRONG, DEMI-GOD-- MY PLACE IS EVER AT MY MOTHER'S SIDE!
THANK THE FATES SHE IS MERELY UNCONSCIOUS--!
THE QUEEN IS YOUR MOTHER?!? THEN TAKE HER SWIFTLY, CHILD-- ABOVE GROUND!
THIS ISLAND IS UNIMAGINABLY HEAVY!
OH? I ONCE READ YOU WERE STRONG ENOUGH TO SUPPORT THE HEAVENS THEMSELVES!
I FEAR THE LEGENDS TEND TO EXAGGERATE--!
NOW GO! TAKE YOUR MOTHER AND FLEE-- WHILE YOU STILL CAN!
GO, CURSE YE-- GO!!
DESPITE HERACLES' PROTESTS, I SEE NOW THE TALES I READ OF HIM IN MAN'S WORLD SPOKE TRUE--!
BEYOND THE BARBARISM THAT ALLOWED HIM TO IMPRISON AND HUMILIATE MY AMAZON SISTERS THOSE LONG CENTURIES AGO--
--THERE IS ALSO HEROISM AND A GREAT NOBILITY IN HERACLES!
IS IT TRULY OVER THEN, SISTERS?
IT WOULD SEEM SO, EUBOEA...
"DOOM'S DOORWAY, WHICH WE HAVE SO LONG BEEN CHARGED TO GUARD WITH OUR VERY LIVES, LIES IN RUINS--
"--THE MONSTROUS TERRORS IT ONCE CONTAINED NOW GONE!"
IT APPEARS THE PRINCESS DIANA SUCCEEDED IN HER QUEST--BUT AT WHAT COST?
AND WHAT OF QUEEN HIPPOLYTE--?!?
SISTERS-- LOOK!
AMIDST THE RUINS-- SOMETHING MOVES--!
4

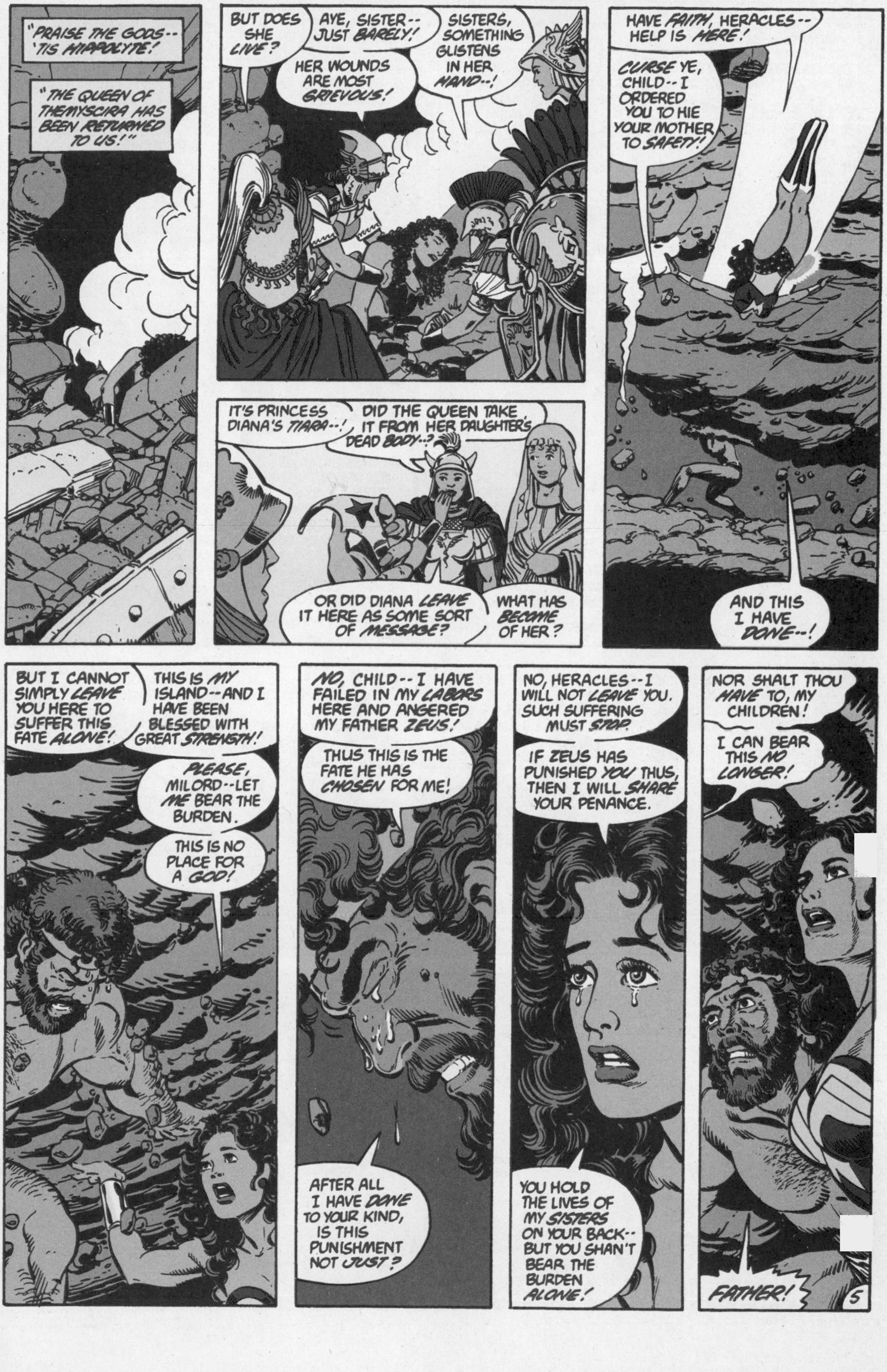
"PRAISE THE GODS-- 'TIS HIPPOLYTE!
"THE QUEEN OF THEMYSCIRA HAS BEEN RETURNED TO US!"
BUT DOES SHE LIVE?
AYE, SISTER-- JUST BARELY!
HER WOUNDS ARE MOST GRIEVOUS!
SISTERS, SOMETHING GLISTENS IN HER HAND--!
IT'S PRINCESS DIANA'S TIARA--!
DID THE QUEEN TAKE IT FROM HER DAUGHTER'S DEAD BODY--?
OR DID DIANA LEAVE IT HERE AS SOME SORT OF MESSAGE?
WHAT HAS BECOME OF HER?
HAVE FAITH, HERACLES-- HELP IS HERE!
CURSE YE, CHILD-- I ORDERED YOU TO HIE YOUR MOTHER TO SAFETY!
AND THIS I HAVE DONE--!
BUT I CANNOT SIMPLY LEAVE YOU HERE TO SUFFER THIS FATE ALONE!
THIS IS MY ISLAND--AND I HAVE BEEN BLESSED WITH GREAT STRENGTH!
PLEASE, MILORD--LET ME BEAR THE BURDEN.
THIS IS NO PLACE FOR A GOD!
NO, CHILD-- I HAVE FAILED IN MY LABORS HERE AND ANGERED MY FATHER ZEUS!
THUS THIS IS THE FATE HE HAS CHOSEN FOR ME!
AFTER ALL I HAVE DONE TO YOUR KIND, IS THIS PUNISHMENT NOT JUST?
NO, HERACLES-- I WILL NOT LEAVE YOU. SUCH SUFFERING MUST STOP.
IF ZEUS HAS PUNISHED YOU THUS, THEN I WILL SHARE YOUR PENANCE.
YOU HOLD THE LIVES OF MY SISTERS ON YOUR BACK-- BUT YOU SHAN'T BEAR THE BURDEN ALONE!
NOR SHALT THOU HAVE TO, MY CHILDREN!
I CAN BEAR THIS NO LONGER!
FATHER!
5

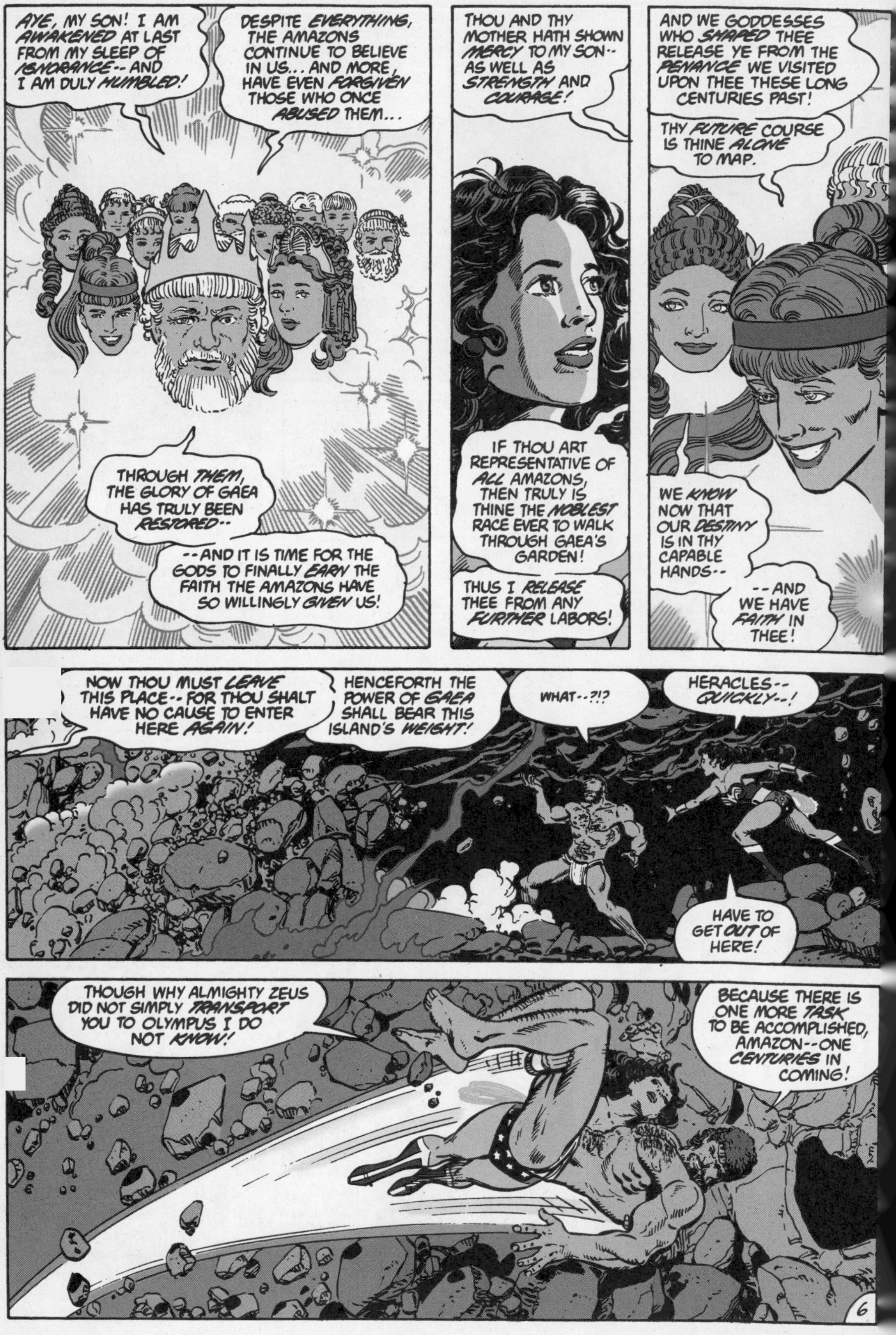
AYE, MY SON! I AM AWAKENED AT LAST FROM MY SLEEP OF IGNORANCE-- AND I AM DULY HUMBLED!
DESPITE EVERYTHING, THE AMAZONS CONTINUE TO BELIEVE IN US... AND MORE, HAVE EVEN FORGIVEN THOSE WHO ONCE ABUSED THEM...
THROUGH THEM, THE GLORY OF GAEA HAS TRULY BEEN RESTORED--
--AND IT IS TIME FOR THE GODS TO FINALLY EARN THE FAITH THE AMAZONS HAVE SO WILLINGLY GIVEN US!
THOU AND THY MOTHER HATH SHOWN MERCY TO MY SON-- AS WELL AS STRENGTH AND COURAGE!
IF THOU ART REPRESENTATIVE OF ALL AMAZONS, THEN TRULY IS THINE THE NOBLEST RACE EVER TO WALK THROUGH GAEA'S GARDEN!
THUS I RELEASE THEE FROM ANY FURTHER LABORS!
AND WE GODDESSES WHO SHAPED THEE RELEASE YE FROM THE PENANCE WE VISITED UPON THEE THESE LONG CENTURIES PAST!
THY FUTURE COURSE IS THINE ALONE TO MAP.
WE KNOW NOW THAT OUR DESTINY IS IN THY CAPABLE HANDS--
--AND WE HAVE FAITH IN THEE!
NOW THOU MUST LEAVE THIS PLACE-- FOR THOU SHALT HAVE NO CAUSE TO ENTER HERE AGAIN!
HENCEFORTH THE POWER OF GAEA SHALL BEAR THIS ISLAND'S WEIGHT!
WHAT--?!?
HERACLES-- QUICKLY--!
HAVE TO GET OUT OF HERE!
THOUGH WHY ALMIGHTY ZEUS DID NOT SIMPLY TRANSPORT YOU TO OLYMPUS I DO NOT KNOW!
BECAUSE THERE IS ONE MORE TASK TO BE ACCOMPLISHED, AMAZON--ONE CENTURIES IN COMING!
6

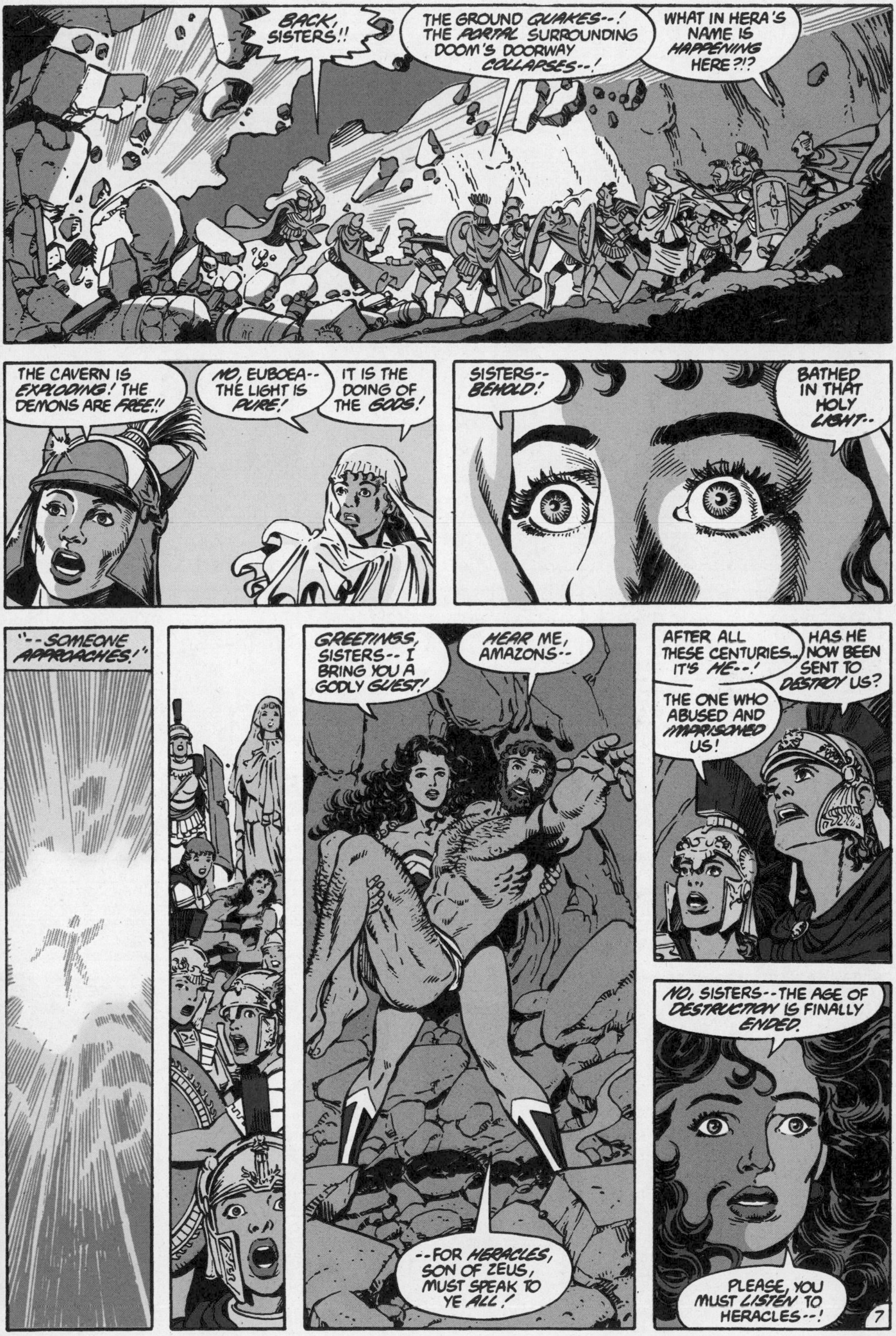
BACK, SISTERS!!
THE GROUND QUAKES--! THE PORTAL SURROUNDING DOOM'S DOORWAY COLLAPSES--!
WHAT IN HERA'S NAME IS HAPPENING HERE?!?
THE CAVERN IS EXPLODING! THE DEMONS ARE FREE!!
NO, EUBOEA-- THE LIGHT IS PURE!
IT IS THE DOING OF THE GODS!
SISTERS-- BEHOLD!
BATHED IN THAT HOLY LIGHT--
"--SOMEONE APPROACHES!"
GREETINGS, SISTERS-- I BRING YOU A GODLY GUEST!
HEAR ME, AMAZONS--
--FOR HERACLES, SON OF ZEUS, MUST SPEAK TO YE ALL!
AFTER ALL THESE CENTURIES... IT'S HE--!
THE ONE WHO ABUSED AND IMPRISONED US!
HAS HE NOW BEEN SENT TO DESTROY US?
NO, SISTERS--THE AGE OF DESTRUCTION IS FINALLY ENDED.
PLEASE, YOU MUST LISTEN TO HERACLES--!
7

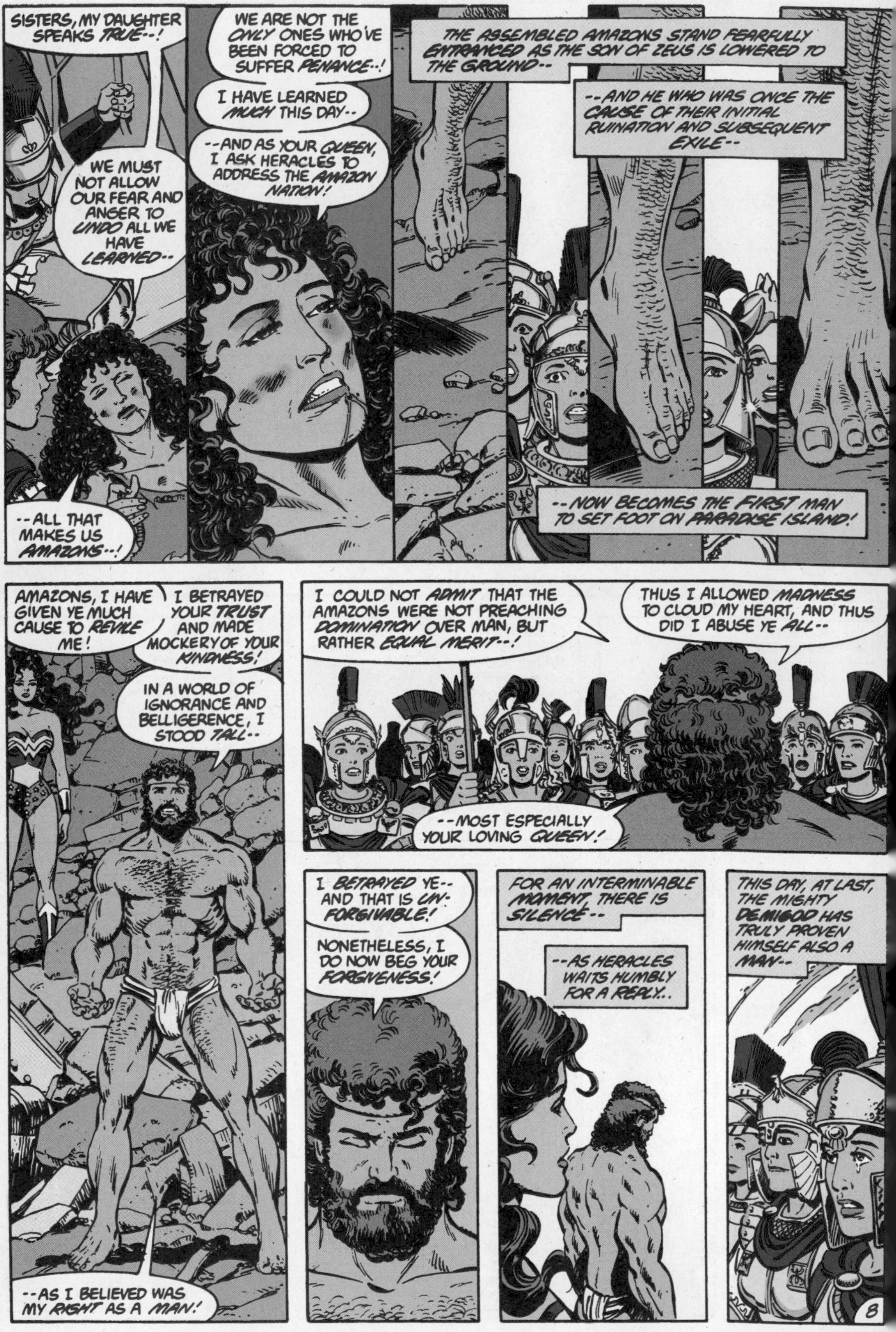

SISTERS, MY DAUGHTER SPEAKS TRUE--!
WE MUST NOT ALLOW OUR FEAR AND ANGER TO UNDO ALL WE HAVE LEARNED--
--ALL THAT MAKES US AMAZONS--!
WE ARE NOT THE ONLY ONES WHO'VE BEEN FORCED TO SUFFER PENANCE--!
I HAVE LEARNED MUCH THIS DAY--
--AND AS YOUR QUEEN, I ASK HERACLES TO ADDRESS THE AMAZON NATION!
THE ASSEMBLED AMAZONS STAND FEARFULLY ENTRANCED AS THE SON OF ZEUS IS LOWERED TO THE GROUND--
--AND HE WHO WAS ONCE THE CAUSE OF THEIR INITIAL RUINATION AND SUBSEQUENT EXILE--
--NOW BECOMES THE FIRST MAN TO SET FOOT ON PARADISE ISLAND!
AMAZONS, I HAVE GIVEN YE MUCH CAUSE TO REVILE ME!
I BETRAYED YOUR TRUST AND MADE MOCKERY OF YOUR KINDNESS!
IN A WORLD OF IGNORANCE AND BELLIGERENCE, I STOOD TALL--
--AS I BELIEVED WAS MY RIGHT AS A MAN!
I COULD NOT ADMIT THAT THE AMAZONS WERE NOT PREACHING DOMINATION OVER MAN, BUT RATHER EQUAL MERIT--!
THUS I ALLOWED MADNESS TO CLOUD MY HEART, AND THUS DID I ABUSE YE ALL--
--MOST ESPECIALLY YOUR LOVING QUEEN!
I BETRAYED YE--AND THAT IS UNFORGIVABLE!
NONETHELESS, I DO NOW BEG YOUR FORGIVENESS!
FOR AN INTERMINABLE MOMENT, THERE IS SILENCE--
--AS HERACLES WAITS HUMBLY FOR A REPLY...
THIS DAY, AT LAST, THE MIGHTY DEMIGOD HAS TRULY PROVEN HIMSELF ALSO A MAN--
8

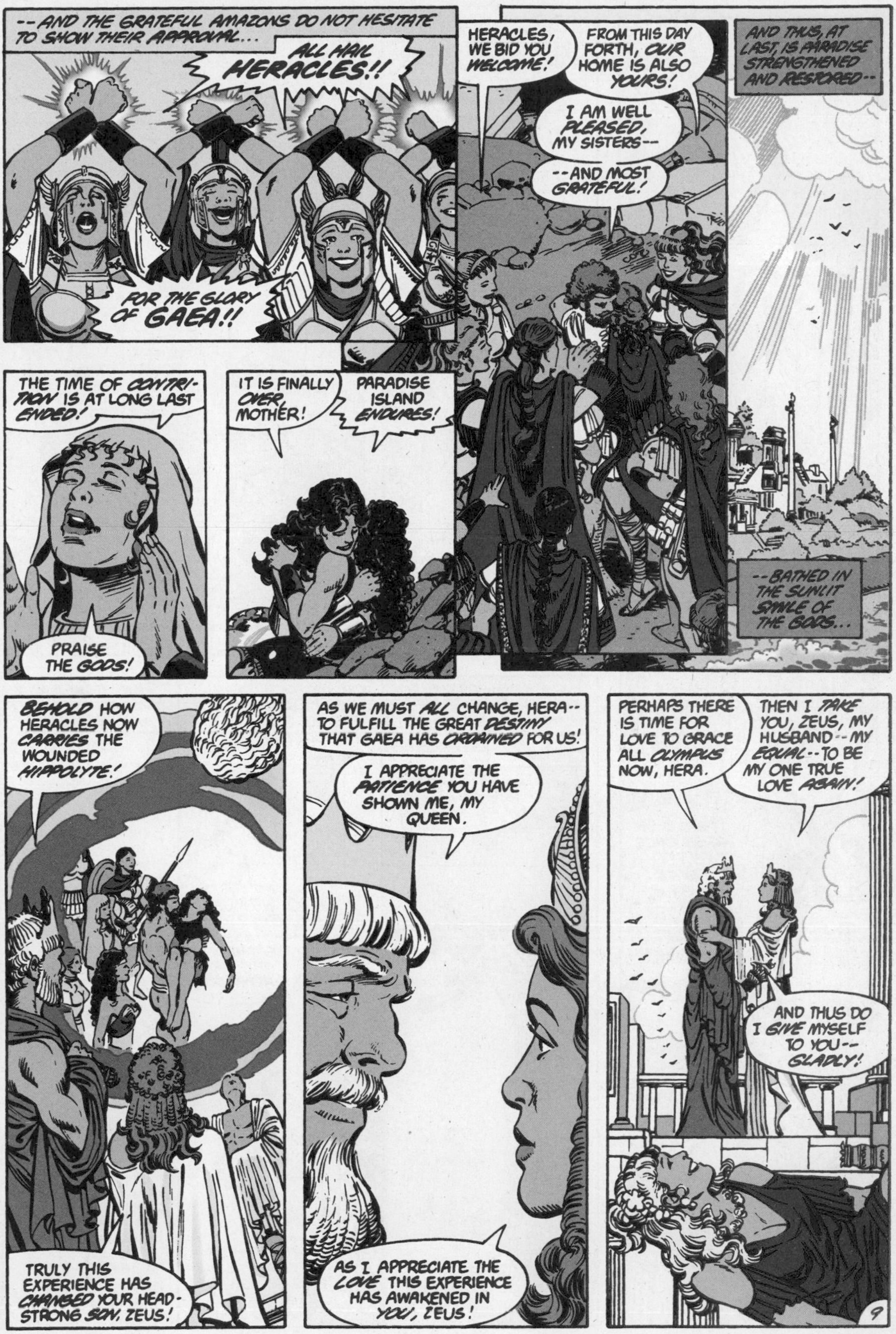
--AND THE GRATEFUL AMAZONS DO NOT HESITATE TO SHOW THEIR APPROVAL...
ALL HAIL HERACLES!!
FOR THE GLORY OF GAEA!!
HERACLES, WE BID YOU WELCOME!
FROM THIS DAY FORTH, OUR HOME IS ALSO YOURS!
I AM WELL PLEASED, MY SISTERS--
--AND MOST GRATEFUL!
AND THUS, AT LAST, IS PARADISE STRENGTHENED AND RESTORED--
--BATHED IN THE SUNLIT SMILE OF THE GODS...
THE TIME OF CONTRITION IS AT LONG LAST ENDED!
PRAISE THE GODS!
IT IS FINALLY OVER, MOTHER!
PARADISE ISLAND ENDURES!
BEHOLD HOW HERACLES NOW CARRIES THE WOUNDED HIPPOLYTE!
TRULY THIS EXPERIENCE HAS CHANGED YOUR HEADSTRONG SON, ZEUS!
AS WE MUST ALL CHANGE, HERA-- TO FULFILL THE GREAT DESTINY THAT GAEA HAS ORDAINED FOR US!
I APPRECIATE THE PATIENCE YOU HAVE SHOWN ME, MY QUEEN.
AS I APPRECIATE THE LOVE THIS EXPERIENCE HAS AWAKENED IN YOU, ZEUS!
PERHAPS THERE IS TIME FOR LOVE TO GRACE ALL OLYMPUS NOW, HERA.
THEN I TAKE YOU, ZEUS, MY HUSBAND--MY EQUAL--TO BE MY ONE TRUE LOVE AGAIN!
AND THUS DO I GIVE MYSELF TO YOU-- GLADLY!
9

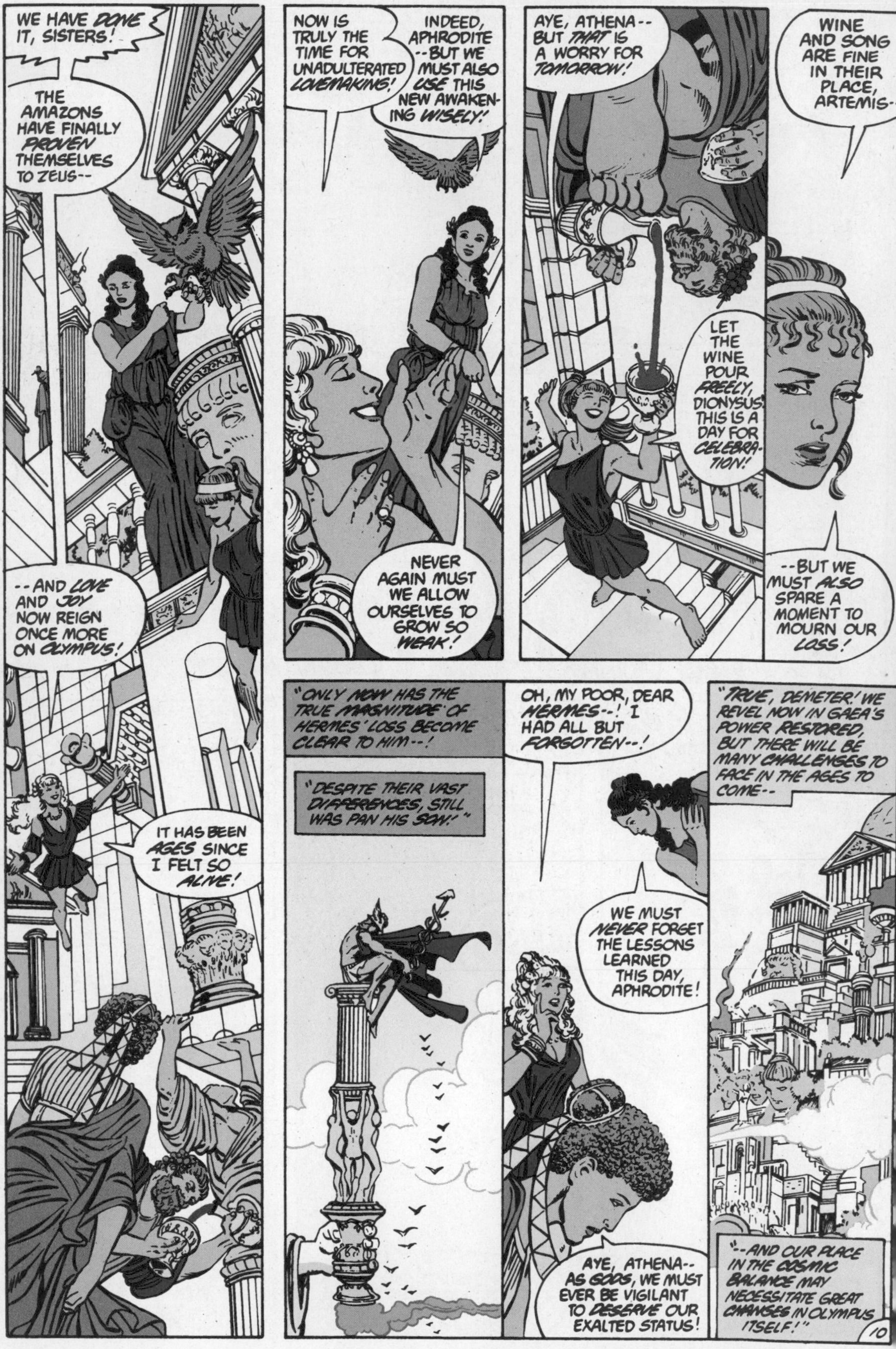
WE HAVE DONE IT, SISTERS!
THE AMAZONS HAVE FINALLY PROVEN THEMSELVES TO ZEUS--
--AND LOVE AND JOY NOW REIGN ONCE MORE ON OLYMPUS!
IT HAS BEEN AGES SINCE I FELT SO ALIVE!
NOW IS TRULY THE TIME FOR UNADULTERATED LOVEMAKING!
INDEED, APHRODITE --BUT WE MUST ALSO USE THIS NEW AWAKENING WISELY!
NEVER AGAIN MUST WE ALLOW OURSELVES TO GROW SO WEAK!
AYE, ATHENA-- BUT THAT IS A WORRY FOR TOMORROW!
LET THE WINE POUR FREELY, DIONYSUS! THIS IS A DAY FOR CELEBRATION!
WINE AND SONG ARE FINE IN THEIR PLACE, ARTEMIS--
--BUT WE MUST ALSO SPARE A MOMENT TO MOURN OUR LOSS!
"ONLY NOW HAS THE TRUE MAGNITUDE OF HERMES' LOSS BECOME CLEAR TO HIM--!
"DESPITE THEIR VAST DIFFERENCES, STILL WAS PAN HIS SON!"
OH, MY POOR, DEAR HERMES--! I HAD ALL BUT FORGOTTEN--!
WE MUST NEVER FORGET THE LESSONS LEARNED THIS DAY, APHRODITE!
AYE, ATHENA-- AS GODS, WE MUST EVER BE VIGILANT TO DESERVE OUR EXALTED STATUS!
"TRUE, DEMETER! WE REVEL NOW IN GAEA'S POWER RESTORED, BUT THERE WILL BE MANY CHALLENGES TO FACE IN THE AGES TO COME--
"--AND OUR PLACE IN THE COSMIC BALANCE MAY NECESSITATE GREAT CHANGES IN OLYMPUS ITSELF!"
10

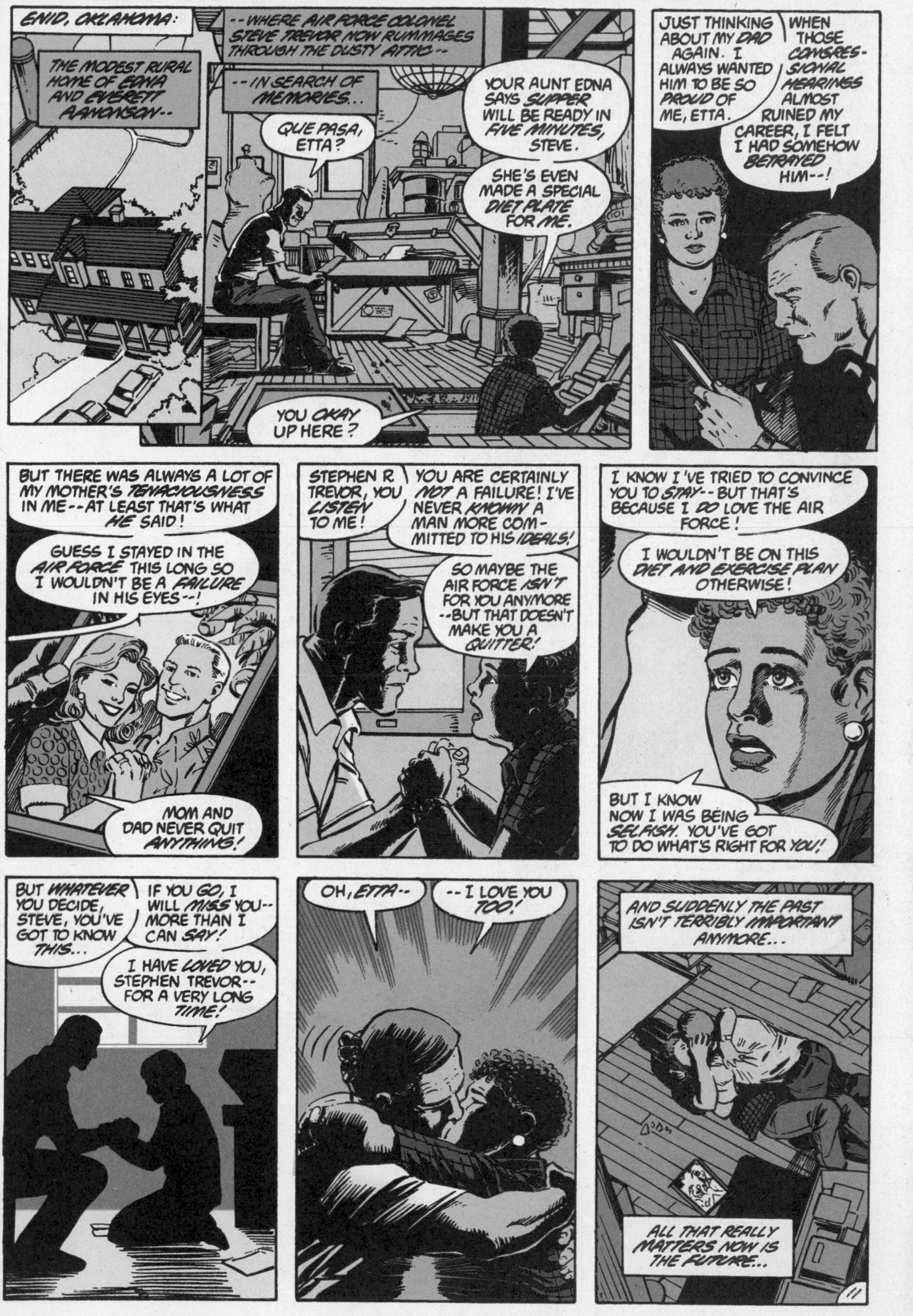
ENID, OKLAHOMA:
THE MODEST RURAL HOME OF EDNA AND EVERETT AAMONSON--
--WHERE AIR FORCE COLONEL STEVE TREVOR NOW RUMMAGES THROUGH THE DUSTY ATTIC--
--IN SEARCH OF MEMORIES...
QUE PASA, ETTA?
YOUR AUNT EDNA SAYS SUPPER WILL BE READY IN FIVE MINUTES, STEVE.
SHE'S EVEN MADE A SPECIAL DIET PLATE FOR ME.
YOU OKAY UP HERE?
JUST THINKING ABOUT MY DAD AGAIN. I ALWAYS WANTED HIM TO BE SO PROUD OF ME, ETTA.
WHEN THOSE CONGRES-SIONAL HEARINGS ALMOST RUINED MY CAREER, I FELT I HAD SOMEHOW BETRAYED HIM--!
BUT THERE WAS ALWAYS A LOT OF MY MOTHER'S TENACIOUSNESS IN ME--AT LEAST THAT'S WHAT HE SAID!
GUESS I STAYED IN THE AIR FORCE THIS LONG SO I WOULDN'T BE A FAILURE IN HIS EYES--!
MOM AND DAD NEVER QUIT ANYTHING!
STEPHEN R. TREVOR, YOU LISTEN TO ME!
YOU ARE CERTAINLY NOT A FAILURE! I'VE NEVER KNOWN A MAN MORE COM-MITTED TO HIS IDEALS!
SO MAYBE THE AIR FORCE ISN'T FOR YOU ANYMORE --BUT THAT DOESN'T MAKE YOU A QUITTER!
I KNOW I'VE TRIED TO CONVINCE YOU TO STAY--BUT THAT'S BECAUSE I DO LOVE THE AIR FORCE!
I WOULDN'T BE ON THIS DIET AND EXERCISE PLAN OTHERWISE!
BUT I KNOW NOW I WAS BEING SELFISH. YOU'VE GOT TO DO WHAT'S RIGHT FOR YOU!
BUT WHATEVER YOU DECIDE, STEVE, YOU'VE GOT TO KNOW THIS...
IF YOU GO, I WILL MISS YOU--MORE THAN I CAN SAY!
I HAVE LOVED YOU, STEPHEN TREVOR--FOR A VERY LONG TIME!
OH, ETTA--
--I LOVE YOU TOO!
AND SUDDENLY THE PAST ISN'T TERRIBLY IMPORTANT ANYMORE...
ALL THAT REALLY MATTERS NOW IS THE FUTURE...
11

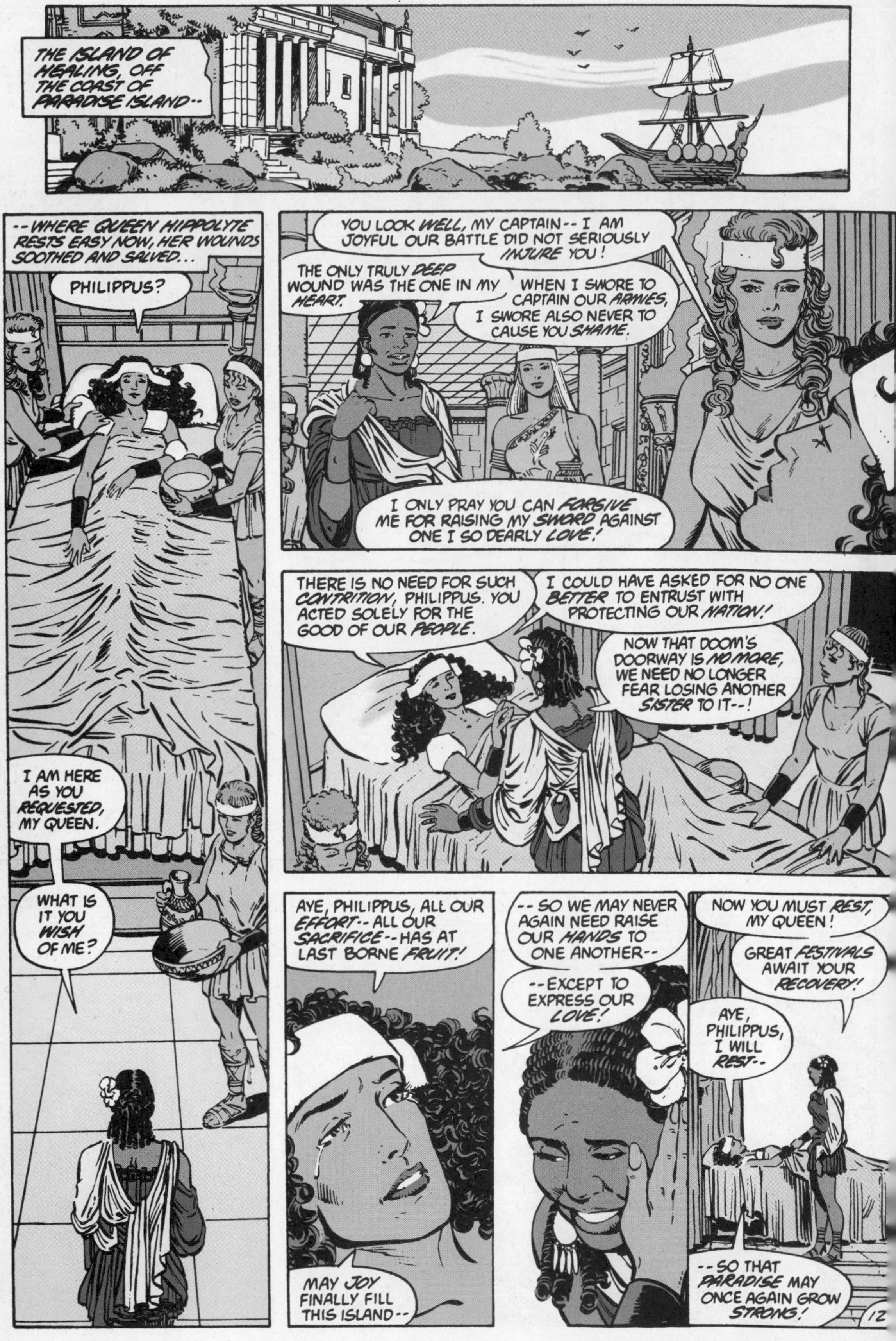
THE ISLAND OF HEALING, OFF THE COAST OF PARADISE ISLAND--
--WHERE QUEEN HIPPOLYTE RESTS EASY NOW, HER WOUNDS SOOTHED AND SALVED...
PHILIPPUS?
I AM HERE AS YOU REQUESTED, MY QUEEN.
WHAT IS IT YOU WISH OF ME?
YOU LOOK WELL, MY CAPTAIN-- I AM JOYFUL OUR BATTLE DID NOT SERIOUSLY INJURE YOU!
THE ONLY TRULY DEEP WOUND WAS THE ONE IN MY HEART.
WHEN I SWORE TO CAPTAIN OUR ARMIES, I SWORE ALSO NEVER TO CAUSE YOU SHAME.
I ONLY PRAY YOU CAN FORGIVE ME FOR RAISING MY SWORD AGAINST ONE I SO DEARLY LOVE!
THERE IS NO NEED FOR SUCH CONTRITION, PHILIPPUS. YOU ACTED SOLELY FOR THE GOOD OF OUR PEOPLE.
I COULD HAVE ASKED FOR NO ONE BETTER TO ENTRUST WITH PROTECTING OUR NATION!
NOW THAT DOOM'S DOORWAY IS NO MORE, WE NEED NO LONGER FEAR LOSING ANOTHER SISTER TO IT--!
AYE, PHILIPPUS, ALL OUR EFFORT-- ALL OUR SACRIFICE--HAS AT LAST BORNE FRUIT!
MAY JOY FINALLY FILL THIS ISLAND--
--SO WE MAY NEVER AGAIN NEED RAISE OUR HANDS TO ONE ANOTHER--
--EXCEPT TO EXPRESS OUR LOVE!
NOW YOU MUST REST, MY QUEEN!
GREAT FESTIVALS AWAIT YOUR RECOVERY!
AYE, PHILIPPUS, I WILL REST--
--SO THAT PARADISE MAY ONCE AGAIN GROW STRONG!
12

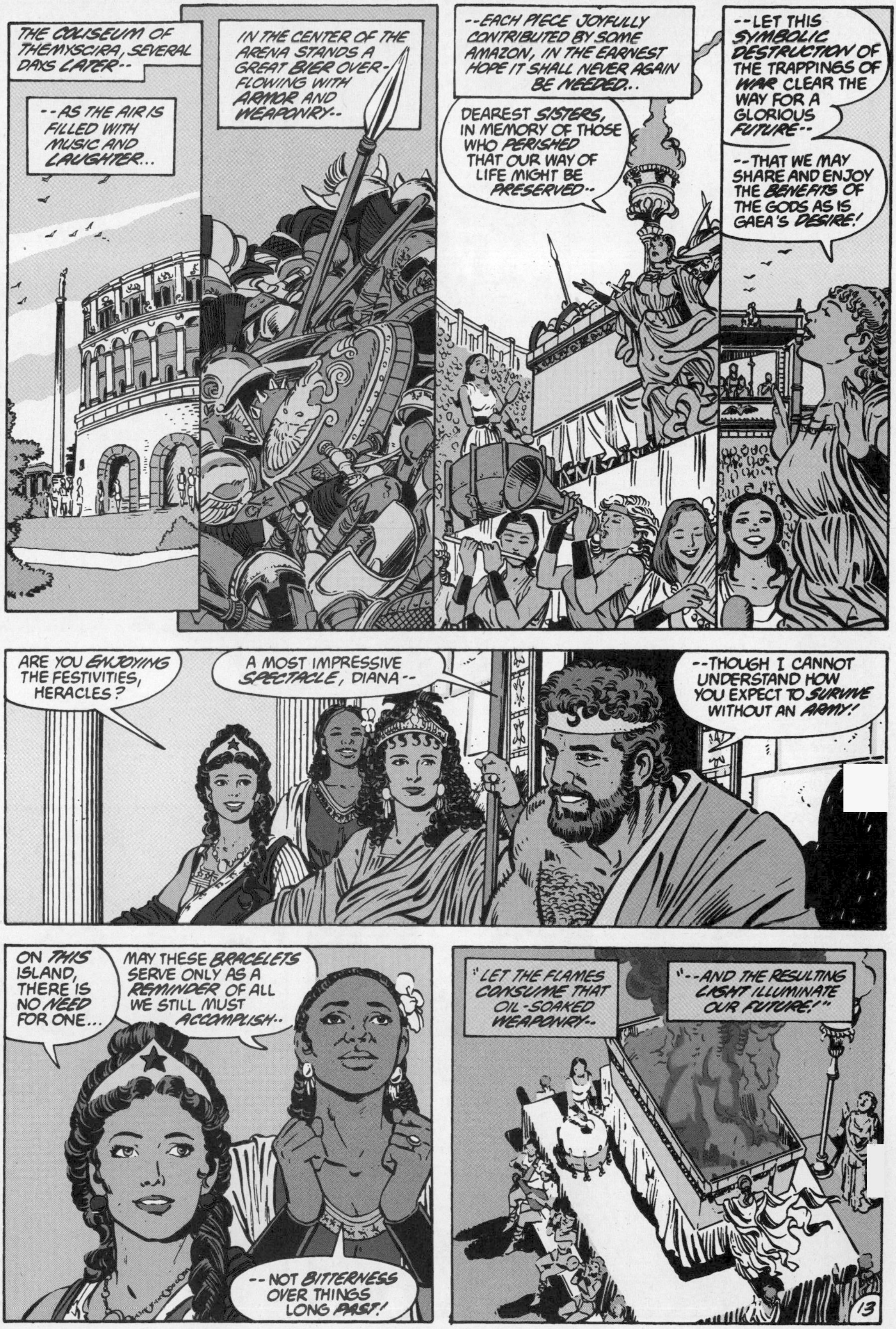
THE COLISEUM OF THEMYSCIRA, SEVERAL DAYS LATER--
--AS THE AIR IS FILLED WITH MUSIC AND LAUGHTER...
IN THE CENTER OF THE ARENA STANDS A GREAT BIER OVER-FLOWING WITH ARMOR AND WEAPONRY--
--EACH PIECE JOYFULLY CONTRIBUTED BY SOME AMAZON, IN THE EARNEST HOPE IT SHALL NEVER AGAIN BE NEEDED...
DEAREST SISTERS, IN MEMORY OF THOSE WHO PERISHED THAT OUR WAY OF LIFE MIGHT BE PRESERVED--
--LET THIS SYMBOLIC DESTRUCTION OF THE TRAPPINGS OF WAR CLEAR THE WAY FOR A GLORIOUS FUTURE--
--THAT WE MAY SHARE AND ENJOY THE BENEFITS OF THE GODS AS IS GAEA'S DESIRE!
ARE YOU ENJOYING THE FESTIVITIES, HERACLES?
A MOST IMPRESSIVE SPECTACLE, DIANA--
--THOUGH I CANNOT UNDERSTAND HOW YOU EXPECT TO SURVIVE WITHOUT AN ARMY!
ON THIS ISLAND, THERE IS NO NEED FOR ONE...
MAY THESE BRACELETS SERVE ONLY AS A REMINDER OF ALL WE STILL MUST ACCOMPLISH--
--NOT BITTERNESS OVER THINGS LONG PAST!
"LET THE FLAMES CONSUME THAT OIL-SOAKED WEAPONRY--
"--AND THE RESULTING LIGHT ILLUMINATE OUR FUTURE!"
13

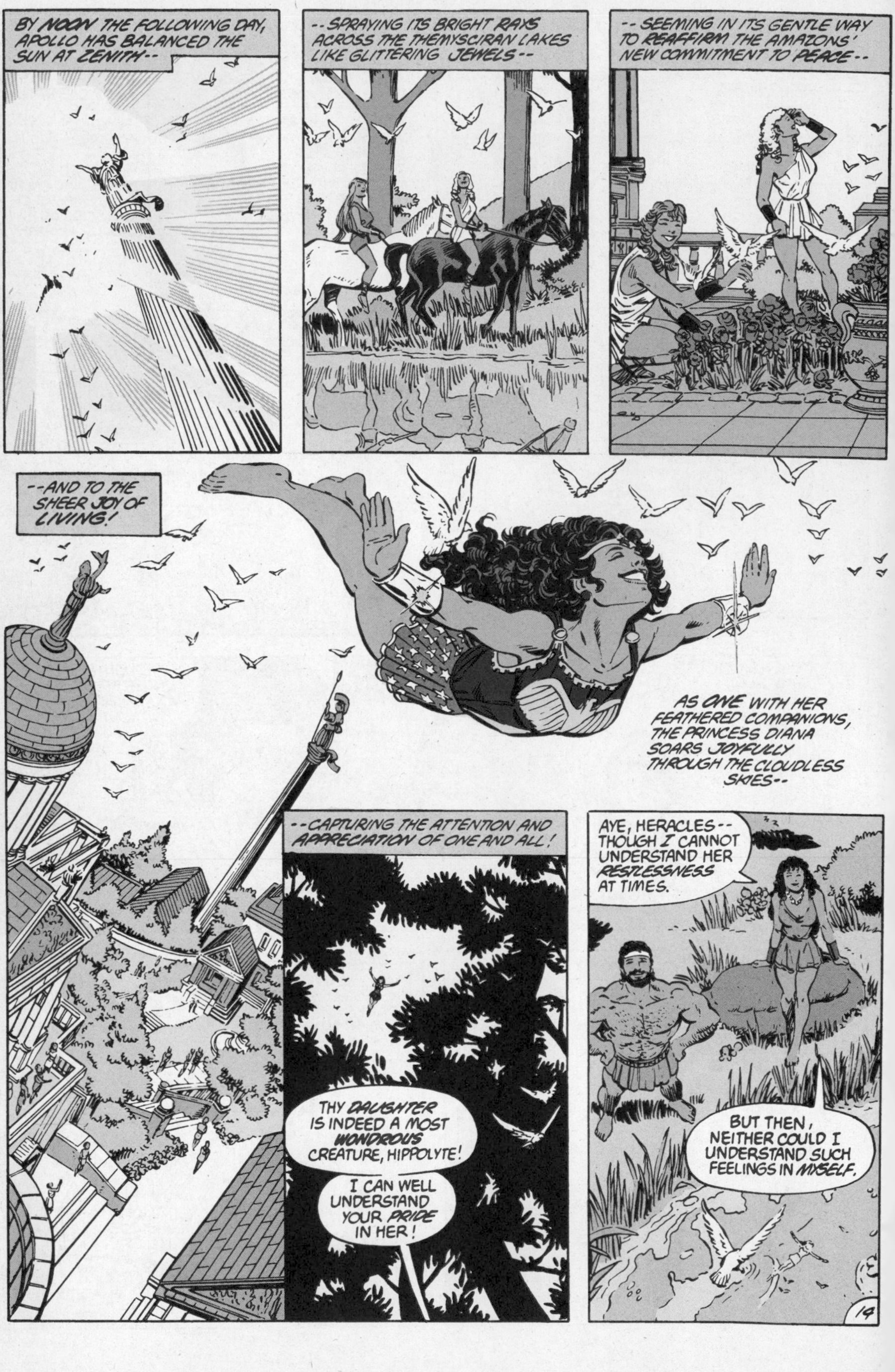

BY NOON THE FOLLOWING DAY, APOLLO HAS BALANCED THE SUN AT ZENITH--
--SPRAYING ITS BRIGHT RAYS ACROSS THE THEMYSCIRAN LAKES LIKE GLITTERING JEWELS--
--SEEMING IN ITS GENTLE WAY TO REAFFIRM THE AMAZONS' NEW COMMITMENT TO PEACE--
--AND TO THE SHEER JOY OF LIVING!
AS ONE WITH HER FEATHERED COMPANIONS, THE PRINCESS DIANA SOARS JOYFULLY THROUGH THE CLOUDLESS SKIES--
--CAPTURING THE ATTENTION AND APPRECIATION OF ONE AND ALL!
THY DAUGHTER IS INDEED A MOST WONDROUS CREATURE, HIPPOLYTE!
I CAN WELL UNDERSTAND YOUR PRIDE IN HER!
AYE, HERACLES-- THOUGH I CANNOT UNDERSTAND HER RESTLESSNESS AT TIMES.
BUT THEN, NEITHER COULD I UNDERSTAND SUCH FEELINGS IN MYSELF.
14

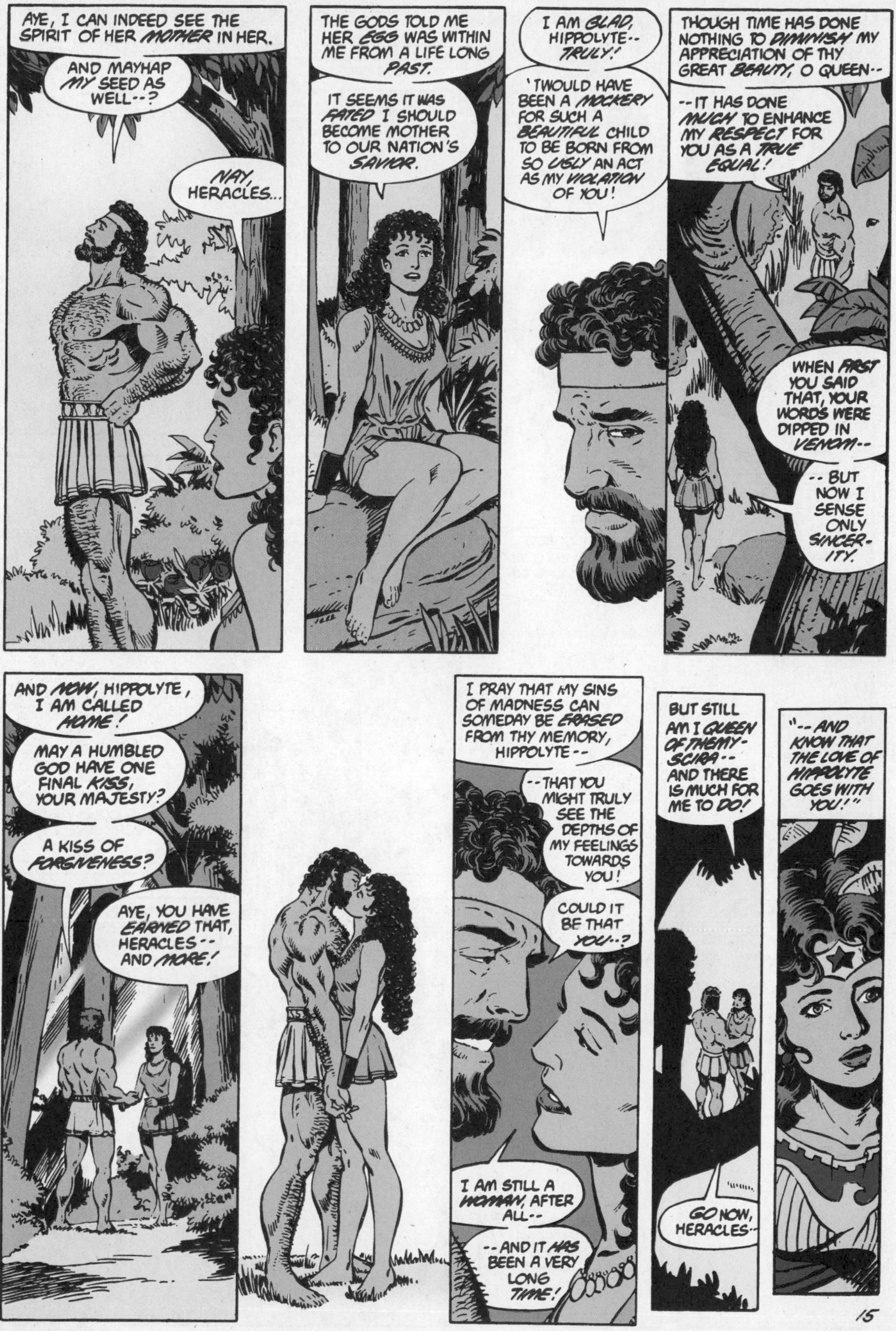
AYE, I CAN INDEED SEE THE SPIRIT OF HER MOTHER IN HER.
AND MAYHAP MY SEED AS WELL--?
NAY, HERACLES...
THE GODS TOLD ME HER EGG WAS WITHIN ME FROM A LIFE LONG PAST.
IT SEEMS IT WAS FATED I SHOULD BECOME MOTHER TO OUR NATION'S SAVIOR.
I AM GLAD, HIPPOLYTE-- TRULY!
'TWOULD HAVE BEEN A MOCKERY FOR SUCH A BEAUTIFUL CHILD TO BE BORN FROM SO UGLY AN ACT AS MY VIOLATION OF YOU!
THOUGH TIME HAS DONE NOTHING TO DIMINISH MY APPRECIATION OF THY GREAT BEAUTY, O QUEEN--
--IT HAS DONE MUCH TO ENHANCE MY RESPECT FOR YOU AS A TRUE EQUAL!
WHEN FIRST YOU SAID THAT, YOUR WORDS WERE DIPPED IN VENOM--
--BUT NOW I SENSE ONLY SINCER-ITY.
AND NOW, HIPPOLYTE, I AM CALLED HOME!
MAY A HUMBLED GOD HAVE ONE FINAL KISS, YOUR MAJESTY?
A KISS OF FORGIVENESS?
AYE, YOU HAVE EARNED THAT, HERACLES-- AND MORE!
I PRAY THAT MY SINS OF MADNESS CAN SOMEDAY BE ERASED FROM THY MEMORY, HIPPOLYTE--
--THAT YOU MIGHT TRULY SEE THE DEPTHS OF MY FEELINGS TOWARDS YOU!
COULD IT BE THAT YOU--?
I AM STILL A WOMAN, AFTER ALL--
--AND IT HAS BEEN A VERY LONG TIME!
BUT STILL AM I QUEEN OF THEMY-SCIRA--AND THERE IS MUCH FOR ME TO DO!
GO NOW, HERACLES--
"--AND KNOW THAT THE LOVE OF HIPPOLYTE GOES WITH YOU!"
15

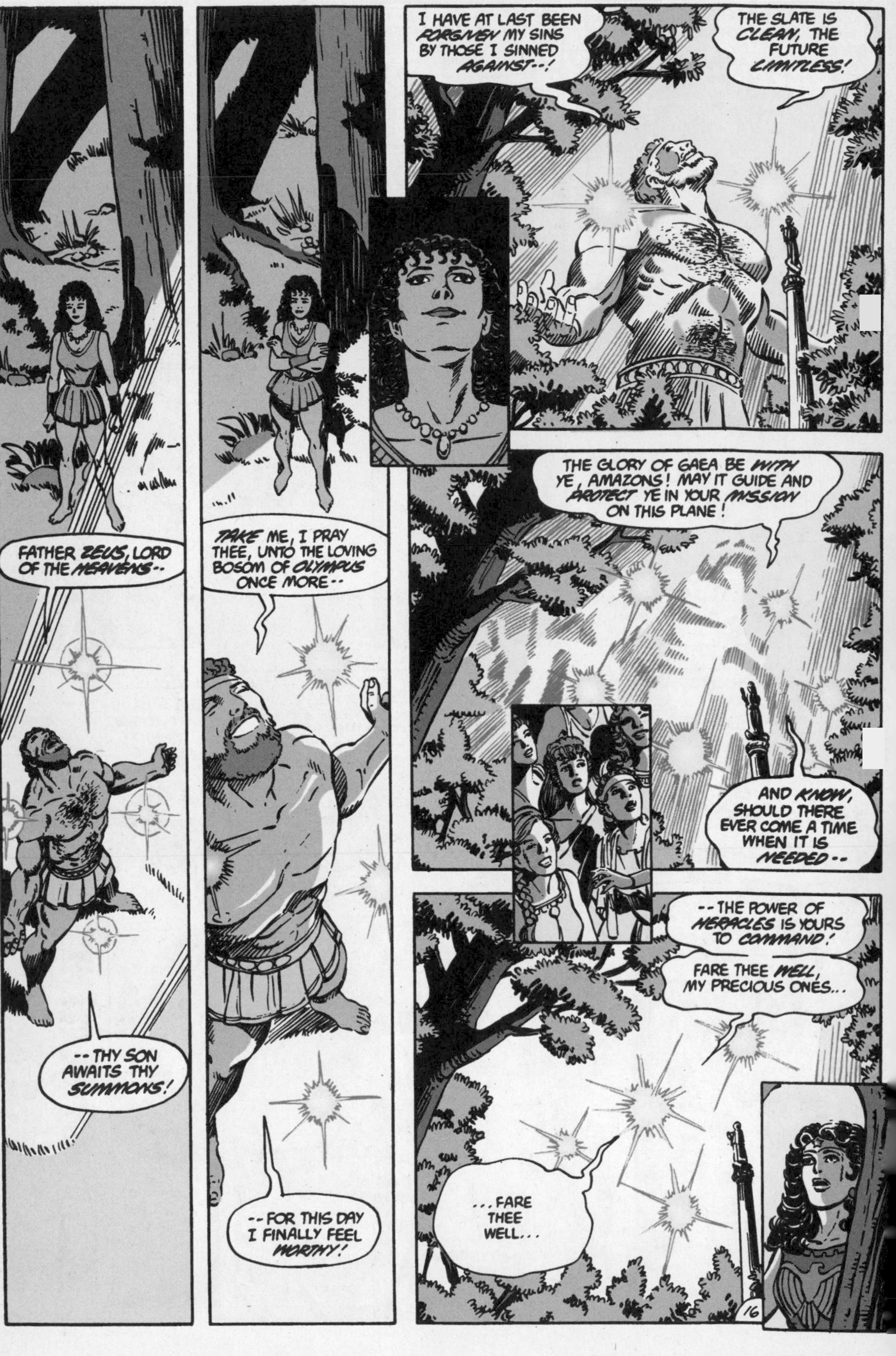
FATHER ZEUS, LORD OF THE HEAVENS--
--THY SON AWAITS THY SUMMONS!
TAKE ME, I PRAY THEE, UNTO THE LOVING BOSOM OF OLYMPUS ONCE MORE--
--FOR THIS DAY I FINALLY FEEL WORTHY!
I HAVE AT LAST BEEN FORGIVEN MY SINS BY THOSE I SINNED AGAINST--!
THE SLATE IS CLEAN, THE FUTURE LIMITLESS!
THE GLORY OF GAEA BE WITH YE, AMAZONS! MAY IT GUIDE AND PROTECT YE IN YOUR MISSION ON THIS PLANE!
AND KNOW, SHOULD THERE EVER COME A TIME WHEN IT IS NEEDED--
--THE POWER OF HERACLES IS YOURS TO COMMAND!
FARE THEE WELL, MY PRECIOUS ONES...
...FARE THEE WELL...
16

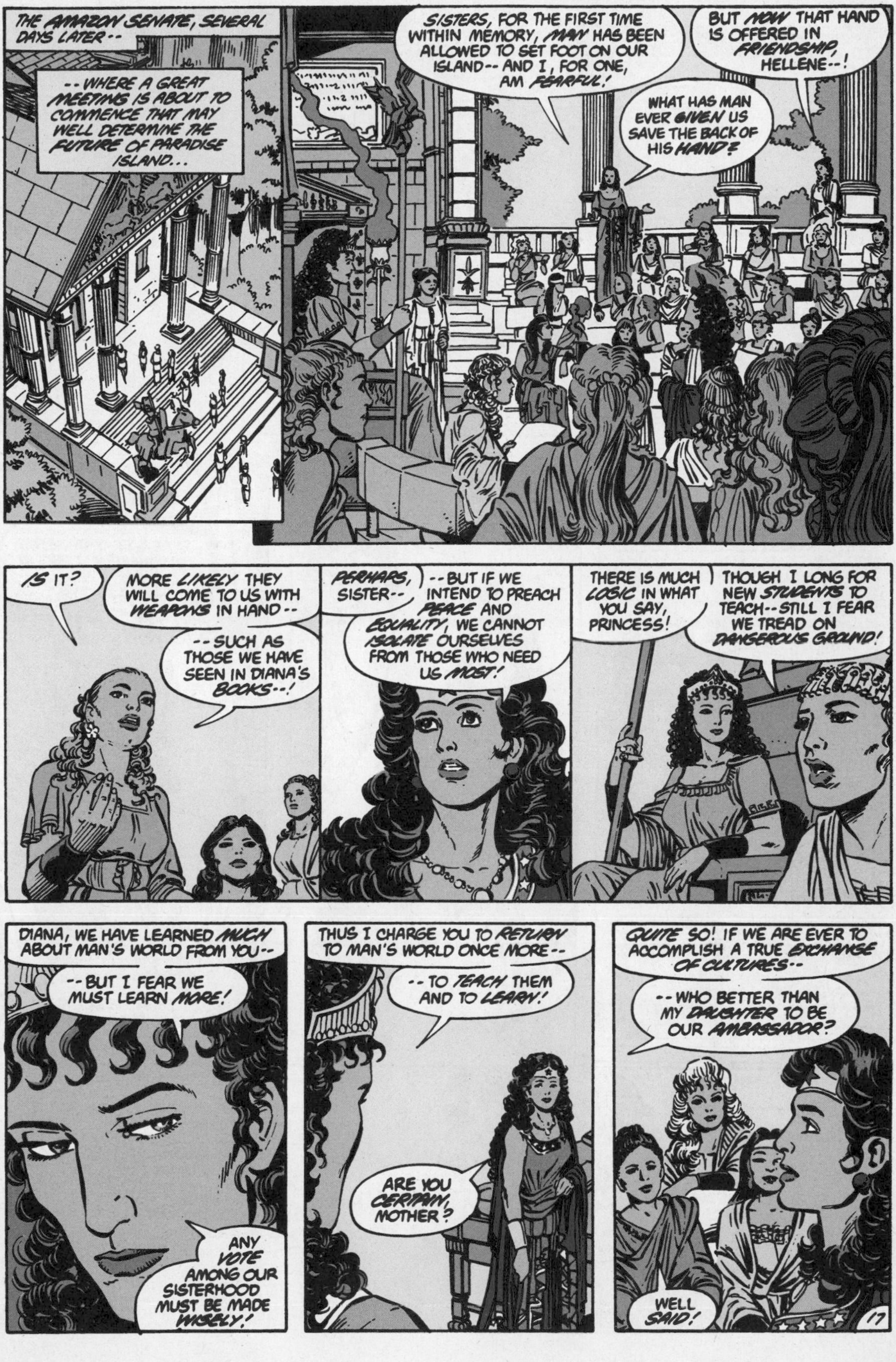
THE AMAZON SENATE, SEVERAL DAYS LATER--
--WHERE A GREAT MEETING IS ABOUT TO COMMENCE THAT MAY WELL DETERMINE THE FUTURE OF PARADISE ISLAND...
SISTERS, FOR THE FIRST TIME WITHIN MEMORY, MAN HAS BEEN ALLOWED TO SET FOOT ON OUR ISLAND-- AND I, FOR ONE, AM FEARFUL!
WHAT HAS MAN EVER GIVEN US SAVE THE BACK OF HIS HAND?
BUT NOW THAT HAND IS OFFERED IN FRIENDSHIP, HELLENE--!
IS IT?
MORE LIKELY THEY WILL COME TO US WITH WEAPONS IN HAND--
--SUCH AS THOSE WE HAVE SEEN IN DIANA'S BOOKS--!
PERHAPS, SISTER--
--BUT IF WE INTEND TO PREACH PEACE AND EQUALITY, WE CANNOT ISOLATE OURSELVES FROM THOSE WHO NEED US MOST!
THERE IS MUCH LOGIC IN WHAT YOU SAY, PRINCESS!
THOUGH I LONG FOR NEW STUDENTS TO TEACH--STILL I FEAR WE TREAD ON DANGEROUS GROUND!
DIANA, WE HAVE LEARNED MUCH ABOUT MAN'S WORLD FROM YOU--
--BUT I FEAR WE MUST LEARN MORE!
ANY VOTE AMONG OUR SISTERHOOD MUST BE MADE WISELY!
THUS I CHARGE YOU TO RETURN TO MAN'S WORLD ONCE MORE--
--TO TEACH THEM AND TO LEARN!
ARE YOU CERTAIN, MOTHER?
QUITE SO! IF WE ARE EVER TO ACCOMPLISH A TRUE EXCHANGE OF CULTURES--
--WHO BETTER THAN MY DAUGHTER TO BE OUR AMBASSADOR?
WELL SAID!
17

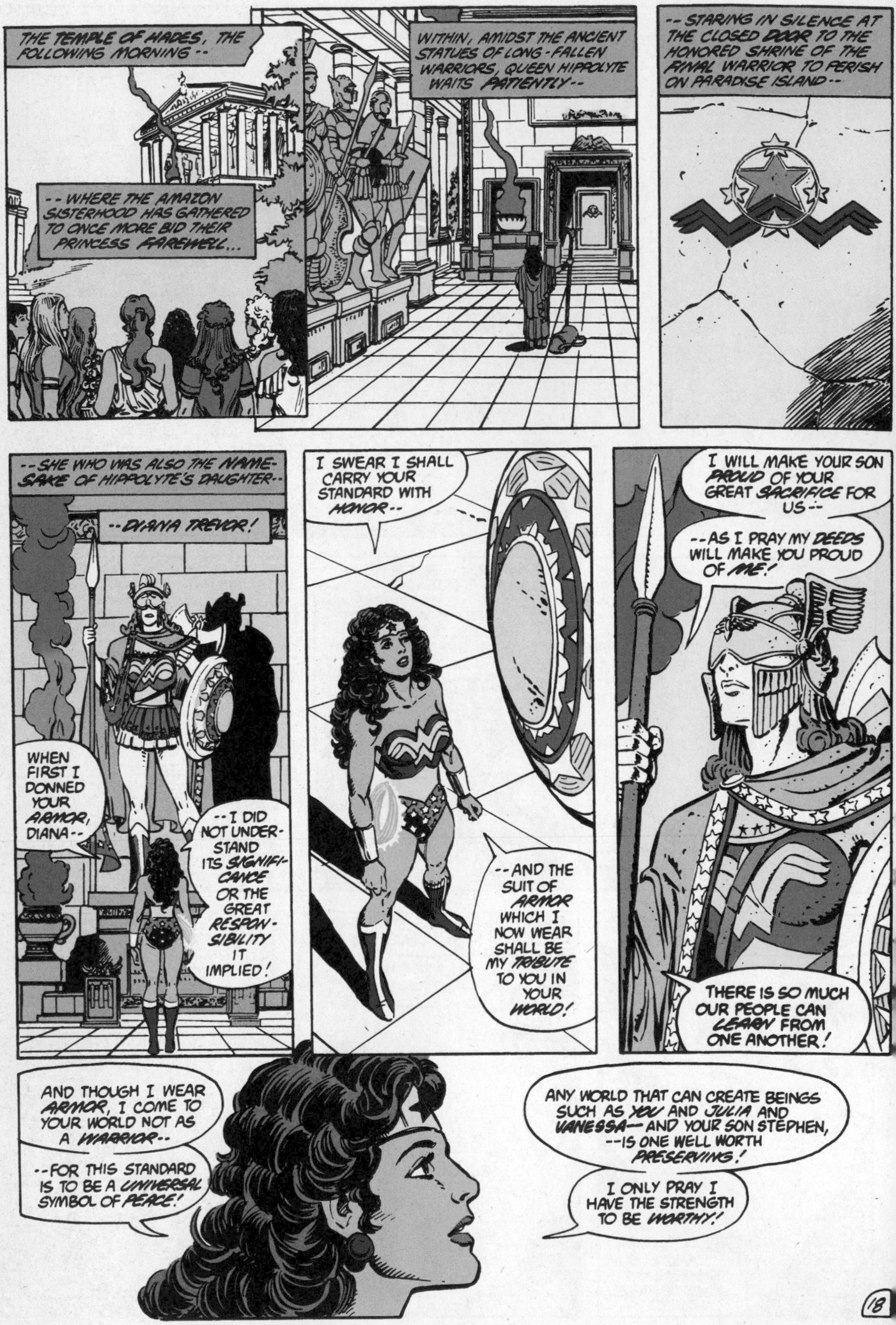
THE TEMPLE OF HADES, THE FOLLOWING MORNING --
-- WHERE THE AMAZON SISTERHOOD HAS GATHERED TO ONCE MORE BID THEIR PRINCESS FAREWELL...
WITHIN, AMIDST THE ANCIENT STATUES OF LONG-FALLEN WARRIORS, QUEEN HIPPOLYTE WAITS PATIENTLY --
-- STARING IN SILENCE AT THE CLOSED DOOR TO THE HONORED SHRINE OF THE FINAL WARRIOR TO PERISH ON PARADISE ISLAND --
-- SHE WHO WAS ALSO THE NAME-SAKE OF HIPPOLYTE'S DAUGHTER --
-- DIANA TREVOR!
WHEN FIRST I DONNED YOUR ARMOR, DIANA --
-- I DID NOT UNDER-STAND ITS SIGNIFI-CANCE OR THE GREAT RESPON-SIBILITY IT IMPLIED!
I SWEAR I SHALL CARRY YOUR STANDARD WITH HONOR --
-- AND THE SUIT OF ARMOR WHICH I NOW WEAR SHALL BE MY TRIBUTE TO YOU IN YOUR WORLD!
I WILL MAKE YOUR SON PROUD OF YOUR GREAT SACRIFICE FOR US --
-- AS I PRAY MY DEEDS WILL MAKE YOU PROUD OF ME!
THERE IS SO MUCH OUR PEOPLE CAN LEARN FROM ONE ANOTHER!
AND THOUGH I WEAR ARMOR, I COME TO YOUR WORLD NOT AS A WARRIOR --
-- FOR THIS STANDARD IS TO BE A UNIVERSAL SYMBOL OF PEACE!
ANY WORLD THAT CAN CREATE BEINGS SUCH AS YOU AND JULIA AND VANESSA -- AND YOUR SON STEPHEN, -- IS ONE WELL WORTH PRESERVING!
I ONLY PRAY I HAVE THE STRENGTH TO BE WORTHY!
18

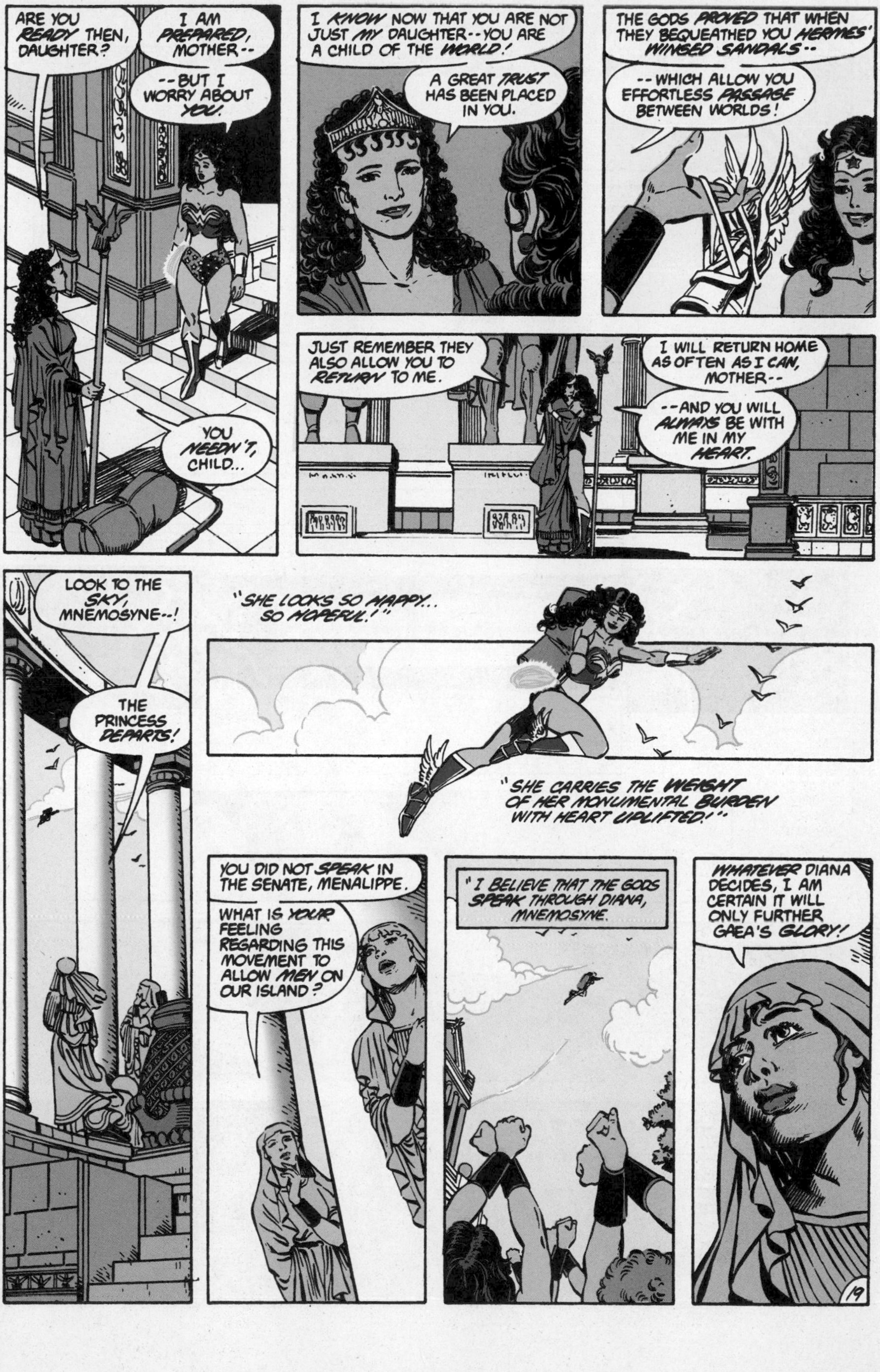
ARE YOU READY THEN, DAUGHTER?
I AM PREPARED, MOTHER--
--BUT I WORRY ABOUT YOU.
YOU NEEDN'T, CHILD...
I KNOW NOW THAT YOU ARE NOT JUST MY DAUGHTER--YOU ARE A CHILD OF THE WORLD!
A GREAT TRUST HAS BEEN PLACED IN YOU.
THE GODS PROVED THAT WHEN THEY BEQUEATHED YOU HERMES' WINGED SANDALS--
--WHICH ALLOW YOU EFFORTLESS PASSAGE BETWEEN WORLDS!
JUST REMEMBER THEY ALSO ALLOW YOU TO RETURN TO ME.
I WILL RETURN HOME AS OFTEN AS I CAN, MOTHER--
--AND YOU WILL ALWAYS BE WITH ME IN MY HEART.
LOOK TO THE SKY, MNEMOSYNE--!
THE PRINCESS DEPARTS!
"SHE LOOKS SO HAPPY... SO HOPEFUL!"
"SHE CARRIES THE WEIGHT OF HER MONUMENTAL BURDEN WITH HEART UPLIFTED!"
YOU DID NOT SPEAK IN THE SENATE, MENALIPPE.
WHAT IS YOUR FEELING REGARDING THIS MOVEMENT TO ALLOW MEN ON OUR ISLAND?
"I BELIEVE THAT THE GODS SPEAK THROUGH DIANA, MNEMOSYNE.
WHATEVER DIANA DECIDES, I AM CERTAIN IT WILL ONLY FURTHER GAEA'S GLORY!
19

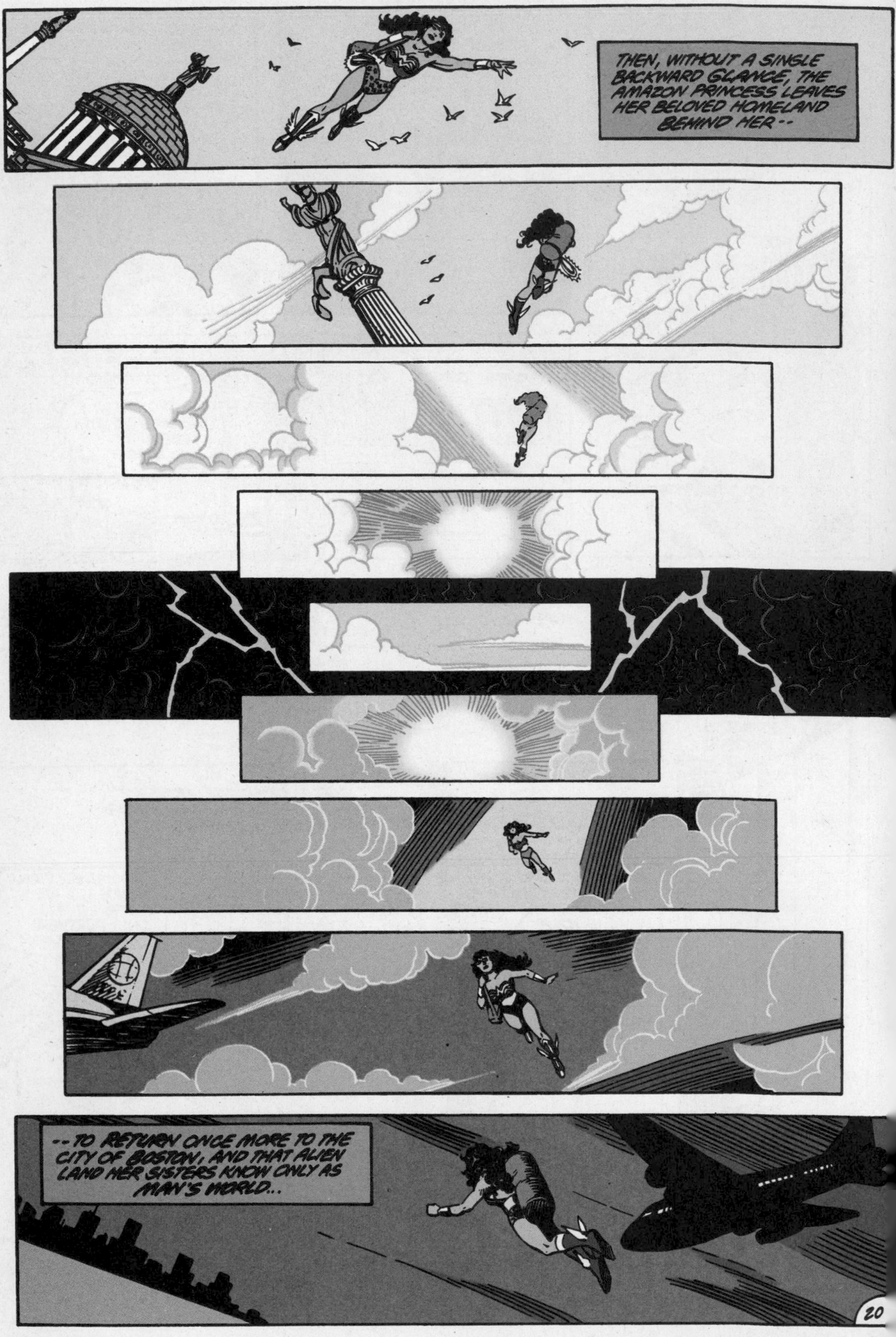
THEN, WITHOUT A SINGLE BACKWARD GLANCE, THE AMAZON PRINCESS LEAVES HER BELOVED HOMELAND BEHIND HER--
--TO RETURN ONCE MORE TO THE CITY OF BOSTON, AND THAT ALIEN LAND HER SISTERS KNOW ONLY AS MAN'S WORLD...
20

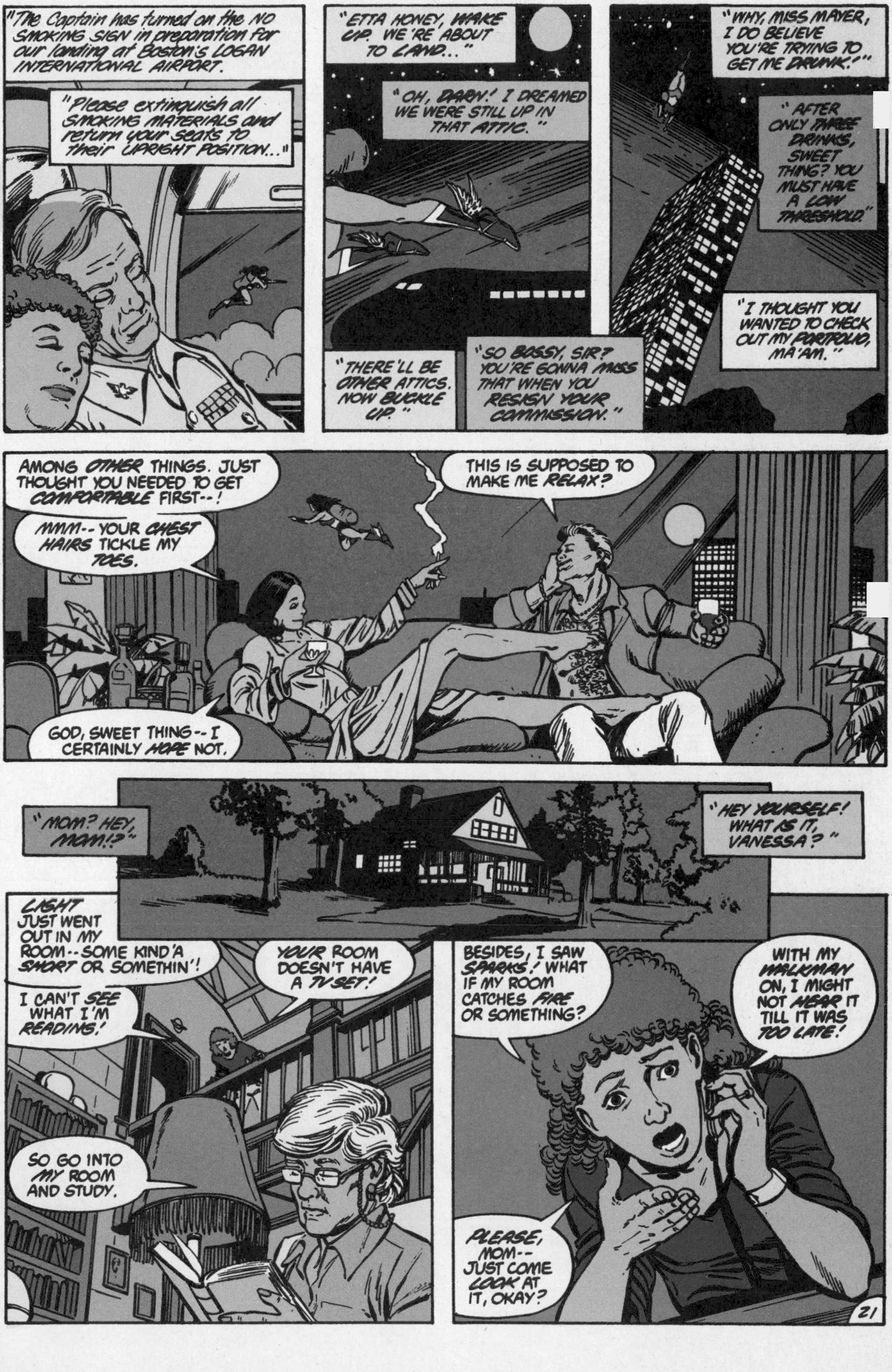
"The Captain has turned on the NO SMOKING SIGN in preparation for our landing at Boston's LOGAN INTERNATIONAL AIRPORT.
"Please extinguish all SMOKING MATERIALS and return your seats to their UPRIGHT POSITION..."
"ETTA HONEY, WAKE UP. WE'RE ABOUT TO LAND..."
"OH, DARN! I DREAMED WE WERE STILL UP IN THAT ATTIC."
"THERE'LL BE OTHER ATTICS. NOW BUCKLE UP."
"SO BOSSY, SIR? YOU'RE GONNA MISS THAT WHEN YOU RESIGN YOUR COMMISSION."
"WHY, MISS MAYER, I DO BELIEVE YOU'RE TRYING TO GET ME DRUNK."
"AFTER ONLY THREE DRINKS, SWEET THING? YOU MUST HAVE A LOW THRESHOLD."
"I THOUGHT YOU WANTED TO CHECK OUT MY PORTFOLIO, MA'AM."
AMONG OTHER THINGS. JUST THOUGHT YOU NEEDED TO GET COMFORTABLE FIRST--!
THIS IS SUPPOSED TO MAKE ME RELAX?
MMM--YOUR CHEST HAIRS TICKLE MY TOES.
GOD, SWEET THING--I CERTAINLY HOPE NOT.
"MOM? HEY, MOM!?"
"HEY YOURSELF! WHAT IS IT, VANESSA?"
LIGHT JUST WENT OUT IN MY ROOM--SOME KIND'A SHORT OR SOMETHIN'!
I CAN'T SEE WHAT I'M READING!
YOUR ROOM DOESN'T HAVE A TV SET!
SO GO INTO MY ROOM AND STUDY.
BESIDES, I SAW SPARKS! WHAT IF MY ROOM CATCHES FIRE OR SOMETHING?
WITH MY WALKMAN ON, I MIGHT NOT HEAR IT TILL IT WAS TOO LATE!
PLEASE, MOM--JUST COME LOOK AT IT, OKAY?
21

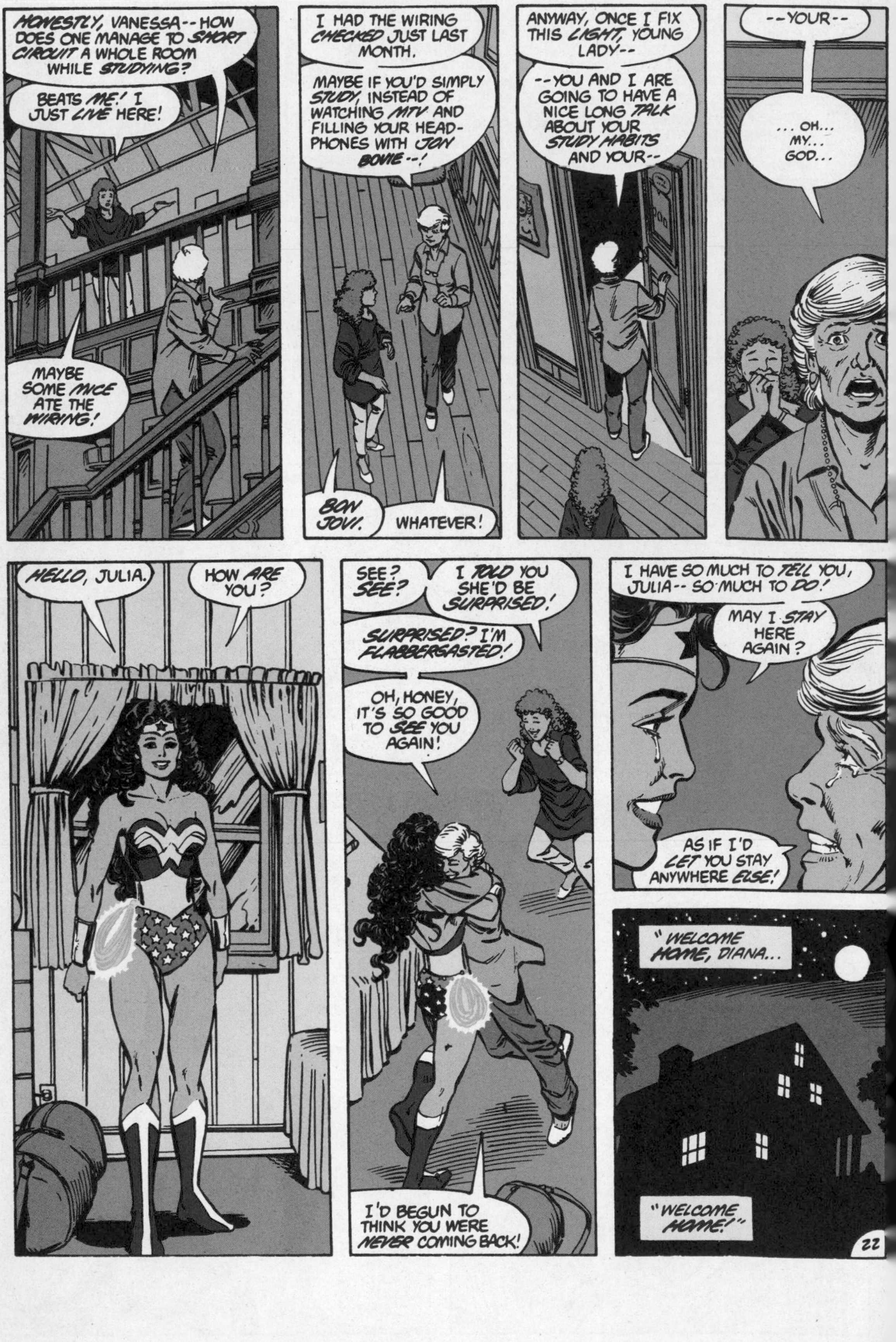
HONESTLY, VANESSA--HOW DOES ONE MANAGE TO SHORT CIRCUIT A WHOLE ROOM WHILE STUDYING?
BEATS ME! I JUST LIVE HERE!
MAYBE SOME MICE ATE THE WIRING!
I HAD THE WIRING CHECKED JUST LAST MONTH.
MAYBE IF YOU'D SIMPLY STUDY, INSTEAD OF WATCHING MTV AND FILLING YOUR HEAD-PHONES WITH JON BOVIE--!
BON JOVI.
WHATEVER!
ANYWAY, ONCE I FIX THIS LIGHT, YOUNG LADY--
--YOU AND I ARE GOING TO HAVE A NICE LONG TALK ABOUT YOUR STUDY HABITS AND YOUR--
--YOUR--
...OH... MY... GOD...
HELLO, JULIA.
HOW ARE YOU?
SEE? SEE?
I TOLD YOU SHE'D BE SURPRISED!
SURPRISED? I'M FLABBERGASTED!
OH, HONEY, IT'S SO GOOD TO SEE YOU AGAIN!
I'D BEGUN TO THINK YOU WERE NEVER COMING BACK!
I HAVE SO MUCH TO TELL YOU, JULIA-- SO MUCH TO DO!
MAY I STAY HERE AGAIN?
AS IF I'D LET YOU STAY ANYWHERE ELSE!
"WELCOME HOME, DIANA...
"WELCOME HOME!"
22

VOLUME TWO

WONDER WOMAN GALLERY

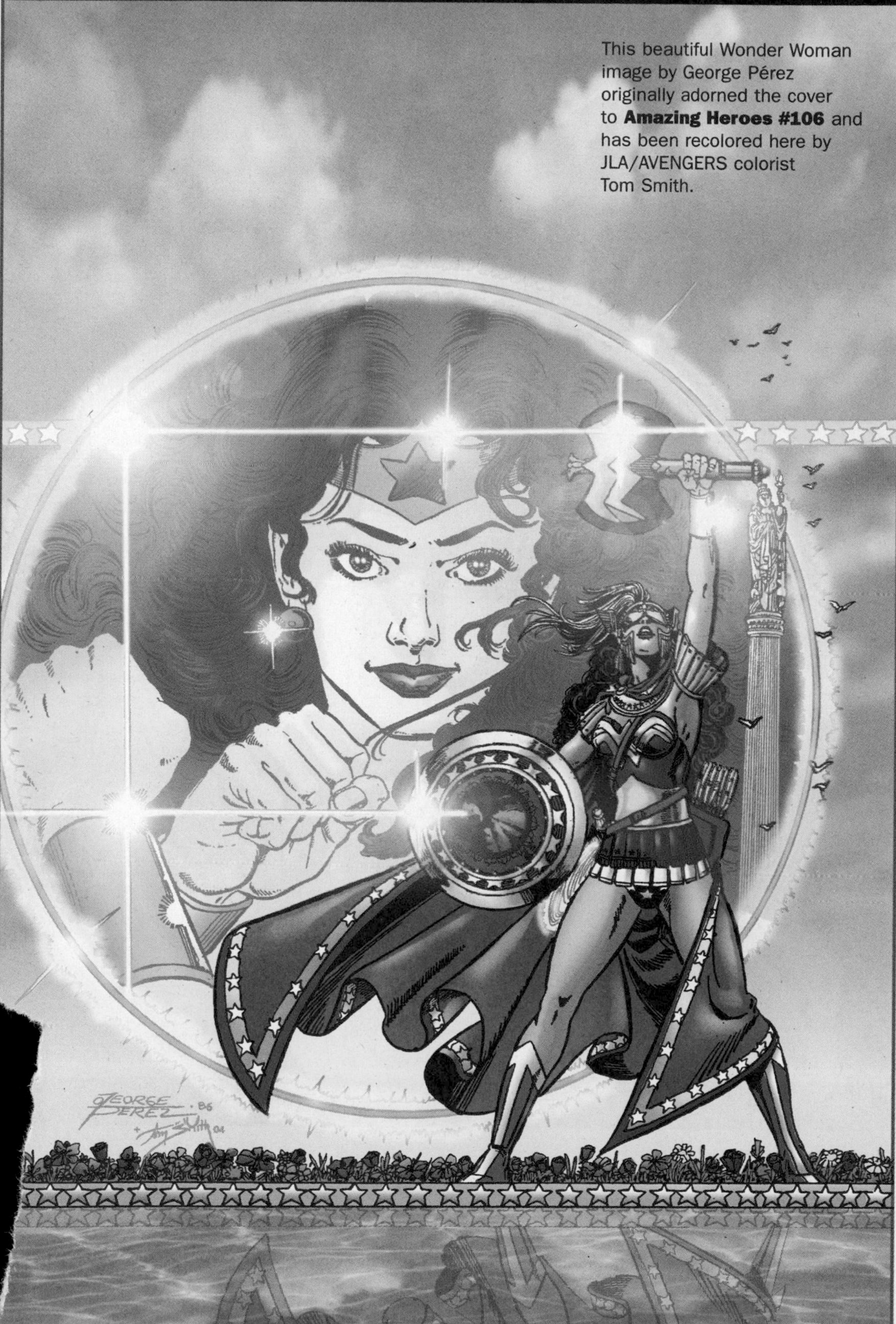

This beautiful Wonder Woman image by George Pérez originally adorned the cover to **Amazing Heroes #106** and has been recolored here by JLA/AVENGERS colorist Tom Smith.

HISTORY

At this writing, little is known of the origin of the new Cheetah save this: Some time ago, archaeologist Barbara Minerva went in search of a legendary lost race of cat-like humanoids. Though she did not find the cat people themselves, in the ruins of their treasure city she found an ancient herb long thought extinct that they had purportedly worshipped and nurtured.

With the aid of her African aide-de-camp, Barbara made an elixir from the leaves of the herb, drank of it from a saucer-like vessel during the reenactment of an ancient ritual, and thus was transformed into the humanoid cat-creature called the Cheetah!

For reasons as yet unexplained, the Cheetah seeks the mystic girdle of the Earth-Goddess Gaea, which has since been transformed by the Olympian God Hephaestus into the golden lasso of truth now wielded by the Amazon Princess Diana, known to the world at large as Wonder Woman.

Though the Cheetah appeared to perish during her first battle with Wonder Woman for possession of the lasso, no trace of her body was found, and thus her current whereabouts remain unknown.

POWERS & WEAPONS

A superior hand-to-hand combatant, the Cheetah is incredibly fast, possessing superhuman agility and strength, unerring night-vision, and razor-sharp claws that are able to pierce bricks as easily as they rend her attackers to shreds. She can also control her tail as an extra appendage to grapple with her foes or strangle them.

C H E E T A H

ALTER EGO: Barbara Ann Minerva
OCCUPATION: Archaeologist, Treasure Hunter
MARITAL STATUS: Single
KNOWN RELATIVES: None
GROUP AFFILIATION: None
BASE OF OPERATIONS: Mobile, principally Europe
FIRST APPEARANCE: (As Barbara Minerva) WONDER WOMAN (second series) #7, (As the Cheetah) WONDER WOMAN (second series) #9
HEIGHT: 5' 9"   **WEIGHT:** 120 pounds   **EYES:** Brown   **HAIR:** Black

TEXT: LEN WEIN
ART: GEORGE PÉREZ
COLOR: TOM SMITH

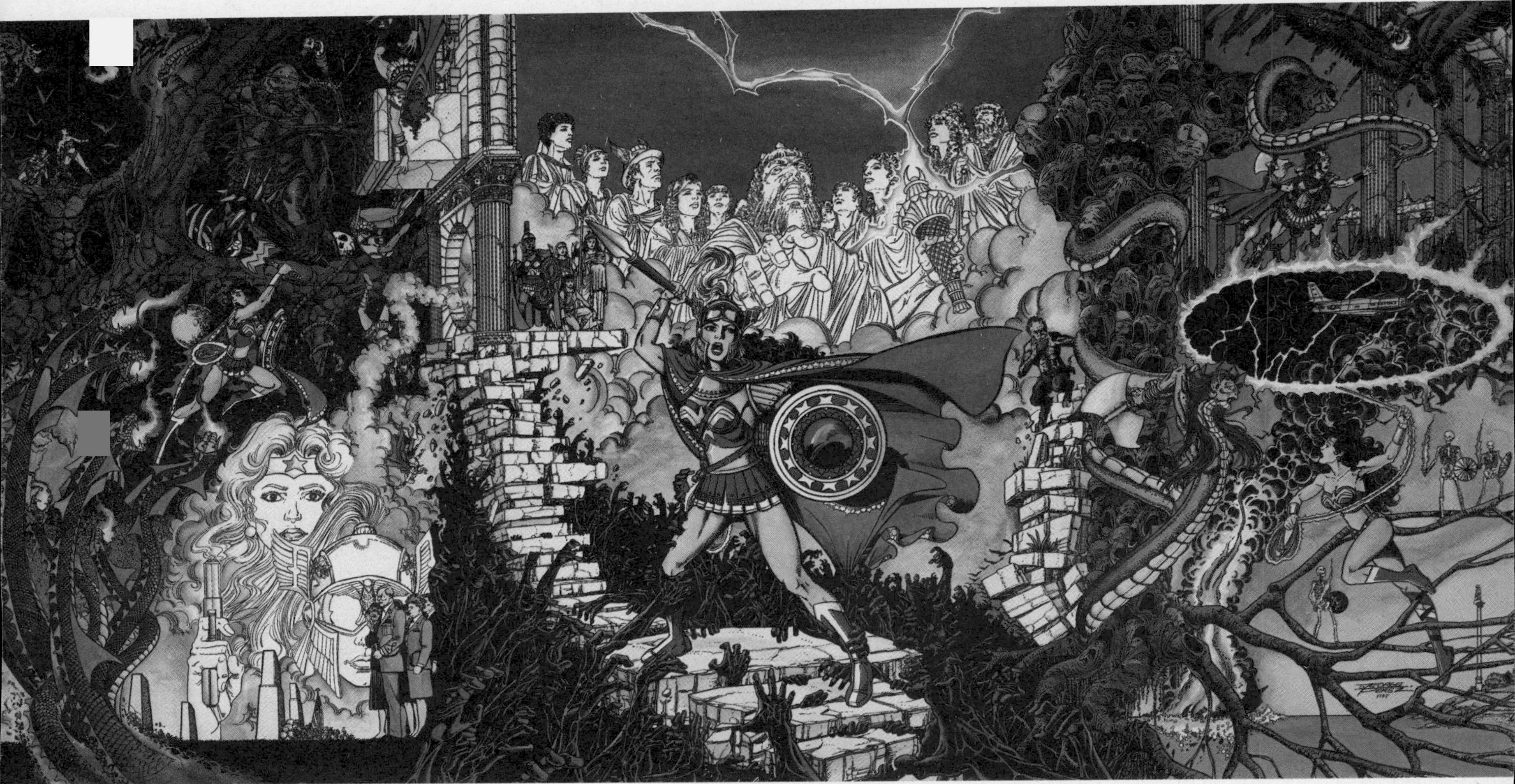

This WONDER WOMAN POSTER image from 1987 is the full version of the gatefold cover that adorned issue #10.

ART: George Pérez [illegible] Ziuko

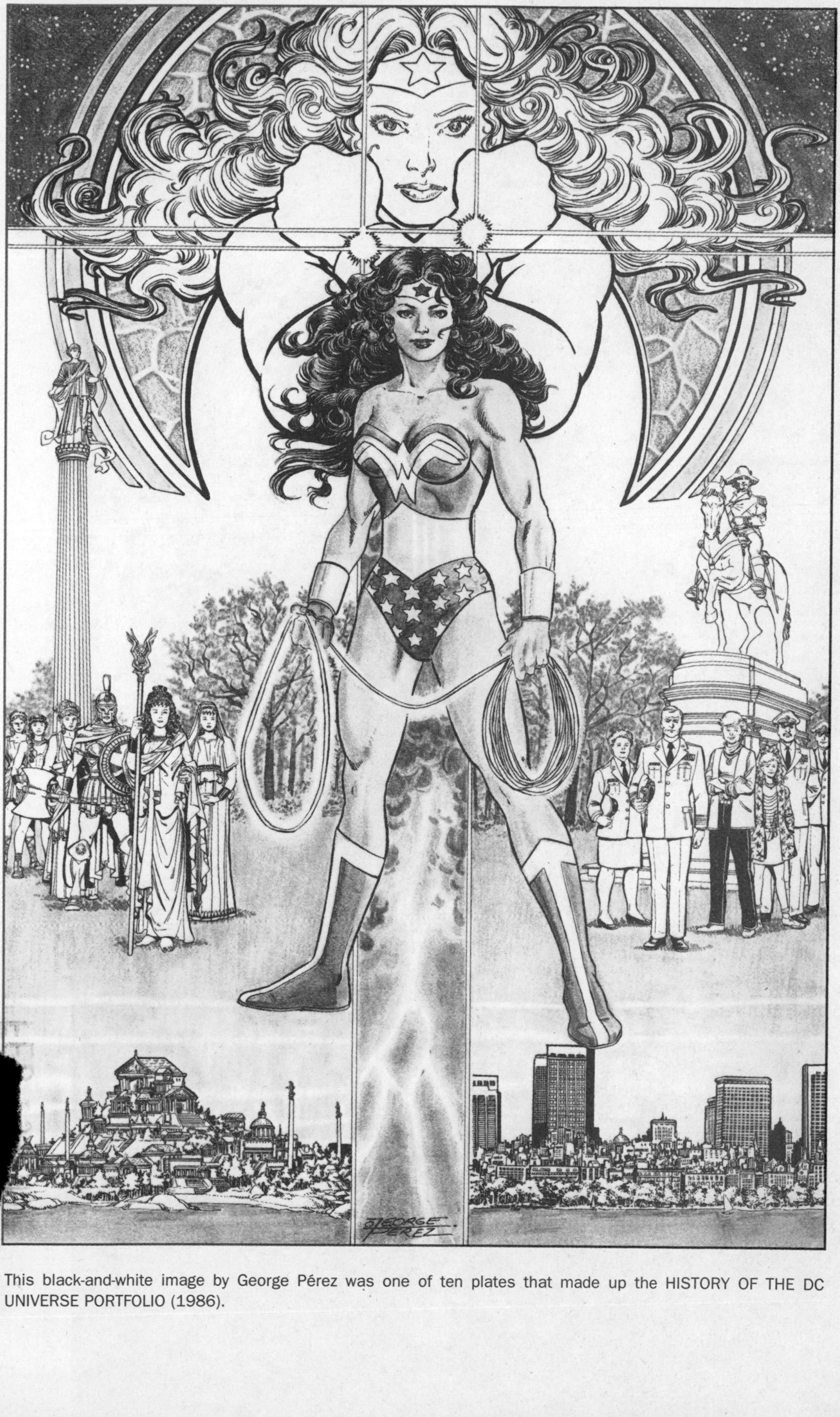
GEORGE PÉREZ

This black-and-white image by George Pérez was one of ten plates that made up the HISTORY OF THE DC UNIVERSE PORTFOLIO (1986).